This is a ground-breaking study of an important and critically neglected body of writing of one of America's twentieth-century literary masters. In spite of the mounting numbers of books and articles examining the art of Hemingway's fiction and the impact of his life and art on twentieth-century culture, remarkably little attention has been paid to the nonfictional pieces that he wrote throughout his career. This study explores his newspaper and magazine journalism, his three books of factual prose, his introductions and prefaces to books by others, his program notes on painting and sculpture exhibitions, and his statements in self-edited interviews. In doing so, it throws a new, oblique light on what has usually been regarded as his major work—his short stories and novels.

In Part One the author surveys Hemingway's career as an essayist from his earliest work to his posthumously published nonfiction. He traces his changing role as a spokesman to the public, showing how he began as an impersonal social commentator and humorist,

sources, analogues, and series of details in the fiction. The details are largely the same in both kinds of writing, but take on different meanings because of changing contexts Part Five the author examines Hemingw concept of the essay as an art form, and evaluates the effectiveness of his style.

Hemingway's public voice in his non tional work constitutes an intermediate vo. between his own private voice and the mask voices of his fiction. Because it begins th process of objectification and creative r arrangement found in the fiction, the publi voice speaks in an especially significant way.

Robert O. Stephens is an associate professor of English at The University of North Carolina at Greensboro.

D1159363

HEMINGWAY'S NONFICTION

The Public Voice

HEMINGWAY'S NONFICTION

The Public Voice

by ROBERT O. STEPHENS

The University of North Carolina Press · Chapel Hill

Copyright © 1968 by
The University of North Carolina Press
Library of Congress Catalog Card Number 68-25912
Manufactured in the United States of America
Printed by The Seeman Printery, Durham, N. C.

PS
3515
.E37
288

HUGH STEPHENS LIBRARY
STEPHENS COLLEGE
COLUMBIA, MISSOURI

For Ginny, Nancy, Melissa, and Rob

120051

Acknowledgments

QUOTATIONS FROM VARIOUS WORKS BY ERNEST HEMINGWAY WHICH appear in this work are protected by copyright and have been reprinted here by special permission of Charles Scribner's Sons and By-Line Ernest Hemingway, Inc., and for distribution in the United Kingdom and the British Commonwealth, excluding Canada, by permission of The Executors of the Ernest Hemingway Estate, Jonathan Cape, Ltd., and William Collins Sons & Company, Ltd.; quotation of "Lines to a College Professor" is by special permission of *Yale Literary Magazine* and the Estate of Sinclair Lewis.

Preface

THIS BOOK IS AN ATTEMPT TO FILL A MAJOR GAP IN HEMINGWAY studies. In spite of the mounting numbers of books and articles examining the art of Hemingway's fiction and the impact of his life and art on twentieth-century culture, remarkably little attention has been paid to the nonfictional pieces that Hemingway wrote throughout his career. Charles Fenton's *The Apprenticeship of Ernest Hemingway* is an exception to the general indifference to this material. Even so, Fenton's purpose was not so much to examine the material for its own sake as to show the early journalism as a stage in the development of the novelist and short story writer. My contention is that Hemingway's work in the essay—my term for his nonfictional writing in magazines, newspapers, books, introductions to others' works, and other such fugitive pieces—was an important and parallel form of writing done throughout his career. In many cases it furnishes insights into what he did in the fiction. In other cases the nonfiction has its own reasons for existence and its own claims to critical notice.

The recent publication of *By-line: Ernest Hemingway*, edited by Professor William White, at last brings to the attention of the public many of Hemingway's nonfictional works. They may gain the recognition they deserve. Gene Z. Hanrahan's *The Wild Years*, a collection of several Hemingway pieces from the *Toronto Star Weekly* and the *Toronto Daily Star*, initiated notice of the material in 1962, but has failed to stay in print with any dependability.

Critically, Hemingway's nonfiction provides a dimension that I have called the public voice. We have some personal data on Hemingway which, if used cautiously, furnishes useful insights into his fiction. This private voice of Hemingway, however, can be misleading if we identify it automatically with the masked voice in his fiction. His public voice in the nonfictional work constitutes an intermediate voice between the private and the masked voices. Because it begins the process of objectification and creative rearrangement found in the fiction, the public voice speaks in an especially significant way for the voice behind the mask of fiction. I have attempted to suggest this relationship in the arrangements of Parts Two, Three, and Four of the study, where the emphasis shifts progressively from man to thought to fiction. Parts One and Five are more general considerations of the man and the work respectively.

Although I have written the study as a sustained argument in support of the thesis stated above, I have also presented the individual chapters in such a way that they may be read separately if one wishes to pursue a specialized interest. This procedure has necessitated at some points a review of matters considered elsewhere in a different context. At such points I ask the indulgence of the reader who follows the argument from start to finish.

Many people and institutions are due thanks for help with this study. I am grateful to Mr. Charles M. Adams, Librarian and Head of the Walter Clinton Jackson Library, The University of North Carolina at Greensboro, for his help in identifying and acquiring many of the fugitive pieces here studied; to Mrs. Mary Walker Mallison of the Acquisitions Department; and to Mrs. Elizabeth Holder and Miss Mary Robert Seawell, reference librarians, for their cheerful help. I owe debts of gratitude also to other university and civic libraries, especially to the Clifton Waller Barrett Collection, The Alderman Library, The University of Virginia; to the many correspondents representing journals and publishing houses answering my inquiries; to Professor Joseph Allen Bryant, Jr., of The University of North Carolina at Greensboro and Professor C. Hugh Holman of The University of North Carolina at Chapel Hill for useful and encouraging conversations; to The University of North Carolina at Greensboro's Research Council for grants to acquire materials and to prepare the manuscript; and to the Duke University-University of North Carolina Cooperative Program in the Humanities for a fellowship and the time to write the study.

ROBERT O. STEPHENS

Greensboro, North Carolina
1967

Table of Contents

PART ONE / *The Public Voice*

I. Hemingway's Career As an Essayist

IN 1956, WHILE WRITING A LOOK MAGAZINE ARTICLE APPROPRIATELY
entitled "A Situation Report," Ernest Hemingway saw himself
in a situation he had frequently confronted and decried throughout his forty-year career of writing for pay. He was writing
journalism when he preferred to be at work on a novel. On the
next day, he promised, he would get back to work on the "long
book" after having been away from it for months in Peru to
oversee the filming of scenes for the movie version of *The Old
Man and the Sea*. In the report he characterized his attitude
toward a kind of writing that consumed a large part of his time
and energy during a long creative career: "As for journalism,
that writing of something that happens day by day, in which
I was trained when young, and which is not whoring when done
honestly with exact reporting; there is no more of that until this
book is finished."[1]

1. *Look*, **XX** (September 4, 1956), 25.

Throughout his writing career Hemingway displayed that ambivalence not only toward journalism but also toward his nonfictional work in general—toward a body of writing that equaled approximately one-third of his total production. He has been properly recognized as he wanted to be—a serious and consummately skillful master of fiction. But he was also a journalist and essayist of considerable stature, and will probably be recognized so in the total perspective of his life and career. One mark of this growing recognition is that while his stories and novels are taking their places in literary collections and anthologies, his essays have begun to appear as models of expository prose in university writing courses.

But this is an outcome Hemingway did not foresee. He always insisted on separating his fiction and poetry from his journalism and critical writing. In 1951 he declared, "The only work of mine that I endorse or sign as my true work . . . is what I have published since *Three Stories & Ten Poems* and the first *In Our Time* [*sic*]."[2] The reason for such a declaration appeared twenty years earlier when he wrote to Louis Henry Cohn, his first bibliographer, that he did not want his quickly written journalism to enter estimates of his literary worth. "If you have made your living as a newspaperman, learning your trade, writing against deadlines, writing to make stuff timely rather than permanent, no one has a right to dig this stuff up and use it against the stuff you have written to write the best you can."[3] So strongly did he want to bury the bones of his apprenticeship in 1931, that he opposed Cohn's preparation of a bibliography. It would locate the early work for the world to see.[4]

Other indications of the slight value he placed on his journalism, including that after 1923, appeared in the magazines and nonfiction books themselves. In one of his *Esquire* articles of 1935 he insisted that while he cared very much about writing good fiction, he took very lightly "the writing of these monthly letters."[5] And from the perspective of *A Moveable Feast*, written in the late fifties, he observed that serious work required the

2. Charles Fenton, *The Apprenticeship of Ernest Hemingway* (New York, 1961), p. 178.

3. Louis Henry Cohn, *A Bibliography of Ernest Hemingway* (New York, 1931), p. 112.

4. *Ibid.*, pp. 10-11.

5. "Monologue to the Maestro," *Esquire*, IV (October 1935), 21.

conducive atmosphere of certain cities and ranch retreats, but he could write journalism anywhere.[6]

His wish to separate expository writing from fiction had internal as well as external reasons. This became plain to him, if we can believe Gertrude Stein, when he showed her a "narrative meditation" about E. E. Cummings' *The Enormous Room* and she informed him that "remarks are not literature."[7] He tried to pass on the insight later in "Monologue to the Maestro" when he told his protégé Arnold Samuelson that news reporting is built around the element of timeliness. But as time passes, he pointed out, so does the event tied to time. When an action is invented, though, it escapes the tie to a passing event and remains as true as when it was first created.[8] About the same time, he was writing in *Green Hills of Africa* that writing against a deadline violates the integrity of a subject by forcing one to find merely facile ways of rendering it. One should write, paint, or hunt, he said, as long as one feels serious about his work and has the skill to do it.[9] And in 1952 he could still lament that memory is the casualty of journalism: "In newspaper work . . . you have to learn to forget every day what happened the day before."[10]

Besides causing timeliness instead of timelessness, journalism and occasional writing, he feared, could lead one to take a quick and unreflective view of events. In 1959, looking back to his newspaper days, he saw that news reporting had taught him to write about what happened but not to explore why.[11] Earlier in Paris, Gertrude Stein had cautioned him to get out of news work because "you will never see things, you will only see words and that will not do, that is if you intend to be a writer."[12] Exactly what that meant was spelled out later in *Death in the Afternoon*. He wanted to make his writing embody what he and the reader really felt, not what they were supposed to feel. The tricks of news writing depended on predictable response, and emotion,

6. *A Moveable Feast* (New York, 1964), p. 7.
7. Gertrude Stein, *The Autobiography of Alice B. Toklas* (New York, 1960), p. 219.
8. *Esquire*, IV (October 1935), 21.
9. *Green Hills of Africa* (New York, 1935), p. 12.
10. Fenton, p. 129.
11. A. E. Hotchner, "Ernest Hemingway Talks to American Youth," *This Week*, October 18, 1959, p. 10.
12. Stein, p. 213.

like memory, had to be intrinsic in the created action where it could be extrinsic in the reported one.[13]

A third objection he had to writing journalism was that it used up materials and energy that should go into creative work. Gertrude Stein had warned that "the one would use up the juice I needed for the other. She was quite right . . . and that was the best advice she gave me."[14] This became a refrain for Hemingway before he finally declared himself free of newspaper work; he lamented to Sherwood Anderson, among others, in 1922 that "this goddam newspaper stuff is gradually ruining me. . . ."[15] In 1924, having left the *Toronto Star*, he still shuddered at the possible losses of usable material. In his "Pamplona Letter" for *the transatlantic review* he complained that photographing, like reporting, denies the essential thing and emphasizes the facade. "And when you destroy the valuable things you have by writing about them you want to get big money for it. Once you put a thing in words, unless you do it 'on your knees,' you kill it. If you do write it 'on your knees' (I forget who said that about knees and it may have been somebody very banal) the thirty francs a page is only a supplementary reward."[16] It is not clear how symbolic he felt the rate of payment to be.

The fourth objection was one learned after years of dispute with newspaper and magazine editors, genteel critics, and Boston censors. In his 1934 "Defense of Dirty Words" he pointed to Ring Lardner as an example of the writer tamed by journalism. Lardner had failed, he charged, to write the true language of his characters because he had been restricted by newspaper and magazine editors. The sportsmen of Lardner's world used four-letter words, and to suggest even by omission that they did not was to lessen the truth of his sketches and stories. Thus journalism not only limited his presentation of the real thing, it conditioned him to accept those limits when he had the relatively greater freedom of book publication.[17] Hemingway's own encounter with Boston censors during the serial publication of *A Farewell to Arms* in *Scribner's Magazine* taught him the relative strength he had in book publication.

13. *Death in the Afternoon* (New York, 1932), p. 2.
14. Fenton, p. 128.
15. *Ibid.*, p. 105.
16. *the transatlantic review*, II (October 1924), 300.
17. *Esquire*, II (September 1934), 19.

If such was the case against journalism in Hemingway's mind, his practice indicated he protested too much to be convincing. Not only did he practice journalism and the writing of occasional essays throughout his career, but he also advised others to take the advantages in journalism, and he found the line between expository writing and the creation of fiction not as great as he imagined. He advised his brother Leicester to work for newspapers to learn to write fluently.[18] And on several occasions he changed his mind about what he had written so that a piece first conceived of as critical or journalistic was reclassified as fiction. His *New Republic* article "Italy, 1927" purported to show the facts of Mussolini's Italy during an actual trip Hemingway and Guy Hickok made through that country in 1927; yet later that same year he called the sketch a story, titled it "Che Ti Dice La Patria?" and put it in his second major short story collection, *Men Without Women*. In *Death in the Afternoon* he presented "A Natural History of the Dead" as a satirically pedantic essay with a dramatized *exemplum* as part of his justification of bullfighting. But in *Winner Take Nothing* he reclassified the essay as a short story, cut several exchanges of dialogue between himself and the Old Lady interlocutor, and reduced, or at least made more implicit, the dramatic context of the essay.

His integrity in expository writing was no less important than it was in fiction and this was seen by Louis Henry Cohn, one of the first to evaluate his career as a writer of both nonfiction and fiction. Cohn pointed out that Hemingway had to ignore the demands of publishers and public for more fiction while he spent years writing *Death in the Afternoon* and *Green Hills of Africa*. He knew that neither book would have the sales that another novel would produce, but they represented something also important to him.[19] The importance concerned the relationship between the observed and analyzed thing and the created thing and it became clear in his foreword to *Green Hills of Africa*: "Unlike many novels, none of the characters or incidents in this book is imaginary. . . . The writer has attempted to write an absolutely true book to see whether the shape of a country and the pattern of a month's action can, if truly presented, compete with a work of the imagination."

18. Leicester Hemingway, *My Brother, Ernest Hemingway* (Cleveland, 1961), p. 156.

19. "Collecting Hemingway," *Avocations*, II (January 1938), 349-50.

In his introduction to *The Writer Observed*, Harvey Breit put Hemingway's journalism and other essays in perhaps the truest perspective. Hemingway, Breit said, had a potentially great career as a reporter and commentator on the world's scene. But he adapted his ability to observe and interpret the world to the demands of fiction, where it undergirded the creative imagination with an authoritative sense of the way the world operates, whether in blow-by-blow accounts of prizefights, in the ritual movements of bullfights, or in the tactical developments of wars.[20]

Before, during, and after the writing of all the fiction from *Three Stories & Ten Poems* to *The Old Man and the Sea*, Hemingway pursued an unacknowledged career as journalist and essayist, critic and commentator. It began, as Charles Fenton has shown, in Oak Park (Illinois) High School where Hemingway simultaneously wrote Lardneresque reports on school athletic events and bloody stories of Indian revenge.[21] "The Judgment of Manitou" and "Sepi Jingan," published in *Tabula*, the school literary sheet, showed his early abilities in fiction; in columns of the school newspaper *Trapeze*, Hemingway wrote sports articles and satirical small-talk pieces. His writing at this time, however, was neither consciously part of a journalistic career nor preparation for a literary one. He intended to follow his father's example in the study of medicine.

After his graduation, though, he decided in favor of cub reporting with the *Kansas City Star* over pre-medical studies at the state university. From October, 1917, to April, 1918, he covered the police station and general hospital beats and summed up the experience this way for George Plimpton in 1958: "On the *Star* you were forced to learn to write a simple declarative sentence. This is useful to anyone. Newspaper work will not harm a young writer and could help him if he gets out of it in time."[22]

Leaving the *Star* to serve with the Red Cross in Italy, he wrote more Lardneresque satire for *Ciao*, a news and gossip sheet published by young Americans with the ambulance group at Schio. In June, 1918, appeared "Al Receives Another Letter,"

20. *The Writer Observed* (New York, 1961), p. 17.

21. Fenton, pp. 22-30.

22. George Plimpton, "The Art of Fiction," *The Paris Review*, XVIII (Spring 1958); reprinted in Carlos Baker (ed.), *Hemingway and His Critics* (New York, 1961), p. 25.

an adaptation of Lardner's brand of humor to the situation of young men still surprised by their rapid elevation to honorary lieutenants in the Italian Army.[23] But the urge to publish stopped when Hemingway was wounded on July 8, 1918, at Fossalta di Piave, and not until after a long convalescence in a Milanese hospital, a hero's return to Oak Park, and an emotional break with the family in late 1919 did he return to the publishing world.

From February, 1920, to December, 1923, except for six months as associate editor with Harrison Parker's *Co-operative Commonwealth* in Chicago, Hemingway worked for the *Toronto Star Weekly* and the *Toronto Daily Star.* He began as free-lance contributor to the *Star Weekly* with a satirical article on art collecting among the bright young set of the city and followed with humorous and satirical accounts about barber colleges, the Toronto mayor's search for votes at the boxing matches, and on the war profiteer's attempt to appear as a veteran after the armistice. After three months his vein of satire wore out and he began a series of straight articles on crime, prohibition and bootlegging, and on the finer points of camping and fishing. "When You Camp Out Do It Right," "Fishing for Trout in a Sporting Way," and "A Fight with a 20-Pound Trout" appeared among such topical articles as "Canuck Whiskey Pouring into U.S." and "Plain and Fancy Killings, $400 Up" from mid-1920 to early 1922. Articles with Chicago angles, such as "The Wild West Is Now in Chicago" and "Gun-Men's Wild Political War On in Chicago," reflect the period he spent with Parker's Chicago house organ. Then, disillusioned with Parker's enterprise, he arranged with the *Toronto Star* to go to Europe as free-lance correspondent for both the *Toronto Daily Star* and the *Star Weekly.*

Despite his complaints about writing against deadlines, Hemingway seldom had a deadline to meet for the *Star Weekly.* While his subjects were current and timely, they were not the type to compete with the latest news break. As Charles Fenton explained, the *Star Weekly* was a feature paper rather than newspaper. Under the editorship of J. Herbert Cranston, the *Star Weekly* emphasized entertainment, social signs of the times, literary notices, sports, and comics. It catered, in short, to a wide range of interests; aside from proscribing overt sex and blasphe-

23. Fenton, pp. 55-56.

my, the editors exercised little control over their contributors. Hemingway found that adoption of a Canadian viewpoint, however, was one of the unwritten rules. Such freedom of topic and treatment was valuable for a young writer trying to develop a serviceable prose style and a new way of rendering experience.[24] That speedy reporting was less a matter of concern than style on the *Star Weekly* can also be seen in Cranston's view of Hemingway as a writer of "good, plain Anglo-Saxon" with a gift for humor and in his willingness to pay the young writer three-quarters of a cent a word initially and a cent a word later instead of the regular rate of half a cent a word.[25]

When Hemingway went to Europe for the *Daily Star*, he had scarcely less freedom. He was paid at regular space rates and received, after acceptance of his material, payment for expenses incurred while getting the stories. He had complete freedom of movement and choice of material and was expected to cultivate a lively, intimate, and subjective approach in his articles. These conditions differed sharply from those imposed on most correspondents for American news agencies, who were expected to submit routine, objective, factual reports.[26]

High points of his early work as a European correspondent were articles in the *Daily Star* on the Genoa Economic Conference of April, 1922; reports on a trip into Germany in the late summer of that year to survey the attitudes of recent enemies; and reports on the rise of Mussolini, complete with warnings of the danger posed by his young Fascists in their war against the ineffectual Socialists and Communists of Northern Italy. During the fall of 1922 he reported on the Greco-Turkish war with vividly written accounts of the retreat of the Greek army and Greek refugees across Thrace. Also during the fall of 1922 and the following winter, he reported the Lausanne Conference for the *Daily Star*. To get extra money for living in expensive Lausanne, he filed additional stories with Universal News Service and International News Service. His reports for both agencies are lost to retrospective study, however, as he telephoned the news to Paris for rewriting there.[27] But his Toronto editors received other perceptive background articles from Lausanne on

24. *Ibid.*, pp. 68-70.
25. *Ibid.*, pp. 72, 74.
26. *Ibid.*, pp. 97, 100-101.
27. *Ibid.*, pp. 150-51.

Mussolini and Tchitcherin, the enigmatic Russian foreign minister.

While this mixture of news and feature writing went to the *Daily Star* in 1922, other articles of more general interest were being sent to the *Star Weekly*. Included in these reports were articles on the absinthe scandal in Paris, riots in Germany, and the antics of American literary people in Europe.

Hemingway's major assignment for the *Daily Star in* 1923 was a trip into Germany and the French-occupied Ruhr districts to provide Canadian readers with an analysis of the causes and effects of the French occupation. His ten-article series on the Ruhr question was his grand coup before he returned to America with his wife in the late summer of 1923 for the birth of their first child. Back in Canada and at work under the sarcastic *Star* editor Harry Comfort Hindmarsh, at work also in a society he found provincial after that in Europe, he began to write more feature material for the *Star Weekly* revealing his nostalgia for Europe. His wide and rather exotic European experiences of bullfighting, hunting and fishing in continental forests and streams, skiing the Alps, of meeting literary notables and seeing the hidden side of European and Asian cities—all became the subjects of stories filed during the fall of 1923. This was the time of such germinal pieces as "Bull Fighting Is Not a Sport—It Is a Tragedy," "Night Life in Europe a Disease," and "Trout Fishing All across Europe"—all articles that dealt with material he would reuse in later fiction and repeat in later essays. It was also a time when he was writing so furiously to get extra money for a return to Europe that he sometimes wrote under the by-line of John Hadley to disguise some of his more flagrant hack-work.[28]

Before Hemingway returned to the United States for the birth of his son, he had made several friendships among the expatriate writers and publishers. Robert McAlmon of the Contact Publishing Company had published *Three Stories & Ten Poems* in the summer of 1923, and William Bird's Three Mountains Press published the Paris edition of *in our time* in January of 1924 while the Hemingways were on their way back to Europe. The poems and stories of these collections indicated Hemingway's link with the *Little Review* and *Poetry* as contributor of experimental forms in verse and sketch; six of the vignettes of

28. *Ibid.*, pp. 198-99.

in our time had first appeared in the *Little Review*. Now his relationship to the experimental magazines was also that of assistant editor and columnist. Besides helping Ford Madox Ford with the editorial chores of *the transatlantic review*, Hemingway contributed to "Chroniques," the section of the *review* devoted to commentary on contemporary life and letters. "And to the United States," in the May-June, 1924, issue, was a miscellany of gossip about writers, critics, composers, literary show-offs, painting exhibits, race horses, and boxers. One significant notice concerned the probable increase in critics from ten critics to one writer to fifty-five to one after the *Dial* award had gone to a critic.[29] Since Hemingway was living off savings and whatever he could make from his writing, the 150 francs an article he was making at the *review* helped, as did most of his journalism, to pay living expenses while he learned about fiction.

Later "Chroniques" satirized the Dadaists and celebrated the Pamplona bullfights for the enlightenment of Latin Quarter readers. In the October, 1924, issue he mourned the recent death of Joseph Conrad and in so doing wrote the first of several prose elegies he would be called on to write throughout his career.[30]

In 1925 he worked with Ernest Walsh on *This Quarter*, contributing "Big Two-Hearted River" and writing an appreciative essay called "Homage to Ezra." In the tribute Hemingway, thinking seriously about the process of creative writing and criticism, reasoned out a position from which he asserted that Pound was a major poet and T. S. Eliot a minor one.[31] It was only one of several occasions Hemingway seized to contradict literary and critical trends and insist upon his personal insights and loyalties.

Following his successes with *In Our Time* and *The Sun Also Rises*, he was finally able to publish in mass-circulation American magazines. This opening of new opportunities included the placing of his nonfiction as well as his stories. While his short fiction began to appear in the *Atlantic Monthly* and *Scribner's*, a miscellany of personal and travel articles appeared in other magazines. "My Own Life," published in the *New Yorker* for February 12, 1927, was satirical literary gossip and parody, but the part called "The True Story of My Break with Gertrude Stein"

29. *the transatlantic review*, I (May-June 1924), 355-57.
30. "And Out of America," II (August 1924), 102-103; "Pamplona Letter," II (October 1924), 300-302; "Conrad," II (October 1924), 341-42.
31. *This Quarter*, I (May 1925), 221-25.

was his first published acknowledgment of the rift between him and his former mentor. "Italy, 1927" first appeared in the May 18 issue of *New Republic* as a vivid and condemnatory sketch of Italian Fascists seen during a ten-day trip Hemingway and Guy Hickok made through Northern Italy. With *A Farewell to Arms*, it was the reason for Italian critics' patriotic outrage and designation of him as *persona non grata* in Italian publishing circles during the 1930's.[32] His article, "The Real Spaniard," in the Paris *Boulevardier* for October, 1927, was a further example of his talent for parody, this time directed against Louis Bromfield's more solemn search for "The Real French" in the previous issue of the magazine. In *Fortune* for March, 1930, he capitalized on his fame as popularizer of bullfighting to write a business-oriented view of the sport, "Bullfighting, Sport and Industry." The economics of the sport, he pointed out, were shaky, overbalanced in favor of the matadors, and weighted against the bull breeders and handlers. The piece was also indicative of Hemingway's new stature in that it was one of the few signed articles allowed in the young but prestigious magazine.[33] It was richly illustrated with color reproductions from Goya, Manet, and Zuloaga.

During the period of his initial success, Hemingway also had to accept the responsibilities of a recognized man of letters. His own ability established, he was called upon by the still-aspiring to write in their behalf, and he began to write introductions and prefaces to others' work. His career as writer of prefaces began in 1929, innocently enough, with an invitation to write a prefatory note to his own story "The Killers" for Henry Goodman's symposium-anthology *Creating the Short Story*. As prefaces go, it was pretty well beside the point, but it was the first of more to come. That same year he wrote an introduction to the memoir *Kiki of Montparnasse*, translated by fellow expatriate Samuel Putnam and published by expatriate Edward W. Titus's press at the Sign of the Black Manikin. Kiki was the acknowledged queen of the Montparnasse district, former prostitute, favorite model of well-known photographers and painters, and, according to Putnam, a moderately good painter herself.[34] Hemingway's introduction certified that the "End of an Era" had

32. Samuel Putnam, *Paris Was Our Mistress* (New York, 1947), pp. 132-34.
33. Cohn, p. 83.
34. Putnam, p. 80.

come by 1929 and that Kiki's was one of the most authentic voices of that lost time.[35] He also swore it would be his last introduction, but it was closer to being the first than the last. In 1934 he was doing another introduction, this time for James Charters' memoir *This Must Be the Place*. Better known as Jimmie the Barman at Lou Wilson's Dingo Bar and at other Paris bars later operated by himself, Charters enjoyed his own legend around the tourists' Paris. He took his title from the frequently heard cry of discovery by flappers seeking out the much talked of gathering place. By 1934 Hemingway had felt the sting of Gertrude Stein's *The Autobiography of Alice B. Toklas* and used his introduction to Charters' book to contrast the manly comforts of the Dingo bar with the jealousy and spite of Gertrude Stein's salon. It was not a pretty piece of prose, but it showed one use Hemingway was willing to make of available pages. The crude harshness of the piece could be partly explained by the fact that Hemingway wrote it while he was suffering from amoebic dysentery on the Serengetti Plains of Tanganyika during his first safari.

A later item that came as a result of Hemingway's expatriate associations with other artists was the published answer to Eugene Jolas' survey in the tenth-anniversary issue of *Transition*. Calling his survey an "Inquiry into the Spirit and Language of Night," Jolas asked several prominent writers about the use of dreams and dream symbols in their work. Some writers pled privacy, others answered but ignored the question, some answered seriously. Hemingway answered seriously about the subjects of his dreams but, true to his belief that talking about such things spoils them, he refused to analyze their role in his work.[36]

In the 1934 *Cahiers d'Art* issue on Joan Miró, he did the first of several introductions to nonliterary arts. In a commentary placed beside a reproduction of Miró's "The Farm," Hemingway explained how he came to own the prize painting. He

---

35. The 1930 edition called *Kiki's Memoirs* with the same Hemingway introduction was published in Paris by Titus and was denied entry into the United States because of customs charges of obscenity. The 1929 *Kiki of Montparnasse* had been published as a pamphlet in New York in an edition of twenty-five copies to secure copyright. See Cohn, pp. 35, 38. Other editions were published in 1950 and 1955 by the Seven Sirens Press and in 1954 by Bridgehead Books under the title *The Education of a French Model*. By 1954 Hemingway made minor revisions to tone down remarks made about writer Julian Green.

36. *Transition*, No. 27 (April-May 1938), 237.

had contracted to buy it from Miró's dealer before the painter had gained fame, and he finally had to borrow money from cafe friends to make the last payment while the dealer waited hoping to foreclose and sell the painting for four times the original price. The note had the effect of identifying him even more completely with the true artists of the twenties—a time that looked better and better as the depression deepened.

While Hemingway's fame gained by *The Sun Also Rises* and *A Farewell to Arms* drew him into the business of promoting others' fortunes, it also brought him enough financial security to finish a job he had proposed for himself years earlier. Soon after his personal discovery of bullfighting, he realized that he had more to learn and say about that complex art than he could say in novels, stories, or even in his articles in the *Toronto Star Weekly* and in *Fortune*. He proposed to Maxwell Perkins as early as 1925 the writing of a book-length treatment of bullfighting, and he continued his observations and readings toward that end in 1926 and resumed them in 1929 and 1931, having sustained his interest while writing his war novel and most of the stories for *Men Without Women*.[37]

Death in the Afternoon, which Arnold Gingrich, later Hemingway's editor at *Esquire* and *Ken*, called the greatest four-word poem in the language,[38] appeared in September, 1932. More than a history or manual of bullfighting, it also became Hemingway's attempt to rationalize the aesthetic plan he had followed in his fiction. His pronouncements on the iceberg theory of writing, his explorations of the principles and emotions underlying bullfighting, painting, and writing, his insights into the key distinctions between Spanish and Anglo-Saxon psychology and culture, and his use of most of the travel writer's opportunities—all showed him to be considerably more erudite than most of his critics could believe. For they had seen only the artfully primitive mask he wore in his fiction. If he sounded like Jake Barnes characterizing morality as how one feels after an experience, in his own voice he provided a considerably more detailed context of thought, if not feeling, than Jake could bring himself to say. *Death in the Afternoon* took its place in Hemingway's nonfictional career as his first extended attempt to show his capacity

37. Carlos Baker, *Hemingway: The Writer as Artist* (Princeton, 1963), pp. 145-46.

38. Leicester Hemingway, p. 130.

for serious, sustained nonfictional treatment of a topic ultimately as important to him as any of his fiction.

In 1933 Hemingway entered one of the most controversial periods of his career. His writing for the new men's magazine *Esquire* drew expressions of disappointment from all levels of readers who thought he had sold out after writing his uncompromising fiction of the twenties. In his review of *Green Hills of Africa* in 1935, Edmund Wilson, indicating what most critics thought of Hemingway's new writing, lamented the "rubbishy articles in the men's wear magazine *Esquire*."[39] So many general readers of the magazine complained of his writing articles rather than fiction that Hemingway took time in his 1935 article, "He Who Gets Slap Happy," to answer them. His critics were, he said, unimaginative and conventional and would end up imitating him and others who did what they liked to do, not what was the expected thing to do.[40]

That Hemingway felt ambivalent about his arrangement with *Esquire* can be seen in his own writing for the magazine. In "Notes on Dangerous Game" after his return from Africa, he apologized to his white hunter and guide, Philip Percival, in an aside: "(Excuse me, Mr. P. You see I do this for a living. We all have to do a lot of things for a living. But we're still drinking their whiskey, aren't we?)."[41] But in "Old Newsman Writes" he seemed to take pride in being a journalist who knew and wrote about the world, and he contrasted his pragmatic knowledge of revolutions with the theoretical knowledge of such matters held by an unnamed "baggy pants" columnist who had to substitute dialectic for experience.[42] By the end of his African trip, Hemingway had begun to like the reader response to his pieces and told Arnold Gingrich that his articles were a bargain for most readers. He was giving them "how-to" information that had cost him thousands of dollars to learn.[43] And as Philip Young has pointed out, Hemingway and others may have been too condescending about the standards and stature of the magazine; in it Hemingway could keep company with Dreiser, Huxley, Fitz-

39. *The Shores of Light* (New York, 1952), p. 621.
40. *Esquire*, IV (August 1935), 19.
41. *Esquire*, II (July 1934), 94.
42. *Esquire*, II (December 1934), 25.
43. Leicester Hemingway, p. 144.

gerald, Dos Passos, Pound, Anderson, and Stein.[44] His ambivalence was indicative of an unresolved conflict between images of the writer as professional and artist.

Hemingway's link with *Esquire* came about through his friendship with Arnold Gingrich, editor of *Apparel Arts* magazine in Chicago and fellow fishing enthusiast. Attracted by Hemingway's cult of manliness in *Death in the Afternoon*, Gingrich sought him for his new journal, which in its first number advertised itself as "A Magazine for Men Only." His purpose, Gingrich noted on the first table of contents page, was to reverse the trend of adapting magazines to the tastes of women readers; rather *Esquire* was to be for men what *Vogue* was for women. His editorial policy for contributors was that he edits best who edits least, and he immediately gained well-known contributors by offering immediate payment and freedom to write more daring articles than the formula magazines allowed. In several cases he bought controversial manuscripts for hundreds of dollars from established writers who would have demanded thousands from the sedately established journals.[45]

Gingrich offered Hemingway a policy of (1) no changes in the author's copy, (2) advance payment of $200 to $250 or more per article as later circumstances permitted, and (3) freedom to write on any subject. As he originally planned to publish *Esquire* quarterly, Gingrich urged Hemingway to plan to submit four articles for the first year and suggested that they be in letter form to take a minimum of Hemingway's time and energy away from his fiction. Hemingway at first suggested that $250 was below his rate and told Gingrich that he had two selling policies: if the publication was noncommercial, he would write *gratis* or take a nominal fee, but he demanded the top price from commercial magazines because they appreciated only their expensive writers. Gingrich assured Hemingway that the $200 per article was the top price and that he would in any case be paid twice as much as anyone else. This two-for-one policy continued until the publication of "The Snows of Kilimanjaro," for which Hemingway received $1,000 compared to the maximum of $500 paid others.[46] By May, 1933, he had agreed to the original offer be-

44. *Hemingway* (New York, 1952), pp. 112-13.

45. Theodore Peterson, *Magazines in the Twentieth Century* (Urbana, 1964), pp. 275, 278.

46. Arnold Gingrich to ROS, January 28, 1966.

cause he began to need additional money for his projected African safari. By the end of his African trip, when *Esquire* was publishing monthly, he was satisfied enough with the arrangements to offer to do ten more letters for Gingrich at the same rate. He received, in fact, $3,000 advance payment for the ten letters, which he then used to buy his fishing boat "Pilar."[47]

Hemingway's "Marlin off the Morro" appeared in the first issue of *Esquire* in the autumn of 1933. It set a pattern for the twenty-four "letters" which followed until May of 1936. The articles were personal, sometimes whimsical, sometimes bitter, filled with technical advice to amateur sportsmen and amateur writers. Some, like "Shootism versus Sport," spelled out the white hunter's code he had learned in Africa and would later incorporate into his African stories. Others recorded his game fishing exploits and, as in "Genio after Josie," told of the psychology needed to stir Cuban boat crews to action. "Defense of Dirty Words" brought him into current literary quarrels, and "Monologue to the Maestro" gave him a chance to say more about the craft of writing. Some of the later articles showed Hemingway as a political pundit and military commentator. "The Malady of Power" repeated much of what he had learned from William Ryall (later William Bolitho) about the underside of European politics, especially about the *hubris* of political power. "Notes on the Next War" foresaw the inevitability of war in Europe because of indecision by Britain and France and the bullying personalities of Hitler and Mussolini. "Wings Always over Africa," written in the manner of his mock treatise "A Natural History of the Dead," was subtitled "An Ornithological Letter" and drew on his earlier experiences with the Italian Fascists and on his African hunting lore to predict the horror Italian troops would face when wounded in Ethiopia and left to the vultures. In all, Hemingway's assumption was that he was a fully masculine, rough, and knowledgeable older brother to his readers, and his articles were shaped according to that image. Even his nonfiction had to adopt some of the more obvious techniques of fiction.

He also published another kind of article in *Esquire* during these years, though it was not part of his contract with Gingrich. His writing of catalogue notes for exhibitions of paintings and drawings was an expectable next step after his introductions for

47. Leicester Hemingway, pp. 132-40.

the memoirists and painters of the Paris years. In December, 1934, he and John Dos Passos sponsored an exhibition of etchings by Luis Quintanilla at the Pierre Matisse Galleries in New York, and each contributed an appreciative note on the artist. At that time Quintanilla was in a Madrid jail charged with participation in the October revolt. Hemingway paid for the show and incidental expenses and contracted to buy fifteen of the etchings if the show failed to sell enough to meet expenses.[48] Announced aims of the show were: (1) to prompt the Spanish government to realize how important an artist it had behind bars and (2) to raise money for securing Quintanilla's release. Hemingway's catalogue note, like his article "Old Newsman Writes" of the same month, distinguished between the easy users of the word "revolution" and those like Quintanilla who had earned the right to use it. The catalogue notes and sample pictures appeared in *Esquire* in February, 1935, with the title "Facing a Bitter World." He wrote a program note for the Cuban artist Antonio Gattorno a few months later. First published in the book *Gattorno* in Havana in April, 1935, it was reprinted with accompanying reproductions of several paintings in *Esquire* for May, 1936. Hemingway saluted a kindred spirit, a fellow primitive with hidden sophistications, and traced Gattorno's spiritual pilgrimage through the art capitals of Europe and back to Cuba.

Green Hills of Africa had its trial in several *Esquire* articles written during and after Hemingway's African safari. The three Tanganyika letters, "a.d. [for amoebic dysentery] in Africa," "Shootism versus Sports," and "Notes on Dangerous Game," came out of the safari experience and were at least partly written before Hemingway began composition of the book in mid-April.[49] In these letters he worked out several of the ideas that would inform the narrative and meditational passages in the book: that African terrain had physical and cultural associations with Spain and the American West; that fine points in the hunting code were based on animal anatomy and human pain and resourcefulness; that close observation is also an art; and that subject and style show their mutual dependence in the nonfictional work as much as in the story. Indeed, *Green Hills of Africa* seems to have

48. *Ibid.,* p. 179.
49. Baker, *Hemingway: The Writer as Artist,* pp. 163-65.

occupied a middle position in Hemingway's mind between the *Esquire* articles and the later African stories. As Carlos Baker has pointed out, Hemingway began the work that would become *Green Hills of Africa* as a short story, analogous in his mind with "Big Two-Hearted River."[50] Only as he progressed through the work did he discover that there was an intermediate level of imagination to be explored—a reordering and resavoring of experience in a new context, but not a re-creation of it into fiction. While he planned to use the African experience in fiction, he also followed the insight he had discovered while writing the conclusion of *Death in the Afternoon*: "The great thing is to last and get your work done and see and hear and learn and understand and write when there is something that you know and not before; and not too damned much after."[51]

Written between April, 1934, and February, 1935, the African account was initially published in serial form in *Scribner's Magazine*, May to October, 1935, and issued as a book in late October of that year.[52] It was the last full-length nonfictional work Hemingway would try for twenty-five years; such books were for exploration of individual enthusiasms, and in 1935 he was again addressing himself to public events demanding briefer, journalistic treatment.

But he wrote three short pieces at this time as afterwords to the sports passages in *Esquire* and in *Green Hills of Africa*. "Marlin off Cuba," a revision and expansion of his first *Esquire* article "Marlin off the Morro," was published as a separate chapter in Eugene V. Connett's *American Big Game Fishing* in 1935. His introduction to S. Kip Farrington's *Atlantic Game Fishing* in 1937 lamented the ruin of sport fishing by the introduction of heavy equipment that did all the fighting and left the sportsmen free to take the credit. Unlike some of the others for whom Hemingway wrote, Farrington was already established as a writer. His introduction to Farrington's book was, so Cohn notes, the first Hemingway wrote without the primary intent of giving the book's author a boost.[53] His sketch in Georges Schrieber's *Portraits and Self-Portraits* (1936) was an exercise in direct self-characterization. It certified his wide and rough range of experience

50. *Ibid.*, p. 165.
51. *Death in the Afternoon*, p. 278.
52. Baker, *Hemingway: The Writer as Artist*, pp. 165, 352.
53. "Collecting Hemingway," p. 354.

and contained the cryptic observation that had he not spent so much time at sports he might have either written more or shot himself. It was also an exercise in either forgetfulness or misstatement: he gave his age incorrectly and said that publication of "Fifty Grand" in the *Atlantic Monthly* was his first American magazine publication. He had published "The Killers," "In Another Country," and "A Canary for One" in *Scribner's Magazine* prior to the July, 1927, publication of "Fifty Grand;" and he was thirty-seven in 1936, not thirty-eight.

While these last statements in behalf of sports were being written, Hemingway was also doing the first of many short pieces showing his concern about the rise of Fascism in Europe and America. He had noted the drift of events in Europe in his later *Esquire* articles, and in the September, 1935, issue of *New Masses* appeared another kind of Hemingway article not seen since his little-magazine days. "Who Murdered the Vets?" was an elegiac accusation of Washington bureaucrats for intentionally failing to remove dissident veterans from the construction projects on the Florida Keys before the September hurricane hit. At the request of *New Masses* he had wired the 2800-word dispatch but refused payment because, as he told Maxwell Perkins, he did not want to make money from murder.[54] He wrote another prose elegy for *New Masses* in 1939 called "On the American Dead in Spain." It was even more in the elegiac tradition as it invoked the fertility cycle as the basis for hope that the volunteers had not died without purpose.

A second occasion for writing about public agonies came when the North American Newspaper Alliance engaged Hemingway to report the Spanish Civil War. In January, 1937, Hemingway contracted with John Wheeler, president of N.A.N.A., to do a three-month series of cable and mail reports on events in Spain. The fee would be $500 per cable dispatch of 250-400 words and $1000 for mailed dispatches of 1200 words, with a maximum payment of $1000 per week. N.A.N.A would receive exclusive newspaper rights.[55] As in the case of Hemingway's *Toronto Star* articles, the N.A.N.A. pieces were to be feature material rather than spot reporting, since N.A.N.A. was not trying to compete with such syndicates as the Associated Press for the quick news

54. Baker, *Hemingway: The Writer as Artist*, p. 201n.
55. Leicester Hemingway, pp. 194-95.

break. Banking on Hemingway's reputation as interpreter of Spain, expert on war, and master journalist, Wheeler wanted Hemingway to tell in his "colorful style" the meaning of recent events, to give the feeling of the war, and to interpret the Spanish people and countryside in war for American readers.[56] Wheeler and Hemingway made a second contract in the summer of 1937 with essentially the same terms except that: (1) while N.A.N.A. would still have exclusive rights to the dispatches, Hemingway would be free to do other work as well; and (2) the contract would be canceled if events in Spain should lose their news value. That Hemingway found the Spanish reporting agreeable can be seen in his exuberant offer to do one free dispatch for Wheeler to show his pleasure in writing for a syndicate serving major American papers.[57] Besides his reports, he was working on the filming and narration of *The Spanish Earth* and preparing to write *The Fifth Column*. He was helping pay for the filming of *The Spanish Earth* with earnings from his N.A.N.A. dispatches.

Besides appearing in major newspapers, Hemingway's N.A. N.A. dispatches gained a degree of permanence when eighteen were republished in four numbers of the *New Republic* between May, 1937, and June, 1938. They gained further permanence when they constituted a complete issue of *Fact* magazine in July, 1938. Among the pieces were individualized portraits of American and British volunteers and of Spanish hotelkeepers and chauffeurs, generalized accounts of Spaniards under siege in Madrid, and sensation-packed reports of the way it feels to be shelled, bombed by aircraft, strafed, or caught in refugee columns. Other dispatches showed Hemingway at the war maps explaining how the Republicans in Catalonia had fought valiantly on the Ebro but let the Fascists come unopposed through the mountains to the north to outflank the Ebro positions.

Closely associated with these dispatches was Hemingway's participation in the development of a new kind of journalism. For the July 12, 1937, issue of *Life* magazine Hemingway supplied captions for the photographic essay "Death in Spain"—a new form of essay then being tried out by the magazine. His captions were for the most part quotations and rephrasings from his dispatches and from the narration for *The Spanish Earth*.

56. Richard Freedman, "Hemingway's Spanish Civil War Dispatches," *Texas Studies in Literature and Language*, I (Summer 1959), 171-73.
57. Leicester Hemingway, pp. 202, 204.

Similarly, in the spring of 1938 he published his essay "The Heat and the Cold" in *Verve*, an art magazine also run by Arnold Gingrich and David Smart. As in the N.A.N.A. pieces, Hemingway attempted here to suggest the feel of war and revolution in terms of its deprivations, hopes, and despairs. Written as a belated response to his work on *The Spanish Earth*, the article appeared as an afternote when the film narration was published as a book.

The Spanish Earth was a hybrid venture. Hemingway gathered much of his N.A.N.A. material while he, Joris Ivens, and John Ferno explored Madrid, the battle areas, and the countryside for sequences typifying the struggle of Spanish workers and peasants to throw off feudal land barons and fight their way into the twentieth century. The project was sponsored by Contemporary Historians, Incorporated, organized by John Dos Passos, Lillian Hellman, and Archibald MacLeish, whose plan was to show the film across the nation and collect contributions for the Loyalist cause. Hemingway's profits from the sale of the book went to the widow of Werner Heilbrun, a Republican doctor who helped Hemingway, Ivens, and Ferno as they filmed the war and who became a casualty of the war in June, 1937.[58]

Although his contract with N.A.N.A. ran out almost a year before the end of the fighting in Spain, Hemingway could foresee the outcome when the insurgents completed their drive to the sea. Changing tactics, he abandoned writing feature stories commenting on particular events in the war and began viewing the war as a whole in a series of articles for the new magazine *Ken*. Conceived by *Esquire* editors David Smart and Arnold Gingrich as a rallying point for liberal opinion, the magazine first appeared in March, 1938, with the declared intention of telling the inside story of the political intrigues at home and abroad, whether Fascist or Communist, American bureaucratic or Japanese imperial. Learning of *Ken*'s aims, Hemingway asked Gingrich to list him as an active editor as well as contributor. However, while in Spain, he began hearing contradictory stories about the editorial policy of the magazine. What the stories were is not clear. But it is either a mark of their virulence or of Hemingway's caution that by the time his first contribution appeared in the April 7 number, he had cabled Gingrich to have an expla-

58. *The Spanish Earth* (Cleveland, 1938), afternote.

nation inserted beside his article stating that he had acted as contributor only and had had no voice in making policy for the magazine.[59]

His *Ken* articles showed Hemingway's increasing concern that America did not realize the implications of the Spanish war. They sometimes had an almost hysterical overtone as he made plainer and simpler, sometimes overly simple, the dangers of Fascism inside and outside the country. It was the closest Hemingway ever came to outright propaganda, but that he believed his own cries of alarm is beyond challenge. If his treatment of European and domestic politics was at times heavy-handed, it revealed a sense of urgency widely at variance with the statements of five years before that he had already served his time for democracy. Typical subjects were "Treachery in Aragon" and "False News to the President."

What more Hemingway could do about the Spanish war he did in speeches, pronouncements, journal articles, and introductory endorsements of works by other survivors of the war. They reflected one of the most urgent but least balanced periods of his nonfictional career. "The Writer and the War," appearing in a symposium on the lessons to be learned from the Spanish conflict, depicted the sorry plight of authors engulfed by a totalitarian state, and warned that war could produce such a condition in America.[60] *Writers Take Sides*, published by the League of American Writers in 1938, contained an anti-Franco statement by Hemingway and a telegram jointly signed by him, Vincent Sheean, and Louis Fischer calling for money contributions to support the Loyalist medical service. And in the 1939 *Direction* magazine article, "The Writer as Writer," based on Hemingway's Barcelona interview with James Lardner, son of the humorist, he told of the need for writers who could infiltrate into Spain and tell what went on there after the Falangist conquest. Hemingway recognized himself as a figure too well-known and too well-identified with the Republican cause to be able to live and work in Franco's Spain.

A second kind of writing about the war that Hemingway did at this time was to provide introductions and commentaries for works in the other arts. For painters and etchers he wrote the

59. Peterson, pp. 279-80; Arnold Gingrich to ROS, January 28, 1966.
60. Henry Hart (ed.), *The Writer in a Changing World* (New York, 1937), pp. 69-73.

preface to the Museum of Modern Art booklet *Luis Quintanilla: Artist and Soldier* (1938) and three prefaces for the Modern Age Books edition of Quintanilla's war drawings *All the Brave* (1939), which included the prefaces written the previous year for Quintanilla. For sculptors he did a word portrait of Milton Wolff, youthful commander of the Lincoln and Lincoln-Washington Brigades, as a catalogue note for an exhibition of sculptures by Jo Davidson on Spanish Civil War heroes. His third group of war writings consisted of introductions to books by veterans of the recent conflict. Joseph North's pamphlet *Men in the Ranks,* sketches of twelve Americans who fought in the Fifteenth International Brigade, was written and published to raise money for the support and defense of Spanish Civil War veterans from America who were imprisoned by Franco or interned at Ellis Island under the terms of the neutrality agreement. Hemingway's foreword spelled out the appeal. His preface to Gustav Regler's novel *The Great Crusade* was written at Camaguey, Cuba, in 1940, and showed the effects of time and distance in his thinking about the Spanish war. Perhaps because of his fictional catharsis in *For Whom the Bell Tolls,* he saw the early days of the war and the exploits of the International Brigades as the time "when all their gold was iron," when the brigades were undergoing their first ordeals, sometimes faltering, but emerging purified and enduring at last. He contrasted the brigades' early heroic optimism, as chronicled by Regler, with the later grim Marxist version of defeat and retreat told by Alvah Bessie. Regler's book, he insisted, was as much factual as invented and the better for its reporting.

The stages of Hemingway's career as essayist often overlapped. While he was still writing about the Spanish war, he began to work on other projects, some reflecting new interests. For more than a year after his return from Spain he worked as a man of letters, continuing and completing projects he had started during the war years. In 1937, for example, he took time from his reporting to write the preface for Jerome Bahr's collection of stories *All Good Americans.* He used the preface, moreover, to talk about himself as well as about Bahr. Thinking, no doubt, of his own early struggle to publish, he noted that many good writers are born to tell short stories rather than to write novels. But their publishers want novels, because novels have the possibility of delayed success that story collections lack. "But when you are a young writer, the only way you can get a book of stories published now is to have someone with what is called, in the trade, a name write a preface to it. Otherwise you must write a novel first."[61] In this mood he wrote the preface to his own collection for the 1938 edition of *The Fifth Column and the First Forty-Nine Stories*. The stories in many cases were victories of integrity over compromise, he noted. While publishers and anthologists had made some of the stories standard reading, there were other stories he valued equally as high, though few readers seemed to share his opinion.

Two other works during this man-of-letters interlude were his program note for Henrietta Hoopes' exhibition of paintings at the Knoedler Galleries in late 1940, and his lyric essay on "The Clark's Fork Valley, Wyoming" in *Vogue* for February, 1939. The Henrietta Hoopes note was almost as gay, surrealistic, and irresponsible as the pictures themselves. The Wyoming sketch was one of four in a nostalgic group on American scenes, with the other three furnished by Irwin Edman ("Red Mountain, Arlington, Vermont"), Archibald MacLeish ("Dry Tortugas"), and Vincent Sheean ("An Illinois Town—Chatauqua Week"). Significantly, the sketch identified Hemingway with native-soil writers of the thirties in spite of his long expatriation. Hemingway and Thomas Wolfe, said editor Frank Crowninshield, had priestlike abilities with "words of power" to "call up the very spirit of America."[62]

The interlude was soon over, though, and Hemingway's writing returned to the subject of war. His literary work during the years of World War II was exclusively essayistic. It also furnished a cross-section of his working media—newspaper journalism, book essays, and magazine features. The first was a series of six articles for the unique newspaper *PM*, following his trip to China in 1941.

His work for *PM* was the result of personal acquaintance and editorial policy. While finishing work on *For Whom the Bell Tolls*, Hemingway fished with *PM*'s Ralph Ingersoll, former editor of *Fortune* and staff man on several Luce publications. While *PM* was still in the planning stages, Ingersoll engaged

61. *All Good Americans* (New York, 1937), p. viii.
62. *Vogue's First Reader* (New York, 1942), p. xiii.

Hemingway to write for the new paper.[63] Ingersoll's *PM* was different in that it appeared with the format and frequency of a newspaper but was a journal of opinion and commentary on current affairs, was free of advertising, and was supported by sales and by subsidies from liberal department-store angel Marshall Field.[64] Although *PM*, like *Ken*, was plagued with rumors of staff infiltration by Communists, Hemingway was ready to fulfill his contract by the spring of 1941. Ingersoll, like John Wheeler of N.A.N.A., valued Hemingway as a master journalist and expert on military affairs from command levels to tactical maneuvers in the field. His articles were to be written after his return from the Far East and were to provide readers with a full perspective and prognosis on Japanese intentions in the Pacific. The contract further provided that if war broke out while Hemingway was in the Far East, he would stay there and report by cable on a day-to-day basis.[65]

With his new wife, Martha Gellhorn Hemingway, a *Collier's* correspondent, Hemingway made the trip a combination wedding journey and fact-gathering expedition. The Hemingways entered China at Hong Kong, went on to Chungking by way of several provincial cities, and, after seeing battle and training areas, followed the Burma Road and its supply routes to Rangoon. Traveling by plane, car, train, sampan, horseback, and on foot to battle areas, they spent weeks talking and listening to Chinese Nationalists and Communists, Russians, British, Americans, and in Hong Kong to Japanese nationals. Hemingway returned by plane from Rangoon to Manila and New York with stops at Kunming and Hong Kong. His wife returned several days later after a stay in Sumatra to gather materials.[66]

The China articles met Ingersoll's expectations. As master journalist Hemingway played Chinese officials against British advisors to learn what each really thought of the other; he used his knowledge of Soviet military advisers gained in Spain to prompt Soviets in China to talk; his portraits of Chiang Kai-shek and other key people caught them in mid-motion while they made

63. Leicester Hemingway, p. 225. Leicester Hemingway was also on the *PM* staff at the time.

64. John Tebbel, *The Marshall Fields* (New York, 1947), pp. 188, 206.

65. Ralph Ingersoll, "Hemingway's Far East Trip to See for Himself if War with Japan Is Inevitable," *PM*, June 9, 1941, p. 6.

66. *Ibid.*, pp. 6-8.

history; his descriptions of walled cities, dust, and caravans juxta-posed a thousand-year view of Chinese history with prospects for the next six months. As military expert he contrasted British, German, and Russian views of the Chinese Nationalist armies and Japanese mobile divisions and looked behind the Japanese timetable to see what moves their logistics requirements would prompt.

As world traveler he informed readers of the relative merits of rice wine flavored with dead snakes and of that flavored with dead cuckoos in the bottom of the jar.

His second venture in war writing of the decade was the editing of *Men at War* and providing an introduction for the anthology of war pieces. Again his reputation as war writer was critical. Solicited by Crown Publishers to carry through on a plan suggested by play anthologist William Kozlenko, Hemingway obtained a release from Scribner's to work on the collection and brought with him Scribner's editor Maxwell Perkins.[67] Substantially reworking Kozlenko's plan, Hemingway used his knowledge of military classics for guidance in selecting the particular battle accounts and working out the scheme of organization—arrangement by themes taken from the maxims of von Clausewitz. Selections ranged from the biblical account of Joshua at Jericho and Livy's "Horatius at the Bridge" to the latest reports from Midway and the Libyan Desert, from Stephen Crane's poetic re-creation of action at Chancellorsville to such historically accurate and verifiable accounts as Admiral George Dewey's "Manila Bay." Hemingway's stance in the introduction was that of the father's generation talking to the sons now fighting another war. Indeed, he dedicated the book to his three sons, one of whom was already the age that Hemingway had been when he first went to war. The intention behind the introduction was pragmatic: to develop fortitude and moral endurance in his armed-service readers by convincing them that, whatever their agonies, other men throughout history had faced them and endured. He gained many nonmilitary readers also and the book appeared on the best-seller lists in November and December of 1942.

His third group of war writings was a series of six articles in *Collier's* in 1944, ranging from the Normandy invasion to the

67. Herbert Michelman to ROS, January 20, 1966.

breaking of the Siegfried Line. This time arrangements with the publisher came about easily because of Martha Gellhorn Hemingway's already existing contract with the magazine. *Collier's* publisher Joseph Knapp, in spite of a dispute over fishing records in 1935, made Hemingway *Collier's* European bureau chief and contracted with him for feature coverage of European battle areas.[68] Hemingway's six articles were frequently vivid, sometimes awkward, always personal. Here more than in any of his other war writing he was self-consciously expert and legendary. Not only did he tell landing boat officers and infantry platoon leaders how to approach Fox Green beach and attack German positions, he also helped create the legend of himself as bearded leader of French guerrillas swaggering into Paris to liberate the Ritz Hotel wine cellar before LeClerc's Free French divisions could enter the city. His reported comment by an American officer after the spectacular capture of their segment of the Siegfried Line ironically characterized Hemingway's work for *Collier's*: it all seemed like something out of a grade-B movie.

After the war Hemingway withdrew from the public arena except for occasional single articles or chapters and isolated prefaces. His pattern during the period was to begin with postmortems on the war, work into another sportsman cycle, and emerge as a more self-conscious spokesman for the arts.

In 1945, John Groth, sometime illustrator for *Esquire* and later war artist, published his *Studio: Europe*, which contained in addition to his battle pictures a memoir on Hemingway in the Siegfried Line and an introduction by Hemingway. Groth's portrait, "Schloss Hemingway," helped keep alive the postwar memory of Hemingway as the old soldier-correspondent calmly deploying gunners to enfilade the approaches to a captured farmhouse in the Hürtgen Forest. The house was known as "Schloss Hemingway" on the maps at the headquarters of the nearby army division. Hemingway's introduction was written out of respect for Groth's work originating in the *Esquire* days and because of the friendship that developed between them during their week together on the battle line in Germany. Requested by Groth to provide the introduction, he certified the credibility of the drawings and prose sketches. It was an act of friendship rather than of inspiration. His 1945 foreword to Ben Raeburn's forum on

68. Leicester Hemingway, pp. 183-84, 229.

postwar problems, *Treasury for the Free World*, showed Hemingway as a Walter Lippmann style commentator, calling for international justice and understanding by the victors in a world just shocked into the age of atom bombs and war trials. Although this piece came close to the Big Thinking he had always decried, it was properly large-minded enough to be reprinted the next year as a keynote article in the United Nations magazine *Free World*.

With the publication of "The Great Blue River" in *Holiday* magazine and "Cuban Fishing" in *Game Fish of the World*, both in 1949, Hemingway resumed the role of public sportsman. The magazine piece showed his ability to write within the *Holiday* travel-escape formula and still keep his own touch. The Great Blue River, his term for the Gulf Stream, was a place, he asserted, where sportsmen could make their last stand against encroaching civilization. The article was filled with "how-to" information, as the *Esquire* articles of the thirties had been, and in addition listed reasons for a sportsman to live in Cuba—reasons which echoed and extended his expatriate thinking. In "Cuban Fishing" the sportsman combined with the amateur naturalist to describe the fighting habits of game fish in Cuban waters; the approach was heavily influenced by the natural history interests of the editors, Brian Vesey-Fitzgerald and Francesca Lamonte, the latter an Associate Curator of Fishes at The American Museum of Natural History. Hemingway followed suit in his 1951 preface to Van Campen Heilner's *Salt Water Fishing*. He saluted Heilner as a sportsman and pioneer in most of the known game fish areas of the world. The highest compliment he could offer Heilner, he said, was to note that in his field he was still learning. A brief coda to the fishing essays was his preface to Charles Ritz's book *A Fly Fisher's Life*, in 1959. As with several other prefaces of the period, the substance was in the signature rather than in the essay itself, an appreciation of an old friend's zest for a vanishing art.

Gradually, however, the sportsman cycle took him again into big game hunting, an interest he followed until the African crashes in late 1953. The transition between Cuban fishing and world-wide big game hunting became evident in his *True* magazine article of April, 1951, "The Shot." In the article Hemingway shifted his attention from the immediate locale of Cuba to a remembered hunt in Idaho. In doing so, he reasserted his belief in the significance of frontier skills even for the mid-twentieth century. If the antelope hunt was typical Hemingway material, it was also quite in line with the *True* formula. Factual, adventurous, humorous, and broadly masculine, the account, as the editors saw, presented Hemingway as model sportsman.[69] Said the blurb, "Mr. Hemingway understands hunting, whether in Cuba or in the high country of Idaho. This is a story about how it's done—but especially about how a sportsman does it—by one of our greatest living writers." His foreword to François Sommer's *Man and Beast in Africa* (1953) was a mixture of technical observation on fire-arms and animal anatomy and of justification of the hunter's instinct. Hunting tastes, he said, came in patterns and a hunter learned from age to age what he could kill with maximum satisfaction. In young manhood he might look for lions, but killing the carrion birds was more important to the older man. He also lamented the abuses practiced by white hunters in East Africa when the safari tended to become a guided tour instead of a life-risking hunt. An oblique comment on the hunter's life appeared that year in the *Ringling Brothers and Barnum & Bailey Circus Magazine*. In "The Circus" he contrasted the dream-like quality of the show animals with the fierce reality of charging lions and of buffalo bulls crashing through the brush. In the pattern of *Death in the Afternoon* and *Green Hills of Africa* thirty years before, he linked his beast mystique to his ideas on art. Animals in circuses, he wrote, furnished allegories for men trying to understand their own caged lives.

That same year, following his popular and critical triumph in *The Old Man and the Sea*, Hemingway contracted with *Look* magazine to do an article based on his return safari to East Africa. Expecting to benefit from the recall value of the country for readers of *Green Hills of Africa*, "The Snows of Kilimanjaro," and "The Short Happy Life of Francis Macomber," he took along *Look* photographer Earl Theissen for extra pictorial effects. While the article obviously intended to profit also from interest in the recent film *The Snows of Kilimanjaro*, Hemingway wrote as though it were a mission to correct mistaken ideas prompted by the film. He contrasted the actual country with that shown in "The Snows of Zanuck" and concentrated on the real Africa

69. Peterson, pp. 312-14.

known by white hunters and game rangers—the Africa of wounded rhinos, orphaned gazelles, and drouth-idled natives.

The "Safari" article was published in *Look*'s January 26, 1954, issue, but by the time of publication, news value of the safari had increased greatly because of two crashes the Hemingways had survived over the Christmas-New Year period. The result was two more African pieces in *Look* in late April and early May. "The Christmas Gift," in two parts, told of the Hemingways' flight along the Kivu-Albert lake system and the Rift Valley and on to Murchison Falls, where they crashed and awaited rescue until they hailed a river steamer below the falls and came back into the world's view. Boarding a plane at Butiaba for flight back to Nairobi, they crashed again and burned, this time barely escaping death and receiving serious injuries. As several notices of his death in the crashes had gone out to the world, Hemingway spent time in press interviews giving the facts of the crashes and at the same time denying the frequently printed claim in obituaries that he had always sought death and finally found it. This confusion, he wrote in "The Christmas Gift," was his reason for writing the two extra articles: "At the time [of the press interviews] I did not wish to ever write anything about the two crashes but since then I have read so many absurd accounts in our various obituaries, especially in the foreign press, that I thought it would be best to give a true and accurate account."[70] He did not crash, he said, as one German paper had claimed, while trying to land on the top of Mount Kilimanjaro.

Hemingway's third postwar vein of writing was represented by the essay that posed him as speaker for the arts. This tendency had appeared early. In 1946 he was one of a series of artists solicited to express congratulations to the Cincinnati Symphony Orchestra on its Golden Jubilee concert series. In 1948 he acted as established man of letters in writing a special introduction for the deluxe illustrated edition of *A Farewell to Arms*. Yet another part of his role was to write more introductions for other writers' efforts, in much the manner as he had written them during his first fame after the original publication of *A Farewell to Arms*. In 1949 his introduction to Elio Vittorini's *In Sicily* praised the novelist at the expense of the critics, certified that Vittorini's ostensible Fascist politics were honorable but ignor-

70. "The Christmas Gift," Part Two, *Look*, XVIII (May 4, 1954), 83.

able, and endorsed his love of Italy. It was probably this type of book that Hemingway spoke of a year later when he said in a *New York Herald Tribune Book Review* interview that besides reading widely in domestic and foreign books, magazines and newspapers, he read several French and Italian books, some in manuscript, which he believed in and tried to get published.[71] The necessity to admit that he was an established man of letters came a step closer in 1950 when he wrote the preface for Lee Samuels' booklet *A Hemingway Check-List*, published by Scribner's the next year. Here he did what he had refused to do twenty years before for Louis Henry Cohn in his 1931 bibliography. Self-recognition here was expressed to the extent that he regretted that some of his early writings were lost to Samuels' listing. He could even joke about Hadley Hemingway's loss, in 1922, of the suitcase containing almost all of his stories and poems written up to that time. Another job of the time reminiscent of the thirties was his 1952 program note "Finca Vigía" for Reginald Rowe's exhibit of paintings at Wellons Gallery in New York. Reginald Rowe, he said, was not only a good neighbor in Cuba but also a sun-drunk artist who could teach one how to see all over again. Hemingway's self-recognition as a literary figure whose conscience the world watched was evident in his 1956 *Look* article "A Situation Report." Noting at the opening of this report that he had taken too much time from his major work in fiction to oversee the filming of *The Old Man and the Sea*, he swore to leave off journalism, movie-making, and seeing too many friends. The thing to do, as Cyril Connolly had urged in *The Unquiet Grave*, was to work for the masterpiece and ignore the distracting small stuff. Only the masterwork finally counted, and a writer ultimately had to live through his work, not through his personal legend.

It was also during this time—the period of the early fifties—that Hemingway began more and more to practice another form of expository comment. The interview became one of his most frequently used vehicles to convey ideas and moods. It was tied closely with his return to public notice through the publication of *Across the River and into the Trees* and *The Old Man and the Sea*. He had used the interview as a form of expression

71. "Important Authors of the Fall Speak for Themselves," *New York Herald-Tribune Book Review*, October 8, 1950, p. 4.

earlier, but not with the thoroughness or frequency he now practiced. He had written some of his *Esquire* articles in the form of interviews and dialogues and in 1940 he had talked war and books with Robert Van Gelder as he finished reading proof on *For Whom the Bell Tolls.* He had talked about his China trip to Ralph Ingersoll in 1941 for the lead article in his series on the Far East and at that time had begun to exercise control over his interviews so that in many cases they can rightly be considered his work as much as that of the interviewer. Ingersoll noted at the time that the interview was recorded by a stenographer and corrected by Hemingway in typescript. It was thus an "authenticated interview."[72] Not all, of course, were exact reports of Hemingway's words. Lillian Ross's "Portrait" in the *New Yorker* for May 13, 1950, was a masterpiece of insinuation and self-incrimination with its Indian talk, but the ideas on paintings, big cities, and critics were consistent with his writings and other interviews. A more extreme example of the interview not accurately reporting Hemingway's words was the specious interview run soon after publication of *The Old Man and the Sea,* which so embarrassed Hemingway with his Cuban fisherman friends that he felt obliged to make a round of the fishermen's cantinas disclaiming any part of the alleged interview.[73] Other interviews, such as Harvey Breit's recordings in the *New York Times Book Review* and *The Writer Observed,* gave Hemingway a chance to talk to the world without writing. Shortly after publication of his sea novel, his letter to Bernard Kalb in interview form was published in the *Saturday Review.* Kalb had written interview questions in lieu of a face-to-face meeting and received essentially the same answers Hemingway was giving others on his writing routines.[74]

A second wave of interviews occurred after Hemingway won the Nobel Prize in 1954. Indeed, his acceptance speech, delivered to the Swedish Academy by American Ambassador John Cabot restated several of the convictions he had written as early as *Death in the Afternoon,* had repeated and developed in his *Esquire* articles, had stated more recently in interviews, and would restate in future essays and interviews. Particularly he emphasized

72. Ingersoll, p. 6.
73. Leicester Hemingway, p. 273.
74. "A Letter from Hemingway," *Saturday Review,* XXXV (September 6, 1952), 11.

that good writing is lonely writing.[75] Although the interviews subsequent to his receiving the Nobel Prize were too numerous and often too emphemeral to canvass, they all contained variations on themes from *Death in the Afternoon* and *Green Hills of Africa*. The basic ideas were the same. Only their application shifted. These pronouncements had by then, of course, the authority of certification by world opinion reflected in the Swedish Academy's prize as well as the self-gained authority of commercial and critical success. Examples of such interviews were those by *Time* editor (later *Atlantic* editor) Robert Manning,[76] *Paris Review* editor George Plimpton,[77] and television writer and boon companion A. E. Hotchner, who was to convert the interview into a method of biography for *Papa Hemingway* in 1966.[78]

All the time he talked for the interviewers, however, Hemingway denied that he took seriously his own remarks. It was the same pattern he had followed in his journalism. At the close of his Nobel Prize speech he observed that writers should write what they have to say, not speak it. He told Robert Manning the same year that his writing was "for good" while the talk was only incidental. And he explained to George Plimpton that talk was exploratory and irresponsible: he often said things to see whether he believed them. But what he wrote he would stand by.[79]

Three other ephemeral pieces appeared during the early fifties, two of which did little to enhance Hemingway's reputation, though they traded on it. The ethical reasoning behind one of the pieces must have been torturous. A probably apocryphal story has it that he turned down a bid from the advertisers of Lord Calvert whiskey to be one of their "men of distinction" on grounds that he did not believe in the whiskey. In November, 1951, and again in September, 1952, however, Hemingway appeared in a Ballantine ale advertisement with his letter certifying the delights of a cool Ballantine after fighting and boating

75. Reprinted in Baker, *Hemingway: The Writer as Artist*, p. 339.
76. "Hemingway in Cuba," *The Atlantic Monthly*, CCXVI (August 1965), 101-8; interviewed in 1954 but not published until 1965.
77. "The Art of Fiction," *The Paris Review*, XVIII (Spring 1958) 61-89; reprinted in Baker, *Hemingway and His Critics*, pp. 19-37.
78. "Hemingway Talks to American Youth," *This Week Magazine* (October 18, 1959), pp. 10, 11, 24; *Papa Hemingway* (New York, 1966), *passim*.
79. Baker, *Hemingway: The Writer as Artist*, p. 339; Manning, "Hemingway in Cuba," 102; Plimpton in Baker, *Hemingway and His Critics*, p. 24.

a big fish.[80] "A Tribute to Mamma from Papa Hemingway" in a *Life* article on Marlene Dietrich saluted "the Kraut" in much the same way Hemingway had talked of her in Lillian Ross's *New Yorker* portrait. Dietrich, he said, was the embodiment of a modern woman living by stricter, but self-derived and self-imposed, ethics than those prescribed by convention.[81] The third piece was more in keeping with Hemingway's usual stance before the public. His tribute to Ezra Pound, published in the 1955 pamphlet *Ezra Pound at Seventy*, was written on the occasion of the poet's birthday and for the purpose of securing the poet's release from St. Elizabeth's Hospital. Joining such other tribute-givers as E. E. Cummings, he further called for the government to permit Pound to return to Italy where he would be respected as a poet rather than condescended to as a possible lunatic or traitor. Pound's crime had been paid for, he claimed, and continued confinement could only be regarded as cruel and unusual punishment.

Hemingway also found that he could use the published letter as a form of preface as well as advertisement for his own work. Louis Henry Cohn had printed Hemingway's letters as part of his own preface to the 1931 bibliography. Hemingway and the editors of *Life* adapted that practice to their own uses in 1952 and again in 1960. The letter "From Ernest Hemingway to the Editors of *Life*" in the issue just prior to the *Life* publication of *The Old Man and the Sea* did for the short novel what his formal introductions had done for such Scribner-published works as *A Farewell to Arms* and *The Fifth Column and the First Forty-Nine Stories*.[82] The story had taken fifteen years to write, he said, and he could testify that it was "a strange damn story" that strongly affected him even after two hundred readings. He used the letter-preface form again for the 1960 publication of "The Dangerous Summer." A "Publisher's Review" page in the August 29 issue of *Life* recounted the circumstances surrounding the composition of the bullfight series and noted that some 35,000 words of the full 63,562-word account would appear in the magazine. In addition to the first installment of "The Dangerous Summer," the next issue also contained a publisher's letter to readers entitled "Two Prideful Rivals and a Prideful 'Life.'"

80. *Life*, XXXI (November 5, 1951), 90-91; XXXIII (September 8, 1952), 56-57.
81. *Life*, XXXIII (August 18, 1952), 92-93.
82. *Life*, XXXIII (August 25, 1952), 124.

Quoting excerpts from Hemingway letters, the article explained the growth of Hemingway's account of the Ordonez-Dominguin rivalry. Invited by *Life* to write a 5000-word news story on the bullfighters and their competition, he had found the account growing and changing in conception. The news article stretched beyond the three installments allowed it by the magazine to book length. Hemingway found it necessary "to make the people come alive and show the extraordinary circumstances" of the events—to show what was valid and timeless in the matadors' confrontations even after they had lost current news value. "Now I can write only one way," he said, "the best I can."[83]

The letter-preface was right, and significant. "The Dangerous Summer" was more than a report on some fifty bull killings and character sketches of the matadors. It developed dramatically the growing rivalry between the established but shaky champion Dominguin and a proud new challenger—a recognizably Hemingwayesque predicament—until the older man was driven by his inner code to the edge of destruction. But it was also a return to the Spain of *Death in the Afternoon* and *The Sun Also Rises*, an updating of the technical details of the bullfight book and a sequel to the "lost generation" novel in the best "son of the hero" tradition. Antonio Ordonez, son of the model for Pedro Romero in the novel, was in Hemingway's eyes a better man than his father. Luis Miguel Dominguin repeated Belmonte's role from the novel, fighting "corrected" bulls, doing decadently ornate capework, and scorning the jeers of a disappointed crowd. The sequel included, as well, the 1959 version of Jake Barnes's Pamplona fiesta, but this time the author had on no fictional mask and the Robert Cohn role was played by a belligerent young journalist who accused the author of losing himself in the roles of his created characters. It was, in addition, a travel account celebrating the handsome women of Malaga, the Sisley-like river scenes at Aranjuez, the surviving storks of Despenaperros, and the garlic snails of the Callejon restaurant in Madrid. Not least, "The Dangerous Summer" was Hemingway's reconciliation with Franco's Spain, a land he had loved and stayed away from since 1939. But by the time of his travels to see the rivalry, there was no feeling against him in Spain, and he recorded how customs

83. *Life*, XLIX (September 5, 1960), 2.

officers paid the duty on his Gibraltar-bought whiskey as a mark of acceptance.

The significance of the letter-preface was that in "The Dangerous Summer" Hemingway was again writing journalism and trying to make it more than journalism. He tried to have it both ways as he disclaimed the seriousness of journalism and at the same time practiced it while writing "the best I can." Critical response to the series also raised the issue of art in journalism. He told his brother Leicester that "The Dangerous Summer" had been unjustly criticized for lacking literary quality when it was explicitly by contract a job of reporting.[84] His doubts about the series, based apparently on his doubtful execution of uncertain goals, finally resulted in his withdrawing the book version from scheduled publication.

Like his journalism, Hemingway's memoir *A Moveable Feast* was a contradiction of previously stated convictions. Early in his career as a writer of nonfiction he had declared himself doubtful about memoirs and autobiographies. In his 1924 "Pamplona Letter" for *the transatlantic review* he said, "It is only when you can no longer believe in your own exploits that you write your memoirs."[85] And in "A Paris Letter" for *Esquire* in 1934, smarting after the sting of remarks in *The Autobiography of Alice B. Toklas* and lamenting the changes in the city hit by world depression, he wrote, "What makes you feel badly here though is not any of the things I mentioned earlier. People must be expected to kill themselves when they lose their money, I suppose, and drunkards get bad livers, and legendary people usually end by writing their memoirs."[86]

Still, no prisoner of consistency, he wrote his memoir of apprentice days in Paris before recognition brought its problems. Like "The Dangerous Summer," the Paris memoir took on a patterned progression that might have served as a kind of plot had he assumed the mask of fiction. A record of the losing of one's innocence to the seducers of the sophisticated life, it nevertheless called real names and referred to legendary actions. Written as his version of events frequently mentioned in others' memoirs of the Left Bank in the twenties, it began with a record

84. Leicester Hemingway, p. 280.
85. *the transatlantic review*, II (October 1924), 301.
86. *Esquire*, I (February 1934), 156.

of those years and carried through an intent to tell "the way it was," given the perspective of thirty years. He began the work as a result of a stop at the Ritz Hotel in Paris after his 1956 trip to Spain. Ritz porters reminded him to claim baggage stored in the hotel basement since 1936 on threat of its being sent to the incinerator. Going through the bags, he found his notes and journals dating from the early twenties in Paris. Upon his return to Cuba he worked through the source material until by 1957 he had written three chapters and was calling it an autobiography by *remate*, a two-wall shot in *jai alai*. While in Spain in 1959 to follow the Ordonez-Dominguin rivalry, he worked further on the sketches and returned to them with additional resolution after his disappointment with "The Dangerous Summer." Except for final revisions of punctuation and perhaps arrangement, he had completed the manuscript by the time of his death and was considering another small volume on Paris. Last revisions and confirmations on names were carried out by Mary Hemingway in 1963, at the urging of Malcolm Cowley and with the advice of Scribner's editor Harry Brague and *Life* photographer Gordon Parks, who did the photographs for the excerpts in that magazine's version in April, 1964.[87] As the culmination of Hemingway's career in the essay, the book was also published in the spring of that year.

Seeing Hemingway's nonfictional career in perspective, one is impressed by its quantity and diversity. Critics of his fiction have charged Hemingway with attempting only a limited and, on the whole, minor range of moods and effects, however excellent their execution was. Such a charge could obviously not pertain to his work in the essay. If it was weighted in favor of war reporting and the active life of the sportsman, it also readily extended into personal introspection, social and political commentary, into aestehtics, and into almost all major subject areas except metaphysics and religion. Those he left for implicit treatment in his fiction. Contrary to his frequently stated fears that use of material in journalism and other kinds of expository writing would exhaust its possible use in fiction, that body of writing acted as a kind of proving ground for many ideas, situations, and verbal effects that later went into his fiction. If he said that

87. Mary Hemingway, "The Making of a Book: A Chronicle and a Memoir," *New York Times Book Review*, May 10, 1964, p. 26.

he talked to explore and then took what seemed to be true for his writing, he similarly tried out ideas and feelings in his essays before they became the stuff of fiction. Travel scenes, dialogue effects, emotional responses, political insights, elegiac moods, and narrative techniques had their showing first in the nonfiction.

Hemingway's fiction rightly claims our primary attention and ultimate concern, but we miss much of what goes on in that fiction if we remain unaware of the part his nonfictional writing played in that work throughout his career. Our best reason for studying Hemingway's essays is to see better Hemingway's art of fiction. To a secondary degree we can find value in the essays per se. Because Hemingway's fiction is expressive and self-exploring, his essays along with his more personal biography must remain key analytical tools for the study of his art.

We can more confidently read Hemingway's nonfiction as a sure indicator of his thought and feeling—particularly as they relate to his art—than we can read what he says from behind the mask of fiction and take it as his own voice. In *A Farewell to Arms* Frederic Henry says that abstract words are obscene, but Hemingway in his public voice as essayist refused to go that far. He might say that he distrusted certain columnists' theorizing about revolution without their having experienced one, and he might prefer Tolstoy's narration in *War and Peace* to his Big Thinking about chance and history, but those declarations were not in the same realm as statements made by created characters. If we are to know with some certainty what Hemingway thought, we have to look to the nonfiction first and follow the alchemy of art on from that point. In effect, there are three levels of ideas to deal with: what Hemingway thought personally, what he expressed publicly and directly in his essays, and what he put into his fiction. The first perhaps was never adequately recorded, even if the Hemingway letters are ever published and Hotchner's *Papa Hemingway* can be verified. The most personal level must inevitably be left to inference. The third involves the necessary complication and transformation of the imaginative mask and can presumably be put into only the roughest equivalent of expository language for critical study. The second he put into the form and language most readily and directly usable for total comprehension. It is that self-explaining, public voice with which this study is concerned.

The Essay as a Vehicle of Personality

II. The Eternal Expert

"MYSELF," SAID MONTAIGNE, "AM THE GROUND WORK OF MY BOOK."
The same could have been said by Ernest Hemingway. As an
essayist in the tradition of the great skeptic, he almost invariably
practiced the art of personal statement—the subjective response.
When we think of Hemingway the novelist's objective narration
and his horror of the intrusive author, we are surprised at the
personal element in the essays. But perhaps we need not be. The
personal force of the narrator in *The Sun Also Rises* or *A Farewell to Arms* is not greatly different in effect from the author's
impact in the essays. It is only that the fictional mask compli-
cates identities. In the essays Hemingway the author is always
present; his influence, his prejudices, his sense of his own identity
hang over all the statements. Much of the reason for his becoming a public personality lies in his self-depiction. And if we are
tempted to identify Hemingway with Jake Barnes or Harry of
Kilimanjaro, we can with less risk, and perhaps no less force,

identify him with the voice of the commentator-observer of "American Bohemians in Paris a Weird Lot," "World's Series of Bullfighting a Mad, Whirling Carnival," or *Green Hills of Africa.*

This way of making his personal views part of the public's life was not, however, wholly Hemingway's invention, though he must have aided its development with his actions as well as his essays. "The private Hemingway was an artist," observed Robert Manning. "The public Hemingway was an experience."[1] Charisma, magnetism, talent, whatever it was—Hemingway made people believe anything marvelous about him, whether he said it or not. Morley Callaghan noted from their shared days at the *Toronto Daily Star* that Hemingway had "that fatal capacity for making men want to tell fantastic stories about him."[2] Even Scribner's editor Maxwell Perkins told a story about Hemingway jumping into the ring and knocking out the middleweight champion of France. Both the *Chicago Tribune* and the *Toronto Star Weekly* ran stories of Hemingway's bull wrestling exploits at Pamplona, with Donald Ogden Stewart, John Dos Passos, and Robert McAlmon incidentally sharing the publicity. The *Star Weekly* quoted him as saying casually that tackling a bull in Spain was like playing rugby. The *Star Weekly* paragraph in September, 1924, also indicated his candidacy for legend well before publication of *In Our Time* or *The Sun Also Rises:* "How Hemingway got into the bull ring is due to his adventurous spirit which seeks a kick in everything from flyfishing in the Pyrenees to following the Turkish army in Macedonia. His bullfighting adventures are no more startling than his turning, when he was rejected because of eyesight by his own army during the late war, to driving a Ford truck ambulance in the Italian army, from which vantage point he managed to secure a commission in the Italian Arditi, their famous shock troops corps, in which he won the Valore medal and a lame leg."[3] The legend of his service with the Arditi was the sort of story Hemingway allowed to circulate without contradiction. As late as 1956, Sylvia Beach wrote her biographical "facts," still uncorrected and contributing to legend that Hemingway had lived a bitter boyhood marked by the early death of his father and by early departure from school to support his mother, sisters, and brothers; that he had

1. "Hemingway in Cuba," *Atlantic Monthly*, CCXVI (August 1965), 148.
2. *That Summer in Paris* (New York, 1964), pp. 62-63.
3. "Tackling a Spanish Bull Is Just Like Rugby; Hemingway Tells How He Surprised the Natives," *TSW*, September 13, 1924, p. 18.

done vagabond newspaper work in his youth and had later enlisted in Canada, was wounded in Italy, and spent two years in army hospitals recovering from his wounds.[4] Knowingly or otherwise, Hemingway perpetuated the legend in 1944 when he wrote in "The Battle for Paris":

During this epoch I was addressed by the guerilla force as "captain." This is a very low rank to have at the age of forty-five years, and so in the presence of strangers, they would address me, usually, as "colonel." But they were a little upset and worried by my very low rank, and one of them whose trade for the past year had been receiving mines and blowing up German ammunition trucks and staff cars, asked confidentially, "My Captain, how is it that with your age and your undoubted long years of service and your obvious wounds (caused by hitting a static water tank in London) you are still a captain?" "Young man," I told him, "I have not been able to advance in rank due to the fact that I cannot read or write."[5]

Such were the force of personality and the climate of public belief that prompted Hemingway to make his essays the vehicle of his personal views for the public world. People wanted to believe in heroes.

Fundamental to Hemingway's use of the essay as a vehicle of his personality was his assumed role as expert. The other roles he might play, the other special interests he might exploit, finally depended on his self-presentation as one who knew both the basic principles and the ultimate refinements of the subject at hand. His right to speak on a topic, whether it was lion-hunting or wine-drinking or fiction-writing, derived from his implied competence and knowledgeability. If logically this technique was one of begging the question, the tactic was still that practiced by anyone whose authority is self-generated rather than conferred. In thinking and writing in this manner Hemingway simply demonstrated his own understanding of how men's minds work and what men accept as reality. Finally it is the force of personality or character that convinces, not logic and not ideology. He could say, as Emerson said in *Nature*, that the self is axiomatic and its assertions, even those about the phenomenal world, are authoritative and convincing if they are consistent with the inner exigencies of the self. If he did not say that much, he

4. *Shakespeare and Company* (New York, 1959), pp. 78-79.
5. *Collier's*, CXIV (September 30, 1944), 86.

wrote and acted as if it were true. The result was that essays displaying this sense of expertness had their own autonomy and in turn corroborated the sense of authority discernible in his fiction. In *The Sun Also Rises* Hemingway's sense of authority is evident in the passage chronicling Jake and Bill's walk after dinner from Madame Lecomte's restaurant, along the Seine, up the Rue du Cardinal Lemoine and on finally to the Café Select. No explanation is given of sights encountered during the walk; simply their notation by Jake is enough. The girl at the kitchen of the Café Aux Amateurs ladles stew from an iron pot onto a plate held by an old man who holds a bottle of wine in his other hand. The familiarity and relevance of such sights are suggested when Jake asked Bill if he wants a drink.[6] Similarly in the essays, the scenes and events and finally their large significance are suggested by their relevance to the controlling consciousness —the awareness of technical and moral processes involved—of Hemingway the expert.

He played the role with four different emphases. First, he presented himself as the model for living one's life "all the way up"—as the man who could teach by example how to live the intense life that was best known to the matadors. Second, he was the man who knew behind-the-scenes facts about the stories told to the public. Third, he was the master of "how to" information, the preceptor of the way to do things to extract the full measure of satisfaction in any act. And finally, he portrayed himself as the giver of expert advice—moral and technical—to those who had to act on knowledge. This last role was always the one that the other three implied as their ultimate result.

Hemingway early cultivated the image of himself as a man of full experience. In his series of reports on the Genoa Economic Conference during the spring of 1922, he told how the unpopular Russians exacted such stiff guarantees of safety from the Italians that they were finally placed at the Imperial Hotel, two hours by car from Genoa, and there were shut off from the world by high walls, cordons of police, and by an Italian commissioner of secret police who refused to honor newsmen's credentials. But Hemingway told how he was able to get into the hotel for a lengthy interview with Soviet delegate Maxim Litvinoff while other newsmen waited outside the walls. Recognizing

6. *The Sun Also Rises* (New York, 1954), pp. 76-77.

the head of the Cheka guard in the street outside the hotel, he had boldly asked for a pass, obtained it, and bypassed the surly Italian police commissioner. That he was in chosen company was indicated by his pass number; he was the eleventh to gain admission behind the guarded walls.[7] In Thrace he was not content, he said, to observe from a train or a roadside the refugee column flowing from Anatolia to Macedonia. At Adrianople he left other newsmen, stayed the night in a mosquito- and lice-infested local inn, and the next day joined the counter-stream of Turkish refugees going from western Thrace to Constantinople. During the day he witnessed Greek cavalrymen beating Turkish cart drivers in the column and later in the day walked back to Adrianople with the Greek refugee column. Only after that authentic and vivid experience could he write his report "Refugee Column Is Scene of Horror."[8]

In his European reporting he depicted himself experiencing some of the lighter moments of the full life. Getting a hot bath in Genoa, he wrote, was almost as hazardous as fighting a war, and the wounds one received were less likely to afford much dignity. He recorded being blown from his bathtub by an exploding water heater and afterwards, while standing cut and bleeding and wrapped in only a towel, being congratulated by the hotel owner for not having been killed. The hotel janitor, the owner casually mentioned, had forgotten to remove the catch from the safety valve on the heater.[9] From Les Avants, Switzerland, he told Canadian readers of the enlargement of experience to be gained by bobsledding down the Swiss Alps. Sliding down the mountain at fifty miles an hour, he said, provided a sensation nowhere else available. It started as a chill at the base of the spine and ended with one nearly swallowing his heart; it was like riding a runaway movie film. Back at the railroad station at the foot of the mountain, he wondered "why people go to Palm Beach or the Riviera in the winter time."[10]

In an otherwise banal piece on the moral implications of the Max Baer-Joe Louis fight of 1935, a fight after which he accused Baer of cowardice resulting from an ignorance of the technical requirements of his job, Hemingway certified, out of the full-

7. "Russian Delegation Well Guarded at Genoa," *TDS*, May 4, 1922, p. 10.
8. *TDS*, November 4, 1922, p. 7.
9. "Getting a Hot Bath an Adventure in Genoa," *TDS*, May 2, 1922, p. 5.
10. "Try Bob-Sledding If You Want Thrills," *TDS*, March 4, 1922, p. 9.

ness of his own experience in the world, his right to talk about fear in other men. He had known its reaches himself: "The one who is writing this has been frightened many times and known plenty of fear of the kind that makes your legs difficult to move and makes your voice so you do not recognize it when you hear it. He is familiar with the sweating deadly fear that you get on a ledge, climbing, the hollow, gone-in-the-stomach fear before a bombardment; the dry, sudden dread of eternity that comes in a flash like the slamming open of a furnace door and leaves you hollow for a month until the dried springs of your courage seep back." But he had not, he asserted, treated the world to a public spectacle of that fear as Max Baer had. Indeed, part of his guise as expert was to suggest that men could live morally satisfying lives if they paid enough attention to technical proficiency in their work. It was their bulwark against chaos.[11]

By the forties and fifties Hemingway could take his role of mentor in the art of living seriously enough to begin a *Holiday* article with a recitation of his reasons for living in Cuba. The sum was that in that sun-mellowed land one could cultivate the art with a minimal restriction by climate or convention. One could raise and train fighting cocks, if that was his desire, and he could fish every day, for the Gulf Stream was never more than thirty minutes from his writing board.[12] Less seriously he could certify his place among the elite of experience and at the same time recognize his claim as the possible subject of parody. After his 1953 air crash in East Africa he wrote that he was an *Ndege* character, one who had "to do intimately with . . . aircraft" and had "certain secret feelings and much undeclared knowledge" about airplanes. "The *Ndege* have a set of ethics which are not publicly declared. If you are one, you are one. If you are not you will be detected and publicly exposed."[13] If the humor did not reach all the way to parody, it at least showed him self-consciously aware of the role he played.

Knowing how to live fully gave Hemingway the right to evaluate others' styles of living. As in any art, the ultimate responsibility was judgment of quality. Thus in his tribute to Marlene Dietrich he cited her ability to live fully and judge accurately and recommended her as one worthy of respect among

11. "Million Dollar Fright," *Esquire*, IV (December 1935), 35.
12. "The Great Blue River," *Holiday*, VI (July 1949), 60-61.
13. "The Christmas Gift," *Look*, XVIII (April 20, 1954), 37.

those who know the world. "Since she knows about things I write about, which are people, country, life and death, and problems of honor and of conduct, I value her opinion more than that of many critics." Besides her sense of tragedy and her gallows humor, he wrote, her ability to know when love truly exists made her worthy of celebration.[14] Among those who did not know the fullness of experience and have the right to judge, he thought, were his journalistic and academic critics. At the time of his African air crashes and his supposed death, some journalists had emphasized his life-long quest for death. But he answered that they were unable to distinguish between a quest for death and a quest for intense life in the presence of death. He thought that was a proper answer too for the academicians who saw his work as an expression of a death wish.[15] As in most paradoxes, the extreme opposites of the question resembled each other more than they did the middle ground.

His second claim to expertness—his claim to have behind-the-scenes knowledge—was part of Hemingway's work as a feature-writing journalist. Because he worked as an interpreter of events, not as a reporter, he was able to linger at the scenes of action long enough to see the consequences of events and to probe into their causes. He could interpret events in terms of their long-range meanings rather than simply chronicle them as the straight news reporter was often forced to do. Thus he could stay to see the face behind the statesman's mask, the intent behind the censor's pencil. Soon after his arrival in Europe in 1922 he looked at the realities behind the inflationary prices in France, Italy, and Austria and found that real prices at Swiss resorts were the same as those in neighboring countries. Hotel-keepers pegged prices at current exchange rates. But tourists receiving fewer Swiss francs than French francs for their dollar thought the over-crowded French resorts cheaper when for the same money they could stay at first-class resorts in Switzerland.[16] From Paris he wrote that American and Canadian tourists were fooled into thinking they saw real French night life at the champagne night clubs. The real thing was in the *bal musettes* where the apaches

14. "Tribute to Mamma from Papa Hemingway," *Life*, XXXIII (August 18, 1952), 92-93.
15. "The Christmas Gift," *Look*, XVIII (May 4, 1954), 37, 86.
16. "Tourists Are Scarce at Swiss Resorts," *TSW*, February 4, 1922, p. 3.

danced and drank, he said, and the real artists were at work in their studios, not in the crowd of poseurs at the Café Rotunde.[17] In "Behind the Scenes at Papal Elections" he saw his insider's view as typical of those held by American reporters in Europe. But the newsmen, restricted by their editors, could not tell the truth. Once a week American and British correspondents in Paris met to talk shop and trade insights on the personalities and motives behind events. "If the world could have a dictaphone in the room it would have such a back-stage view of European politicians, conferences, coronations, and world affairs that it would spin very fast for quite a time from the shock." The pope, they said, was crowned on a plain pine-board throne put together for the occasion, and the coronation resembled nothing so much as a fraternity initiation.[18]

The Greco-Turkish war of 1922 and the Mudania Conference following it were also fertile events for under-the-table stories. Hemingway keyed readers for exposés by giving them echoes of insiders' lingo. Constantinople was called "Constan" by old-timers, he confided, just as Gilbraltar was called "Gib." And the public at home, he noted after the conference, had been inadequately informed because of capricious and unintelligent censorship by British officials. With only one cable and one cable office in Constantinople, British censorship was complete. Irregular censor office hours, haphazard deletion, and the censors' belief that something had to be cut from each message led to gross distortions in the news. Only after several weeks had passed were correspondents able to tell about British threats to burn the city if Kemal allowed a massacre of Christians or about the British fleet's pursuit of a Turkish submarine furnished by the Soviets. And after checking with his Turkish informants, Hemingway offered another view of Mustafa Kemal, the man the British saw as spokesman for all Turkey. Kemal, he wrote, was viewed by many of his own people as an atheist undedicated to recapture of the old Ottoman empire by holy war. And this charge of atheism was more dangerous to Kemal than other rumors that he had Jewish blood. Turks, Hemingway found,

17. "Wild Night Music of Paris Makes Visitor Feel Man of the World," *TSW*, March 25, 1922, p. 22; "American Bohemians in Paris a Weird Lot," *TSW*, March 25, 1922, p. 15.
18. *TSW*, March 4, 1922, p. 3.

HUGH STEPHENS LIBRARY
STEPHENS COLLEGE
COLUMBIA, MISSOURI

were always ready to believe in another's atheism, and "there is no blacker crime in the Mohammedan world."[19]

In brief, Hemingway's mind in 1922 and 1923 was particularly keyed to establish his credentials as a foreign correspondent by showing the realities behind the masks of Europe's politicians. The climax of his *Daily Star* series on the French occupation of the Ruhr in 1923 was an article describing French officials taking a party of American churchmen on "an impartial investigation" of the Ruhr while speeding through the area at 40 m.p.h. in a French staff car. Elsewhere in the article he reported the French genius for public deception, if not for industry. While a French movie company took film sequences for a propaganda show, the French miners energetically shoveled coal and the customs officials busily inspected cargoes; but when the cameras stopped, the miners put down their shovels and the customs men slumped against a wall to smoke their pipes.[20] The descriptions were only the more dramatic instances of public pose and private deception he had seen in his investigation of the Ruhr occupation. That kind of insider's knowledge helped feed Hemingway's distrust of politicians later in his career.

During the thirties he looked back at the lessons of the twenties and at the events that had prompted adoption of his role as the man with inside but unwelcome knowledge and decided that editors and readers did not really want to know the inside story: ". . . after having very frank and prophetic interviews with Mussolini before the march on Rome buried opposite the financial page; and an interview with Clemenceau in which the old man was very bitter and for once very loquacious returned by a great Canadian paper with this notation, 'He can say these things but he cannot say them in our paper'; your correspondent learned that when, through following something closely, you were positive something was going to happen, the thing to do was to discover some way of betting that it would happen and keep your mouth shut about it."[21] Where he could,

---

19. " 'Old Constan' in True Light; Is Tough Town," *TDS*, October 28, 1922, p. 17; "Censor Too 'Thorough' in the Near East Crisis," *TDS*, October 25, 1922, p. 7; "Destroyers Were on Lookout for Kemal's One Submarine," *TDS*, November 10, 1922, p. 12; "Turks Beginning to Show Distrust of Kemal Pasha," *TDS*, October 24, 1922, p. 17.
20. "French Register Speed When Movies Are on Job," *TDS*, May 16, 1923, p. 19.
21. "a.d. Southern Style," *Esquire*, III (May 1935), 25.

120051

though, he found journals that would print the uncomfortable truth and continued publishing in them.

Particularly during the Spanish Civil War he turned to *Ken*, a magazine, wrote the editors, dedicated to identifying the intrigues that make events, not to reporting the events themselves.[22] Thus, in "Fresh Air on an Inside Story," Hemingway told how a prominent American journalist had come to besieged Madrid convinced that a reign of terror was underway in the city and talked and wrote of corpse-littered streets though he had not ventured outside his hotel after arrival. Finally he had tried to trick an unsuspecting newswoman into smuggling out stories of the supposed purge, had been cornered by Hemingway and other journalists and forced to admit his stories were false reports written to fit an editorial policy agreed upon by him and his paper.[23]

As late as "The Dangerous Summer" of 1960 Hemingway continued his practice of giving the expert's inside view on popular deceptions. He explained then how matadors and their managers tampered with bulls' horns so they were not as dangerous as appearances suggested and the matadors not as daring as the deluded public imagined.

Hemingway's preoccupation with noting the way things happen—the process, the right technique for carrying out an action—was not only the third key to his self-presentation as expert but also an important key to his way of seeing, understanding, and ultimately of writing. Indeed, his aesthetic principles and practice were derivations of his ability to see while doing; as an element of expertness, it constantly informed his essays. In his early journalism concern with technique furnished him a subject. In the mature period it became a necessary part of an established manner, and at last it was a self-conscious tool, itself open to comment and analysis.

When he began contributing to the *Star Weekly* in early 1920, what he had to sell was an understanding of how people managed and manipulated to get what they wanted, not a handful of interesting but inert facts. His first article was an account of how the smart set of Toronto arranged for, paid for, and circulated original art works. His second told how to get a free shave at the local barber college. His third chronicled gesture

22. "In the Editorial Ken," *Ken*, I (June 30, 1938), 4.
23. *Ken*, II (September 22, 1938), 38.

by gesture and smile by smile Toronto Mayor Church's technique for recruiting votes at the local sports arena. The fourth was step-by-step advice, satirically given, to the war slacker on how to disguise himself as a war veteran. But also quite early he saw that technical proficiency was applicable to sports, and in one article on fishing told the reader what to buy and how much to pay for a rod, gut leaders, line, reel, and hooks, suggested the proper bait for different seasons and streams, and told how to "horse in" a trout rather than jerk it out of the stream.[24] In "Fishing for Trout in a Sporting Way" he contradicted the sporting magazine myth that only fly fishing with expensive equipment was sporting. The magazines were supported by advertisers of expensive equipment suitable for use in under-stocked, over-fished streams of the Eastern United States. Bait fishing, he asserted, was more suitable for most streams, and he told how and where to dig for fishing worms, how to approach a fishing area, and how to bait a hook and let the current carry the bait.[25] In another article on camping he instructed his readers on the fine points of making camp beds, arranging mosquito netting, and cooking over coals instead of a blazing fire.[26] One needs only to remember the deliberate details of "Big Two-Hearted River" to see how the expertise of these articles became the stuff of authoritative fiction.

By the thirties Hemingway's emphasis on technique had become a recognized and expected element of his writing. The confusion of author and protagonist in his fiction and the declarations by such characters as Jake Barnes that knowing how was better than knowing why in the world prepared the way for Hemingway the expert in *Esquire*. In his letter-articles for the magazine he consciously purveyed expert knowledge as an extension of his public mind and a further development of his writing skills. As he learned new techniques in big game hunting and deep-sea fishing, he proved to himself that he had learned them by writing them down, that he had seen them imaginatively while doing them. In the first of his *Esquire* letters, "Marlin off the Morro," he described the four basic ways marlin hit a bait and told the proper ways to play them.[27] In "Marlin off Cuba," a

24. "Are You All Set for Trout?" *TSW*, April 10, 1920, p. 1.
25. *TSW*, April 24, 1920, p. 13.
26. "When You Camp Out, Do It Right," *TSW*, June 26, 1920, p. 17.
27. *Esquire*, I (Autumn 1933), 8, 39, 97.

1935 expansion of the *Esquire* letter, he added advice to new yachtsmen on where to find and what to pay guides and instructions on how to bait for deep-running marlin and what weights and lengths of line to use.[28] In later *Esquire* letters he wrote on ways to shoot fleeing and charging game animals and suggested in several articles, as he did later in "The Short Happy Life of Francis Macomber," that the first part of bravery is skill. It was significant that during the thirties most of his essays and much of his fiction dealt with actions that lent themselves to technical treatment. He was becoming increasingly conscious of its aesthetic possibilities.

His emphasis on technique rested not only on his full experience but also on his knowledge as an amateur naturalist. On several occasions he advanced technical instruction against a background of biological knowledge. In his preface to François Sommer's *Man and Beast in Africa*, he advised hunters to watch as their kills were skinned and dressed so they could learn the anatomies of the various game animals. The hunter, like the surgeon, he wrote, should know the laws of the body before he alters its functioning. He called on his knowledge of carrion bird behavior in "Wings Always over Africa" to advise the wounded left on the battlefield, particularly Italian wounded in Ethiopia, on how to save their eyes and faces. And in two *Esquire* articles, "Out in the Stream" and "Genio After Josie," he suggested that greater knowledge of marlin age characteristics and sexual behavior was necessary for intelligent hunting of the species. Significantly, he cited studies by Henry W. Fowler of the Philadelphia Academy of Natural History for support of his recommendation.[29] For readers of his fiction, though, the importance of these technical concerns was the authority given his later sea novel. Santiago is there able to assume knowledge of the things Hemingway the essayist labored to establish.

Just as he could characterize the full life for readers to subscribe to, Hemingway was also ready to spell out the code governing hunters and fishermen, including himself, as they achieved the full life. He had noted the code governing bullfighters in *Death in the Afternoon*, but the matadors formed such an ex-

28. Eugene V. Connett (ed.), *American Big Game Fishing* (New York, 1935), pp. 57-59, 71, 79-81.
29. *Esquire*, II (August 1934), 19, 156; II (October 1934), 22.

clusive group that magazine-reading admirers of the full life could hardly identify with them except in fiction. Hunting and fishing, though, could be practiced with style by the many if they only knew the style-setting code. And Hemingway could convey that in his nonfiction. His statements on sports fishing were illustrative. Fundamental to an understanding of the code was its definition, which he provided in the essay "Marlin off Cuba": "As I see big-game fishing with rod and reel it is a sport in which a man or woman seeks to kill or capture a fish by means which will afford the fisherman the greatest pleasure and best demonstrate the speed, strength and leaping ability of the fish in question; at the same time killing or capturing the fish in the shortest time possible and never for the sake of flattering the fisherman's vanity, using tackle unsuitable to the prompt capture of the fish."[30] Some of the key phrases of the definition were spelled out in other essays. In his introduction to S. Kip Farrington's *Atlantic Game Fishing*, he explained that true sportsmanship obligated the fisherman to use tackle appropriate to the game. It should not be so light that the fish could escape wounded, to be destroyed later by sharks, because the angler had tried for a light-tackle record. Nor should the equipment be so massive and foolproof that it took all the risk from the sportsman.[31] The code, in short, was a delicate balance of considerations for both man and game. Moreover, the sportsman was to get clear what was meant by game fish. Fish were not game in the sense that a fighting cock is game; they did not fight back. Rather they made more or less intelligent and powerful attempts to escape, depending on their type, age, and health. But the "game" was in the sportsman. The degree to which he adapted himself to the moral and psychological demands of the struggle determined the gameness of the fight. Not until he worked with a hook in his mouth, jaw, or stomach, Hemingway insisted, could the sportsman rightly call the struggle a fight.[32]

In "Shootism versus Sport" and "Notes on Dangerous Game" he explained the hunter's code. The role of the expert for Hemingway was complicated at this point, however, by the knowledge that his version of the code would be read by his mentor,

30. Connett, p. 70.

31. *Atlantic Game Fishing* (New York, 1937), pp. xvii-xviii.

32. "Cuban Fishing," *Game Fish of the World*, Brian Vesey-Fitzgerald and Francesca Lamonte (eds.) (New York, 1949), p. 157.

the white hunter Philip Percival, as well as by subway readers. Still, he had further expertness at work for him. One not only had to know and practice the ethics of hunting, he had to render them in convincing form as well. That meant conveying the meaning of the code by showing its relevance in action. His account of shooting the black-maned lion in "Shootism versus Sport" was authentication of his knowledge and practice.

The code itself was based on, among other things, the lion's eyesight, the terrain over which the lion would be hunted, and the mutual responsibilities of sportsman and guide. The basic point of honor was that one did not assassinate the lion by shooting from a car or blind or platform. One approached lion terrain by car and picked his lion while the animal did not distinguish hunter from car. But the hunter had to get out of the car and let the lion recognize him as hunter before he shot. A kind of primitive recognition between antagonists was thus involved. The lion's recognition of the hunter would immediately cause him to run for cover, and only the hunter's steadiness and marksmanship gave him his chance before the lion escaped, ran wounded into cover, or dropped. If the wounded lion reached cover, the hunter had an even chance of being mauled while flushing the lion from the thicket. In this context he stated the code as clearly as it was ever to be stated. Its keynote was mutual responsibility:

In the ethics of shooting dangerous game is the premise that the trouble you shoot yourself into you must be prepared to shoot yourself out of. Since a man making his first African shoot will have a white hunter, as a non-native guide is called, to counsel him and aid him when he is after dangerous animals, and since the white hunter has the responsibility of protecting him no matter what trouble he gets into, the shooter should do exactly what the white hunter tells him to do.

If you make a fool of yourself all that you get is mauled but the white hunter who has a client wounded or killed loses, or seriously impairs, his livelihood. So when a white hunter begins to trust you and let you take chances, that is a mark of confidence and you should not abuse it. For any good man would rather take chances any day with his life than with his livelihood and that is the main point about professionals that amateurs never seem to appreciate.[33]

33. "Notes on Dangerous Game," *Esquire*, II (July 1934), 19.

That is, the true advocate of the code would rather deal with the moral questions of life, death, skill, and courage than with the lesser questions of profit and loss. If the essay version was different in the writing from what Philip Percival might have conveyed during a lion hunt, it was the marked point, nevertheless, from which further transformations might be made for use later in "The Short Happy Life of Francis Macomber."

Hemingway's war reports demonstrated his expertness as well as any other group of his writings. In addition to showing him as adviser on military actions, both strategic and tactical, they included most of the other ways he claimed special skill and authority. The major period of his war writing, 1937 to 1944, was also the time when he was most self-consciously the knower. It was a propitious time for showing his expertise: his lifelong interest in military history and campaigns came into practical focus, and the world was ready to recognize his special understanding. The early stages of his education in war were over. He had gained credentials from his own service and wounding, he had reported war in the Near East, he had made his understanding of war classic in the short stories and *A Farewell to Arms,* and he had built up his own collection of war studies.[34] Publishers of the North American Newspaper Alliance, *PM,* and *Collier's* recognized his credentials and authority. His role as war expert was a near perfect matching of talent and task.

In his introduction to *Men at War* (1942) Hemingway cited his own special military experience—his participation in the first world conflict and his having gone through the trial of suffering and surviving wounds—as his credentials for writing on war and for collecting the best voices in the world on the subject. He was one of many, he said, who had participated in the great disillusionment of the century and learned that wars do not end wars. As a moral evaluator of wars, he warned in the same introduction against the tendency to accept an enemy's ethics while learning his techniques. Americans should adopt the Germans' blitzkrieg tactics, he noted, but not their Fascism.[35] As an expert at the rifleman's level of war, he recorded in one of the Spanish Civil War dispatches how he helped a Loyalist infantryman at

34. Mary Hemingway to ROS, May 25, 1964.
35. *Men at War* (New York, 1942), pp. xi-xiii.

the siege of Teruel free a jammed bolt on his rifle.[36] Also at Teruel he demonstrated his awareness of the risks in a fluid battle line. As he did not know the countersign during the Loyalists' entry into the just-captured stronghold, he determined to stay close to uniformed officers to avoid being mistakenly shot as an insurgent. And, as he noted during his work with cameramen Joris Ivens and John Ferno while filming sequences for *The Spanish Earth*, he had to keep an eye on shifts in the battle to keep them from getting into needlessly exposed positions. Even that battlefield know-how posed its moral problems, he found, for he had to decide constantly whether his holding them back was "necessary and just prudence, based on experience," or "the not so pretty prudence of the burnt monkey who dreads the hot soup."[37]

His recognition of the military realities of terrain served Hemingway again during the 1944 invasion of France. In "Voyage to Victory," his *Collier's* account of D-Day landings at Omaha Beach, Normandy, he saw from the deck of the attack transport "Dorothea M. Dix" the "highly defensible" beach and reported asking the ship's captain, Commander Leahy, if the assault was really only a diversionary attack in force. His criticism of high-command decisions was only implied in the wartime article, but he foresaw extreme casualties resulting from an attack over such terrain.[38] In the assault boats he helped the boat officer decide amidst the confusion of contradictory instructions which was the assigned beach and did so by recognizing key features of terrain: " 'This has got to be Fox Green,' I said to Andy. 'I recognize where the cliff stops. That's all Fox Green to the right. There is the Colleville church. There's the house on the beach. There's the Ruquet Valley on Easy Red to the right. This is Fox Green absolutely.' " As the boat was about to touch the beach, he dissuaded the infantry lieutenant aboard from going in, pointing out the machine gun emplacements enfilading their landing area and was confirmed moments later when machine guns and anti-tank guns opened fire on them. At his suggestion the boat cruised parallel to the beach until destroyers steamed in close and blasted

36. *Fact*, No. 16 (July 15, 1938), 47-48.
37. *The Spanish Earth* (Cleveland, 1938), p. 59.
38. *Collier's*, CXIV (July 22, 1944), 13.

the gun positions. Then the infantry splashed ashore with minimum losses.[39]

In "Battle for Paris" he reported how his knowledge of terrain and tactics served again, this time with French guerrillas instead of American regulars. Noting that the advance to Paris was held up by road blocks and heavy fighting at Rambouillet, he set out to find a way around the fighting. His years of residence in France helped. He had learned the country by bicycling through it, he said, and bicycling taught one how to use and avoid terrain that one ignores when riding in a car. Even the lowest hills are significant to cyclists. So his accurate memory of the contours of the countryside enabled him to lead the guerrillas into Paris by an undefended back way. Along the way the guerrillas continued to occupy a small village after American units had been pulled back. He knew, he said, that German tanks were prowling the area, had observed the American withdrawal, and would advance to make contact. To protect the village from being shot up by the tanks, he persuaded the guerrilla captain to put out a screen of units to provide contact with the tanks outside the village. And by that tactic they held the town until American forces had regrouped and advanced.[40]

As code-sayer Hemingway also recorded his response to the Geneva Convention governing the conduct of war correspondents. If they were forbidden to bear arms or command troops, they were not required to be passive or neutral. Besides advising both regular-army men and guerrillas, he noted in "Battle for Paris," he helped conduct French guerrillas to army command posts so they could provide information on deployment of German tanks and guns.[41] But above all it was the correspondent's responsibility to get back with the story. What he saw had validity when it reached the readers. Like the artist, he had to reduce his information and insight to a recorded sequence to complete its meaning. The code of prudence was as important for the correspondent entering the captured city as it was for the lion-hunter entering the thicket. So when he returned to Paris, he was, he said, careful to take cover during the street fighting and to keep someone behind him when he dodged into

39. *Ibid.*, 13, 54.
40. *Collier's*, CXIV (September 30, 1944), 11, 84.
41. *Ibid.*, 83.

the entrances of apartment houses. A dead expert, he knew, was a contradiction of terms.[42]

Although he mostly identified himself with action at the rifleman's level, Hemingway also recorded that he advised commanders. In Spain he delivered a report to Loyalist General Lucasz on the criminally negligent planning by the Hungarian commander of the Fifteenth Brigade. The brigade had been mauled at the Jarama River as a result of the poorly conceived attack, and Hemingway expressed satisfaction that the Hungarian had been relieved of his command and shot upon his return to Russia, regretting that he had not been shot at the time of the attack.[43] Asked by Madame Chiang Kai-shek during his tour of interior China if he thought the Soviets would withdraw aid to the Nationalists, once the Russo-Japanese security pact was signed, he drew on his Spanish Civil War experience to answer that Soviet aid would continue as long as Soviet military advisors in China thought the Nationalists could keep the Japanese occupied and away from Russian frontiers.[44] His expert's view of the Far East, though, was finally as much a matter of understanding the force of character as of understanding geopolitics. Ralph Ingersoll of *PM* had stipulated that Hemingway was to write a prognosis for the China theater as well as reports on actual conditions there, and he complied by stating he foresaw no defeat for the Chinese during the next two or three years. "Nor, if you want my absolute opinion, having seen the terrain, the problems involved and the troops who will do the fighting, will the Japanese ever defeat the Chinese army unless they are sold out. So long as the U.S.A. is putting up the money to pay and arm them and the Generalissimo is in command, they will not be sold out. But if we ceased to back them or if anything ever happened to the Generalissimo, they would be sold out very quickly."[45]

It was a suitably positive statement and fully in character with Hemingway the expert. It becomes clear finally that Hemingway's claim to expertness in matters of technique and judgment was a function of his personality as much as of his experi-

42. "How We Came to Paris," *Collier's*, CXIV (October 7, 1944), 67.

43. *The Great Crusade* (New York, 1940), pp. vii-viii.

44. "Russo-Jap Pact Hasn't Kept Soviets from Sending Aid to China," *PM*, June 10, 1941, p. 4.

45. "After Four Years of War in China, Japs Have Conquered Only Flatlands," *PM*, June 16, 1941, p. 6.

ence. Other men might have run his gamut of experience and still lacked his authority, still not had the right to make their expertness part of the record. What Hemingway had besides experience was the creative mind that saw how events were relevant to human feelings and how they could become the stuff of journalistic reporting and later of created accounts in his fiction. His expertness was ultimately based not on his apprehension of external events but in his ability to read the mind in conflict.

III. The Travel Writer

LIKE MANY AMERICAN NOVELISTS, HEMINGWAY APPROACHED FICTION through an apprenticeship in travel writing. Like Hawthorne, Cooper, Twain, Howells, and James he also returned to travel-writing at intervals throughout his productive career. If the *Toronto Star* was his *Alta California* at the beginning, *Death in the Afternoon* was his *Life on the Mississippi* at mid-career, and later "The Dangerous Summer" his counterpart to *Following the Equator*. Besides, travel writing, nearly always profitable, kept the words flowing while plots thickened. Not only did his travel work serve as warm-up and source book for his fiction, it served equally well as a device to clarify the larger world for Hemingway and his readers. It enabled him to gain a sure hold on the outer world of event and scene, both intellectually and stylistically, before he extended his explorations to the inner world of feeling. For the subjective life was always fed and corrected by knowledge from outside; this was his control against having feeling become sentimentality. One of the roles Hemingway played in person before going behind the mask of novelist was that of portrayer of the world's face.

Exactly what travel writing meant to Hemingway appeared near the end of *Green Hills of Africa* when he presented a partial apologia to Philip Percival: "If I ever write anything about this [safari] it will just be landscape painting until I know something about it. Your first seeing of a country is a very valuable one. Probably more valuable to yourself than to anyone else, is the hell of it. But you ought always to write it to try to get it stated. No matter what you do with it. . . . I'd like to try to write something about the country and the animals and what it's like to some one who knows nothing about it."[1]

That Hemingway recognized his travel writing as part of an established literary tradition can be seen by his remarks on other travel writers and their works. In the early *Toronto Daily Star* reports on the Greco-Turkish crisis, he took time from political articles to sketch Constantinople for Canadian readers. It was not the exotic city depicted by romantic wanderers, he wrote, but a ghetto of alleys and scurrying rats. Constantinople with a population of over one and a half million, crammed with Czarist refugees and Kemalist infiltrators, was doing its dance of death. Kemal Pasha had sworn to stop all drinking, gambling, dancing, and night life when he captured the city, and in the last days before capitulation foreigners and citizens kept up a prolonged orgy in the Galata district. When one walked through the streets at night, one saw rats scuttling and stray dogs poking at street garbage, heard late revelers behind closed blinds, and smelled the offal in the streets.

In the morning when you wake and see a mist over the Golden Horn with the minarets rising out of it slim and clean towards the sun and the Muezzin calling the faithful to prayer in a voice that soars and dips like an aria from a Russian opera, you have the magic of the east. When you look from the window into the mirror and discover your face is covered with a mass of minute red speckles from the latest insect that discovered you last night, you have the east. There may be a happy medium between the east of Pierre Loti's stories and the east of everyday life, but it could only be found by a man who

1. *Green Hills of Africa* (New York, 1935), pp. 193-94.

always looked with his eyes half shut, didn't care what he ate, and was immune to the bites of insects.[2]

True to his journalistic practice, he followed the conventions of travel-writing while denying their validity.

Death in the Afternoon showed that he was also aware that his version of Spain was different from that of other writers. Particularly he saw Waldo Frank's *Virgin Spain* (1926) as the sort of travel book that produced more confusion than sense. Full of pseudo-scientific jargon and false mysticism, it was, charged Hemingway, an example of "erectile writing"—subjectively distorted writing by an author supposedly "having a vision." It was to him a kind of writing too prevalent for the day, a derivative school of writing produced by poor observation and worse thinking.[3] In "A Natural History of the Dead," also part of *Death in the Afternoon*, he showed his awareness of travel literature by both satirizing and parodying it. The essay begins as a mockery of the scientific school of travel writing, Latinate and heavily pedantic, that seeks to justify itself by providing natural history and natural theology rather than aesthetic impressions for readers:

It has always seemed to me that war has been omitted as a field for the observations of the naturalists. We have charming and sound accounts of the flora and fauna of Patagonia by the late W. H. Hudson; the Reverend Gilbert White has written most interestingly of the Hoopoe on its occasional and not at all common visits to Selbourne and Bishop Stanley has given us a valuable, although popular, *Familiar History of Birds.* Can we hope to furnish the reader with a few rational and interesting facts about the dead? I hope so.

. . . .

With a disposition to wonder and adore . . . as Bishop Stanley says, can no branch of Natural History be studied without increasing that faith, love and hope which we also, every one of us, need in our journey through the wilderness of life? Let us therefore see what inspiration we may derive from the dead.[4]

The beginning of "The Dangerous Summer" also saw bullfighting accounts as a form of the genre and protested its abuses. He would, he wrote, try to avoid "peppering, larding and truffleing

2. "'Old Constan' in True Light: Is Tough Town," *TDS*, October 28, 1922, p. 17.
3. *Death in the Afternoon* (New York, 1932), p. 53.
4. *Ibid.*, pp. 133ff.

[*sic*]" the account with Spanish terms usually found in "newly erudite" writers on the art. Scorning such terms as Manoletinas, Giraldillas, Pedresinas, and Trincherillas, he observed that "any pass that ends in *ina* or *illa* is probably phony and was invented to impress a gullible public."[5] And in *Green Hills of Africa* he recorded Philip Percival's complaint that safari books were always filled with "bloody rot about shooting beasts with horns half an inch longer than some one else shot. Or muck about danger."[6] Aware of the pitfalls in the travel-writing tradition, Hemingway thought he could practice it more honestly than some.

Unlike many nineteenth- and twentieth-century American travelwriters, Hemingway seldom wrote travel pieces with the explicit aim of marveling at the monuments or customs of Old World civilization. He would not return again and again to some gallery, as did Bayard Taylor or Hawthorne or James, to absorb the spirit of a particular painting—absorb it, that is, for its "civilizing" influence. He studied paintings at the Louvre, he recorded in *A Moveable Feast*, to learn how to see and to write, but such sorties were not parts of his travel pieces. His travel essays were incidental to utilitarian purposes. His role was not travel writer per se, but in the early days that of reporter, later that of *aficionado*, and still later that of sportsman-hunter or fisherman. Even when he wrote of events from a vacation trip, he reported the travel adventures as they provided insights for social analysis. His fishing trips of the early twenties in the Black Forest, for example, celebrated the pleasures of finding silvery trout and clear streams but were part of the larger picture of inflationary and bureaucratic bungling in postwar Germany.

Reporting on conditions in Alsace-Lorraine in 1922, Hemingway recorded details of life in Strasbourg that contrasted new ways and old. Taxi drivers spoke French; horse-cab drivers spoke German. But among remarks on official languages and exchange values, he managed to include other details showing nostalgia for the medieval German past of the city and often touched them with whimsy. "Strasbourg is a lovely old town with streets of houses that look so much like old German prints that you keep looking up at the chimneys for storks' nests. Little rivers cut

5. *Life*, XLIX (September 5, 1960), 86.
6. *Green Hills of Africa*, p. 194.

through it and there are picturesque quays where men sit fishing and women bend their backs to their laundering. It seems a very fine division of labor from the male standpoint, but I think the women are revenged because I have never seen any of the men catch any fish and imagine it is the soapsuds that keep them from biting." Like other travel writers, he recorded dubious local legend. At a cafe across from the great single-spired cathedral at Strasbourg, he inquired why the local beers were so tall and narrow and was told by a nearby priest that they were influenced by the cathedral spire. While ostensibly concerned with the slipping power of the German mark, Hemingway also described in sensuous detail the dinner he bought so cheaply with francs. Chronicling all the courses including the plum brandy at the end, he also evoked, in the best reflective tradition of travel writers, the presence of the past in the scene: "We ate on the first floor in a low wood paneled room that seemed to reek of flagons of ale, poniards stuck in the table and quarreling Brandenburgers and women with those sort of head-dresses that go way out to a point like a long slanted back dunce's cap and have a veil draping down."[7] And inevitably his evaluations of people involved in the economic and political tangles of postwar Europe were influenced by his treatment as a traveler, as he showed in his condemnation of the surly Bavarian innkeepers.

As a newsman, Hemingway also recorded scenes of French life that were more properly travel observations than news items. In "Wild Night Music of Paris" and "Night Life in Europe a Disease," both for the *Toronto Star Weekly*, he provided thumbnail evaluations of night life more useful for cocktail-party opinions than for hard facts on world conditions. "Paris night life is the most highly civilized and amusing, Berlin is the most sordid, desperate and vicious. Madrid is the dullest, and Constantinople is, or was, the most exciting." His details noted that, contrary to Americans' belief, only a few oases of night life— Montmartre cafes, Jean Cocteau's Boeuf-Sur-Le Toit, Moulin Rouge, a Russian place called the Caucasian, and Florence's American Negro Club—stayed open past 12:30 midnight. The Montmartre places were filled with fake artists and fake champagne, both strictly for American tourist consumption. Cocteau's place was for insiders only, was crowded, and depended on local

7. "The Old Order Changeth in Alsace-Lorraine," *TDS*, August 26, 1922, p. 4.

art gossip for entertainment. At Florence's the Negro dancers and waiters had lost their original primitive jollity, now were sophisticated and pretended to be of Choctaw descent. In "Rug Vendor Is Fixture in Parisian Life" Hemingway, on pretext of describing the economic plight of Algerians in Paris and of possible traps for tourists, presented a variation on the familiar sketch of aggressive salesman and helpless victim. After heaping all the abuse he could think of on the Arab vendor, Hemingway acknowledged he came away forty francs poorer and holding a shedding "tiger skin" rug he knew was goat. But tourists, he observed, bought the rugs daily for three or four times the price he paid.[8]

During the fall of 1923 in the *Toronto Star Weekly*, Hemingway published his first lyric tribute to bullfighting—a topic that afforded him a lasting subject in his second kind of travel writing and gave him a second vehicle for travel tips and observations. The portentous words on his first bullfight came this way:

It was the first bullfight I ever saw, but it was not the best. The best was in the little town of Pamplona, high up in the hills of Navarre, and came weeks later. Up in Pamplona, where they have held six days of bullfighting each year since 1126 A.D., and where the bulls race through the streets of the town each morning at six o'clock with half the town running ahead of them. Pamplona, where every man and boy in town is an amateur bullfighter and where there is an amateur fight each morning that is attended by 20,000 people in which the amateur fighters are all unarmed and there is a casualty list at least equal to a Dublin election.

These ominous words came in his article "Bull Fighting Is Not a Sport—It Is a Tragedy," when Hemingway's first period as reporter was virtually over and he was about to enter the second one as aficionado. It was a role that lasted intermittently until the end of his writing career. In late 1923, though, he wrote two articles on the bullfights he had experienced during the season of 1923. The second, also on the Pamplona fiesta, ended on the true note that Hemingway had sounded—that of the travel writer longing for the place of his delight: "That was just three months ago. It seems in a different century now, working in an office. It is a very long way from the sun-baked town of Pamplona,

8. *TDS*, August 12, 1922, p. 5.

where the men race through the streets in the mornings ahead of bulls to the morning ride to work on a Bay-Caledonia car. But it is only fourteen days by water to Spain and there is no need for a castle."[9]

While following bullfights to mature his knowledge of that art, Hemingway also incidentally developed his powers as a travel writer. Moving about Spain as an *aficionado*, he learned about good cafes, pleasant hotels, breath-taking landscapes, famous paintings, eccentricities of people from diverse provinces, the places to get the best paella and to see the most handsome women, and the ritual to follow during the day of the bullfights to make the events of the arena the climax of a perfectly arranged day. Nowhere did Hemingway play the expert better than when he conducted his explicit listener, the Old Lady in *Death in the Afternoon*, or his implicit companion, the reader, on excursions both inside the bull ring and outside.

His descriptions of Aranjuez, Ronda, and Valencia detailed more than the bullfight seasons there. At Aranjuez one arrived by special bus from Madrid, walked through the town to see the *plaza de toros* on the edge of town, bought fresh strawberries and ate grilled steaks or roasted chicken and drank Valdepeñas at the feria booths for only five pesetas. Seeing the picturesquely different market place and the rows of beggers lining the way to the arena, Hemingway placed the whole experience in a pictorial frame: "The town is Velasquez to the edge and then straight Goya to the bull ring." At the ring he instructed the reader on the fine art of spotting and complimenting the local beauties by expert use of field or opera glasses. Part of the instruction was being able to distinguish between the amateur and professional ladies. Hemingway's notations were of the same order as Melville's description of the nymphs of Typee almost a century earlier:

This girl inspection is a big part of bullfighting for the spectator. If you are near-sighted you can carry a pair of opera or field glasses. They are taken as an additional compliment. It is best not to neglect a single box. The use of a good pair of glasses is an advantage. They will destroy for you some of the greatest and most startling

9. "Bull Fighting Is Not a Sport—It Is a Tragedy," *TSW*, October 20, 1923, p. 33; "World's Series of Bull Fighting a Mad, Whirling Carnival," *TSW*, October 27, 1923, p. 33.

beauties who will come in with cloudy white lace mantillas, high combs and complexions and wonderful shawls and who in the glasses will show the gold teeth and flour-covered swartness of some one you saw last night perhaps somewhere else and who is attending the fight to advertise the house; but in some box you might not have noticed without the glasses you may see a beautiful girl. It is very easy for the traveller in Spain seeing the flour-faced fatness of the flamenca dancers and the hardy ladies of the brothels to write that all talk of beautiful Spanish women is nonsense. Whoring is not a highly paid profession in Spain and the Spanish whore works too hard to keep her looks. Do not look for beautiful women on the stage, in the brothels or the canta honda places. You look for them in the evening at the time of paseo when you can sit in a chair at a café or on the street and have all the girls of the town walk by you for an hour, passing not once but many times as they walk up the block, make the turn and come back, walking three or four abreast; or you look for them carefully, with glasses in the boxes at the bull ring.[10]

If Hemingway characterized Aranjuez as a good place to see one's first bullfight because of its picturesqueness, Ronda had romantic views from the plateau on which the town plaza was located, comforts of fine hotels, good seafood, good wines, short walks, and a historic bull ring. His label for Ronda was within the travel-tip tradition if not that of genteel convention: "That is where you should go if you ever go to Spain on a honeymoon or if you ever bolt with anyone."[11]

Valencia, besides being the home of several famous matadors, was in Hemingway's eyes more properly the home of memorable paella—so memorable he had Pilar repeat in *For Whom the Bell Tolls* most of his lyric to Valencia. Like good travel literature, it spoke through the senses:

Valencia is hotter in temperature and sometimes hotter in fact when the wind blows from Africa, but there you can always go out on a bus or the tramway to the port of Grau at night and swim at the public beach or, when it is too hot to swim, float out with as little effort as you need and lie in the barely cool water and watch the lights and the dark of the boats and the rows of the eating shacks and the swimming cabins. At Valencia too, when it is hottest, you can eat down at the beach for a peseta or two pesetas at one of the eating pavilions where they will serve you beer and shrimps and a

---

10. *Death in the Afternoon*, pp. 40-41.
11. *Ibid.*, pp. 42-44.

paella of rice, tomato, sweet peppers, saffron and good seafood, snails, crawfish, small fish, little eels, all cooked together in a saffron-colored mound. You can get this with a bottle of local wine for two pesetas and the children will go by barelegged on the beach and there is a thatched roof over the pavilion, the sand cool under your feet, the sea with the fishermen sitting in the cool of the evening in the black felucca rigged boats that you can see, if you come to swim the next morning, being dragged up the beach by six yoke of oxen.

This was the city too that, he observed, when it turned on one of its local matadors after his several disasters, named as a monument to him one of the public urinals.[12]

Because Hemingway understood bullfighting as one of the performing arts, his aesthetic impressions carried over into his travel observations. His Spain was that of the Prado as well as of cafes and arenas. For him the Prado and the bull plaza were the essence of Madrid. The buildings of unpretentious plainness, the galleries of untheatricalized masterpieces, the understatement and austerity of the whole effect were Hemingway's reasons for preferring Castile to all the other regions of Spain. Velasquez, Greco, and Goya best captured the different aspects of Spanish life, but because Goya depicted bullfights and wars he was closest to Hemingway's Spain. "Goya did not believe in costume but he did believe in blacks and greys, in dust and light, in high places rising from plains, in the country around Madrid, in movement, in his own cojones, in painting, in etching, and in what he had seen, felt, touched, handled, smelled, enjoyed, drunk, mounted, suffered, spewed-up, lain-with, suspected, observed, loved, hated, lusted, feared, detested, admired, loathed, and destroyed. Naturally no painter has been able to paint all that but he tried."[13]

Like Goya, the bullfighter represented the fully experienced life that was Spain for Hemingway. The lyrical last chapter of *Death in the Afternoon* made clear that it was a book about the total Spanish experience. Bullfighting was only the vehicle for carrying those observations. The last chapter was Hemingway's attempt to suggest all the experiences that he was unable to focus on during his discussion of Tauromaquia: "If I could have made this enough of a book it would have had everything in it. . . . It

12. *Ibid.*, pp. 44-46.
13. *Ibid.*, pp. 204-5.

should make clear the change in the country as you come down out of the mountains and into Valencia. . . . It should have the smell of burnt powder. . . . It should, if it had Spain in it, have the tall thin boy. . . . There ought to be Astorga, Lugo, Orense, Soria, Tarragona and Calatayud, the chestnut woods on the high hills. . . . What else should it contain about a country you love very much?" In the fashion of other great travel writers he concluded that he had to tell about the country as he experienced it, not only because good experience could slip from memory but also because the world itself was changing. He wanted to celebrate how it was before people forgot the old ways.

Hemingway's third role as travel writer was that of hunter and safarist. But except for a very few incidental observations on the popularity of Islam among East Africans, a brief sketch of the Masai and their country, and a tendency to see patches of country as if they were painted by André Masson, *Green Hills of Africa* was not the work that best showed Hemingway as travel writer and safarist. It was much too concerned with his self-explanation and justification, too philosophically concerned with animals and hunting as the proper interests of a writer, too much occupied with terrain as a tactical problem to serve as a travel book. Few readers learned about the face of Africa from *Green Hills of Africa*. It took the works of the fifties to render Hemingway's Africa. Even there, it was terrain and animals that concerned Hemingway, not Africans. In 1953 he wrote that he preferred studying animals to studying Mau Mau extremists because something might happen to the animals while the Mau Maus would be around for a long time. His observations of African life included, however, notes on comparative conduct of tribes in the Nagadi Nguruman escarpment area. He described how the aristocratic Masai, avoiding tedious work wherever possible, hired the M'Bulus to dig their wells at a price of one cow per well. And he depicted Masai readying themselves for a lion hunt by drinking a potion brewed from tree bark.[14]

But African animals more than Africans themselves were his subject because the animals reminded him that they would vanish as the region ceased being a frontier. Accordingly, he acted as guide through time as well as space. At a Masai watering hole he noted: "There was a flock of more than six thousand guinea

14. "Safari," *Look*, XVIII (January 26, 1954), 20, 30-34.

fowl and we shot only what we needed for meat. The sand grouse came to drink at the water in the mornings in pairs, singly, and in scattered bunches. They also came in flocks that were dense as the passenger pigeons around Petoskey before Michigan ever was a state."[15] His description of giant crocodiles along the Victorian Nile hinted that the time reference was primordial rather than frontier:

Formerly in Southern Tanganyika along the great Ruaha River, the only sight we ever had of a crocodile was the tip of his nostrils in the water. These crocodiles along the Nile were on the banks and with their heads facing the shore rather than the water. . . . I counted seventeen of the length of 12 feet and over (remember this is done from the air and therefore you cannot have complete accuracy—they might have been much longer), but they were extremely large crocs and they were together and under the brush or trees along the side of the river. As well as being very long, they were very broad and the plane did not disturb them at all. We began to consider that this was a fairly rough country.[16]

One reason that Hemingway was more active as a travel writer in the fifties than he was during the thirties was that he was later more vacationer than hunter. Most of the game animals the fiftyish Hemingway shot were the same kinds of animals he had shot so memorably years before. Mary Hemingway's wish to fly over the Belgian Congo and the lake system northward to Murchison Falls was the occasion for significant African travel in the fifties. Chronicling their Christmas flight, Hemingway recorded impressions of magenta-colored Lake Natron with herds of buffalo, Ngorongoro Crater, the gorilla sanctuary of Ruanda Urundi, the "Mountains of the Moon," flights of ibis, herds of hippos, elephants, and buffalo at Lake Albert, and of fishermen catching a two-hundred-pound Nile perch. His celebration of the hotel comforts and the view of Lake Kivu at Costermansville was properly in the travel writer's mood: with its islands, broken shore line, and its deep blues, it was, he said, using the travel writer's technique of evocation by comparison, "as beautiful as Lago Maggiore or Lago di Garda."[17]

His role as returner to old grounds was a key one for the

15. *Ibid.*, 20.
16. "The Christmas Gift," *Look*, XVIII (April 20, 1954), 31.
17. *Ibid.*, 31.

older Hemingway, but he had played it before. It was particularly appropriate for the quietly elegiac mood that hovered over his later work and showed the man without his fictional mask. That he had used it before only made it seem fully realized at last. While reporting in Italy for the *Toronto Daily Star*, he had returned to the Piave and the town of Schio where he had been billeted before being wounded in 1918. Even by 1922, he noted, the area was so rebuilt and the grass grown over the fought-over grounds that an old veteran had trouble believing he had ever lived some of the key moments of his life at the place. His conclusion at the time was that it was better to visit someone else's old battle front than one's own. Memory and imagination had a better chance then to reconstruct old scenes. Stopping by Spain in 1933 on his first trip to Africa, Hemingway again saw saddening change. The old Café Fornos was being torn down to be replaced by an office building. And by the fifties he found that even the terrain of Africa was not as remembered and described earlier. In the country back of Mombasa he found the erosion of a two-year drouth. "This had been a gray or tawny land when I had known it in the old days. Now it was gray or red with dust that dragged in clouds behind the cars or trucks that moved along the road and soon our faces were masked by it."[18] By the time he returned to Pamplona for the fiesta in 1959, he could describe with gusto the dancing and drinking, the afternoons at the arena, and the capture of pretty girls as fiesta prisoners. But it was a determined gesture to evoke rather than quiet old memories. If age and slowed reflexes prevented his savoring the experiences as vividly as before, his own memories that had become public memories sustained the fiesta for him and his cocelebrants, and he could declare that the old thing was still there if one knew how to find it. That too could become public experience through his account.

If travel writing has a formula, Hemingway was enough aware of it to observe several of its conventions. According to Willard Thorp, the nineteenth-century travel accounts ordinarily included such elements as these:

The author must begin with the excitements of the ocean voyage itself and devote at least a portion of a chapter to the thrill, so long

18. "Safari," 20.

anticipated, of setting foot on foreign soil. From this point on he should mix architecture and scenery with comment on philanthropies, skillfully work in a little history cribbed from Murray's Guides, taking care to add a touch of sentiment or eloquence when the occasion permitted. If the essay or book required a little padding, it was always possible to retell an old legend or slip in an account of dangers surmounted in crossing the Alps.[19]

Hemingway's practice of pursuing an object other than outright travel narrative was reason enough for his not following closely the pattern that veteran travel readers might expect, not to mention the constant infusion of his own personal force and his awareness of twentieth-century sensibilities. Still, in his way he left-handedly observed and used the available patterns.

Particularly he was a connoisseur of approaches to cities and ports. On his first trip to Europe as a correspondent he described the Spanish port of Vigo in chromo terms for Canadian readers. "Vigo is a pasteboard looking village, cobble streets, white and orange plastered, set up on one side of a big, almost landlocked harbor that is large enough to hold the entire British navy. Sunbaked brown mountains slump down to the sea like tired old dinosaurs, and the color of the water is as blue as a chromo of the bay at Naples."[20] Later making his first approach to Constantinople via the Orient Express, he described his coming across a treeless plain and past the Marmora shores with Asia in the distance, his passage through zones of tenements and dirty white minarets, finally his passing through the reddish old Byzantine wall of the city. In 1959 on his return to Spain he recorded passing by the brown bulk of Gibraltar and coming to "anchorage off the friendly-looking Moorish white town of Algeciras spread up the green hill. . . ." Days later at Aranjuez he again was savoring the scene in both sensuous and reflective terms. It was a passage worthy of the most appreciative of travel writers: "We had stopped at Aranjuez and while the car was being filled with gasoline and serviced we ordered asparagus and a bottle of white draft wine at the old restaurant and café built along the south bank of the Tajo River. The river was green, narrow and deep. Trees grew along its banks and weeds swung in the current and there were no customers for the open launches that

19. "Pilgrim's Return," *Literary History of the United States,* ed. Robert E. Spiller *et al.* (New York, 1955), p. 831.
20. *TSW,* February 18, 1922, p. 15.

carried holiday makers upstream to the old royal gardens. Aranjuez was quiet in the early chilly spring and the restaurant was like a painting by Sisley of a place by the Seine beyond Bas-Meudon."[21]

Hemingway's scene-painting, however, occurred as the background for strenuous action, and his appreciation of architecture was limited mostly to the design of ski huts and cafes with terraces. The foreground of his sketches depicted Hemingway sampling the sports experiences of an area rather than the "views." For Canadian readers he described the luge as the Swiss version of bobsled, flivver, canoe, horse and buggy, and pram, and the Alps as the place to luge. His description of Swiss social customs also centered on riding the luge; on bright days one could see both grandmothers and small children sailing down a frozen road, their feet stuck out at the sides of their luge, and going between twelve and thirty miles-per-hour. Swiss railways also adapted to the sport, running special trains to the Col du Sonloup, four thousand feet high, so that whole families could make day-long luge-outings on the run down to Montreux. He used the sport as occasion also for comment on national character. Seeing the ex-governor of Khartoum skim down the Chamby-Montreux road, hands behind his back, muffler flying behind, and a cherubic smile on his face while being cheered by Swiss children, Hemingway commented, "It is easy to understand how the British have such a great Empire after you have seen them luge."[22] Similarly he described tuna fishing at Vigo, Spain, and told how a true fisherman, after working at a nauseating strain for six hours to boat a fish, might find himself pronounced worthy to enter unabashed among the fishing gods in the brown hills above Vigo. That he was ashore there for only an hour and thus unable to achieve such glory for himself does not appear in the account.

A second dimension of his sampling the sports available in an area was his historical perspective. Fishing in the Rhone canal near Aigle, he savored the slow coming of evening onto the scene by noting the lights and shadows on the overhanging glacier and reflected, in the best travel manner, on other historical per-

21. "The Dangerous Summer," *Life*, XLIX (September 5, 1960), 88, 94.
22. "Flivver, Canoe, Pram and Taxi Combined Is the Luge," *TSW*, March 18, 1922, p. 15.

sons who might have stopped there to fish—Helvetians from Roman road gangs, Napoleon's batman seeking a trout for the general's breakfast, even the light-traveling Huns taking time out from their encroachment on the Roman Empire to fish the Rhone canal.[23] He completed his celebration of the perfect evening by recording his walk down the chestnut tree-lined road to Aigle, stopping at the train station cafe with the galloping gold horse on top, and drinking a dark beer. Hemingway's use of the "ideal day" motif achieved another standard dimension of the travel sketch in "Christmas on the Roof of the World." There he described the near-perfect way to observe Christmas in Switzerland. Starting in the morning when the German maid came in to build a fire in the porcelain stove while the Hemingways still lay in bed, he described their dressing, quick breakfast, ride on the skier-filled train up the mountain, their further climb to a cattle barn, lunch out of a rucksack with white wine, a nap and the long glide down in the afternoon, climaxing with a hot Christmas dinner of turkey, side dishes, wine and the accompanying Christmas tree. "It was," he saw, "the kind of Christmas you can only get on top of the world."[24]

Hemingway's further modification of the travel formula involved substituting a near-legendary view of African animals for the usual legends about castles and old trees. In both "The Christmas Gift" and "Safari" he took a view of lions, leopards, wildebeests, and some small deer that echoed qualities attributed to them in the bestiaries. In "Safari," for example, he described the assault of a hawk on a flight of guinea fowl and the struggles of one guinea to escape while the hawk flew away with it, already starting to feed on its prey. For Hemingway, the allegory was cultural. "They were obviously of different tribes. Watching this action I was not wholly sure of the white man's role in Africa."[25] In "The Christmas Gift" he celebrated night as "the loveliest time in Africa"—lovely because "the animals are quite transformed." The lion gives up his daytime silence to cough and roar, the hyena's laugh takes on a pleasant note, the wildebeest gives off terrifying noises to seem dangerous, the bat-eared foxes come out, and the hunting leopard coughs messages to the baboons along the river. Hemingway's characterization of Mr. Chui

23. "There Are Great Fish in the Rhone Canal," *TDS*, June 10, 1922, p. 5.
24. *TSW*, December 23, 1922, p. 19.
25. "Safari," 34.

the leopard on a hunt, reminiscent of Kipling and perhaps Rousseau, evoked half-men, half-beast images for an enchanted jungle. It was like an afterglow of his dreamlike circus animals written about the previous year for the *Circus Magazine.*[26]

Following the tradition of those travelers who wrote not only on what they saw but how cheaply they saw it, Hemingway wrote in 1922, "A Canadian with One Thousand a Year Can Live Very Comfortably and Enjoyably in Paris." He wrote, of course, in keeping with his time as well, a time when favorable exchange rates allowed Canadians and Americans to see Europe at all; he also wrote in keeping with his own instinct for technique. For the key to living cheaply in Paris, he explained, was not only in taking advantage of the eleven-to-one exchange rate on francs from Canadian dollars but also in knowing where and how to live there. Right Bank hotels were as expensive as those in New York, but one could live on the Left Bank and eat at restaurants in the area around the Academy of the Beaux Arts for two weeks on what a weekend on the Right Bank would cost. And Paris was anything one wanted to make it—rainy, cold, beautiful, crowded, lonely, or exciting—and cheap, he wrote, provided one knew how.[27]

In the tradition of those travel books written to describe cultural landscapes, Hemingway's travel writing abounded with observations on national character. Such observations were fundamental to his remarks on politics, economics, military analysis, and even bullfighting. But though he practiced making generalizations on European and Asian national character for his Canadian readers, he began by telling them about themselves and their "Yank" neighbors. In 1920 he contrasted the views of each other held by Canadians and United States Americans, lamented the lack of understanding between the two nations, and concluded that United States citizens admired Canadians for the wrong reasons while Canadians, influenced by warmongering Hearst papers, refused to credit Americans with having sacrified sufficiently in the recent war. Americans needed to lower their voices, he said, and Canadians to lower their pride.[28]

In later sketches he characterized the French as exclusively

26. "The Christmas Gift" (May 4, 1954), 34.
27. *TSW*, February 4, 1922, p. 16.
28. "The Average Yank Divides Canadians into Two Classes—Wild and Tame," *TSW*, October 9, 1920, p. 13.

France-oriented and highly sensitive about the war dead, called
them geniuses in the arts of good living and hard fighting but
fumblers in big business. He contradicted the myth of French
cosmopolitanism when he explained how foreigners could pass
themselves off in Paris as champions or experts when they were
failures at home. "This state of affairs exists because of the extreme provinciality of the French people and the French press.
Everyone in Canada knows the names of half a dozen French
soldiers and statesmen, but no one in France could give you the
name of a Canadian general or statesman or tell who was head
of the Canadian government. By no one, I mean none of the
ordinary people; shopkeepers, hotel owners and the general bour-
geois class. For example, my femme de menage was horrified
yesterday when I told her there was prohibition in Canada and
the States. 'Why have we never heard of it?' she asked. 'Has it
just been a law? What, then, does a man drink?' " To explain
how a French government could almost be toppled by a picture
of Premier Poincaré laughing, or smiling, at the Verdun Cemetery, he had to explain the French attitude toward the dead. No
man, regardless of his fame, was immune from criticism in France.
There were too many divergent views on politics, religion, and
ethics in France to permit that. But once dead, any man rated
respect. Frenchmen doffed hats at every funeral, paused respectfully for even the most straggling funeral hearse. If they thought
even the Premier could be light about French war dead, that
was enough to topple him from office. And explaining the French
debacle in the Ruhr occupation and their failure to bring out
enough coal to pay for German war reparations, he again cited
national character. "The French have a genius for love, war,
making wine, farming, painting, writing and cooking. None of
these accomplishments is particularly applicable to the Ruhr, except making war." It took business genius to operate the Ruhr
at all and took more than the French had to operate it at a
profit.[29]

In *Death in the Afternoon* Hemingway had to explain Spanish national character to account for the complex feeling behind
bullfighting. On several occasions he had to remind American
readers of a psychology different from theirs. In sports Ameri-

29. "The Mecca of Fakers Is French Capital," *TDS*, March 25, 1922, p. 4; "Did
Poincaré Laugh in Verdun Cemetery?" *TDS*, August 12, 1922, p. 4; "French
Register Speed When Movies Are on Job," *TDS*, May 16, 1923, p. 19.

cans and British were dominated by ideas of fair play and victory. They could hardly look on a bullfight as anything more than an unequal match, without fair play for both antagonists or hope of victory for one. But for Spaniards the bullfight was not sport or spectacle but a ritual offering and avoidance of death. It predicated a cult of death that neither English, nor French, nor even some kinds of Spaniards could understand: the Englishman lived for this world, he wrote, and considered death a thing not to be talked about or to be risked except for patriotism, adventure, or reward. Although the French had a "cult of respect for the dead," they lived for such material things as family, position, and good foods and wines. They would kill "for the pot," but not to celebrate death as a mystery. Even Catalonians and Galicians were too commercial and too practical to see death and bullfighting as Castilians and Andalusians did. But Castilians had a different sense of reality: "The people of Castile have a great common sense. . . . They know death is the inescapable reality, the one thing any man may be sure of; the only security; that it transcends all modern comforts and that with it you do not need a bath tub in every American home, nor when you have it, do you need the radio. They think a great deal about death and when they have a religion they have one which believes that life is much shorter than death. Having this feeling they take an intelligent interest in death and when they can see it being given, avoided, refused and accepted in the afternoon for a nominal price of admission they pay their money and go to the bull ring. . . ."[30]

Part of his military analysis of the China-Burma theater of war in 1941 was also based on a reading of national character. As he explained the situation, the two keys to the effective Chinese tying-down of Japanese divisions in China, while the United States and Britain built their Pacific defenses, were continued aid to the Nationalists via Burma and survival of Chiang Kai-shek with his will to resist both the Japanese and the Chinese Communists. Both of these estimates depended on national character. Aid through Burma was complicated by Burmese habits. Burma he described as a land of "complete and utter red tape . . . worse than France before the fall." Burmese bureaucrats combined the "worse features of Hindu Babu and the French pre-fall function-

30. *Death in the Afternoon*, pp. 22, 166.

ary." In China the complication was "the age-old Chinese custom of squeeze." Where not money but engineering and labor were key factors, as for example in the building of landing strips for American-aid bombers, projects operated with technical efficiency. But when money was involved, as in the pilfering and black marketing of gasoline shipped in by the Burma Road, centuries of Chinese business custom and ethics undercut the war effort.[31] When he talked with American Ambassador Nelson Johnson, he learned further that for the Chinese all present problems existed in a context of a thousand years; and even such seemingly essential figures as the Generalissimo might readily be sacrificed or betrayed by Chinese politicians acting in their long tradition of regional loyalties.[32] In either case, political planners had to consider the intangible of national character.

Besides doing variations on nineteenth-century travel conventions, Hemingway wrote during his formative period as travel author in the manner of Mark Twain, exploiting the New World and democratic prejudices of his Canadian audiences. Again, it was a case of ambivalence—restless desire to see and admire the Old World and willingness to mock the Old World's claims of superior and sophisticated civilization. That Hemingway consciously appealed to Canadians' prejudice, even at the expense of their American neighbors, appeared in such recorded comments as that by a Swiss hotelkeeper. When Hemingway asked how he told the difference between Canadians and Americans, he replied that "Canadians speak English and always stay two days longer at any place than Americans do." Hemingway appealed to Canadians' democratic prejudices when he sketched the lumpy families of French war profiteers flocking to Swiss resorts to preen ridiculously in the company of old-line aristocrats. Poetic justice even had a chance of working when the wolflike young men lurking at the card tables of the resorts fleeced the profiteers, who may have been wolves in their business practices but were sheep at the watering places.[33]

As for the famed architecture and customs of Europe, they

31. "Story of Ernest Hemingway's Far East Trip to See for Himself If War with Japan Is Inevitable," *PM*, June 9, 1941, p. 8.
32. "Ernest Hemingway Tells How 100,000 Labored Night and Day to Build Huge Landing Field for Bombers," *PM*, June 18, 1941, p. 18.
33. "Queer Mixture of Aristocrats, Profiteers, Sheep and Wolves at the Hotels in Switzerland," *TSW*, March 4, 1922, p. 25.

could be seen through the eyes of another Westerner abroad. Switzerland, said Hemingway, was an up-and-down country with hotels of the cuckoo-clock school of architecture much like the Canadian "iron dog on the front lawn" period. French politeness had "gone the way of absinthe, pre-war prices and other legendary things." French cab drivers made more by intimidating passengers to give large tips than they did from fares, Frenchmen grabbed bus seats when Americans rose to offer them to women, museum officials refused to honor their own announced visiting hours and snarled insults at tourists who innocently asked admission to the museums, and passport officials insulted tourists who wanted the change from their passport charges even when no-tipping signs were present. German family life, he wrote, failed to match the popular legends of happy domesticity. On a train he saw a German husband eat an hour-and-a-half lunch in the dining car, complete with several beers, and then go back to his wife in the coach bearing only a few rolls stuffed with cheese. With that, Hemingway observed, "The family [had] dined." In another part of the train, when a heavy rucksack fell on a German wife's head, the husband curtly informed her, "You're not hurt." And on a bus a German husband grabbed a seat from an old lady, leaving his wife to stand embarrassed and blushing.[34]

Even Twain-like phrasing appeared in some sketches, phrasing that held implicit the vestiges of frontier cruelty and exaggeration. In Spain Hemingway found that tipping the postman insured delivery of one's mail. Once, giving an especially generous tip, he found the postman so overcome that he produced another letter he had been saving back for another day's *propina*. But he learned to accept such tricks in spite of his American desire to correct the world: "The climate is so soft and gentle that it makes it seem not worthwhile to kill the postman. Life is so mellow in Spain."[35] Describing the French custom of taking aperitifs—"the hour before lunch and the hour before dinner, when all Paris gathers at the cafés to poison themselves into a cheerful pre-eating glow"—he characterized the liqueurs as "patented mixtures" having "a basic taste like a brass door knob."

34. *Ibid.*; "French Politeness," *TSW*, April 15, 1922, p. 29; "Hubby Dines First; Wife Gets Crumbs!" *TDS*, September 30, 1922, p. 9.
35. "How'd You Like to Tip the Postman Every Time?" *TSW*, March 11, 1922, p. 13.

When aperitif manufacturers slipped forbidden absinthe into one liqueur named Anis Delloso, it gained immediate popularity, giving "the slow, culminating wallop that made the boulevardier want to get up and jump on his new straw hat in ecstasy after the third Delloso." But the government discovered the reason for Delloso's new popularity, and dullness returned to the boulevards: "The boulevardier waits in vain for the feeling that makes him want to shinny up the side of the Eiffel Tower. For it is not absinthe any more."[36]

If, as Willard Thorp has indicated, the fundamental question American travel writers have had to confront is what to think about Europe,[37] Hemingway's answer was to see Europe as background for his own growth and for knowledge of himself and the world. His records of travel, though written incidentally, showed him becoming increasingly knowledgeable and sure of his right to full experience. Whether as reporter, *aficionado*, safarist, or returner to old grounds, he found the world's affairs and his personal interests to be good companions; and his personal requirements and those of the travel-writing tradition gave mutual aid and insight. So much at home was he with the tradition that even when he transformed personal and public knowledge into fictional statement, he retained vestiges of his travel-writing techniques. Early and late he honed passages of fiction that showed protagonists with the traveler's eye. Jake Barnes in *The Sun Also Rises* explains the customs of the country to his friends and remarks to himself perhaps ironically on the differences between Spanish friends and those in France. His French friends always have a sound financial basis for friendship; but his Spanish friends, true to their national character, have their secret reasons that have to do with quaint ideas of honor and death. Both Frederic Henry and Catherine Barkley in *A Farewell to Arms* know enough of the tourist clichés about architecture and painting to mock them. Robert Jordan's only book is on his ten-year travels in Spain, but it provides him with an insight into Spanish character and customs as they operate in war. And in *Across the River and into the Trees* Richard Cantwell, approaching Venice with his army driver, sounds momentarily like a guide book to the city even if he later mocks the Baedeker tourists there. That

36. "Latest Drinking Scandal Now Agitates Paris," *TSW*, August 12, 1922, p. 11.
37. "Pilgrim's Return," p. 834.

Hemingway recognized his tendency to carry over travel-writing techniques into his fiction appeared in his account of writing *The Sun Also Rises*: "I showed the first draft to Nathan Asch, the novelist, who then had quite a strong accent and he said, 'Hem, vaht do you mean saying you wrote a novel? A novel huh. Hem, you are writing a travel buch.' I was not too discouraged by Nathan and rewrote the book, keeping in the travel (that was the part about the fishing trip and Pamplona) at Schruns in the Vorarlberg at the Hotel Taube."[38] First and last, in journalism and in fiction, he was an unapologetic practitioner of the art of recording experience in travel.

38. Carlos Baker (ed.), *Hemingway and His Critics* (New York, 1961), p. 31.

IV. Hemingway at War

WHEN HE WROTE THE INTRODUCTION TO HIS 1948 EDITION OF *A Farewell to Arms,* Hemingway used the occasion to explain why he had spent so much of his creative energy writing about war:

Some people used to say: why is the man so preoccupied and obsessed with war, and now, since 1933 perhaps it is clear why a writer should be interested in the constant, bullying, murderous, slovenly crime of war. Having been to too many of them, I am sure that I am prejudiced, and I hope that I am very prejudiced. But it is the considered belief of the writer of this book that wars are fought by the finest people that there are, or just say people, although the closer you are to where they are fighting, the finer people you meet; but they are made, provoked and initiated by straight economic rivalries and by swine that stand to profit from them.[1]

The statement was central and symptomatic; suggesting both the ambivalences and the ambiguities of Hemingway's thinking,

1. (New York, 1948), p. x.

it emphasized his paradoxical notion that wars are fought by the best of people for the worst of reasons. It suggested his moral intuition, often only informally understood by himself, that good can come out of evil while acting as the agent of evil; suggested his ambivalence in both hating and following enthusiastically the great crimes of the century, of emotionally doing best what he was mentally reluctant to do at all. It implied his sometimes admitted emotional preference for the rifleman with the enemy over his gun sight to the godlike general miles behind the front with his maps and mental, rather than sensational, comprehension of the war. And it suggested his assumption, frequently not recognized by him, that war is the real experience of the century—the experience that makes a man feel incomplete if he misses it, and an experience to be known directly, sensuously, and emotionally rather than abstractly.

That he was present at the wars, and had a right to be, he frequently certified. In the 1942 introduction to *Men at War* he presented as his credentials not only that he had taken part in the First World War and had been wounded but that he had also passed through that initiation of war which is the key to understanding much of the century's experience. Badly wounded, he had lost his illusion of personal immortality. But in losing that illusion, and suffering because of the loss, he had gained that other insight that men of war must have: "I had a bad time until I figured it out that nothing could happen to me that had not happened to all men before me. Whatever I had to do men had always done. If they had done it then I could do it too and the best thing was not to worry about it."[2] Accompanying American tankmen in Northern France after the breakthrough from Paris in 1944, he stood with them while artillery softened the German antitank positions, and as they watched, one tank soldier made the comment central to Hemingway's presence at the wars: "What are you doing here if you don't have to be here? Do you do it just for the money? . . . There ain't the money in the world to pay me for doing it."[3]

Hemingway was there because he had to be. Witnessing and reporting wars, he was living up to his discovery that war is essentially a state of mind, a condition of the will and the emo-

2. (New York, 1942), pp. xiii-xiv.
3. "The G.I. and the General," *Collier's*, CXIV (November 4, 1944), 44.

tions. One does well to describe the movement, clash, dirt, blood, and fatigue of war, but the ultimate meaning is emotional. He recorded this insight in his 1940 preface to Gustav Regler's novel on the Spanish war, *The Great Crusade*: "The Spanish Civil War was really lost, of course, when the Fascists took Irún in the late summer of 1936. But in a war you can never admit, even to yourself, that it is lost. Because when you will it is lost, you are beaten. The one who being beaten refuses to admit it and fights on the longest wins in all finish fights; unless of course he is killed, starved out, deprived of weapons, or betrayed. All of these things happened to the Spanish people. They were killed in vast numbers, starved out, deprived of weapons and betrayed."[4] Saying this, he was well within the tradition of classic war commentary, especially that of Prussian General Karl von Clausewitz, whose treatise *On War* he quoted and referred to on several occasions and from which he derived maxims to serve as the organizing principle for *Men at War*. Such Clausewitzean notions as the maxims that courage to decide as well as courage to strike or resist is fundamental for the soldier and that resolution to act as well as firmness or staunchness in resistance is a key military virtue—these he not only quoted for his readers of *Men at War* but also applied them to his own presentation of the century at war. He used them, for example, to explain the Italian debacles at Brihuega and Guadalajara during the Spanish Civil War. The other basic concept from Clausewitz, that war is an extension of politics by means of force, he realized and hated as he cursed the politicians for their betrayal of soldiers. Whether it was the politicians' betrayal of French military planning by allowing German possession of Spanish airfields after French war industries had been moved away from Germany and into the South of France, or the French manufacturers' continuing to manufacture 37 mm. antitank guns after the Spanish Civil War had shown the need for heavier weapons, Hemingway saw what Clausewitz meant. And he hated the "mismanagement, gullibility, cupidity, selfishness and ambition" that produced war even as he admired the men who prosecuted the war.[5] That hatred was part of the emotional tangle of war.

He recognized another facet of the emotional course of war

4. *The Great Crusade* (New York, 1940), p. vii.
5. *Men at War*, p. xi.

when he wrote of having cried at the death of Republican General Lucasz: "And about crying let me tell you something that you may not know. There is no man alive today who has not cried at a war if he was at it long enough. Sometimes it is after a battle, sometimes it is when someone that you love is killed, sometimes it is at the disbanding of a corps or a unit that has endured and accomplished together and now will never be together again. But all men at war cry sometimes, from Napoleon, the greatest butcher, down."[6] When he wrote the introduction to *Men at War*, it was a time when survival was the issue, and he could propose emotionally, even if sober thought might rule it out, that Germans be sterilized after the war to destroy their war-making potential.[7] Later in the war, after describing how American "wump" guns shattered Siegfried Line bunkers and knowing serenely that victory was in reach, he could feel almost regretful sorrow at all the Germans' frustrations and all their plans gone wrong.[8]

It was clear to Hemingway that not only an individual war but also a century of war had its emotional course, and his being able to witness the wars of the century gave them an emotional pattern mirrored in his own experience. His characterizations of the different wars derived from his differing responses to them. Although his response to the First World War was the impulse for much of his best fiction, it gained only incidental mention in his essays. He told in *Men at War* that it was, however, the occasion for his loss of the illusion of personal immortality and his learning to hate the politicians whose corrupt policies had their denouement in the great slaughters of the Somme, Verdun, and the Vittorio-Veneto. It was the war of disillusionment, with a personal climax for him in the summer of 1918—the time of his wounding—but with a general emotional climax and disillusionment in 1917—the time of the incipient mutiny in the French army and the Caporetto disaster in Italy. In a more retrospective vein, he recorded in "A Veteran Visits Old Front" that even the old magic of scarred battlefields, made somehow significant by the near presence of the buried dead, was dissipated when the dead were reburied in military cemeteries and the trenches filled,

6. Regler, *The Great Crusade*, p. ix.
7. p. xxiii.
8. "War in the Siegfried Line," *Collier's*, CXIV (November 18, 1944), 73.

the old bunkers leveled and grown over.[9] For all his reporting on the Greco-Turkish war of 1922, he saw the effects of war rather than the war itself. He heard reports from Captain Wittal of the Indian cavalry on the battles in Anatolia—the incompetence of the Greek Constantine officers and the Greek artillery's firing into its own infantry—but he actually saw the Greek army retreat across Thrace and Thracian refugees clog the roads to Macedonia. He recognized the betrayal of the Greek armies by British and Greek politicians but this time cynically, as a confirmation of what he had sensed during the previous war. His chief response was pity for the suffering refugees.

His acquaintance with the Italian-Ethiopian war of the thirties was vicarious and distant, but his service with the Italians in the First World War provided him with insight into the minds of the Italian soldiers caught in the African campaign. He saw that young Fascists sent into the Ethiopian bush would go with the propaganda-inspired zeal of neo-Romans, would even praise *il Duce* if they received only flesh wounds; but if hit in the bone or sickened by malaria or dysentery, they would quickly relinquish their dream of military glories and recognize their new betrayal by politicians.[10] In Hemingway's eyes it was a political war started by a bully hoping to accrue cheap military glory and some loot.

The Spanish Civil War had a strong emotional pattern for Hemingway. His emotional investment in the country, great because he had lived and written there, was made more poignant because many of his friends from the bullfight days were on the wrong side; most of the matadors supported the Francoist insurgents. And the Soviets supporting the Republic were more acceptable politically and intellectually than emotionally. The simplified feeling that he was finally able to work out toward the war had its basis in his long-felt loathing for Mussolini and in his reconciliation with liberal friends like John Dos Passos and Archibald MacLeish more than in a clear emotional commitment to one side or the other in Spain. But as the Republican cause became "our" cause, he absorbed the partisan mind. It was focused by the surprise Republican victories at Brihuega and Guadalajara and the successful defense of Madrid. Consistent

9. *TDS*, July 22, 1922, p. 7.
10. "Wings Always over Africa," *Esquire*, V (January 1936), 31.

with his predilection for the underdog and the lowly rifleman, it became for him the people's war against the generals. Then came the time of caution, of regrouping and retraining, when anarchist battalions were replaced by battalions trained and led by peasant generals, though their field methods suspiciously resembled those taught in Soviet military academies. The second emotional high point occurred when the insurgent stronghold at Teruel was captured in the winter of 1937. Though the rebel drive to the sea was temporarily thwarted by the capture of Teruel, the war by spring of 1938 took on a mood of inevitability as superior rebel forces pushed toward Barcelona. Hemingway's dispatches from the Ebro front soon began to hold a note of desperate and anxious determination to see the Fascist offensive stopped. When the drive reached the sea and Catalonia was cut off, the road to Valencia left only technically open, he began to record the relief of Spanish Republican commanders who now had only their local battles to fight, only their regional loyalties to recognize. Tacitly accepting the inevitable end of Republican resistance, he began to write of the lessons of Spain for the rest of Europe and America. His response finally was fear that non-Fascist Europe and America would again betray the soldiers who would have to fight the coming war, that politicians would give away all the military advantages.

Turning in 1941 to the Far East, Hemingway toured the Sino-Japanese war theatre, but his aim was not so much to report the war going on there as to analyze it for signs of the Pacific war to come. In the Spanish war he had been more concerned with the bullying personalities of Mussolini and Hitler than with Spanish reform and reactionary groups as the causes of war, whereas in the Far East his analysis was primarily economic and only incidentally concerned with such individual persons as Generalissimo Chiang Kai-shek. He concentrated on what raw materials the Japanese needed from Southeast Asia and the Dutch East Indies and what they would have to do before moving toward those materials. He saw the hands of both Hitler and Stalin at work in the Sino-Japanese war and, in so noting, saw the applicability of von Clausewitz's maxim that war is the continuation of policy by means of force. Hitler wanted the Japanese to move against the British base at Singapore and thus relieve him from pressures by the British fleet and Far Eastern reserves.

Stalin wanted the Japanese to move against the British, Dutch, and Americans and free him from the threat at his back door. Hemingway's response to the tour was again fear that American politicians would fail to aid China enough to tie down Japanese divisions there while British, Dutch, and American military men built up their Pacific defenses. But he had his smallest emotional investment in this war; he tacitly accepted the Japanese need for expansion toward greater raw materials.

His two responses to the Second World War were as much mental as emotional. Although he had already expended during the Spanish war much of his hate for Mussolini, Hitler, and Neville Chamberlain, whom he saw as the chief movers toward war, his residue of emotion, if we are to believe *Men at War*, was directed toward Allied military commanders who refused to adapt to a new kind of war and who wanted to hide behind lies forced onto the reporters of the war. He was really talking about morale, however, and not technology. "Covering up errors to save the men who make them can only lead to a lack of confidence which can be one of the greatest dangers a nation can face."[11] The second response was to see the century as a whole, with the events of the second war as the vantage point for perspective. What he saw was the emotional course of history:

This war is only a continuation of the last war. France was not beaten in 1940. France was beaten in 1917. Singapore was not really lost in 1942. It was lost at Gallipoli and on the Somme and in the mud of Passchendaele. Austria was not destroyed in 1938. Austria was destroyed in the battle of Vittorio-Veneto at the end of October in 1918. It was really lost and gone when it failed to beat Italy after Caporetto in the great Austrian victory offensive of the 15th of June, 1918. . . . All of history is of one piece and it is ourselves, who bore the least weight of casualties in 1917 and 1918, who have to bear the most to defeat Germany this time. Once a nation has entered into a policy of foreign wars, there is no withdrawing. If you do not go to them then they will come to you. It was April, 1917 that ended our isolation—it was not Pearl Harbor.[12]

He would have endorsed Dick Diver's statement in *Tender Is The Night* that Europe lacked the emotional reserves to fight another Battle of the Somme.

11. *Men at War*, p. xxxi.
12. *Ibid.*, p. xxiii.

Hemingway's other assumption, "that wars are fought by the finest people," is more than a restatement of the Darwinian maxim that the fittest are sent to fight the wars of nations. He came closest to explaining what he meant in a passage from *The Spanish Earth*: "This is the true face of men going into action. It is a little different from any other face you will ever see. Men cannot act before the camera in the presence of death."[13] It was appropriate for him to write that in 1937. As he told in *Death in the Afternoon*, he had used bullfighting as an emotional equivalent of war during the twenties and early thirties. But at the end of that book, he had found that matadors could posture before the crowd in the presence of death at the arena. Or because of the decadence in bullfight practices, one could never tell whether he was in the presence of death or only of a tampered-with bull. By the time of the Spanish war it had become clear to him that death was the true measurer of human qualities and that, while "death is still very badly organized in war," it is, in war, beyond human tampering. The corrupted bullfight managers might find their moral equivalent in the politicians, but the politicians' mismanagement did not intrude into the testing of men at the front. So he went to the battle fronts of his time and reported how men really are.

Assuming that men are at their finest the closer they are to battle and to the testing of their resources against death, Hemingway showed his strong leaning toward primitivism. In this case, though, death's agent was other men rather than nature. Hemingway's war writing was a continued celebration of men's resourcefulness—in mental, emotional, and physical efforts—when death was the stake. It is striking how seldom he disparaged the "enemy," for the enemy too was a man functioning at his highest powers in the presence of death. At the end of his account of the Normandy landings in "Voyage to Victory" Hemingway balanced his praise for American successes with a tribute to German defenses. "It had been a frontal assault in broad daylight against a mined beach defended by all the obstacles military ingenuity could devise. The beach had been defended as stubbornly and as intelligently as any troops could defend it. But every boat from the Dix had landed her troops and cargo. No boat was lost through bad seamanship. All that were lost were

13. (Cleveland, 1938), p. 23.

lost by enemy action. And we had taken the beach."[14] Later in the Hürtgen Forest he admired the ingenuity demonstrated in the German bunker emplacements at the same time he admired the Americans' ingenuity in destroying them with self-propelled 105 mm. "wump" guns brought to the rear of the bunkers and fired point-blank at the bunker doors. During the Spanish war he admired the Moors and Civil Guards who held the University City salient against repeated Loyalist minings and counterattacks.

Although he preferred the intensity of feeling and sensation at the front, Hemingway also recognized that the strategy of war as well as the tactics of battle called for the clearest thinking and judgment, and he was a reporter on generals as well as machine gunners. His own full reading in military history enabled him to act as critic of strategies for his readers. In "Wings Always over Africa" he saw Ethiopian strategy as a plan of retreat to keep the Italian army unengaged in the field while the Italian line of communications and support stretched dangerously long, to keep the Italians in the bush until the rainy season caught them, and to keep the Italians involved by not allowing them a decisive victory while money and the morale of Mussolini's unreliable African allies drained away. If the plan worked, he wrote, it would produce a repetition of the Italian debacle at Adowa (Adua) in 1896. He could point to the example of German Colonel von Lettow-Vorbeck's successful guerrilla tactics in East Africa during the First World War as precedent for the Ethiopian guerrilla war strategy.[15] In Spain he saw a determined and resourceful stand by Republican forces at the Ebro negated by their strategic error of leaving undefended the valleys to the north of Tortosa. The northern sector, he noted, was "the backdoor to all Catalonia." A young divisional commander thought he could still block the drive, Hemingway reported, but the result was a successful Fascist drive to the sea and the cutting off of the principal manufacturing area of Spain.[16] In China he talked to Chinese commanders and British and Soviet advisers and saw the conflict between Japan and China as one of economic strategies. Japanese mobile divisions had already captured the flat country, but had bogged down in the mountains where the vast

14. *Collier's*, CXIV (July 22, 1944), 57.
15. "Notes on the Next War," *Esquire*, IV (September 1935), 156.
16. *Fact*, no. 16 (July 15, 1938), 60-62.

numbers of minimally equipped Chinese regulars and irregulars were holding and where mobile divisions lost their tactical advantage. The Japanese would need additional petroleum, rubber, and quinine from the Dutch East Indies to complete their conquest of China and would have to accept war with the Netherlands and risk war with Britain and the United States to get those additional supplies. The United States and Britain, needing time to build defenses in the Pacific, needed to supply China by way of the Burma Road so that China could keep Japanese forces occupied. Japan, caught between continuing expenditures of materials in China and increasing diversion of East Indian supplies to British and American bases, would have to move southward. Only the timing was conjectural, but for the generals and admirals, the ambassadors, and the aid officials concerned, it involved calculations measured against national survival.[17]

Both Spain and China illustrated another part of Hemingway's assumption that war was where men lived most fully. To live next to death they had to learn to live nimbly, to accept the discipline of a situation, and to adapt themselves mentally, emotionally, and physically to new situations. He saw men stretch their powers and adapt as often as terrain, weapons, or comrades changed. In Spain he recognized the need for Soviet-trained divisions of regular Republican troops in place of the unwieldy anarchist divisions. In China he admired Chinese regular units trained by Germans on the Prussian model, and he approved a strict discipline that not only decreed heavy punishment for the usual army crimes of theft and insubordination but also shot entire sections that failed to follow their officers into combat. Trained to eat little and to "know that death is certain from behind but only possible from in front," they had, he said, "the best of the inhuman qualities that make a man a good soldier."[18] For contrast, he pointed to the failure in training and disciplining Chinese pilots. They came mostly from the Chinese gentry and were more concerned with the superiority that being pilots supposedly gave them than with developing their knowledge of combat tactics. The result in one instance was that all sixteen planes in one Chinese group of sixteen were shot down by formation-

17. *PM*, June 10, 1941, pp. 4-5; June 18, 1941, pp. 16-17.
18. "After Four Years of War in China, Japs Have Conquered Only Flatlands," *PM*, June 16, 1941, p. 6.

flying Japanese near a Szechwan airfield.[19] He said explicitly concerning freedom and discipline in China what he sometimes made only implicit in his reports on wars in other countries before and after: "There is much argument whether China is or is not a democracy. No country which is at war remains a democracy for long. War always brings on a temporary dictatorship."[20]

He saw that besides learning new disciplines, men at war had to stay mentally nimble to avoid being tagged by death, and in his role of war observer Hemingway reiterated this theme constantly in his accounts of the Spanish war and of the Second World War. In some cases adaptability consisted of going back to older forms of combat; in some cases to the newly found. At Belchite in the early days of the Spanish war he told how American volunteers crawled Indian-style through woods to attack the town. But after the Republican victory at Brihuega he declared, "It is the coordination of these planes, tanks and infantry which brings this war into a new phase," and believed that "Brihuega will take its place in military history with the other decisive battles of the world."[21]

In *Men at War* he urged that Americans learn from experience as the Germans had. Germans had profited from World War I by changing their concept of war from stalemate to blitzkrieg, while the French, thinking they had won the war, prepared themselves for defeat. Similarly he urged learning from Japanese successes in the Pacific that navies meant airplanes as much as ships.[22] And in "The G.I. and the General" he recorded approvingly how American tankmen learned from German tankmen: "If we used cover like those damned Krauts, a lot more guys would get to Paris or Berlin or wherever it is we're going."[23]

On the other hand, he warned against over-reliance on machines. Human will, zeal, and flesh could sometimes go where machines failed. Republican troops took Teruel in December, 1937, while a blizzard halted all tanks, planes, and even horses. Only men could stand such weather, he wrote. "One thing remains. You need infantry still to win battles and impregnable

19. "China Needs Pilots as Well as Planes to Beat Japs in the Air," *PM*, June 17, 1941, p. 5.
20. "Aid to China Gives U.S. Two-Ocean Navy Security for Price of One Battleship," *PM*, June 15, 1941, p. 6.
21. *Fact*, 43, 34.
22. *Men at War*, pp. xii, xxii.
23. "The G.I. and the General," 11, 14.

positions are impregnable as the will of those that hold them."[24] After the battles in the Hürtgen Forest he wrote that claims about which armored unit was first on German soil were irrelevant. The real truth was that the infantry broke the Siegfried Line. "They cracked it on a cold rainy morning when even the crows weren't flying, much less the Air Force."[25] And in *Men at War*, after discussing the illusion of power that horses once had given and that tanks now gave, he wrote: "The moral of this digression is, as stated above, that a horse will carry a man in his first action where his legs might not go; and a mechanized vehicle will carry him further than a horse will go; but finally no mechanized vehicle is any better than the heart of the man who handles the controls. So learn about the human heart and the human mind in war from this book."[26] For his military readers he recommended a very secret kind of learning which he had come by the hard way. To live effectively and fully in the presence of death, one had to avoid worry: "Learning to suspend your imagination and live completely in the very second of the present minute with no before and no after is the greatest gift a soldier can have."[27]

While Hemingway often referred to his own wounding as an event that others could learn from, he recognized during the Spanish war to what degree his experience was generally applicable. Encountering a wounded American, Jay Raven, at the Valencia Road Hospital in Madrid, Hemingway learned that he had been a social worker in Pittsburgh and had been blinded and burned by a grenade burst while helping to regroup a routed unit on his right flank in the trenches outside Madrid. Hearing Raven's account and seeing his unmilitary person and manner, Hemingway could not believe his story though he did not say so to the wounded man. It was too much the story that men would want to tell about how they had been wounded. "In the war that I had known, men often lied about the manner of their wounding. Not at first, but later. I'd lied a little myself in my time. Especially late in the evening." But later meeting Jock Cunningham, Raven's unit commander, Hemingway learned that Raven's story was true, though possibly understated. Out of

24. *Fact*, 46.
25. "War in the Siegfried Line," 18.
26. *Men at War*, pp. xix-xx.
27. *Ibid.*, p. xxvii.

many things one learned in war, he wrote, this was one of the most important—that an unsoldierly type could perform so well the acts of war. "This is a strange new kind of war where you learn just as much as you are able to believe."[28]

The emotional intensity of living by death's dispensation was also Hemingway's subject. He noted it on the command level as well as the popular level. Robert Van Gelder reported that in an interview with Hemingway and Gustavo Duran, one of Hemingway's favorite Republican generals of the Spanish war, when Duran talked of the agonies of military decision-making Hemingway exclaimed that was what *For Whom the Bell Tolls* was about.[29] In his own essays he recorded war's emotional wear on commanders. In "How We Came to Paris," for example, he noted French General LeClerc's curt dismissal of French guerrillas on the outskirts of the city and observed, "In war, my experience has been that a rude general is a nervous general."[30] In "The G.I. and the General" he noted a division general's understanding of the fatigue of his troops when the troops did not realize the feelings were recognized outside their own unit. But the true agony of command became evident when, in spite of the general's attempts to gain a four-day rest for his troops, they had to fight again because of a German counterattack.[31] Perhaps one of the best examples of the mystery of command came from his Spanish Civil War experience. Republican General Mangada, he recalled, was a successful eccentric who planned his battles while sitting in a tree in advance of his own lines, scanning enemy terrain through his field glass and talking to spirits.[32]

Occasionally he wrote sketches of commanders who recognized the emotional basis of command. Of Chiang Kai-shek he said, "The Generalissimo is a military leader who goes through the motions of being a statesman. This is important. Hitler is a statesman who employs military force. Mussolini is a statesman who is unable to employ military force. The Generalissimo's objectives are always military. For 10 years his objective was to destroy the Communists. He was kidnapped under Communist

28. *Fact*, 20-23.
29. "Ernest Hemingway Talks of Work and War," *Writers and Writing* (New York, 1946), p. 97. The interview was on August 11, 1940.
30. *Collier's*, CXIV (October 7, 1944), 14.
31. "The G.I. and the General," 47.
32. "Good Generals Hug the Line," *Ken*, II (August 25, 1938), 28.

auspices and agreed to give up fighting the Communist and fight the Japanese. He has never given this up. I think that somewhere inside of him he has never given the other objective either."[33] Part of Chiang Kai-shek's command problem, he noted, was having to endure collaborators and potential betrayers about him while he worked for both immediate and distant goals.

But because the people rather than the generals were close to the front, Hemingway wrote mostly about their wars. In Madrid, as in Thrace, the people included civilians as well as soldiers. Hemingway's astonishment and admiration was that men could behave so well around death. While his stories and sketches were often of the panic and cowardice of men at war, his war reports themselves were of people who suffered but did not panic—no Nick Adamses, no Pablos, no Bonellos. Whether they were refugees at Adrianople or Tortosa, infantry at Usera or tankmen in the Schnee-Eifel complex, most had found that extra dimension that put them among the finer people. Near Gandesa in Catalonia, for example, Hemingway saw a Frenchman standing beside his overturned but intact load of oranges and pleading with passing soldiers and refugees not to shortweight him as he was responsible for the load when it arrived in France. The result was that "nobody touched his oranges, and they lay a shining yellow tribute to something as we pulled out of there."[34]

When he wrote of the mass of people, Hemingway was concerned with morale and those general ideas people had of themselves and their allies or enemies. Quite early in his war reporting he explained the effects of faltering morale:

Kemal whipped the Greeks as everyone knows. But when you realize that he was fighting a conscript army whose soldiers the barren country they were fighting to gain hated, who had no desire as men to conquer Asia Minor, and who were thoroughly fed up and becoming conscious that they were going into battle to die doing a cat's paw job, it was not the magnificent military achievement that it is made out to be. Especially is that shown when you realize that Kemal's troops were fanatical patriots anxious to drive the invaders out of their country. The ratio of effectiveness of well-trained, well-armed, highly fanatical patriots fighting in their own country against

33. "Aid to China Gives U.S. Two-Ocean Navy Security," p. 6.
34. *Fact*, 57.

half-hearted, poorly-officered, homesick conscript invaders is some-where about ten to one.[35]

During the Spanish war he saw the force of morale again but had to recognize its limits against advanced weaponry. The well-equipped Italians broke at Brihuega, when opposed by nearly equal numbers of Republicans in tanks and planes, because they lacked zest for the Spanish war. Many had volunteered to work in Ethiopia, not fight in Spain, he explained, and he cited stories of despair learned from prisoners and from letters found on the dead.[36] He saw the Moors and Civil Guards at the University City salient, for all their bravery and tenacity, as professional soldiers opposed to "a people in arms" and likely to be defeated except for a constant supply of arms furnished them by Italy and Germany.[37]

In China he saw a different concept of morale. It was the result of friction between allies and consisted of an all-things-are-possible attitude because so many things were wrong. The Nationalists were not only in conflict with the Communists but also bitter because the Communists received better mention in the world's press. The Nationalists received British aid and mili-tary advice but felt the contempt of the British so strongly that their own response was contempt. To the British verdict that "you can't depend on Johnny [John Chinaman] to take the offen-sive," the Chinese answered that they did better without planes or artillery than the British had done in Norway. A Chinese gen-eral summed up the Chinese attitude when he told Hemingway that British officers wore monocles so that they would not see more than they could understand.[38] In Szechwan province he saw 100,000 Chinese laborers build a thousand-acre airfield for Flying Fortresses under the direction of a thirty-eight-year-old engineer, Chen-Lo-Kwan. The remarkable thing for Hemingway was that Chen-Lo-Kwan worked under a "finish by March 30 or else" order from Chiang Kai-shek. Neither the engineer nor the coolies thought of the threat as anything other than normal.[39] It

35. "Russia to Spoil French Game with Kemalists," *TDS*, October 23, 1922, p. 13.
36. *The Spanish Earth*, pp. 46-47.
37. *Ibid.*, p. 34.
38. "Russo-Jap Pact Hasn't Kept Soviet from Sending Aid to China," *PM*, June 10, 1941, pp. 4-5.
39. "Ernest Hemingway Tells How 100,000 Chinese Labored Night and Day to Build Huge Landing Field for Bombers," *PM*, June 18, 1941, p. 16.

was morale based on total fatalism, a kind he had not encountered in Europe.

When he wrote of individuals in war, it was to study them for both their unique and typical responses to danger. The succession of chauffeurs he and Sidney Franklin had in Madrid was a study of responses to war. The first was Tomas, a dwarf and a man of feeling but useless once he had seen tanks bombed by planes. After that he always had trouble starting the car in the mornings for another day's run through the battle areas and was finally sent back to Valencia as a coward. The second driver was pure rogue, who ran away to Valencia with forty liters of valuable gasoline. The third was David, brave, foul-mouthed, and unable to drive except at a crawl or a dash. His eccentricity was his pleasure in hearing shells whistle overhead until one day he saw seven women in a food line hit by a shell. After that his response was overwhelming sadness. He provided insight into typical Spanish profanity and the profane response to war. "David was an Anarchist boy from a little town near Toledo. He used language that was so utterly and unconceivably [*sic*] foul that half the time you could not believe what your ears were hearing. Being with David has changed my whole conception of profanity." The fourth was Hipolito, a trade-union man for twenty years, veteran of the assault on the Montana Barracks and a believer in the Republic. "He made you realize why Franco never took Madrid when he had the chance. Hipolito and the others like him would have fought from street to street, and house to house, as long as anyone of them was left alive; and the last ones would have burned the town. They are tough and they are efficient. They are the Spaniards that once conquered the Western World." With Hipolito at the wheel, theirs was the only car on the streets the day Madrid was hit by three hundred shells.[40] When he wrote his portrait of Milton Wolff, youthful commander of the Lincoln-Washington Battalion in Spain, Hemingway found Wolff's resourcefulness unique and his career reminiscent of youthful colonels during the American Civil War.[41] With French guerrillas near Rambouillet on the road to Paris, Hemingway celebrated one of the more classic responses. When they

40. *Fact*, 25-33.

41. "Milton Wolff," *An Exhibition of Sculptures by Jo Davidson* (New York, 1938), p. 22.

were shunted aside by LeClerc's Free French armored division, the guerrillas retired to a crossroads bar to sing and drink. Their response was partly the result of Hemingway's unsubtle peacekeeping methods: "In those days I found that the production of an excellent bottle of any sort of alcoholic beverage was the only way of ending an argument." But their insouciance before death as well as their hard drinking was admirable in the eyes of Hemingway's driver: "Best outfit I ever been with. No discipline. Got to admit that. Drinking all the time. Got to admit that. But plenty fighting outfit. Nobody gives a damn if they get killed or not. *Compris?*"[42] With British pilots trained to intercept German robot bombers in England in 1944, Hemingway celebrated a response both new and old. The Tempest interceptors were so new that nothing could be told of their performance data, but the pilots' response to their new tools of war was in an old pattern: "You love a lot of things if you live around them, but there isn't any woman and there isn't any horse, nor any before nor any after, that is as lovely as a great airplane. . . . A man has only one virginity to lose in fighters, and if it is a lovely plane he loses it to, there his heart will be forever."[43]

For his readers, though, the real Hemingway at war was not so much interpreter or even reporter of events and moods, but renderer of the sensations of war. There is little doubt that this is what John Wheeler wanted for N.A.N.A., Ralph Ingersoll for *PM*, and Joseph Knapp for *Collier's*. They wanted him to do for their journals what he had done in his fiction: make the experience so palpable that every reader could have it as his own.

His primary appeal was by visual imagery. His narration accompanying the film *The Spanish Earth* furnished verbal scenes to supplement and intensify those on the screen. In one sequence showing Republican infantry advancing over a broken field, he wrote: "The infantry in the assault [go] where cameras need much luck to go. The slow, heavy-laden undramatic movement forwards. The men in echelon in columns of six. In the ultimate loneliness of what is known as contact. Where each man knows there is only himself and five other men and before him all the great unknown."[44] At Coruna Heights, outside Madrid,

42. "How We Came to Paris," *Collier's*, CXIV (October 7, 1944), 65-67.
43. "London Fights the Robots," *Collier's*, CXIV (August 14, 1944), 17.
44. *The Spanish Earth*, p. 51.

he took the reader into the field, flopped belly down in "the grey, olive-studded broken hills" to watch infantry advancing and see "tanks as they moved like ships up the steep hills and deployed into action."[45] Climbing a height in company of a Republican officer, and implicitly the reader, Hemingway viewed the area after the battle. Fascist soldiers were building machine-gun nests on a tableland across the valley. Below was the road that government forces had wanted to push forward on after routing the Italians, but which was so destroyed that tanks could not advance on it, and now government forces were content to build up strong positions overlooking the valley.[46]

At Brihuega he found intensity in the visible evidence of past violence:

There is nothing so terribly sinister as the track of a tank in action. The track of a tropical hurricane leaves a capricious swathe of complete destruction, but the two parallel grooves the tank leaves in red mud lead to planned death worse than any hurricane leaves. The scrub oak woods north-west of Palace Ibarra, close-angling the Brihuega-Utande road, are still full of Italian dead which burial squads have not yet reached. The tank tracks lead to where they died, not as cowards, but defending skillfully constructed machine gun and automatic rifle positions where the tanks found them and where they still lie. The untilled field and oak forest are rocky and the Italians were forced to build up rocky parapets rather than dig soil where a spade would not cut and the horrible effect of shells from the guns of sixty tanks which fought with infantry in the Brihuega battle, bursting in and against these rock piles makes nightmare corpses.[47]

During the Normandy landings he again used comparisons, this time historical and legendary, to intensify visual imagery. Troops in the landing craft watched the battleship "Texas" move closer to fire its fourteen-inch guns point blank at shore installations. "Under the steel helmets they looked like pikemen of the Middle Ages to whose aid in battle had suddenly come some strange and unbelievable monster."[48]

Another kind of visual image of war appeared in vignettes reminiscent of those from *In Our Time*. They occurred like

45. *Fact*, 10-11.
46. *Fact*, 13.
47. *Fact*, 12.
48. "Voyage to Victory," *Collier's*, CXIV (July 22, 1944), 12.

suspended moments in the flow of refugee columns, the noise and movement of battle. Near Gandesa, for example, Hemingway found a madonna-in-flight glimpse of war: "On a mule piled high with bedding rode a woman holding a still freshly red-faced baby that would not have been two days old. The mother's head swung steadily up and down with the motion of the beast she rode and the baby's new jet black hair was drifted grey with dust. A man led the mule forward, looking back over his shoulder and then looking forward at the road."[49] A vignette during the final assault on Teruel added auricular appeal to visual imagery: "We saw the armoured cars go with the troops to attack a fortified farmhouse a hundred yards from us, the cars lying alongside the house and whang, whang, whanging into the windows while the infantry ducked into it with hand grenades."[50]

The sound as well as the sight of exploding bombs was part of Hemingway's impression of the Spanish war. It was part of that new experience the world had to learn about. With Joris Ivens and John Ferno he was helping film the assault on Coruna Heights in April, 1937, when he learned about the new bombing. Trying to convey the experience to a public not yet at war, he wrote: "We were stopped within 300 yards of the front line in some thick woods, but as we were in a hollow of these woods we could not see anything of the general fighting except the sudden appearance of Government bombing planes which came over and dropped their clutches of eggs, boom, boom, boom, boom, then boom, boom, boom, boom just beyond us. The rapidity and irregularity of suddenly falling bombs was [*sic*] completely unlike artillery fire, and black clouds of smoke from the bombs shot up over the trees which were newly dressed in early spring green."[51] Describing the sounds of artillery shells passing over or hitting close by became another of Hemingway's specialties. Whether it was a crash in the street outside his Madrid hotel, "the metal ziffing and the dirt clods lobbing over" him on the battle front, or hearing "the fragments sing around you on the rocky, dusty hillside, your mouth . . . full of dust," Hemingway was careful to make it a very real sensation of war. Other observations included the pragmatic notes that "the close ones

49. *Fact*, 53.
50. *Fact*, 48.
51. *Fact*, 14-15.

have a zipping whisper and the really close ones crack," and the sound of one's own battery firing overhead was a "crack and the chu-chu-chu-ing air-parting rustle" or a "noise like tearing silk." While it was not a new sound in war, the sound of shells was one that riflemen remembered most.

But an even more terrible sound, especially in Madrid under siege, was the silence after the patter of debris had ended. Hemingway found a way to convey that silence through sentences that stopped talking while the meaning went on. Showing bread lines in *The Spanish Earth*, he commented: "You stand in line all day to buy food for supper. Sometimes the foods run out before you reach the door. Sometimes a shell falls near the line and at home they wait and wait and nobody brings back anything for supper." Or showing a body sprawled on the pavement, he said: "This is a man who has nothing to do with war. A bookkeeper on his way to his office at 8 o'clock in the morning. So now they take the bookkeeper away, but not to his office or to his home." Another scene of boys in the streets of Madrid ended thus: "Boys look for bits of shell fragments as they once gathered hailstones. So the next shell finds them. The German artillery has increased its allowance per battery today."[52]

Tactile, gustatory, and olfactory images of war occurred randomly. The note at the end of *The Spanish Earth* was an example. After seeing the film, he wrote that many of the most memorable sensations could not be conveyed on film: "The first thing you remember is how cold it was; how early you got up in the morning; how you were always so tired you could go to sleep at any time . . . and how we were always hungry. It was also very muddy . . . nothing of that shows on the screen except the cold when you can see the men's breath in the air in the picture." To stave off hunger, he and the camera crew carried raw onions to munch on during the day and washed them down with whiskey from a silver flask.[53] A special account of tactile adventure occurred when the Lincoln-Washington Battalion was overrun at Gandesa and during the ensuing night survivors filtered back through Fascist lines to escape down the Ebro River. One volunteer, reported Hemingway, stepped on a sleeping German's hand

52. *The Spanish Earth*, pp. 41, 46.
53. *Ibid.*, pp. 55-56.

in the dark and stumbled across an open field while being sniped at by shouting Germans.[54]

Perhaps some of Hemingway's most vivid impressions of war were descriptions of battles in progress when seen from a particular vantage point. At the final assault on Teruel he told how he and other correspondents on the assault line were pinned down by machine gun fire while government artillery fired at the fortress of Mansueto, standing like a battleship prow over the sloping valley. They could hear the government shells coming over with a "noise like tearing silk" and see "the sudden spouting black geysers of high explosive shells pounding at the earth-scarred fortifications of Mansueto." Then the infantry assault began. "On our left an attack was starting. The men bent double, their bayonets fixed, were advancing in the awkward first gallop that steadies into the heavy climb of an uphill assault. Two of them were hit and left the line. One had the surprised look of a man first wounded who does not realize the thing can do this damage and not hurt. The other knew he had it bad." As the rebel trench mortars went to work on the attack wave, shell bursts spouted among the infantry and "one man ran out of the seeming center of the smoke in a half circle, first naturally, wildly back, then checked and went forward to catch up with the line. Another lay where the smoke was settling." He then watched the rebel front line withdraw while their machine guns raked the assault line. When the defenders had been driven back to the fortress wall, Republican children's brigades planted charges under the east wall, and following the giant detonation, the assault wave, with Hemingway, Herbert Matthews of the *New York Times*, and Sefton Delmer of the *London Daily Express* in their midst but sticking close to Republican officers to ensure recognition as correspondents, poured into the smoking town.[55]

At Amposta on the Ebro delta, after the Fascist breakthrough at Gandesa had driven back government lines, Hemingway witnessed that fluid time on a newly forming battle front when men are more interested in getting into position than in fighting. Republican infantry were digging foxholes behind a railroad track on the river bank and thrusting their rifles over the track toward the Rebels across the river. Rebel guns were firing at

54. *Fact*, 55.
55. *Fact*, 47-50.

random while their observation posts were getting located. Hemingway watched straggling Republican soldiers slip across the river near an old white house on the bank and for the moment they were not fired on by Fascist machine guns. Hemingway could walk across the area immune from bombing or strafing by overhead German planes because he was not yet part of a target assigned them. Finally contact between the armies was established, almost as a relief, and when men slipping across the river were fired on by Italian machine guns, he knew the dress rehearsal was over, the battle on, and it was time to stop walking about the area. His last sight of the area was that of the infantry at the river bank, now with bayonets on their rifles as they faced the Fascists across the Ebro.[56]

His account of the opening of the battle for the Siegfried Line was particularly effective in conveying the feel of coming battle, of changing gears emotionally for a time of fatal testing:

Then, suddenly the rat race [across Northern France] was over and we were on a high hill, out of the forest, and all the rolling hills and forests that you saw ahead of you were Germany. There was a heavy, familiar roar from the creek valley below as the bridge was blown, and beyond the black cloud of smoke and debris that rose, you saw two enemy half-tracks tearing up the white road that led into the German hills.

Our artillery was blasting yellow-white clouds of smoke and dust ahead of them. You watched one half-track slither sideways across the road. The other stopped in the turn of the road after trying twice to move like a wounded animal. Another shell pounded up a fountain of dust and smoke along side the crippled half-track and when the smoke cleared, you could see the bodies on the road. That was the end of the rat race, and we came down a trail in the woods and into the ford over the river and across the slab-stoned river bed and up the far bank into Germany.

We passed the unmanned old-fashioned pill boxes that many unfortunate people were to think constituted the Siegfried Line, and got up into good high ground that night. The next day we were past the second line of concrete fortified points that guarded road junctions and approaches to the main Westwall, and that same night we were up on the highest of the high ground before the Westwall ready to assault in the morning.[57]

56. *Fact,* 65-67.
57. "War in the Siegfried Line," 18.

Behind all the sensations of war, though, were the potential sensations of one's own death, and secondarily, one's response to the death of those in his vicinity. Hemingway's rendering of this response occurred most often in his Spanish war writing. By World War II he wrote with more concern about adapting one's thinking and emotions and learning to win. But the Spanish conflict was his most emotional war. What he felt then, he told. In Madrid, as the shells landed without apparent pattern or target, people learned, he said, a fatalism before the explosion and a relief afterwards; and people stepped out of doorways into which they had dodged, looked at the dead, and walked on. "And everyone has the feeling that characterizes war. It wasn't me." After a shell hit the front of the Florida Hotel, Hemingway was able to get a "beautiful double corner room" for less than half what others were paying for smaller rooms on the lee side of the hotel; he again celebrated that absurd feeling of immunity. "It wasn't me they killed. See? No, not me. It wasn't me anymore." After seeing wounded Americans, he again sounded the refrain "And it still isn't you that gets hit but it is your countryman."[58] In his afternote to *The Spanish Earth*, written away from the falling shells, he concluded: "When you were young you gave death much importance. Now you give it none. You only hate it for the people that it takes away. . . . Death is still very badly organized in war, you think, and let it go at that."[59]

To Hemingway they were not simply soldiers' wars that he observed. They were writers' wars too. The problem was not only to experience human response to a supreme challenge but also to express it. He spelled out the problem in his essay "The Writer and War" when, in the midst of the Spanish Civil War, he acknowledged that the writer's problem is not only to find out the truth but also to tell it in such a way that it becomes part of the reader's experience. The possibility of his death would force a writer to decide whether the rewards were worth the risk. The rewards, besides financial, were a chance to keep history ungarbled. Some writers, he charged, preferred to maintain positions won by the typewriter and consolidated by the fountain pen. But there were wars enough for those who chose to find

58. *Fact*, 18-22.
59. *The Spanish Earth*, p. 60.

out the truth about them.[60] He implied in the opening pages of *Death in the Afternoon* that a writer could learn his craft in war; and when the wars were in recess, he had to go to the bull rings to find the emotional equivalent of war, to find the sequence of elementary events that both produced a sensation of basic reality and suggested the means for seeing it analytically and for rendering it.[61] But war was more complex than bullfighting. To observe violent death in war, one had to get into the ring with the antagonists, and that introduced another dimension of subjectivity. Moreover, the focal points in war were multiple. It was not a duel but a melee. When he wrote in *Green Hills of Africa* of war as the best school for writers, he recognized it not only as "one of the major subjects" but also as a great cross-section of experience and thus "one of the hardest [subjects] to write truly of."[62] In his war reporting he accepted the probability of an incomplete rendering of experience. He indicated so in his summing up of the Normandy landing: "There is much that I have not written. You could write for a week and not give everyone credit for what he did on a front of 1,135 yards. Real war is never like a paper war, nor do accounts of it read much the way it looks. But if you want to know how it was in a LCV(P) on D-Day when we took Fox Green Beach and Easy Red Beach on the sixth of June, 1944, then this is as near as I can come to it."[63]

During the Spanish war and the Second World War he recognized the further complication that a writer, like a soldier, had to accept discipline, that he could not write all he knew. To avoid helping the enemy he had to censor himself or accept external censorship. Implicitly, he acknowledged that a publishing writer gave up reportorial objectivity to be on one side or the other for the duration of the war. To know the immediate sensation of war he sometimes had to forfeit telling what he learned, and sometimes forfeit criticism. After a war all could be told, but the sensation was no longer there. And sensation, or emotion, recollected in tranquillity was likely to be another thing. He noted the treason of memory in *Death in the Afternoon*. The

60. *The Writer in a Changing World*, ed. Henry Hart (New York, 1937), pp. 69-73.
61. *Death in the Afternoon* (New York, 1932), pp. 2-3.
62. *Green Hills of Africa* (New York, 1935), pp. 70-71.
63. "Voyage to Victory," 57.

thing to do, he said, is to "write when there is something that you know; and not before; and not too damned much after."[64] He supplemented that advice in *Men at War*: "If, during a war, conditions are such that a writer cannot publish the truth because its publication would do harm to the State he should write and not publish."[65] Hemingway chose to write—and publish—the partial view in his war reports, to sacrifice completeness of vision for the immediacy and intensity of experience. He saved the fictional critiques for afterwards but recognized, and urged his readers to recognize, that his fictional voice on war was different from his public voice.

64. *Death in the Afternoon*, p. 278.
65. *Men at War*, p. xv.

V. The Feudist

IN ADDITION TO USING THE ESSAY AS A VEHICLE FOR CERTIFYING HIS own general expertise, for chronicling his travels, and for depicting himself as a writer on war, Hemingway made his nonfiction a part of the career-long feud he had with critics in general and with certain literary adversaries in particular. For him the essays were like sparring jabs made to keep the critics at their distance. He understood that his fiction would be the knockout blow. His stance was always that of the primitively strong man of simple integrity who tries to hold to plain virtue and plain language while buffeted by attackers who change their masks and identities with shifting literary fashions. And in the process, they were usually depicted as somehow less than fully virile, or less than completely feminine.

Writing in 1938 to review Hemingway's career up to that point and to recommend his work as worthy of being collected, Louis Henry Cohn explained how many of the literary ephemera resulted from Hemingway's critical battles:

His worst fault is his quick temper leading to a certain causticity in his remarks and in his written comments causing breaks with many of his early friends and most sincere admirers including a number of critics. This is naturally in line with his greatest virtue which is an unsurpassed intellectual honesty. It would have been the course of diplomacy to have ignored the animadversions of those critics who for one reason or another, oft-times personal, vented their spleen upon him and his work. But that has rarely been his mode of conduct. He has never had the slightest hesitancy about responding when he considered the criticism unfair. His responses moreover do not usually take the form of the retort courteous. And this unfortunately does not make for a genial glow in the breast of the critic assailed when he next has occasion to review a Hemingway book.[1]

Perhaps Cohn gave Hemingway credit for allowing his critics the first blow more often than the evidence admits, and certainly he was generous in attributing the recriminations solely to "intellectual honesty." While Hemingway's instincts on literature might be thought generally sound, his feuding dealt in personality and character as much as in reasonable discourse. If his critics frequently spoke out of a vast range of critical opinions—and sometimes prejudices—that they never bothered to make explicit, Hemingway characteristically retorted with a dramatized caricature that also failed to reduce the quarrels to really arguable issues. In short, in spite of the poses, there were low blows on both sides.

Early and late, Hemingway took the stance as defender of the integrity of literature against dilution of the art by the popular media. In "Condensing the Classics" in the *Toronto Star Weekly* in August of 1921, he began early to satirize the tendency of journalists and book condensers to oversimplify. In an amateurish and heavy-handed vein, he suggested that, endowed by Andrew Carnegie, condensers could reduce great novels and poems to a headline and lead-paragraph version of the old thing for the edification of tired businessmen. For example, Don Quixote could become "CRAZED KNIGHT IN WEIRD TILT":

Madrid, Spain (By Classics News Service) (Special)—War hysteria is blamed for the queer actions of "Don" Quixote, a local knight who was arrested early yesterday morning when engaged in the act of

1. "Collecting Hemingway," *Avocations*, II (January 1938), 349.

"tilting" with a windmill. Quixote could give no explanation of his actions.

Other easy ones would be from Blake ("Big Cat in Flames"), Coleridge ("Albatross Slayer Flays Prohibition—Not a Drop to Drink"), *Pagliacci* ("Riot in Sicily, 2 Dead, 12 Wounded"), and *Othello* ("Slays His White Bride—Society Girl, Wed to African War-Hero, Found Strangled in Bed").[2]

Again in the satirical vein, Hemingway sent the poem "Valentine" and a covering letter to the faltering *Little Review* in 1929, this time mocking the capitulation of the big-money magazines in New York and Boston to him after years of refusing his work. The poem was an obscene "valentine" for critics—"Mr. Lee Wilson Dodd and any of his friends who want it"—waiting to pounce on a slipping author. In the covering letter he noted that "there is a great demand for my work by the *Atlantic Monthly* and kindred periodicals and wd. not like to disappoint these editors when I have a piece so emminently [*sic*] saleable."[3]

Another dilution of literary value in Hemingway's eyes was the literary anecdote, which he practiced satirically and commented on frequently. Back in Toronto in late 1923 after his first period as a foreign correspondent and intimate of Paris artists, Hemingway reported on the W. B. Yeats visit to Toronto to lecture and capitalize on the prestige of a recent Nobel Prize. He depicted Yeats staying up late to recite literary anecdotes and to chant Erse sagas and his own poems while his host sat hollow-eyed from sleepiness. The article turned the feeling against Yeats and his anecdotes by showing how he departed in confusion the next day, leaving pajamas and toilet articles to be forwarded to him in New York. To his host he was not nightingale but night-hawk or nightmare.[4] This same distaste appears in *Green Hills of Africa*, where the Austrian Kandisky wants to hear Hemingway talk about the brilliant people of Paris and Berlin. But Hemingway spares him the disillusionment of knowing the truth behind gossip. Later in the book Hemingway and Phillips, the white hunter, ridicule each other for talking literary gossip.[5] "We're going to chuck all this . . . and both be writers," Phillips

2. *TSW*, August 20, 1921, p. 22.
3. *Little Review*, XII (May 1929), 41.
4. "W. B. Yeats a Night Hawk; Kept Toronto Host Up," *TSW*, December 22, 1923, p. 35.
5. *Green Hills of Africa* (New York, 1935), pp. 195-98.

tells Mrs. Hemingway after listening to some of Hemingway's stories about James Joyce. "Give us another anecdote. . . . By God, I tell you the literary life's the thing. . . . You can't beat it."[6] And in his *Esquire* article "Notes on Life and Letters," Hemingway called literary anecdoting a vice, but vice or not, he thought he would tell one of those "devastating anecdotes" on Alexander Woollcott.[7]

African accounts seemed to be a favorite place for Hemingway to voice his feeling on literary pretensions. As late as 1954 he recorded in the *Look* article "The Christmas Gift" his scorn of the vulgarization of African books by movies and popular magazines. Flying north from Costermansville in the Belgian Congo, Hemingway, with his wife and his pilot Roy Marsh, saw the Ruwenzori Range "known through my reading of *Life*, and through hearsay about the all-girl safari, as 'The Mountains of the Moon.' . . . I believe this original title came from the late Sir Rider Haggard."[8]

But Hemingway had bigger and frequently more specific targets. In the midst of Dadaists, Marxists, Freudians, followers of T. S. Eliot, admirers of Michael Arlen, and disciples of Faulkner or Saroyan, Hemingway presented himself as the steadfast point in a shifting world of literary fashions. The implication for him was always that the fluctuating fashions were somehow evasions of artistic integrity, violations of the fundamental obligation of the writer to face his material without synthetic bolsters, failures of the artist finally—to use one of Hemingway's favorite phrases— "to bite on the nail."

In *the transatlantic review* article "And to the United States," Hemingway not only mocked critics as "the eunuchs of literature" but also called spades on literary fashion-makers: Dada, he said, was dead, though Tristan Tzara would not admit it. In the next issue of the *review* he had more to say on Dadaists as poseurs. In the headnote to Ring Lardner's play *I Gaspiri*, Hemingway said that Dadaists, whether French (Cocteau), American (Seldes), or Rumanian (Tzara), all pretended to know languages they had not really mastered. Thus, if Cocteau could pretend to translate *Romeo and Juliet* without really knowing English, he should try his Dadaist hand at *I Gaspiri*. "Our only regret is that Mr. Tzara

6. *Ibid.*, pp. 196-97.
7. *Esquire*, III (January 1935), 21.
8. *Look*, XVIII (April 20, 1954), 31.

will be unable to read it. But there may, ultimately, be a translation. By that time though, Mr. Tzara will probably be too
busy on a translation of Marlowe or some other Elizabethan for
next year's Cigale to bother."[9]

As an advocate of the plain style, Hemingway also came into
conflict with the new admirers of the obviously erudite style of
T. S. Eliot. This conflict in allegiances was evident in his championing Joseph Conrad in a tribute on the occasion of the novelist's death. His best appreciation of Conrad was, he thought, to
show how much better a model was the novelist's work than that
of the poet Eliot. Hemingway's comparison, now famous, also
touched satirically, if lightly, on the poet's use of fertility myths
and rebirth themes: "It is agreed by most of the people I know
that Conrad is a bad writer, just as it is agreed that T. S. Eliot
is a good writer. If I knew that by grinding Mr. Eliot into a fine
dry powder and sprinkling that powder over Mr. Conrad's grave
Mr. Conrad would shortly appear, looking very annoyed at the
forced return and commence writing, I would leave for London
early tomorrow morning with a sausage grinder."[10] But that
Hemingway's literary judgment was based on personal loyalty as
much as on consistent principle could be seen in his championing
Ezra Pound over Eliot. In his appreciative essay "Homage to
Ezra" for *This Quarter*, Hemingway suggested that the intricate
Eliotic style might be a cover-up for having little to say. Pound,
he asserted, was a major poet while Eliot, like Marianne Moore
and Wallace Stevens, was a minor one. Minor poets, he explained, do not fail because they do not attempt the major thing.
"They have nothing of major importance to say. They do a
minor thing with perfection and the perfection is admirable."[11]
Perhaps more than coincidentally, Faulkner made this same
charge against Hemingway some twenty-five years later.[12]

Hemingway was even more concerned with fashions in novels,
and his concern over rivals frequently provoked his sharpest judgments. In *A Moveable Feast* he recorded an earlier response to
Michael Arlen's work—a response which in the long perspective
of Hemingway's career seems to be a tacit admission and explicit

9. *the transatlantic review*, I (May-June 1924), 355-57; II (August 1924), 103.
10. "Conrad, Optimist and Moralist," *transatlantic review*, II (October 1924), 341-42.
11. *This Quarter*, I (May 1925), 222-23.
12. Harvey Breit, *The Writer Observed* (New York, 1961), p. 184.

denial of Arlen's impact on him. He told of riding from Lyons to Paris with Scott Fitzgerald and listening to Fitzgerald's admiration for the brilliant people and brilliant style of Michael Arlen. Arlen was the man to learn from, Fitzgerald said. But though Hemingway's first major novel had the same sort of beautiful but damned heroine as Arlen's *The Green Hat* and Hemingway's dialogue and Arlen's were both praised as brilliant, Hemingway remembered telling Fitzgerald he could not read Arlen's books.[13] He seldom found his masters among contemporaries. When William Saroyan in his ebullient and impudent 1934 preface to *The Daring Young Man on the Flying Trapeze* claimed the ability to write like (and presumably as well as) other writers, Hemingway linked him with "another bright young Arminian [*sic*]" who was too facile to learn, "and he turned out to be Michael Arlen." Saroyan, Hemingway warned in "Notes on Life and Letters," needed to observe the world, stop writing about himself, and write for himself. "Anybody can write like somebody else. But it takes a long time to get to write like yourself and then what they pay off on is having something to say." And experience, not imitativeness, was the basis of having something to say: "You've only got one new trick and that is that you're an Arminian [*sic*]. Now you see us, the people you can write like and better than, and some of us have been shot, and some of us have been cut, and all of us have been married, and we've been around a long time and we've been a lot of places that you haven't seen, Mr. Saroyan, and that you won't ever see because the things are over and lots of places aren't there any more."[14] Saroyan's work, he thought, should be to look for the truth and idiom of his own generation.

Hemingway's awareness of William Faulkner as a literary rival and hence one worthy of attacking seems to date from the early thirties. Perhaps knowing that they shared a common starting point in the apprentice pages of the *New Orleans Double-Dealer* in 1922 emphasized Hemingway's recognition of Faulkner as rival as well as contemporary advocate of a totally different approach to writing. He told the Old Lady in *Death in the Afternoon* that there was a current appetite for sensational stories of the abnormal—"the kind of stories Mr. Faulkner writes," she

13. *A Moveable Feast* (New York, 1964), pp. 174-75.
14. *Esquire*, III (January 1935), 21, 159.

called them. But before telling her a sample story of homosexual seduction, he noted that such stories of perversion lack drama because they are predictable, though "no one can predict what will happen in the normal. . . ."[15] In the *Esquire* article "On Being Shot Again" he parodied the Faulknerian manner. When his angling for galano sharks went badly, Hemingway mocked Faulkner's polysyllabic diction and noted parenthetically he had been "reading, and admiring *Pylon.*" His bad fishing luck, he said, was embodied in "the two lengths of double line which now streamed in catfishlike uncatfishivity. . . ."[16] In "The Sights of Whitehead Street" he jabbed obliquely at Faulkner's handling of Negro characters. Apparently he had both *Light in August* and the recent Scottsboro case in mind when he wrote the article in early 1935. His house, he noted, had been listed as sight-seeing stop number 18 on the Key West tourist map; and one day when a literary tourist invaded the place to ask questions about his work, including writing about Negroes, Hemingway answered, "Well, we've tried to avoid it on acount of the instability of the Southern market. . . . You just get a character popularized and he makes some mistake and they lynch him."[17] By the time Faulkner had won the Nobel Prize for 1950 Hemingway was sensitively aware of his rival, and he kept the rest of the rivalry out of the public record. When Harvey Breit decided against asking Hemingway to write an introduction for his collection of interviews, *The Writer Observed,* Hemingway wrote him suggesting that Breit get Faulkner to do an introduction, for which Hemingway would pay $350, "while he, for no financial consideration at all, would write a rival introduction based on an interview with the Deity, which he was almost certain he could obtain, once he explained the circumstances and the high honor being afforded Him of appearing there with Dr. Faulkner."[18] Significantly, it was in an interview with Breit that Faulkner down-ranked Hemingway for being nearly perfect in small works because he never tried the more ambitious projects.

If Hemingway came out scarred from his two-decade rivalry with Faulkner, he fought a longer and perhaps more successful

15. *Death in the Afternoon* (New York, 1932), pp. 179-82.
16. *Esquire,* III (June 1935), 25.
17. *Esquire,* III (April 1935), 156.
18. Leicester Hemingway, *My Brother, Ernest Hemingway* (Cleveland, 1962), p. 277.

battle with critics. Here the point of contention for Hemingway was not so much an attempt to cut down a competitor as to provide a dissenting opinion against what were temporarily the massive leaders of critical thought. In *Green Hills of Africa* Hemingway announced himself as a man out of tune with his time when he insisted on working alone, not in a school or coterie. "Writers should work alone," he said, and see each other, if at all, after their writing is done. Attempting to draw help for their work from others made writers as cozy and ineffectual as worms in a bottle. They tried to get nourishment from others as sterile as themselves or from a sterile bottle called art, economics, or religion. The fate of a true writer, he insisted was to be lonesome.[19] He dramatized this sterility in *To Have and Have Not* two years after *Death in the Afternoon.* In the novel Richard Gordon, a novelist temporarily following the critical dicta of Marxist writers, scorns the suffering Marie Morgan as a dull lump of insensitivity and chooses instead to invent a firm-breasted, full-lipped Jewess agitator as heroine of his strike novel. That he is thinking in clichés is certified scenes later when Herbert Spellman, another follower of literary fashions, hearing that Gordon is writing a strike novel, asks if it has a "beautiful Jewish agitator."[20]

To Hemingway it was not Marxist criticism per se that was objectionable. It was letting something as extraneous as political or economic doctrine dictate what should happen in a story. He insisted many times that only the writer's sense of the validity of events and emotions could dictate that action. In "Old Newsman Writes" he spelled out how distinct political writing is from writing for oneself: "Now a writer can make himself a nice career while he is alive by espousing a political cause, working for it, making a profession of believing in it, and if it wins he will be very well placed. All politics is a matter of working hard without reward, or with a living wage for a time, in the hope of booty later. A man can be a Fascist or a Communist and if his outfit gets in he can get to be an ambassador or have a million copies of his books printed by the Government or any of the other rewards the boys dream about. Because the literary revolution boys are all ambitious."[21] He seized the occasion again in

19. *Green Hills of Africa*, pp. 21-22.
20. *To Have and Have Not* (New York, 1937), p. 197.
21. *Esquire*, II (December 1934), 26.

his preface to *The Fifth Column* to note that Marxist critics tend to be more interested in ideologically sound plots and themes than in stories shaped by a writer's individual sense of reality. Fanatical defenders of the Spanish Republic, he anticipated, would be offended because he showed fifth columnists being shot by Marxists. But the nobility and dignity of the Spanish people's cause would be served best by his telling as much truth about the struggle as perspective allowed and by showing human motives and conduct, not ideological allegories.[22]

Another variation on his wars with politically minded critics was his ridicule of politically extreme points of view in "United We Fall." Mockingly placing himself among the "real fighters" of the times, he led the attack on *Ken* magazine for its criticisms of Marxist foibles as well as of Fascist intrigues. Urged by numerous letter writers to denounce *Ken* as he returned from Spain, Hemingway reported himself always glad to denounce but wanted someone to make plain what he was supposed to denounce. It was like that old war dream of being pushed out of the trucks and told to attack, but he always woke up shouting, "We will attack all right. But will you please explain the positions." Given the chance, he said, he "could lead an assault against *Ken* which would be so daring that even those veteran campaigners of the *Nation* and the *Times* literary supplement would have to turn their heads away in horror as it swept by." And he would do this for his critic friends even though the casualties were "very restrained; very, very restrained."[23]

The Freudian critics apparently did not stir Hemingway until fairly late—if his essays are accurate indication. But by the time of his two plane crashes in Africa in late 1953 and the resulting premature obituaries depicting his career as the expression of one long death-wish, Hemingway was ready to answer them both directly and satirically. He admitted his pleasure in reading his death accounts in the world press; but the real pleasure was in having outflanked his Freudian interpreters, not, he said, in flirting with a harlot named Death: "It was at this point that I commenced that strange vice which I believe could become extremely destructive to one's general equilibrium and cause one, perhaps, to lose one's status as a completely well-adjusted person

22. *The Fifth Column and the First Forty-Nine Stories* (New York, 1938), p. vi.
23. *Ken*, I (June 2, 1938), 38.

though various tin horn biographers had attempted to prove otherwise."[24] Apparently Philip Young's 1952 study of the traumatic bases of Hemingway's art had had is effect on both the writer and his critics.[25] So snared was Hemingway by the Freudian analyses that he offered later in the same article a dream for the Freudians to interpret. He depicted himself in the dream as a barefoot aborigine spear-hunting for wild dogs and meeting Senator McCarthy in the moonlight while the Senator hunted for subversives and talked about losing Schine or Cohn—the talk was confused—and McCarthy complained of losing Schine to the army. "What a fate for a professional loyal American!" Hemingway remarked.[26] The Freudian critics, he implied, attempted to exercise the same immunity that the Senator did as they hunted and sighed as plaintively as the Senator when caught in their own contradictions.

It was not just the schools of creative writing but also those of critical persuasion that Hemingway decried. He doubted, in fact, the general function of critics. This attitude was particularly clear in his late writing. Where before he had been concerned with spurious directions taken by artists, whether Dadaists or Marxists, he now put the burden of guilt on critics for misleading the writers. In his introducion to Elio Vittorini's novel *In Sicily* in 1949, Hemingway contrasted professional creative writing and professional criticism to make the point:

Rain to an academician is probably, after the first fall has cleared the air, H_2O with, of course, traces of other things. To a good writer needing something to bring the dry country alive so that it will not be a desert where only such cactus as New York literary reviews grow dry and sad, inexistent without the watering of their benefactors, feeding on the dried manure of schism and the dusty taste of disputed dialectics, their only flowering a dessicated criticism as alive as stuffed birds, and their steady mulch the dehydrated cuds of fellow critics; such a writer finds rain to be made of knowledge, experience, wine, bread, oil, salt, vinegar, bed, early mornings, nights, days, the sea, men, women, dogs, beloved motor cars, bicycles, hills and valleys, the appearance and disappearance of trains on straight and curved tracks, love, honor and disobey, music, chamber music and chamber

24. "The Christmas Gift," *Look*, XVIII (May 4, 1954), 83.
25. See Philip Young, *Ernest Hemingway: A Reconsideration* (University Park, Pa., 1966), pp. 1-22.
26. "The Christmas Gift," 86.

pots, negative and positive Wassermans, the arrival and non-arrival of expected munitions and/or reinforcements, replacements or your brother.

His reference to "New York literary reviews" was in fact more pointed when he first wrote the preface. He originally directed his attack on the *Partisan Review*, but because the editors of the magazine were personal friends of James Laughlin, publisher of New Directions books and of the Vittorini novel, Hemingway consented to Laughlin's suggestion to make the target less particular. He saw, as Laughlin explained, that it would antagonize Vittorini's potential critics and jeopardize reception of the book in this country. So at the expense of his own critical antagonisms, he toned down the reference.[27] But he restated the view in his conversation with Harvey Breit in 1950. In light of critical disapproval of *Across the River and into the Trees* he asserted that critics were so far behind novelists that they did not understand what writers were doing. He welcomed the dull thud of critics falling from limbs they had gotten themselves out on and looked forward to the time when critics learned to read books rather than attack personalities.[28] In his remarks to Robert Manning in 1954, Hemingway thought critics should point modern writers to great ones now dead and indicate what could be learned from them rather than address themselves to living writers.[29] And in *A Moveable Feast*, in comments that reflected early feeling modified by later perspective, he remembered thinking how he had written stories so completely implicit that editors and critics could not understand them. "But they will understand the same way that they always do in painting. It only takes time and it only needs confidence." If Hemingway could remember having finally succeeded, he also remembered his acquaintance Hal, whom he advised to go into criticism when he could not create. Then Hal, he said, could always be read and respected by his fellow critics. He had to be careful, though, not to set for himself standards too high for even a critic to reach.[30]

Besides expressing general dissent from creative and critical fashions, Hemingway fought several bitterly personal feuds. In

27. James Laughlin to ROS, February 8, 1966.
28. "Success, It's Wonderful," *New York Times Book Review*, December 3, 1950, p. 58.
29. "Hemingway in Cuba," *Atlantic Monthly*, CCXVI (August 1965), 104.
30. *A Moveable Feast*, pp. 75, 95.

most cases Hemingway's part of the recriminations was made public in his essays. In a few instances, he preferred keeping his retort private, though he had been attacked in public. Such was the case with Max Eastman's attack on his artistic integrity, "Bull in the Afternoon," first printed in *New Republic* for June 7, 1933, and reprinted in *Art and the Life of Action* for 1934. Reacting to Hemingway's mystique of courage and cojones in *Death in the Afternoon*, Eastman charged that Hemingway protested too much his masculinity and thus begot "a literary style, you might say, of wearing false hair on the chest."[31] Hemingway's answer was the much-disputed scuffle in Maxwell Perkins' office at Scribner's on August 11, 1937, and a Hemingway inscription on a copy of Eastman's book, presented to Arnold Gingrich, which pointed to a smudge on the book as the place which struck Eastman's nose during the melee.[32]

But several clashes were conducted more publicly. One early example was his half-serious tilt with Louis Bromfield in the pages of *The Boulevardier*. For the September, 1927, issue of the magazine Bromfield chronicled in his essay "The Real French" his disgust with American Francophobes and Francophiles, both of whom he charged with substituting prejudice for observation. The first group he dismissed as bores. The second group he sought to correct because they missed the attributes of actually existent Frenchmen in their search for the "real French"—some mysterious archetype never found in actual French persons. Hemingway's article on "The Real Spaniard" in the same magazine the following month parodied Bromfield's essay, not because it attacked stereotyped thinking but because it was done sentimentally. It had, in fact, much of the ingenuous naïveté of Sherwood Anderson, whose attitude and method he had satirized the year before in *The Torrents of Spring*. Bromfield wrote of having spent the war years as an attaché in the French army and having lived in dunghills, dugouts, and châteaux, while Hemingway wrote that he had spent the war as an attaché in the Spanish army and had slept in "dunghills and châteaux and the like, but to me the Spanish never seemed real. Somehow they didn't. They seemed like cathedrals." And after Bromfield finally saw a sterile, crotchety, opinionated couple of old Bourbonists who he realized

31. In John K. M. McCaffery (ed.), *Ernest Hemingway: The Man and His Work* (New York, 1950), p. 59.
32. Carlos Baker, *Hemingway: The Writer as Artist* (Princeton, 1963), p. 233n.

were the "real French" spoken of by the Francophiles, he rejected the identification in favor of his own cook from Normandy, his chambermaid from the Nièvre, and his chauffeur from La Villette. They were, he declared, "the realest of the *real* French." Hemingway accordingly conducted his search for the real Spaniard and, carrying the joke one step further, discovered that he himself was the real Spaniard. ". . . I knew that my search too, like that of good old Brommy for the real French, had ended in the home."[33] If Hemingway laughed at Bromfield, however, it is not clear how much of the parody can be attributed solely to him. He told Louis Henry Cohn, supposedly in a serious vein, that the article was partly written by *Boulevardier* editor Arthur Moss, who thought he improved work sent to the magazine by inserting funny lines of his own.[34]

Hemingway's feud with the Boston censors, both constabulary and literary, was of longer duration. It was more than two years before he answered them, but the answer was fierce at last. When *Scribner's Magazine* began serialization of *A Farewell to Arms* in May, 1929, Boston police chief Crowley had the issue suppressed in June and July. Public comment, however, overwhelmed Crowley so that he did nothing to suppress the sale of the book in Boston in September. But in an article-review entitled "What Is Dirt?" in the November issue of the *Bookman*, novelist Robert Herrick compared *A Farewell to Arms* unfavorably with Remarque's *All Quiet on the Western Front* and said that, while latrine scenes and attempts to give privacy to a briefly united married couple in the German novel were significant literary materials, scenes showing Frederic Henry's vomiting from drunkenness and others chronicling his "irresponsible" affair with "the Scotch nurse" were gratuitous sensation and "garbage" in the Hemingway novel.[35] Herrick's attack was answered and modified by *Bookman* editor Seward Collins in the February, 1930, issue of the magazine[36] and partially refuted in a two-page argument "Is It Dirt or Is It Art?" by M. K. Hare in pages purchased in the *Bookman* by Scribner's.[37] Not only did the *Bookman* publish Herrick's attack, it also became a voice for the New Humanists,

33. *The Boulevardier* (Paris), I (September 1927), 6, 50, 52; (October 1927), 6.
34. *A Bibliography of the Works of Ernest Hemingway* (New York, 1931), p. 83.
35. *Bookman*, LXX (November 1929), 258-62.
36. "Chronicle and Comment," *Bookman*, LXXI (February 1930), 641-47.
37. *Bookman*, LXXI (March 1930), xiv-xv.

as Norman Foerster points out in *Humanism in America,* and
their cry was against current naturalism and its picture of man
as animal. By the time Hemingway published *Death in the Afternoon* in 1932, he had an answer in "A Natural History of the
Dead." Mockingly using the mask of a pedantic essayist, he reduced to possible absurdity the New Humanists' picture of an
absolute moral universe. And in that context of exploded values
he answered Herrick's claim that the love-sex scenes were irrelevant. Death and sex are both indecorous acts of people, he admitted, but neither can be censored away:

So now I want to see the death of any self-called Humanist because
a persevering traveller like Mungo Park or me lives on and maybe
yet will live to see the actual death of members of this literary sect
and watch the noble exits that they make. In my musings as a
naturalist it has occurred to me that while decorum is an excellent
thing some must be indecorous if the race is to be carried on since
the position prescribed for procreation is indecorous, highly indecorous, and it occurred to me that perhaps that is what these people
are, or were; the children of decorous cohabition. But regardless of
how they started I hope to see the finish of a few, and speculate how
worms will try that long preserved sterility; with their quaint pam-
phlets gone to bust and into foot-notes all their lust.[38]

He noted to his Old Lady listener at this point that he had
learned to use the Marvell allusion by reading T. S. Eliot. In
effect, he turned the technique of one of the school against itself in his answer.

His other answer came two years later in the *Esquire* article
"Defense of Dirty Words," this time in rejoinder to Westbrook
Pegler. "Dirty Trend after War Not Essential to Success, and
Foolish to Try Justification" said Pegler's headline. In contrast,
Ring Lardner was a great writer without messing himself with
dirty words, the columnist argued. But Hemingway pointed out
that Lardner felt superior to the sports world he knew best, and
his failure to use the real language of that world was his weakness, not his claim to greatness. Both Lardner and Pegler wrote
to gain intellectual status and consequently felt contempt for
those who got their hands dirty. A writer on war or sports, Hemingway insisted, had to achieve complete integration of dirty subject and dirty language: "No true idea of war can be conveyed

38. *Death in the Afternoon,* p. 139.

without the true words, nor can any true pictures of professional sport be given without using the words."[39]

The feud with Sinclair Lewis was, for Hemingway, a bomb with a long fuse. While Lewis's part in the dispute was a mixture of praise and blame, Hemingway's was unhappily all caustic and probably among the least fairly conducted of all his feuds. He began the conflict early with a snide article in the *Toronto Star Weekly* for August 5, 1922. "Expecting Too Much in Old London Town" was the headline, and the text was an anecdote circulated in Paris and accepted as true to character if not comfirmable as fact. While in London working on a novel, Lewis, catering to his taste for the lurid, went to see Rotten Row but was disappointed with its smallness, and so informed his driver. To which the disgusted groom replied, "Well sir. . . . You cawn't expect the bloomin' prairies 'ere sir."[40] All the laugh was at Sinclair Lewis' expense, as Hemingway saw it, and he obviously catered to his Canadian readers' anti-Yankee sentiment in giving one of the king's own the last word. Lewis, though, named Hemingway as one of the deserving young American novelists in his 1930 Nobel Prize speech and wrote an appreciative preface to the 1942 Limited Editions Club version of *For Whom the Bell Tolls*.

His attacks on Hemingway's legend, however, had the cutting edge that Lewis had made well-feared in his novels. In his essay "Rambling Thoughts on Literature as a Business" published in the 1936 centennial number of the *Yale Literary Magazine*, he ridiculed Hemingway's *Green Hills of Africa* for its literary evaluations and its enthusiasm for shooting game animals. Lewis also drew on Hemingway's reputation for using raw language and rawer situations in his novels when he presented his "Lines to a College Professor":

> Mister Hemingway
> Halts his slaughter of the kudu
> To remind you that you may
> Risk his sacerdotal hoodoo
> If you go on, day by day,
> Talking priggishly as you do.
> Speak up, man. Be bravely heard
> Bawling the four-letter word!

39. *Esquire*, II (September 1934), 19.
40. *TSW*, August 5, 1922, p. 17.

And wear your mind decolleté
Like Mister Ernest Hemingway.[41]

And in his 1948 sketch "Mr. Eglantine," written for a Bell Syndicate series on Italy, Lewis satirized expatriate artists in Europe as a type and noted their debt to Hemingway. His grubby protagonist Vernon Eglantine and his wife Mitzi finally find a victim to buy them drinks and make small loans. After the first Strega "Verny and Mitzi sighed and smiled and felt good—like a Hemingway hero after the seventh beer—and they knew that in Europe there would never be a time when Americans too sensitive to cope with high schools and tarpon fishing and gum and air-conditioning will not be able to find somewhere an asylum where the less-hairy Whitmans will sit together from 22:30 to 2 and tell one another how superior they are to all the Babbitts in Iowa and Ireland and Oslo and South Uruguay."[42] While Hemingway had made this same point in "American Bohemians in Paris a Weird Lot"[43] and *The Sun Also Rises* as well as in several short stories, he could not accept its being made in a style to parody his code and manner. Besides, in 1948 and 1949 he was apparently in some doubt about his ability to write again and had begun his return to former haunts to write *Across the River and into the Trees*. One of those places was the Italy of Mr. Eglantine. His reply to Lewis' portrait of Mr. Eglantine occurred not in an essay but in his description of the pock-marked, Baedeker-toting tourist of the Venetian novel, which was recognizably and unflatteringly that of Sinclair Lewis. If he ducked behind his fictional mask to complete what he had begun in his essays, the move only showed again the connection between the stories and essays. They were alternate weapons in the war of literary one-upmanship.

The feud with Gertrude Stein was perhaps the most personally vicious of all, and probably the viciousness was partly reaction against early mutual fascination by both writers. What originally began the antagonism is perhaps a matter for biographical study rather than analysis of public essays to discern. Both wrote memoirs, however, as matters of public record, and

41. Reprinted in *The Man from Main Street*, ed. by Harry E. Maule and Melville H. Cane (New York, 1953), pp. 193-97.
42. *Ibid.*, pp. 289-92.
43. *TSW*, March 25, 1922, p. 15.

their claims can be examined. *The Autobiography of Alice B. Toklas* reported that Hemingway guiltily reappeared after an absence of months with the announcement that he could not review *The Making of Americans* even though he had read proof for *the transatlantic review* portion of the book and had tried to find a publisher for the entire manuscript.[44] In *A Moveable Feast* Hemingway reported that as a still illusioned young man, he was initially shocked by Stein's remarks on homosexuality and later was overwhelmed by accidentally overheard importunities.[45] But his satirical use of Stein's manner in *The Torrents of Spring* in 1926 certified and perpetuated a break that had already happened. The first epigraph to *The Sun Also Rises* was apparently too subtly ironic to be understood at first, and many readers failed to pierce the fictional mask to see that the "lost generation" statement by Gertrude Stein was to be taken as a piece of "splendid bombast." But by the time of his 1927 article, "My Own Life," in the *New Yorker*, Hemingway told for literary insiders an archly humble version of "The True Story of My Break with Gertrude Stein." Gertrude's maid had met him at the door, struck him with a bicycle pump, and sent him on his way, he said, and that was how he knew he and Gertrude were no longer friends.[46]

After the publication of *The Autobiography of Alice B. Toklas* in 1933, however, all the humor was gone for Hemingway. After Gertrude Stein charged him with Rotarianism and said he learned from her and Sherwood Anderson to write, without understanding what he was doing, Hemingway took every opportunity available to deny her honesty, competence, and womanliness. After that she was not an alienated friend but a capricious and possessive parasite laboring under delusions of her own genius. When he wrote an appreciative note about Joan Miro's painting "The Farm" for a special Miro number of *Cahiers d'Art* in 1934, he used the occasion not only to talk about how he and Evan Shipman had been able to save the painting from a greedy dealer but also how the painting was a true, seminal, and un-Stein-like work. Noting that it had taken Miro nine months to paint "The Farm," Hemingway wrote: "No one could look

44. *The Autobiography of Alice B. Toklas* (New York, 1933, 1960), p. 220.
45. *A Moveable Feast*, p. 118.
46. *The New Yorker*, II (February 12, 1927), 23.

at it and not know it had been painted by a great painter and when you are painting things that people must take on trust it is good to have something around that has taken as long to make as it takes a woman to make a child (a woman who isn't a woman can usually write her autobiography in a third of that time) and that shows even fools that you are a great painter in terms you understand. . . . If you have painted "The Farm" or if you have written *Ulysses,* and then keep on working very hard afterwards, you do not need an Alice B. Toklas."[47] Again that same year in his introduction to James Charters' *This Must Be the Place,* he reported how one managed to gain mention in the memoirs of a salon woman. Three acid paragraphs explained that such a woman mentioned names if dropping such names added to her brilliance, if one had been loyal to her whims, if one had sold her paintings or drawings which would increase in value when mentioned in memoirs, and especially if one had been alienated and gotten the treatment expectable from one of the girls around the Dôme or Select. "However, if you go to the salon you must expect to be in the memoirs."[48]

In *Green Hills of Africa* (1935) Hemingway still seethed and attempted to answer the charges in *The Autobiography of Alice B. Toklas* more specifically. In his account of talks with Kandisky, he used Gertrude Stein as an example of what was wrong with contemporary American writers: "The women writers become Joan of Arc without the fighting. They become leaders. It doesn't matter who they lead. If they do not have followers they invent them. It is useless for those selected as followers to protest. They are accused of disloyalty."[49] And later he envied the white hunter Phillips because "he doesn't have to read books written by some female he's tried to help get published saying how he's yellow." Then he struck a note of sorrow which he maintained later in his 1958 talk with George Plimpton and in *A Moveable Feast*:

"It's a damned shame, though, with all that talent gone to malice and nonsense and self-praise. It's a god-damned shame, really. It's a shame you never knew her before she went to pot. You know a funny thing; she never could write dialog. It was terrible. She learned how to

47. "The Farm," *Cahiers d'Art,* IX (1934), 28.
48. (London, 1934), pp. 11-12.
49. *Green Hills of Africa,* p. 24.

do it from my stuff and used it in that book. She had never written like that before. She could never forgive learning that and she was afraid people would notice it, where she'd learned it, so she had to attack me. It's a funny racket, really, but I swear she was damned nice before she got ambitious."[50]

It is at this point irrelevant to try to determine the truth of the opposing claims. What is important to note, though, is that the essay was Hemingway's best method of providing external evidence of his growth beyond the Stein technique, whatever might have been the original debt. In *For Whom the Bell Tolls* he has Robert Jordan offer a judgment on the ultimate significance of Gertrude Stein—a judgment that coincides with the view in the essays. Looking at the onion he is eating for breakfast, Robert Jordan muses aloud that: " 'An onion is an onion is an onion,' Robert Jordan said cheerily and, he thought, a stone is a Stein is a rock is a boulder is a pebble."[51]

Hemingway's response to the ridiculing given him by Lillian Ross in her *New Yorker* "Portrait" was relatively mild and was perhaps due to his knowledge that part of the portrait was the result of acting on his part. At least this is suggested by Ross's introductory note in her later edition of the interview. Other people were more concerned that the portrait was unflattering than Hemingway was, she says.[52] Both the act and the portrait were an understood joke. Still, in his 1954 interview with Robert Manning of the *Atlantic Monthly*, Hemingway observed, "Now if you find me talking in monosyllables or without any verbs, you tell me, because I never really talk that way." And, significantly, he talked of Ross in the same way he talked of Gertrude Stein, as one who attacked him after he had helped get her material published—in this case an article on the Brooklyn bull-fighter Sidney Franklin.[53] Hemingway's reaction to Lillian Ross's portrait was not perhaps as mild as he pretended in interviews. Again he went behind the mask of fiction to say the last word. The bloody-whiskered lioness in the fable "The Good Lion," published a year after the *New Yorker* profile, was suspiciously

50. *Ibid.*, pp. 65-66.
51. *For Whom the Bell Tolls* (New York, 1940), p. 289.
52. *Portrait of Hemingway* (New York, 1961), p. 15.
53. "Hemingway in Cuba," 102.

suggestive of Lillian Ross with her reputation for doing the savage *New Yorker* portraits.[54]

The type of attack Hemingway was subject to as he became famous for a second generation appeared in his encounter with the young American journalist in "The Dangerous Summer." Confronting Hemingway in the streets of Pamplona, the journalist berated him for trying to relive the events of thirty-five years before and for trying to be a public personage instead of a working writer. Hemingway's answer in the bullfight account was to note the lines of bitterness in the young journalist's face and to comment that the young man could never lose the old feeling because he could never have it. "It was all there and he had been invited to it but he could not see it." The biblical overtone may have been unintentional.[55]

Portraits of F. Scott Fitzgerald, Ford Madox Ford, and Ernest Walsh in *A Moveable Feast* were all destructive enough, and admirers of these figures found them mostly vicious. They seem, however, to be purely personal sketches, of greater use to the biographer than to the follower of Hemingway's career as a literary in-fighter in the essay. Their value within the context of the whole book can best be seen as moments of illumination for an innocent who was learning every day that writers are not as admirable as their writing. They were as distracting to the earnest young apprentice as were the false leads furnished by literary fashions. But the book was permeated with the knowledge that he had survived those distractions and, looking back with more than thirty years' perspective, he could simultaneously congratulate himself on surviving and regret the loss of such fellow learners along the way.

Hemingway's ultimate adversary in the literary world, though, was the public, including his non-writing friends and admirers. The public would not leave him alone to do his writing. Nor, as he complained in 1930 in a letter published in a bibliographical pamphlet by Walden Book Shop, would they believe that he and his belongings were not public property.[56] He could not keep copies of his books around his house; even the potentially valuable first editions had been taken. In his *Esquire* article "The Sights of Whitehead Street" he complained under the

54. *Holiday*, IX (March 1951), 50.
55. *Life*, XLIX (September 12, 1960), 75.
56. *Bibliographical Notes on Ernest Hemingway* (Chicago, 1930), p. [3].

guise of humor that the tourists in Key West stopped by his home so often he had to hire an old Negro, ostensibly with leprosy, to stand at the gate of the yard and tell the tourists the Hemingway stories they had come to hear.[57] And as late as 1956 he wrote in his "Situation Report" that ". . . Mary and I live here and work until visitors interrupt work so much we have to leave. It was a nice life here for a long time, and it still is a nice life when we are left alone and we will always come back here from wherever we go."[58]

As he traced it, his career indeed had been one of searching for a place to work free from distractions and for the state of mind free from false leads urged by critics and contemporaries. He never pretended that he wrote his nonfictional attacks on other writers without some grim joy in the pain they caused, but his attacks always reflected his insistence that writing stay close to the personal realities. And he was intuitionist enough to believe that his grasp of reality was certain, that he should not be dissuaded from it by literary fashions or strong personalities. In a way, his literary sharpshooting could be taken as a long plea for the conditions conducive to honest work in the arts in the twentieth century.

57. *Esquire*, III (April 1935), 25.
58. "A Situation Report," *Look*, XX (September 4, 1956), 24.

VI. The Man of Letters

ONCE HE HAD GIVEN UP HIS PLACE WITH THE TORONTO STAR AND
associated himself with the new school of writing in Paris, Hemingway had to accept the role of man of letters, whether or not
he liked all the connotations of the term. Writing for such little
magazines as *the transatlantic review* and *This Quarter*, he had
to be aware of the events of the literary world as much as he had
earlier noted political and military events. Writing editorially,
instead of reportorially as in the feature articles, he became the
speaker for literary occasions. But for the public occasions he
adopted the personal voice, not the editorial plural. The sense
that his personal response to an occasion was a valid one was
fundamental in his writings. Also fundamental was his search
for the personal dimension of a literary event, whether it was the
occasion for a tribute, an elegy, or the evaluation of a work.

"Homage to Ezra," published in *This Quarter* for May, 1925,
was Hemingway's first excursion into the tribute form, though

earlier he had written an unsigned tribute-like article for the *Toronto Star Weekly* when the Nobel Prize for 1923 was awarded to W. B. Yeats.[1] In the Yeats article he defended the Irish poet's subtle genius against the admirers of the Robert W. Service-Bliss Carman-Alfred Noyes-John Masefield school of poetry but admitted that "there is little use in attempting to convert a lover of coca-cola to vintage champagne." On the other hand, he thought the award was only partial recompense by the Nobel Prize committee for their critical errors in past awards to such lightweights as Maurice Maeterlinck and Rabindranath Tagore, whose poetry Hemingway found "a little syrupy." The occasion for "Homage to Ezra" was Pound's move to Italy from Paris and the discovery of his absence by numerous admirers in the new generation, many of whom had come to Paris to meet the man scorned by their elders. The pseudo-occasion was Pound's death—his having arrived at fame and his removal from admirers. Hemingway's assignment from *This Quarter's* editor was to write an appreciation of Ezra Pound "as though Pound were dead." Hemingway's response, though, was to write of the man, not of his works, as he would have for a dead man. He celebrated Pound as a man of many geniuses who spent only one-fifth of his time writing poetry, the rest of it advancing the fortunes of his friends, defending them from attack, getting them into magazines and out of jail, lending them money, selling their pictures, arranging their concerts, introducing them to wealthy women, sitting at their bedsides, witnessing their wills, dissuading them from suicide, and sometimes not being knifed by them at first opportunity. That one-fifth effort, Hemingway argued, brought Pound rank as a major poet because of his productivity, skill and insight; and the quality of mind that prompted such achievement was "the temperament of a *toro di lidia* [*sic*] from the breeding establishments of Don Eduardo Miura." "No one ever presents a cape, or shakes a muleta at him without getting a charge. Like Don Eduardo's product too he sometimes ignores the picador's horse to pick off the man and no one goes into the ring with him in safety." But Pound hid that spirit behind shyness, strange haircuts, a "patchy red beard," and a fondness for playing tennis. His critics in America erred when they saw the obviously un-

1. "Learns to Commune with the Fairies, Now Wins the $40,000 Nobel Prize," *TSW*, November 24, 1923, p. 35.

poetic tennis playing and "decided there could not be anything in the Pound legend and that he was probably not a great poet after all." But Hemingway could certify that he was not dead and that he did not suffer. "He is no masochist and this is one more reason why he is not a minor poet."[2] Though he had fathered the generation, he would not be limited by its admirations.

Although this was Hemingway's first attempt at the prose elegy, he found later use of the form. It began with the death of Joseph Conrad. Not having known Conrad, but having heard Ford Madox Ford's stories about him, Hemingway wrote an elegiac lament for a writer of "bad stories" that could keep him awake reading all night. It was part of an elegiac issue of Ford's *transatlantic review* on Conrad's death. As spokesman for the visceral school of readers, Hemingway anticipated such ready editorial phrases to be used for the occasion as "remarkable story teller," "stylist," "deep thinker," "serene philosopher"—and rejected them. Other essays in the issue bore out his anticipation of standard phrases and standard evaluations. He noted the ease with which one in critical circles could be ostracized by an incautious opinion, and he saw that the standard opinion among the *cognoscenti* was that Conrad was a bad writer, T. S. Eliot a good one. But after dismissing Eliot as an "acknowledged technician," he compared Conrad's artistic skills and courage to those of Manuel "Maera" Garcia, his touchstone among Spanish matadors. Besides offering that personal standard of measurement, he cited his own reading history of Conrad. Having learned he could not reread Conrad but that he could find no better first reading, he saved up several Conrad stories to read when he "needed them badly, when the disgust with writing, writers and everything written of and to write would be too much." That time came during his last return to Canada. Finally *The Rover* was his last unread Conrad, and on an assignment at the mining town of Sudbury, Ontario, he read it in one night when he had planned to make it last for days. "When morning came I had used up all my Conrad like a drunkard . . . and felt like a young man who has blown in his patrimony."[3] Conrad probably received no more personal statements of indebtedness than Hem-

2. *This Quarter*, I (May 1925), 222-25.
3. "Conrad," *the transatlantic review*, II (October 1924), 341-42.

ingway's, even if Hemingway, in proper elegic fashion, talked more about himself than about the dead.

On at least two more occasions he spoke as an elegist. "Who Murdered the Vets?" in *New Masses* for September, 1935, was labeled "A First-Hand Report on the Florida Hurricane," but after reading the first sentence one knew it was a lament, not a report. Hemingway's mask was that of angry mourner as he figuratively stood overlooking the washed-out work camp and bloated bodies and asked accusing rhetorical questions:

Whom did they annoy and to whom was their possible presence a political danger?

Who sent them down to the Florida Keys and left them there in hurricane months?

. . . .

But what happened on the Keys?

. . . .

Why were the men not evacuated on Sunday, or, at latest, Monday morning, when it was known there was a possibility of a hurricane striking the Keys *and evacuation was their only possible protection?*

Who advised against sending the train from Miami to evacuate the veterans until four-thirty o'clock on Monday so that it was blown off the tracks before it ever reached the lower camps?

. . . .

Who left you there? And what's the punishment for manslaughter now?[4]

Between the questions, Hemingway suggested what had happened, basing his answers on his own experience during the hurricane. He pointed out that the wealthy and the government officials knew well enough about hurricanes at the Key and did not go there with their yachts to fish during the season of big fish and big hurricanes. He described his own move-by-move preparations at Key West but could only imagine what went on at the Lower Matecumbe work camp. That imagining, though, was both vivid and applicable to whoever was responsible for the debacle—the man who didn't want to face up to any more bonus marches and Anacostia Flats episodes. He hoped the man responsible would know how it was "to hang on to something until you can't hang on, until your fingers won't hold on, and it is dark. And the wind makes a noise like a locomotive passing, with

4. *New Masses*, XVI (September 17, 1935), 9-10.

a shriek on top of that, because the wind has a scream exactly as it has in books, and then the [road] fill goes and the high wall of water rolls you over and over and then, whatever it is, you get it and we find you, now of no importance, stinking in the mangroves." After reconstructing the curse-invoking, nightmare-producing scene, Hemingway returned to elegiac calm with the rhetorical questions.

If his questions were loaded with implicit political accusations, they were nevertheless bolstered by Hemingway's sensuous comprehension of experience and by a quotation from Shakespeare to provide additional literary connotation. He compared the used-up veterans to Falstaff's peppered ragamuffins, first shot up, then left alive to beg and now, Hemingway added, condemned to drown.

"On the American Dead in Spain" showed a slightly different rhetorical method. Briefer and more obviously an elegy, the tribute was written for the "Lincoln Brigade Number" of *New Masses*, published approximately at the time of Lincoln's birthday anniversary in 1939. Hemingway's real tribute here was to the Spain that the Lincoln Battalion volunteers died defending. Their heroism was confirmed on the Jarama heights which they held for four and a half months, but their immortality, wrote Hemingway in one of his very few mentions of the embarrassing abstraction, was guaranteed by the continuation of the Spanish earth and seasons. While the concept was not strange for Hemingway, he wrote in an elevated manner alien to his habits of expression. In spite of the solemn, measured cadence, the lament had that far-off sound of a man speaking more for this audience than for himself:

The dead sleep cold in Spain tonight. Snow blows through the olive groves, sifting against the tree roots. Snow drifts over the mounds with the small headboards.

The dead sleep cold in Spain tonight and they will sleep cold all this winter as the earth sleeps with them. But in the spring the rain will come to make the earth kind again.

For our dead are a part of the earth in Spain now and the earth of Spain can never die. Each winter it will seem to die and each spring it will come alive again. Our dead will live with it forever.[5]

5. *New Masses*, XXX (February 14, 1939), 3.

When we recognize how often Hemingway linked the American and Spanish Civil Wars and referred to Spanish battles as our later Gettysburgs, his use of the Gettysburg Address here as an informing model seems fairly probable.

The kind of occasion Hemingway responded to most often though was the publication of a favored book, the exhibition of work by a favorite artist, or later the publication or republication of his own work. His work as a man of letters made him in many ways a man of prefaces. He began, after his own recognition as successful novelist, to do prefaces or introductions for memoirs by his Paris friends. The first were for Kiki, the well-known model, sometime prostitute, and later painter of Montparnasse and for Jimmie the Barman, keeper of the Dingo Bar. By the mid-thirties he was writing program notes for exhibits by painters Antonio Gattorno and Luis Quintanilla, introductions and prefaces for books on game fishing, and by the end of the thirties, prefaces for friends from the Spanish Civil War. After the Second World War he wrote other prefaces for books on game fishing and game hunting and for a few novels and short story collections by young authors he thought needed encouragement or a boost with the reading public.

Hemingway's approach to preface writing was highly personal and at first either ignorant of or indifferent to the several conventions comprising the art of the preface. As he wrote more, though, he gradually worked out a formula for prefaces and introductions which brought his own closer to those conventional ones. The tension in his prefaces, indeed, was the balancing of his highly personal approach and comment against the conventions. It made for some unusual patterns.

Of the things Hemingway found to say about the author or painter whose work he was introducing, the most frequently recurring item was a citation of the artist's credentials. Indicative perhaps of his own standards for judging the worth of a book or picture, the certification emphasized the artist's personal experience as his best credential. Hemingway's kind of book was a rendering of one's direct encounter with the world, whether told factually or through the mask of fiction or through pictorial reordering. John Groth's war drawings in *Studio: Europe*, said Hemingway, were roughed in while the artist was under fire: "But if John would have made them from any closer up front he would have had to have sat in the Krauts' laps." His personal voucher of Groth's firsthand experience was also a part of the credential: "I saw him make them on good days and bad days, when it was quiet and under really heavy artillery fire. None of us understood the sort of short hand he sketched in. Most of us thought he was crazy. All of us liked him. All of us respected him. It was a very great pleasure to find what fine drawings they were when we finally got to see them."[6] He certified Luis Quintanillas' war etchings by telling how Quintanilla had lost his pre-war frescoes to Fascist bombing, had led the attack on Montana barracks to thwart the Fascist capture of Madrid, and had studied military tactics at night while commanding troops during the day in the Guadarrama Mountains, on the Tagus plains, and in the streets of Toledo.[7] Gustav Regler's authority for writing the Spanish Civil War novel *The Great Crusade*, Hemingway pointed out, was his participation in the action chronicled in the novel. "No one has more right to write of these actions which saved Madrid than Gustav Regler. He fought in all of them." That the novel could be read as a *roman à clef* was indication of the writer's authority: "There was Regler, who is the Commissar of this book. There was Lucasz, the General. There was Werner Heilbrun, who is the Doctor in this book. There were all the others. I will not name them. Some were Communists, but there were men of all political beliefs."[8]

A second kind of credential Hemingway cited for his authors was personal expertness. Van Campen Heilner could write with authority on *Salt Water Fishing* because he had been a pioneer of big game fishing on both East and West Coasts and had fished at Bimini "long before most of today's famous fishermen had ever heard the name of the place." He had, moreover, "kept up with the major developments in heavy game fishing" and had served as Vice-President of the International Game Fish Association, helping to authenticate all major game fish records.[9] For François Sommer's *Man and Beast in Africa*, Hemingway certified that Sommers had earned the right to be heard because he had hunted throughout Equatorial Africa for years and had paid attention to historical and technical problems in describing game habits

6. *Studio: Europe* (New York, 1945), pp. 8-9.
7. *All the Brave* (New York, 1939), p. 7.
8. *The Great Crusade* (New York, 1940), pp. vii-viii.
9. *Salt Water Fishing* (New York, 1953), p. viii.

and hunting equipment. His face, said Hemingway, was his passport in the hunting areas of Africa.[10]

Besides experience that authenticated the author's or artist's work, Hemingway looked for personal qualities that influenced the work. He found it meaningful to give the reader an insight into the kind of person the book's author or picture's creator might be. Describing the Gattorno behind the paintings for which he wrote a program note, he told of a young Cuban of strong feelings, a strong color sense, and a strong sense of mystery. Gattorno had made his artistic pilgrimage from Cuba to Italy and Paris, had been drawn to the Italian primitives and to the new painting in Paris. Modigliani and his group Gattorno knew instinctively—"There is no mystery when you are part of the mystery." Because he had essentially a primitive mind, Gattorno admired his intellectualist opposite: "But he found Galicia very sad. He is quite proud of this because it makes him feel like an intellectual and like all people who are not intellectual he is very proud when he is that way."[11] He found full-bearded John Groth "like some one who was understudying the man who would play Our Lord in a stream-lined Passion Play with North Germans instead of Bavarians."[12] Elio Vittorini, author of *In Sicily*, had the outlook of the young man who had run away from home at seventeen and, like his American counterparts, had learned his country sensuously and totally. Reginald Rowe, Hemingway's Cuban neighbor for whom he wrote a note for a painting exhibit catalogue, was a man familiar in the neighborhood for his old straw hat, paint-smeared shorts, many canvases showing the wonders of Cuban light, and the adulation given him by the children and dogs of San Francisco de Paula village.[13] Lee Samuels, compiler of the 1951 checklist of Hemingway's work, was a man of astonishing distinterestedness, who found and collected an author's works and gave them to a library, instead of selling them for profit to book dealers. "It is such a disinterested action that it is impressive to the point of being almost incredible in these times."[14]

Hemingway's third critical point in celebrating the occasion

10. *Man and Beast in Africa* (London, 1953), pp. 5-6.
11. "Gattorno," *Esquire*, V (May 1936), 111, 141.
12. *Studio: Europe*, p. 8.
13. "Finca Vigia," *Reginald Rowe* (New York, 1952), p. [2].
14. *A Hemingway Check-List* (New York, 1951), p. 5.

of others' work was to note the significance of the work's appearance or its inception. These comments ranged from the cynically practical to the historically perceptive, and in many cases they involved explanation of Hemingway's part as a man of letters. As he explained in the preface to Jerome Bahr's *All Good Americans*, publishers would bet on a beginning novelist; but for a beginning writer of short stories, they wanted a name known in the literary world to introduce the work. He apologized for pointing out excellences in Bahr's work that would be noted anyway without an economically motivated preface.[15] For Gattorno's exhibit of paintings in New York, he explained that Cuba could not support the artist either financially or spiritually, that he had to work and exhibit in New York because in Cuba he could "never see any great painting to wash his mind clear and encourage his heart. . . ."[16] The compelling occasion for Van Campen Heilner's *Salt Water Fishing*, wrote Hemingway, was the threatened end of a great era in game fishing because the sport was being taken over by a generation less heroic than Heilner's—one that followed the well-fished lanes and depended on heavy equipment instead of skill and heart to boat their record-sized fish. In a more droll mood he announced the end of an era also with Jimmie the Barman's *This Must Be the Place*. That a barkeeper of Montparnasse would write his memoirs of the people who once drank at his place was evidence that the great period of Montparnasse was over. It was also a sure sign of the decline of Western Civilization when a bartender violated the confidences of barflies. "It is only a step from abolishing the right of sanctuary in the Republic of San Marino to permitting bartenders to write their memoirs," he lamented. But at that he considered the barman's advice better than much he had received in Montparnasse literary salons. The advice: "You should go home, sir, shall I get a taxi?"[17] In a larger mood he wrote for Ben Raeburn's *Treasury for the Free World*, just after the close of the Second World War, that the symposium on war-engendered problems was timely because it came at a watershed period of history. It was, he said, a time to see established problems—basically those of lands held by other than their own peoples—in a new light. The symposium articles, he noted, were

15. *All Good Americans* (New York, 1937), p. viii.
16. "Gattorno," 141.
17. James Charters, *This Must Be the Place* (New York, 1934), pp. 12-13.

written before men's minds were newly complicated by the release of atomic energy. They would remind readers that the problems were long-lived and difficult of solution, that atomic bombs caused urgency but did not provide solutions.[18] "We must study . . . and remember that no weapon has ever solved a moral problem."

In his three prefaces for Luis Quintanilla's *All the Brave*, Hemingway combined cynical comment on the book trade with a sense of historical moment. The three prefaces were a symptomatic record of Hemingway's struggle with his role of man of letters. Part of the struggle was indicated by the fact that there were three prefaces instead of one. The first was a brief, 314-word sketch of Quintanilla, his losses and his heroisms during the early days of the Spanish war. The second, dated five weeks later, explained that the publisher insisted on the originally agreed upon 1000-word preface, would not settle for 314 words, and threatened to cancel publication of Quintanilla's book if Hemingway's preface did not arrive soon. What followed was a surly, grudging, and self-conscious scraping together of prefatory elements: "At this point in the introduction there should be a little literature about what it means to a man to have his life's work destroyed. . . . Now what comes next in an introduction? Certainly: this is it. The comparison with Goya. . . . So what comes now in an introduction to drawings of war? There certainly should be some reference to war itself. . . ."[19] The cause of his bitter catechism was outside Hemingway's tent as he wrote: "You see there are quite a lot of Americans strung out along the Ebro too, along with Belgians, Germans, Frenchmen, Poles, Czechs, Croats, Bulgarians, Slovenes, Canadians, British, Finns, Danes, Swedes, Norwegians, Cubans, and the best Spaniards in the world. They are all waiting there for the decisive battle of the war to commence . . . [and] everything except the Ebro seems very unimportant tonight."[20] The third preface was gratis. An overt apology to Quintanilla and an implicit one to the publisher, it was written after the battle of Ebro and sadly reported that the Republican left flank had collapsed after a seeming victory over the Italians at Cherta. It closed with a certification that Quin-

18. *Treasury for the Free World* (New York, 1946), p. xiv.
19. *All the Brave*, pp. 8, 9.
20. *Ibid.*, pp. 9-10.

tanilla's true rendering of war set a high standard for war writers to match. For there was now likely to be a bigger war for Europe.

The fifth item on Hemingway's check list for prefaces and introductions called for comments on the qualities of the work itself. Mostly laudatory, as they were written to encourage appreciation, they nevertheless provided insight into the standards Hemingway found applicable. In almost every case he ended by admitting that values found in a work by the critic or introducer were less meaningful than those found by the viewer or reader directly. Paintings, he said of Miro's "The Farm," are to look at, not write about. In the Quintanilla prefaces he conceded that one could write of authors and painters better than one wrote of their work. Whatever he might say of Henrietta Hoopes' water colors, her paintings were the completion of any moods or meanings he might suggest, he noted in his comments on her exhibit. Still, granting that the work is the thing, he wrote his insights to provide initiative for readers and viewers. And his insights had some common denominators. Miro's painting of a Spanish farm, he said, had in it "all that you feel about Spain when you are there and all that you feel when you are away and cannot go there."[21] On Gattorno's paintings of his "long, sad, over-foliaged island," he said the artist "each time he painted a picture . . . tried to get all of it in; no matter what the size of the picture nor whether it had only two figures in it he tried to put all Cuba in it."[22] Louis Quintanilla's etchings of Spanish life suggested another criterion; the artist's relation to his subject determined his authority in the work. The Goya-esque figures of cheap whores, drunken workers, and bloated businessmen were not theoretical judgments on them. "He does not judge them; only presents them because he has led them in action. If you follow, you idealize. If you have led, you present and criticize, you have the right to satirize, and when you hate, you hate intelligently."[23]

Hemingway's criticisms of verbal works varied between literal and figurative judgments. He characterized Sommer's *Man and Beast in Africa* as a book useful and trustworthy for hunters and those generally interested in Africa, one sound and healthy in its approach to hunting because it did not deal in false thrills sought for their own sake. He similarly commended Charles

21. *Cahiers d'Art*, IX (1934), 28.
22. "Gattorno," 141.
23. "Facing a Bitter World," *Esquire*, III (February 1935), 27.

Ritz's *A Fly Fisher's Life* (1959) for its inclusion of sound advice and actual experience without the intrusion of cheaply impressive technical data and terminology. About this same time he was scorning in his own work, "The Dangerous Summer," those commentators on bullfighting who dazzled general readers with so many technical terms they lost sight of the action. He resorted to figurative language to characterize Elio Vittorini's novel *In Sicily*. The "fancy writing," he said, was only packaging to disguise the content from Fascist censors in 1937. "But there is excellent food once you unwrap it." To characterize the imagination within the work, though, he shifted metaphors. Vittorini's imagination was the rain that fertilized experience: "I care nothing about the political aspects of the book. . . . But I care very much about his ability to bring rain with him when he comes if the earth is dry and that is what you need." It was an ability, he noted, lacking in too many novelists and critics of the time.

Perhaps his most extended criticism of others' works occurred in the introduction to *Men at War* (1942). A critique of war writing in general and of selections chosen for the anthology in particular, the introduction indicated that Hemingway's central criterion for evaluating war pieces was the writers' abilities to tell "how it was" to be in war—a criterion particularly suitable to his purpose of initiating his military readers into the mysteries of the human heart during armed crisis. His secondary criterion was to distinguish between writings that rendered war honestly and those that provided intellectualized critiques of military actions. Tolstoy's battle scenes in *War and Peace* were supremely convincing, he said, but his "messianic thinking" on the roles men played in shaping events was dubious and discardable theory. No perceptive and honest writing on war was done during the 1914-1918 conflict, Hemingway believed, except for work by a few poets. Honest prose writing had to wait until after the war, when veterans like Frederic Manning ("Private 19022") wrote *Her Privates We* and similar works. Hemingway certified Manning's version of trench warfare as one of the most truthful accounts, so real that he annually reread parts of the book to remember how it was when he was wounded. And he remembered being told by Evan Shipman during the Spanish Civil War that he had been prepared for the experience of being strafed and wounded by reading Stephen Crane's *The Red Badge of Courage,* "that great boy's dream of war" that was truer than even the facts of war. Of pieces not anthologized Hemingway cited John William De Forest's "forgotten" *Miss Ravenel's Conversion* as one of the most convincing to come out of the American Civil War. Of pieces included in the anthology, he recommended General Marbot's accounts for insight into the battle experience of Napoleon's great cavalry leaders. And in all the war writings, collected or not, he judged their truthfulness by their fidelity to soldiers' language as it was used during battle— by the plain and four-letter words used, not by passing slang or post-battle, elevated versions of the words of war.

A sixth item for comment, and one closely allied to his characterization and evaluation of the works, was Hemingway's tendency to identify the works as part of an artistic tradition. It was perhaps another way of characterizing by allusion. He indicated some of the usefulness of the aesthetic tradition for understanding particular works when he described Gattorno's spiritual pilgrimage:

There is simply good painting which, when it is good enough, is always ageless. But it can be more important if the painter knows the painting that is behind all good painting and the line of descent that all good painting has followed. Gattorno had the luck to go to Italy as a barbarian at a time in his life when the primitives seemed to be painted by his contemporaries. He had never met any contemporaries of his own and in Italy he saw good painting and grew up with it feeling that these were the painters that were his friends and that he could call them all *tu* and *toi*. It was a strange thing that they had all been dead for many centuries but that is the way it is in painting when you are born to be a good painter.[24]

His comments indicated that he felt the painting tradition and the writing tradition were parts of the same whole. He could visualize Waldo Peirce's Pamplona fiesta pictures in the Goyaesque tradition and see *Kiki's Memoirs* in the reminiscing courtesan tradition of Defoe's *Moll Flanders* and *Roxanne,* but to evoke the essential quality of Jerome Bahr's stories in *All Good Americans* he cited their "Pieter Breughel quality of the country and the people." He depended on more recent traditions for larger meanings in some of his introductions to war works.

24. "Gattorno," 111.

He held Gustav Regler's *The Great Crusade* against the run of Marxist-oriented books on the Spanish Civil War. In this case he saw the individual book as a corrective on the tradition. Too many books, like Alvah Bessie's account in *Men in Battle* of heroism in defeat during the last campaigns of the war, were true only of the decline of the Spanish Republic. Regler's book, he emphasized, was necessary to correct that tradition of grimness and to show that there was a golden period of optimism for the Republic during much of the war. To accept Bessie's viewpoint as typical would be like making the retreat from Moscow typical of Napoleon's campaigns. John Groth's battle drawings in *Studio: Europe,* he noted, shared something of the tradition of Bill Mauldin's cartoons but were also "different . . . as Watteau's [drawings] differ from Daumier's."

Hemingway's formal practice of the art of the preface for his own work began several years after he had practiced it for others. Informally he wrote oblique comments about his work as early as 1927 for the Walden Book Shop bibliographical pamphlet of 1930, and his letters on being bibliographed by Louis Henry Cohn were included as a pseudo-preface to Cohn's 1931 *Bibliography.* But not until the publication of *The Fifth Column and the First Forty-Nine Stories* in 1938 did he write a bona fide introduction to his own work. In that introduction and subsequent ones for *Men at War* (1942), the 1948 edition of *A Farewell to Arms,* the 1951 edition of Lee Samuels' *A Hemingway Check-List,* and in public letters on his work printed in *Life* magazine, he made it clear that the rules were different for his work. He apparently recognized, as H. J. C. Grierson says of prefaces and introductions, "that what is the first page of a book for the reader was the last for the author, and that a perusal of the preface may shed light on the whole book that will obviate later misunderstandings, give the reader a glimpse of the writer's mind as he drew to a close, as he saw his work in final perspective. . . ."[25] Because he approached his works with a different perspective, he had different things to talk about. There was, for example, much more explanation of personal experience behind the works, and the evaluations were more likely to be statements of personal preference.

25. "Introduction," *The Personal Note,* ed. by H. J. C. Grierson and Sandys Watson (London, 1946), p. 1.

In the introduction to *Men at War* he cited three personal reasons for making the book as helpful as he could make it for young men going to war: he had been wounded at war during his youth and had learned to hate war; he had lost his illusion of immortality when wounded and had needed someone to give him something in its place—"I would have given anything for a book like this which showed what all the other men we are a part of had gone through and how it had been with them." And he had three sons eligible to fight in the wars of the century.[26] In his introduction to *A Farewell to Arms* he cited other experiences that had helped shape the mood and events of the book: "During the time I was writing the first draft my second son Patrick was delivered in Kansas City by Caesarian section and while I was rewriting my father killed himself in Oak Park, Illinois."[27] He was even more explicit about the influence of personal events on *The Fifth Column*. The Hotel Florida in Madrid, where he wrote the play, was hit by "more than thirty high explosive shells. So if it is not a good play perhaps that is what is the matter with it. If it is a good play, perhaps those thirty some shells helped write it."[28]

He cited as also significant the places he had found stimulating for work: Madrid, Paris, Key West in the cool months, Kansas City, Chicago, Toronto, Havana, a ranch near Cooke City, Montana; Piggott, Arkansas; Sheridan and Big Horn, Wyoming. "Some other places were not so good but maybe we were not so good when we were in them." Indeed some places were better for original writing and others for revising. Paris, Key West, Piggott, and Kansas City were good for writing *A Farewell to Arms*, but only Key West and Paris gave perspective enough for finishing it. Madrid and Paris were good places for writing stories about America, but he wrote war stories close to the scene. "The Old Man at the Bridge" was written in Barcelona soon after he saw the prompting scene, and the play about the siege of Madrid was written in Madrid. Timing was important too. The play was written and sent out of Spain before the battle of Teruel. It was a time of grim defense before the revival of optimism occurred with the taking of Teruel. Time and place com-

26. *Men at War* (New York, 1942), pp. xi, xiv, xxvii.
27. *A Farewell to Arms* (New York, 1948), p. vii.
28. *The Fifth Column and the First Forty-Nine Stories* (New York, 1938), p. v.

bined to suggest the name and content of the play. The Fascist claim that four columns had converged on Madrid and that another of espionage agents had infiltrated it prompted the moods of ferocity and betrayal permeating the play. "If many of the Fifth Column are now dead, it must be realized that they were killed in a warfare where they were as dangerous and as determined as any of those who died in the other four columns."[29]

He cited a long time perspective for *The Old Man and the Sea* when he wrote pre-publication letters to the editors of *Life* magazine. The short novel had fifteen years of learning about men and fish and the sea behind it, and he had delayed writing "because I did not think I could. . . . But I had good luck with this all the way and maybe I will have luck again. . . ."[30] Reason for his dread of writing and his celebration of luck could be seen in his desire for a particular effect in the work. "Whatever I learned is in the story but I hope it reads simply and straight and all the things that are in it do not show but are with you after you have read it." The expressed hope was apparently an indirect instruction on how to read the novel.

When he wrote the preface to Lee Samuels' check list of his work in 1951, Hemingway had to deal with the even more self-conscious process whereby a recognized man of letters counts up his editions and sees the arrangement of his work as a whole. He turned the occasion into one of personal victory and loss. While noting that what he wrote often had more value on the collectors' market than on the publishers' lists, he also lamented the ways a writer's properties could be lost to him. Little magazine publishers who had paid almost nothing for his writing, pleading their literary responsibility more than their financial responsibility, had kept his manuscripts, even when asked to return them, and had sold them to collectors for considerably more than they had paid for the rights to print them. Others of his editions had been taken by house guests; others had been inadvertently lost to rats, roaches, and mildew when improperly stored by members of his own household. And then there was that sickening time when his suitcase of manuscripts had been stolen at the Gare de Lyon in Paris while his wife, who was taking them to him in Switzerland, had stepped out of the train compartment to

29. *Ibid.*, p. vi.
30. *Life*, XXXIII (August 25, 1952), 124.

buy a bottle of Vittel water.[31] Appropriate to a check list, it was a preface citing occasions for losing rather than of writing works.

The evaluation of his own works was a question of relative value, for, as he noted in the preface to *The Fifth Column and the First Forty-Nine Stories,* he did not publish any stories that he did not believe in. Measured against his own personal demands of a story, however, some were more successful than others. When he reread stories like "The Short Happy Life of Francis Macomber," "The Snows of Kilimanjaro," "In Another Country," "Hills Like White Elephants," "A Way You'll Never Be," "A Clean Well-Lighted Place," and "The Light of the World," he could hardly believe he had been able to write that well. Similarly, when he wrote the editors of *Life* about *The Old Man and the Sea,* his evaluation was really a statement of wonder at his good luck: "Don't you think it is a strange damn story that it should affect all of us (me especially) the way it does? I have had to read it now over 200 times and every time it does something to me."[32] His recognition of evaluation by others occasionally served as a foil to his own self-evaluation. In the preface to his collected stories he recognized that some had become such standard examples of modern narration that they were reprinted regularly in anthologies for study by apprentice writers and, while he appreciated the royalties, he felt embarrassed at such canonization. Satisfaction at his good writing luck with *The Old Man and the Sea* and at prospect of a general admiration of the book because of publication in a mass circulation magazine, he told *Life* editors, was preferable to the recognition coming from a Nobel Prize. As he had not then received a Nobel Prize but T. S. Eliot and William Faulkner had, and they were two writers whose versions of literature Hemingway had disparaged, his disclaimer was perhaps to be interpreted as a desire for popular acclaim instead of critical success. He was betting apparently that literary immortality was to be decided by masses of readers rather than by a critical few. And he was putting himself in the conservative tradition of plain storytellers rather than among revolutionists of form. For his type of man of letters, it was not a bad bet.

31. *A Hemingway Check-List,* pp. 5-6.
32. *Life,* XXXIII (August 8, 1952), 124.

Thus, although he recognized in his prefaces and introductions that finally the artistic work had to exist on its own merits, particularly on its power to evoke a wider and more meaningful experience than it actually presented, he also recognized that external commentary had its uses. Introductions and prefaces could encourage the reader to approach the painting or the story on the artist's terms; and where memoirs and factual narratives were an invitation to see experience as the authors had seen it, prefatory comments could introduce the reader to the memoirist and his world. The man of letters acted as voucher for the new—as established middleman whose judgment could be accepted contingently by the reader or viewer. Acting as his own middleman when prefacing his own works, Hemingway indicated the value of a public voice for the man of letters who mostly had to speak from behind the mask of fiction.

PART THREE / *"Think Pieces"*

The Essay as a Vehicle of Thought

VII. Hemingway's Cultural Thought

Antaeus and the Great Frontier

WHETHER THE CONVERSATION WAS FACTUAL OR APOCRYPHAL, Hemingway's remark to Morley Callaghan was consistent with his career-long announcement and practice: a writer, he said, always got in trouble when he started thinking on the page.[1] It was especially true when the page was a fictional one. Both Leo Tolstoy and Aldous Huxley, he maintained on several occasions, diluted their pages with Big Thinking. Put in another way, his view, as A. E. Hotchner told it, was that he could always do a story better than a "think piece."[2]

But to say that Hemingway shied from the discourse of reason is not to say that he worked without intellectual convictions.

1. Morley Callaghan, *That Summer in Paris* (New York, 1964), pp. 97-98.
2. *Papa Hemingway* (New York, 1966), p. 19.

It was only that he kept them implicit in his fiction and spoke them incidentally in his nonfiction. He did his thinking before writing his page; and when he did not use his page for presentation of fictional people, he used it for self-presentation. But thought was in the background, and not so distant that it could not be inferred and often reconstructed. The quality of that thought could best be described as pragmatic and inductive. In his essays he gave no evidence of formulating generalized concepts and working out their implications. Rather his practice was to sense the cogent action or situation, whether for himself or for his fictional people, and when time for reflection came later, to suggest general ideas and their implications which justified or explained accomplished fact. His thinking on cultural patterns, politics, or aesthetics can best be understood then as a kind of apologia.

Reporter, featured columnist, or man of letters, Hemingway observed the events of his time and silently saw them fall into a Spenglerian pattern. That he should do so was perhaps consistent with his time. The postwar period was ripe for news of *The Decline of the West* (1918, 1923). The groups of young artists in Paris discussed the idea of a rise, flourishing, and decay of civilization; it was evident in such works as Archibald MacLeish's "You, Andrew Marvell," in the reverberations of Eliot's *The Waste Land*, and perhaps in the implications of Yeats' gyre poems. Hemingway's specific mention of such a pattern of events did not occur until the late twenties, through the fictional voice of Count Greffi in *A Farewell to Arms* and in more direct statements during the mid-thirties. But his notations of events in Europe and America during the early twenties indicated recognitions that would later prompt and fit the Spenglerian explanations.

Perhaps one of Hemingway's strongest early statements of decadence in Europe was written soon after his return to Toronto from Europe in 1923. While the article "King Business in Europe Isn't What It Used to Be" was obviously slanted to appeal to Canadian anti-continental prejudices, it also noted details and motifs typical of Hemingway's cultural observations. In the article he told how a fellow reporter interviewing King George of Greece saw the king's own unhappiness as puppet of his ministers, learned of his preference for exile in London or Paris to living in a royal palace in Greece, and took his picture on a hay binder so the pose would appeal to newly powerful Americans. Other kings, in similarly unhappy situations, demonstrated the slipperiness of their European footings. Ferdinand of Rumania, uneasy behind his whiskers, waited for his Peace Conference-given kingdom of non-Rumanians to fall apart while his queen scuttled about Europe looking for alliances and recognition of her daughter as queen of Greece, and while Rumanian army officers wore cosmetics and corsets. Boris of Bulgaria also wanted to leave his country but was virtual prisoner of a pro-German army, politicians, and intellectuals who needed him as a buffer between them and Socialist Premier Stambuliski, jailed during the war but now free and head of the pro-French government. Alexander of Yugoslavia was a Serbian king over a nation of Serbs, Croats, and Slovenes. Victor Emmanuel of Italy was the most popular king in Europe but had recently turned over his army and navy to Mussolini. And Alfonso of Spain, when not racing cars, faced strikes and mutinies.[3] It was not that Hemingway was a defender of royalty. His accent was on Europe's loss of certitudes which neither all the kings' horses nor men could re-establish after the war.

His reports on France, for all their appeal to the traveler's instincts, showed a country losing its integrity while maintaining a fair face. It was a country, he noted, that accepted all sorts of fakes and frauds from other parts of the world because it refused to notice what the rest of the world was doing. An American girl whose former stage experience was a small part in an American musical was billed and accepted in Paris as "America's best known and best loved dancer." Jack Clifford was billed in France as the light-heavyweight champion of the United States until beaten in Vienna by a third-rate boxer. Russians, because of their obscured past, were able to make and find credit for almost any claim to former distinction in Czarist Russia.[4] Paris, like much of Europe, was infested with Russian aristocrats living off false hopes of a counter-revolution and selling their jewels to keep from going to work.[5] The Legion of Honor, meanwhile, was becoming a farce. More than 95,000 had been awarded and the government planned to confer hundreds more on the coming

3. *TSW*, September 15, 1923, p. 15.
4. "The Mecca of Fakers Is French Capital," *TDS*, March 25, 1922, p. 4.
5. "Influx of Russians to All Parts of Paris," *TDS*, February 25, 1922, p. 29.

occasion of the 1922 Molière tercentenary celebration—planned to, that is, until one outraged member of the Chamber of Deputies cried enough and temporarily shamed the government into conscience.[6] Even French traditions in drinking were being shaken. Anti-liqueur posters by the Anti-Alcohol League showing rampant, drink-crazed husbands stared across the street at drinkers in the Café des Deux Magots in the Latin Quarter, and students from the Quarter slanted anxious glances at pictures of diseased livers and tuberculosis victims, while wondering if they should accept the wine-beer-and-cider program of the League. "It is only a question of time," Hemingway thought, till a revolution of drinking occurred.[7] But if Paris did not care about the rest of the world until it got to Paris, it was willing to pander to any taste that could be supported by money. Hemingway and Evan Shipman noted it as a sign of the times when the owners of the Closerie des Lilas decided to get their share of the American tourist trade by putting in an American bar and requiring the waiters to wear white jackets and shave off their mustaches. Hemingway saw the sure loss of French integrity when the waiter Jean had to shave off his long dragoon mustache to meet the new demand.[8] Overcrowding and tripled rents in the French capital had forced many to live in houseboats on the Seine. He also noted the "callousness of republics" in France as the country ignored Spartan old Georges Clemenceau and longed for a less imperious premier to carry it to prosperity and more sidewalk cafes.[9] And he saw French complacency indicated in the case of Monsieur Diebler. Known to his Paris suburb neighbors only as a jovial man with some undefined position in the Ministry of Justice, Diebler was in fact one of the most feared men in France, the public executioner. Every so often he would be out of town for a few days, during which time he with his assistants took their special railroad car containing a guillotine to a siding near one of the prisons, there did their job, and returned to their Paris suburban homes where Diebler's neighbors welcomed the jolly man back and wondered vaguely what he did

6. "95,000 Now Wearing the Legion of Honour," *TDS*, April 1, 1922, p. 7.
7. "Anti-Alcohol Leagues Active in France," *TDS*, April 8, 1922, p. 13.
8. *A Moveable Feast* (New York, 1964), pp. 138-39.
9. "Takes to Water; Solves Flat Problem," *TDS*, August 26, 1922, p. 8; "Builder, Not Fighter, Is What France Wants," *TDS*, February 18, 1922, p. 7.

for a living.[10] A decade later, during the mid-thirties, Hemingway again reported on the French, found the French respectable bourgeoisie complacently drinking in their rediscovered Montmartre haunts while refugees from Nazi purges and Nazi spies, the only foreigners now in the cafes, crowded the Dome.[11]

In Germany Hemingway found restrained panic, desperation, and xenophobia, the indices of national decay. Inflation was the technical cause of German problems, but he was more interested in the waste of German morale than of German credit. Watching French housewives and children stream across the frontier from Strasbourg to Kehl where they gorged themselves on cheap German pastries, he noted the disconsolate Germans in the shops, the "swinish" French at the counters, and observed that "it gave you a new aspect on exchange." Farther into Germany, a year later in 1923, he found at Cologne the "amateur starvers," aged middle-class Germans living on fixed incomes and trying, in five documented cases, to live for a year on incomes adequate for barely two weeks under new monetary values. But because they kept out of sight and did not flaunt their poverty like Neapolitan beggars, the casual picture of Cologne was one of clean streets, British officers in colorful mess uniforms, and German children dancing in the streets to music from the officers' ball.[12] Hate was a more immediately perceivable thing. Traveling with his wife and also William Bird and his wife in Bavaria in 1922, Hemingway was refused accommodations at one *Gasthaus* because they were *Ausländers*; and at another, where they were eating dinner, they were objects of sneering remarks by German tourists at the next table but were saved from a fight by German workmen nearby who scorned the German tourists as profiteers.[13] It was a new German attitude, he noted. Formerly the Germans' hatred of the French had led them to cultivate other nationals as possible future friends; but with the mark going beyond help, they took satisfaction in making everyone suffer during their own ruin. Storekeepers insulted heir foreign buyers while selling

10. "Much Feared Man Is M. Diebler," *TDS*, April 1, 1922, p. 7.
11. "A Paris Letter," *Esquire*, I (February 1934), 156.
12. "Crossing to Germany Is Way to Make Money," *TDS*, September 9, 1922, p. 4; "Amateur Starvers Keep Out of Sight in Germany," *TDS*, May 9, 1923, p. 17.
13. "German Inn-Keepers Rough Dealing with 'Auslanders,' " *TDS*, September 5, 1922, p. 9.

them goods, and they felt, Hemingway guessed, like people at a fire sale having to sell to an arsonist.[14]

Writing for a Canadian paper, Hemingway exploited the anti-American prejudices of his Canadian readers, but the Spenglerian assumptions behind his observations held just as truly for the United States and Canada as they had for Europe. The national self-deception he saw in Paris had already appeared in Chicago, epitome of life below the border for Hemingway's readers. In 1920 and 1921, before he went to Europe as *Star* correspondent, he had noted the easy fraud of American prohibition and the violence of crime in the United States. While United States congressmen decried the loss of thirty-two American lives in Mexico yearly, killings in Chicago for a year were ten times as great, he told the Canadian readers. Whiskey was available anywhere in Chicago for $20 a bottle, and it came from Kentucky, not Canada. Gambling flourished with stakes higher than at Monte Carlo. It was, he observed, a carry-over from lawless American frontier habits, a condition missed by Canada because the Mounted Police had kept a lawless west from ever happening in Canada.[15] After his return from European travel, Hemingway wrote a disconnected series of Chicago vignettes which presented with greater clarity if not less complexity his view of lost vitality in America. "So This Is Chicago" was in fact one of his last articles in the *Star* before he shook the dust of both countries from his feet to sail again for Europe. It combined the moods of Old Testament prophets standing over fated Babylon and of the German Expressionists looking at demoralized Berlin. Some examples:

> Seven miles of dirty, wooden houses all alike stretching out on the great west side.
>
> .   .   .   .
>
> Three fat men in the canyon of LaSalle Street painted like Indians, war bonnets on their heads, shivering in the cold wind and shouting "Buy a string of beads. Real Indian beads. Make somebody happy."
>
> .   .   .   .
>
> All the best looking debutantes at a dance with their hair cut like members of the Brooklyn National League ball team.

14. "Germans Are Doggedly Sullen or Desperate Over the Mark," *TDS*, September 1, 1922, p. 23.

15. "The Wild West Is Now in Chicago," *TSW*, November 6, 1920, p. 15; "Chicago Never Wetter Than It Is To-day," *TSW*, July 2, 1921, p. 21.

.   .   .   .

The boys who went into LaSalle Street when you first went on a newspaper now all driving their own cars, lunching at the club, and asking gloomily if you think there is any possible way they could make a living in Paris.[16]

But he let Canadians know things were not much better in Toronto or its environs. Whether he wrote of the tawdry mining towns at Sudbury, the frenetic and mindless activity that passed for comedy in Toronto theatres, or the shipping of out-of-fashion clothes from Toronto department stores to their back-country outlets, the edge of the comment was always that the real thing had gone out of their lives.[17] As in ancient Rome, the women at the prize fights shrieked for blood when they could no longer believe in their men: "Is it the magic name Arena that brings back to the alleged gentler sex their old Roman attributes? Lecky, the historian, says that the majority of the old Gladiatorial crowds were women."[18] As in Paris, the value and meaning of military medals were gone, the acts of valor and sacrifice they signified forgotten in Toronto. A medal was worth only its value as base metal; and after a survey of Toronto's pawn shops, Hemingway found that pawnbrokers, not heroes, determined that. "You could evidently sell a broken alarm clock. But you couldn't sell an M. C. You could dispose of a second-hand mouth-organ. But there was no market for a D. C. M. You could sell your old military puttees. But you couldn't find a buyer for a 1914 Star. So the market price of valor remained undetermined."[19] If he was humorous about fishermen's stories, he was also serious about Torontonians' readiness to substitute talk for action. More fish were caught in Toronto's dinner clubs and cafeterias, he noted, than were ever taken from all the streams in Christendom. Using a turn of Twain's black humor, he observed, "That's where indoor fishing has it on outdoor fishing.

16. *TSW*, January 19, 1924, p. 19.

17. "Search for Sudbury Coal a Gamble," *TDS*, September 25, 1923, p. 4; "It's Time to Bury the Hamilton Gag; Comedians Have Worked It to Death," *TSW*, June 12, 1920, p. 1; "Stores in the Wilds the Graveyards of Style," *TSW*, April 24, 1920, p. 11.

18. "Toronto Women Who Went to the Prize Fights Applauded the Rough Stuff," *TSW*, May 15, 1920, p. 13.

19. "Lots of War Medals for Sale, But Nobody Will Buy Them," *TSW*, December 8, 1923, p. 21.

It is cheaper and the fish run bigger."[20] The article that was his farewell to Toronto, counterpart of the vignettes for Chicago, was perhaps more personally bitter than its mate. "Much Wear Hats Like Other Folks If You Live in Toronto" recorded Hemingway's experience of wearing a floppy German hat on a Toronto bus and of being tittered and jeered at by the provincial-minded locals. When he retorted sarcastically, one rider offered to hit Hemingway for the satisfaction of the others. Hemingway's point was that the hat had seen much more of the world than had the smug Torontonians. It had been bought in Germany, faded in Thrace, chafed by snow glasses in the Alps, and thrown into Spanish bull rings. He concluded, however, with the realization that the Torontonians' attitude was likely to be typical of all Western civilization. After the incident he bought a hat like all the others in Toronto. "But I know very well that if I ever try and wear it in Europe, somebody will want to take a poke at me."[21]

That Hemingway's Spenglerian mood was a continuing thing became clear in later writings, some of which made the point more strongly if not more frequently than those during the twenties and thirties. If people after the second war insisted on seeing a reprieve, possibly a renaissance, for Western Civilization, Hemingway was at best dubious and sometimes sure there would be a decline. His sense of a cyclical pattern in events told him that what was a pattern of renewal for nature could, if abused by men, become a cycle of futility, of repeating old mistakes. Writing for Ben Raeburn's *Treasury for the Free World* in late 1945, he called for both introspection and retrospection to avoid repeating a cycle of errors. He could already cite evidence that the past was being helplessly imitated. American military government courts had demonstrated a vengeful double standard of justice by hanging a sixty-year-old German woman for helping kill a downed American pilot during the war but had done nothing to pilots who had gratuitously strafed German villages while returning from other missions. It was vengeful Versailles all over again. War and postwar actions, he insisted, had to be different. One fought total wars, but afterwards people had to see wars as another time, another world, and had to re-educate themselves according to different values. Both the pilots and the Ger-

---

20. "A Fight with a 20-Pound Trout," *TSM*, November 20, 1920, pp. 25-26.
21. *TSW*, January 19, 1924, p. 33.

man woman had acted according to the values of that other world. The new era should learn the lessons, not the patterns, of the past.[22]

But he doubted that the future would be that way. In his introduction to the 1948 edition of *A Farewell to Arms* he cited the century's compulsion to violence and decadence. At a New Year's party in Sun Valley he had watched rich socialites trying to dance or crawl on their backs under a stick and compared his present company with lost, and to him heroic, friends of a better time—Scott Fitzgerald, Thomas Wolfe, James Joyce, John Peale Bishop, and Maxwell Perkins: "I knew it was a bad year from much uncorrelated, as yet, observation, and the sight of the wealthy and the gay crawling on their backs under this stretched cord or wooden stick did nothing to reassure me."[23] His tribute to Marlene Dietrich in 1952 concentrated on his belief that her moral heroism was atypical of the times. Her beauty and talent would allow her to do whatever she wanted, but her self-made standards of conduct and decency, "no less strict than the original ten," caused her, in his admiring view, to live nobly. To live so was, he said, one of the mysteries of the age.[24] The conduct of Senator Joseph McCarthy was, he feared, more typical. During the auto ride from Masinde to Entebbe following his African crashes in late 1953, he speculated on the senator's probable conduct in the jungle where his artificial immunities would not count: "I wondered if without his senatorial immunity he would be vulnerable to the various beasts with whom we had been keeping company."[25]

The standard against which he judged McCarthy—that is, trial by nature, not society—was indicative of Hemingway's basic cultural values. So much has he been identified as expatriate and, as Carlos Baker has called him, "citizen of the world," that Hemingway's essential identity as American, with American dreams and assumptions, has been ignored to the point of denial.[26] He faced the issue in Cuba in his 1956 article "A Situation Report" and emerged with a clear self-identification. "There is the mat-

22. (New York, 1945), p. xiv.
23. (New York, 1948), pp. ix-x.
24. "Tribute to Mamma from Papa Hemingway," *Life*, XXXIII (August 18, 1952), 92-93.
25. "The Christmas Gift," *Look*, XVIII (May 4, 1954), 80.
26. Carlos Baker (ed.), *Hemingway and His Critics* (New York, 1961), pp. 1-18.

ter of being expatriots. It is very difficult to be an expatriot at 35 minutes by air from Key West and less than an hour, by faster plane, from Miami. I never hired out to be a patriot but regularly attend the wars in which my country participates and pay my Federal taxes. An expatriate (I looked up the spelling) is, consequently, a word I never cared for."[27] But his voluntarily living outside his native land all but ten years of his adult life, to be consistent with his claim to American identity, obviously pointed to the need for clarifying his meaning of the term. That clarification he furnished first through his actions and afterwards by his self-explanation. For to Hemingway, being American had a cluster of meanings which derived from his Spenglerian view of the West.

One meaning he evoked in his 1923 reports on Lloyd George's visit to the United States and Canada. To him, the ex-prime minister was a cultural hero, the man who tried to save Europe from itself at the Genoa Conference the year before and had succeeded in keeping the delegates negotiating until he had been called back to England. Only then had the conference collapsed. He admired George as an orator in the tradition of great prophets, one with a "hammered gold" voice and, hearing him speak, thought how it must have been to hear Peter the Hermit call for the Crusades. He was, besides, a fighter and knew the truth of D'Annunzio's statement: " 'Moire non basta.' 'It is not enough to die.' You must survive to win." And like a legendary figure George had survived most of his Genoa Conference antagonists. Walter Rathenau had been shot while riding in a car in Berlin; Vorovsky had been murdered at his dining table in Lausanne; Stambuliski had been hunted down in the fields and shot by his own soldiers; Greek premier Gournaris had been taken from his bed, sick with typhoid, and executed by a firing squad; Lord Northcliffe, his bitterest English rival, had died before George had left office. As for George, "the political sword that will kill him has not yet been forged." He was a man who learned from history, telling Americans that the real founder of the British Empire was George Washington, who forced the British to learn how to forge an empire of free, self-governing commonwealths. But the clearest indication of that meaning—survival—appeared in Hemingway's imagined thoughts for Lloyd George as the states-

27. *Look*, XX (September 4, 1956), 30.

man prepared to leave the "Mauretania" for his 1923 entry into New York: "No one knows what he was thinking about, but one may venture the opinion that as he thought of the world, it must have come into his mind that he, David Lloyd George, is the one great survivor of the wreck of the Old World."[28]

That view of America as the world's second chance had its specific meaning for Hemingway when he saw the frontier as the essential American experience. To him cities were European, and often in the worst sense of machines and swarms of people. The frontier meant nature and a man testing himself against nature. And, to use Frederick Jackson Turner's scheme, Hemingway's frontier was the hunter's and explorer's frontier, sometimes the rancher's, but hardly ever the small farmer's, and never the miner's. For unspoiled nature was the key to unspoiled man. When asked by the editors of *Vogue* in 1938 to write "a geographic profile about some spot in America dear to him," Hemingway wrote of Clark's Fork Valley, Wyoming, and it was the life of the hunter and fisherman he described: catching heavy trout in a stream near the cabin, waiting in the mornings for the sun to warm the stream, taking in the view across the hay and sage meadows to the mountains and noting the deceptively clean lines of the mountains at a distance, the rugged climb up the mountain and the shooting of the ram in the juniper bushes, watching the young rams wait for the older one to get up, tracking the grizzly bear that tore into the cabin every time it was left unoccupied, listening to the elks bugle across the valley in the fall, watching children learn to ride bareback, seeing the pack train against bare trees, and feeling the frosty saddles of winter.[29]

He looked for vital men to fit such a setting and accepted gladly the view of the frontiersman as crude, loud, boastful, resourceful, technically skillful, and morally naïve as the fulfillment of that quest, just as long as, Antaeus-like, he kept in touch with the earth. That his image of the frontiersman responded to popular concepts of the type could be seen in his admiration for such literary frontiersmen as Stewart Edward White's Andy Burnett and A. B. Guthrie's Boone Caudill, latter-day incarnations of Leatherstocking, as indeed, Arthur Mizener has suggested,

28. "Lloyd George Up Early As Big Liner Arrives," *TDS*, October, 5, 1923, p. 14; "Wonderful Voice Is Chief Charm of Lloyd George," *TDS*, October 6, 1923, p. 17.
29. "The Clark's Fork Valley, Wyoming," *Vogue*, XCIII (February 1939), 68, 157.

was Hemingway's Nick Adams.[30] In any case, Hemingway recorded his admiration for the frontier hunter type wherever he met him. In *Green Hills of Africa* he himself acted according to his concept of the type. After the Austrian Kandisky had asked him all kinds of personal questions at their first meeting, then left, Hemingway realized that he had not asked the Austrian anything: "I do not like to ask questions, and where I was brought up it was not polite."[31] He acted according to the primitive braggart tradition associated with frontier hunters when he boasted to his guide that he was "Bwana Fisi, the hyena slaughterer" and killed with his bare hands. Later during the trip, at the fireside after killing his prize kudus, he bragged to another guide of his hunting exploits by naming off his major kills: " 'Simba, Simba, Faro, Nyati, Tendalla, Tendalla' . . . and I named the six cartridges again. 'Lion, lion, rhino, buffalo, kudu, kudu.' "[32] Early and late in his writing career he practiced the frontiersman's art of exaggeration and telling tall tales. In one of his 1920 *Star* articles about camping he said he and his camping partner were "so far out in the tall and unsevered that there wasn't even an echo. An echo would die of lonesomeness out there." In his 1951 *True* article on antelope hunting in Idaho he reported that the old-timer, whose cabin the hunting party used as a base camp, "had been raising the more hardy insects instead of cattle" and had a scent so powerful "you had to keep windward [of him]." He similarly characterized members of the hunting party by their riding and hunting skills. His son Gregory, he said, rode a horse "as though his mother had dropped him into the saddle," and his hunting friend Taylor Williams could kill at 300 yards with a borrowed rifle. He celebrated the party's night on the town in Goldberg as they acted the role of vital barbarians, including breaking one man's jaw in a Saturday night brawl.[33] He also played the role when he sat for Lillian Ross's *New Yorker* portrait. Then he told her that he got along better with animals than with people and had once in Montana lived with a bear, got drunk with him, and considered him a

---

30. *Green Hills of Africa* (New York, 1935), p. 197; Robert M. Manning, "Hemingway in Cuba," *The Atlantic Monthly*, CCXVI (August 1965), 104; Arthur Mizener, *The Sense of Life in the Modern Novel* (Boston, 1964), p. 205.

31. *Green Hills of Africa*, p. 9.

32. *Ibid.*, p. 241.

33. "When You Go Camping Take Lots of Skeeter Dope and Don't Ever Lose It," *TSW*, August 5, 1920, p. 11; "The Shot," *True*, XXVIII (April 1951), 28.

close friend.[34] The role of frontiersman came almost as a cultural memory for him.

Playful or serious, he cited the return to the purifying frontier from the cities of unmanly leisure as fundamental to the vitality of the frontier type. In the Idaho hills, hunting antelope, he remembered: "We had come up from Sun Valley, Idaho, and were a little softened up by the swimming pool, nights in The Ram, and wheels of Ketchum; but the Old-timer fixed that. We rode to the top of the range where we could look over all the way into the Middle Fork of the Salmon, across the loveliest mountains that I know."[35]

In contrast, Hemingway noted and lamented the changes that had come into the American landscape. Edwin Fussell has maintained that the West ceased to exert an influence on the imagination of Americans well before Hemingway's time because the idea survived only while there was an actual frontier.[36] But Hemingway found his pockets of lingering frontier in both Michigan and Illinois during his childhood and considered himself one who had seen the transition from frontier to a world of cities. It was a loss to which he was never able to become reconciled. It still haunted him in 1934 when he wrote:

I came by there [the prairie near Oak Park, along the Des Plaines River] five years ago and where I shot that pheasant there was a hot dog place and filling station and the north prairie, where we hunted snipe in the spring and skated on the sloughs when they froze in the winter, was all a subdivision of mean houses, and in the town, the house where I was born was gone and they had cut down the oak trees and built an apartment house close out against the street. So I was glad I went away from there as soon as I did. Because when you like to shoot and fish you have to move often and always further out and it doesn't make any difference what they do when you are gone.[37]

Similarly, he reported in Africa to Philip Percival during the thirties that frontier values had been abandoned in urbanized America. People were living on borrowings, not savings, were giving up work in natural settings to build more cities, were

34. Lillian Ross, *Portrait of Hemingway* (New York, 1961), p. 27.
35. "The Shot," 28.
36. Edwin Fussell, *Frontier: American Literature and the American West* (Princeton, 1965), p. 24.
37. "Remembering Shooting-Flying," *Esquire*, III (February 1935), 21.

denying the values of work to go on relief.[38] Because of the trend he saw doom for all the places left where men could hunt or fish. In 1934 he wrote that fishermen were lucky to be able to fish for marlins. "This time next year they may have gotten out a law against it."[39] And he saw the special importance of Charles Ritz in 1959 in his having lived at a time when he could fish all the major streams of Europe. "As the world is run now few people can fish as far as Monsieur Charles fishes."[40]

Indeed, for Hemingway the difference between a few people and many was more qualitative than quantitative. Something happened to people in masses to make them unreal and unnatural. "I had loved country all my life," he wrote in *Green Hills of Africa*; "the country was always better than the people. I could only care about people a very few at a time."[41] Even in Paris he limited his contacts to a few people. People, not weather, could spoil a day, and they were always limiters of happiness.[42] He saw overcrowding as a tragic trend in "The Dangerous Summer" when he contrasted his Pamplona of 1959 with that of 1923: "I've written Pamplona once and for keeps. It is all there as it always was except forty thousand tourists have been added. There were not twenty tourists when I first went there nearly four decades ago. Now on some days they say there are close to a hundred thousand in the town."[43] It was consistent with his habits in such a circumstance to retire to the Irati forests during the days of the fiesta to avoid the abrasive fatigue of crowding and to come back to town in time for the bullfights.

But he indicated his feeling more fully in another passage of the African book when he explained that one could sense the reality beyond human institutions only when alone and aware of the secret flow in nature. Then one was willing to "exchange the pleasant, comforting stench of comrades for something you can never feel in any other way than by yourself." His metaphor for the secret force in the world was the Gulf Stream, and the transitory achievements of nations—"all the systems of governments, the richness, the poverty, the martyrdom, the sacrifice

38. *Green Hills of Africa*, p. 191.
39. "Out in the Stream," *Esquire*, II (August 1934), 158.
40. Charles Ritz, *A Fly Fisher's Life* (London, 1959), p. 7.
41. *Green Hills of Africa*, p. 73.
42. *A Moveable Feast*, p. 49.
43. "The Dangerous Summer," *Life*, XLIX (September 12, 1960), 73.

and the venality and the cruelty . . . the palm fronds of our victories, the worn light bulbs of our discoveries and the empty condoms of our great loves"—were the garbage sinking into the always flowing stream.[44]

He saw crowded cities as centers of sophisticated depravity, traps for his morally naïve frontiersman. Hemingway found such an idea congenial from the first. One of his early articles on camping jocularly saw insect pests of the wilderness as a device of the devil to concentrate people in cities "where he could get at them better."[45] More seriously, in *A Moveable Feast* he still saw cities as the lairs of the rich who periodically sortied, shark-like, to snare the vital few whose innocence was the source of their vitality. Such was his view of his own experience after successful publication of *The Sun Also Rises*. The ravagers came out of the cities to find him in the mountains. "Those who attract people by their happiness and their performance are usually inexperienced. They do not know how not to be overrun and how to go away. They do not always learn about the good, the attractive, the charming, the soon-beloved, the generous, the understanding rich who have no bad qualities and who give each day the quality of a festival and who, when they have passed and taken the nourishment they needed, leave everything deader than the roots of any grass Attila's horses' hooves have ever scoured."[46]

That he saw himself as both writer and son of the frontier was clear. He saw this as a potential identification for other American writers—men whose vitality of vision and spirit the rest of the world needed—but at the same time he saw them trapped, as he had been, by the values of the cities. Explaining to Kandisky in Africa why American writers failed to mature their careers and present lives full of distinguished works to the world, he said that writers were destroyed when they accepted the metropolis standards of monetary and critical success as measures of their work instead of maintaining their own uninstitutionalized visions. Instead of recognizing their primitive individual, Antaean vitality as their key strength, they accepted the mass vision, which turned out to be reformist, genteel, economic, political, or any other massive category, but not individual or

44. *Green Hills of Africa*, pp. 148-50.
45. "When You Camp Out Do It Right," *TSW*, June 26, 1920, p. 17.
46. *A Moveable Feast*, p. 208.

natural or vital.[47] Yet if one asked him to explain or analyze what he meant by such terms, he would not, indeed could not, define them. The meanings could hold strong, the feelings keep their authority, only if they were not killed by analytical dissection. The meaning was in action and the instinct that prompted action. He would find the meaning by doing what he sensed should be done, then tell what he had done in terms of actions, not intellectual categories.

If Hemingway's Wordsworthian and Rousseauist ideas on the value of the individual and nature found their culmination in a Spenglerian view of history, his response to such a view followed lines of action which Walter Prescott Webb has described and formalized in *The Great Frontier*. According to Webb, the frontier for Europe and Europeanized America was not only the American West but any of the undeveloped areas remaining in the world, such as Andean South America, backlands Australia, and equatorial Africa. In the larger view of history running from A.D. 1500 to 1900, Europe served as the metropolitan area of the world; and the areas where nature, not man, was the prime factor were the frontier. In areas where men were posed against nature rather than against other men, the basic values were individual resourcefulness, the power to seize rather than to negotiate, the emphasis on ego rather than humility, and the ability to endure an unceasing struggle against passive nature rather than a sharp but decisive struggle against dynamic men as in battles or wars. But most important was the condition in which land was more plentiful than labor and which gave the individual his importance. In Webb's view individualism had a parabolic development during the four centuries after the discovery of the New World frontier but, with the growth of metropolitan populations and the diminishing of land, had given way by the twentieth century to the corporate principle in government, business, and society.[48]

If Hemingway was committed to a pre-twentieth-century cluster of values while living in the twentieth century, he nevertheless sought and found, for himself at least, a way in which he could live by frontier values. That way was to seek the great frontier, to find areas of the world that still resembled the Ameri-

47. *Green Hills of Africa*, pp. 19-24.
48. Walter Prescott Webb, *The Great Frontier* (Boston, 1952), pp. 11-50, 106-26.

can West of the hunter and fisherman, and to refuse to believe that the world frontier had closed because the American West had ceased to exist as a frontier. To the extent that he identified such frontier values as American, he continued, in his own view, to be essentially an American when he could live in a frontier area, wherever its geographical location.

But Hemingway's protest against the encroaching metropolis and his quest of frontiers were not blind and hopeless defiance of the times, not stiff-necked refusal to see the facts. Besides his gun and fishing rod, Hemingway had another weapon for finding and holding his great frontier. It was his concept of reading and writing. It is significant that in several passages he links reading and writing with fishing and hunting as key passions of his life. What we can further see is that for him, such reading and writing were functions of the frontier sense, not the metropolitan mind. He established the link explicitly in his *Esquire* article "Remembering Shooting-Flying:" "When you have loved three things all your life, from the earliest you can remember; to fish, to shoot, and, later, to read; and when, all your life, the necessity to write has been your master, you learn to remember and when you think back you remember more fishing and shooting and reading than anything else and that is pleasure."[49] But to him not all reading was a function of the frontier sense nor certainly were all writers capable of understanding the frontier mind. When he talked with Kandisky at the East African camp and defended hunting as a function of the artist, he also refrained, he said, from disillusioning the Austrian about all those brilliant literary people he believed in back in the metropolises of Paris and Berlin.[50]

The reading Hemingway looked to as a function of the frontier was the kind that transcended time, that let one feel "the way it was" when the time in the reading was that of frontiers. He reported in *Green Hills of Africa*:

. . . Russia of the time of our Civil War . . . [was] as real as . . . Michigan or the prairie north of town and the woods around Evans's game farm. . . .

. . . I still had the Sevastopol book of Tolstoi and in the same volume I was reading a story called "The Cossacks" that was very

49. "Remembering Shooting-Flying," 21.
50. *Green Hills of Africa*, pp. 7-8, 16-19.

good. In it were the summer heat, the mosquitoes, the feel of the forest in the different seasons, and that river that the Tartars crossed, raiding, and I was living in that Russia again.

. . . For we have been there in the books and out of the books— and where we go, if we are any good, there you can go as we have been. A country, finally, erodes and the dust blows away, the people all die and none of them were of any importance permanently, except those who practiced the arts. . . . A thousand years makes economics silly and a work of art endures forever, but it is very difficult to do and now it is not fashionable. . . . So I would go on reading about the river that the Tartars came across raiding, and the drunken old hunter and the girl and how it was then in the different seasons.[51]

Reading then was, like hunting and fishing, a way of finding that time beyond time by finding the secret current of nature. Back of Hemingway's social thought was that long-used stream-flow-ing-into-the-sea metaphor for time and timelessness, but the dif-ference was that the stream—the Gulf Stream—was already in the sea, and the sea was not a static realm but the vital place where all the streams converged and flowed together.

Hemingway's quest for the great frontier took him first to Paris. That he should head for the virtual center of the great metropolis seems contradictory to the purpose of the quest, but in light of his growing awareness of art as a frontier, his move was not incomprehensible. Indeed, if Malcolm Cowley's inter-pretation is right, Europe was for American exiles of the twenties the newer prairie of the mind, the place where Americans could better learn about being American than they could in their na-tive land.[52] This paradox opened itself to Hemingway, as he recorded in his memoir of Paris, that after a thorough firsthand experience one knew a place better while away from it and saw it clearly enough to give it that extra dimension available in writing: "Maybe away from Paris I could write about Paris as in Paris I could write about Michigan."[53] But the resemblance between Paris, or Europe in general, and the frontier was not all symbolic or paradoxical. There were, in fact, pockets of fron-tier conditions in Europe better preserved than in exploited America. Hemingway wrote for the Toronto *Star* that, contrary to the popular conception of Europe as overcrowded and over-

51. *Ibid.*, pp. 108-9.
52. Malcolm Cowley, *Exile's Return* (New York, 1956), pp. 79, 83-84.
53. *A Moveable Feast*, p. 7.

hunted, Europe contained more game animals in reach of the cities than did Canada; there were more dangerous big game animals within twenty miles of Paris than within twenty miles of Toronto. While bears, boars, and wolves were scarce in Ontario, they flourished in Europe. The Black Forest in Germany had excellent deer hunting, he reported, and the Rhine area provided some of the best duck, quail, plover, and pheasant shooting he had ever seen. Switzerland had hunting for chamois and game birds; Italy had excellent fox hunting near Milan, bear hunting in the Abruzzi, and wolf hunting on the Roman Campagna. The reason for continued good hunting in Europe while game in most parts of Canada and the United States were exterminated, he explained, was that European governments owned and protected forests and enforced closed seasons. The result was not only abundance of game but great areas of virgin and rebuilt forests—a strong contrast with American exploitation of nature. "To-day there is hardly a patch of virgin timber in the upper peninsula of Michigan. . . . But France will always be a game country. For there are forests in France that were there in Caesar's time. More important still, there are now forests in France that were not there in Napoleon's time. Even more important, there will be new forests, a hundred years from now, where to-day M. Poincaré has looked on only scarred hillsides. And all the forests will be full of game."[54] The implicit call for the metropolis to save remaining frontiers was not merely a sophisticated complication of the metropolis-frontier dialectic. It was another way in which artful action achieved the frontier condition for the twentieth century.

Hemingway's search for the great frontier took him beyond Paris. As a grazing area for the mind, Paris both fed and poisoned Hemingway and his friends. The site of personal and aesthetic discoveries, of long literary talks and many beers with "Chink" Dorman-Smith after Paris boxing events, of lonely but honest encounters with his self-faith and talent in his writing room, Paris was also the place where marriages came apart and mentors and protégés quarreled. It was a place of first literary successes but a trap also, tempting one to repeat his lessons learned in success rather than prompting him to go on to different trials.

54. "More Game to Shoot in Crowded Europe Than in Ontario," *TSW*, November 3, 1923, p. 20.

For the frontier, like art, involved change as well as continuity, variety as well as pattern. As he noted in "A Paris Letter" of 1934, Paris was a place to outgrow: "It was a fine place to be quite young in and it is a necessary part of a man's education. We all loved it once and we lie if we say we didn't. But she is like a mistress who does not grow old and she has other lovers now. She was old to start with but we did not know it then. We thought she was just older than we were, and that was attractive then. . . . But me, I now love something else. And if I fight, I fight for something else."[55] And he saw Paris, like New York, discredited by the world depression. The place to miss that depression was on the ranch in Montana, or the retreat at Piggott, Arkansas, or in Key West or the Dry Tortugas or East Africa. So he wrote in *Green Hills of Africa* that the pattern of the artist-frontiersman was to outgrow some countries and go on to others.[56]

Spain was his next frontier. There were three reasons for it to be so. One was that the country was like that in the American West. The hills and plateaus of Castile, Aragon, and Andalusia suggested to Hemingway the mountains of Wyoming and Montana; and the forest of the Irati was always that forest remembered from childhood, whether it was real in Michigan or remembered from books.[57] The second reason was that his Spain was bullfighting Spain, and the raising and handling of bulls was like a return to the American ranching frontier. Spanish bulls were branded and tested on the range as were American range cattle. But most important, the bulls were a link with the ancient and primitively vital past. They were the embodiment of primeval strength kept intact well into the twentieth century. "The fighting bull is to the domestic bull as the wolf is to the dog. . . . Bulls for the ring are wild animals. They are bred from a strain that comes down in direct descent from the wild bulls that ranged over the Peninsula and they are bred on ranches with the thousands of acres of range where they live as free ranging animals."[58]

But because bullfighting was finally an institution that corrupted many men and because Spanish governments altered mountains and rivers, Spain was a frontier also to outgrow. As

55. "A Paris Letter," 156.
56. *Green Hills of Africa*, p. 280.
57. *Death in the Afternoon* (New York, 1932), p. 274.
58. *Ibid.*, p. 105.

he noted in the closing chapter of *Death in the Afternoon*, the wildness was bred out of the bulls and the heroism out of the matadors. And as for the terrain, Spaniards cut down the Irati forests as the lumbermen had those of Michigan. "They ran logs down the river and they killed the fish; or in Galicia they bombed and poisoned them; results the same; so in the end it's just like home except for the yellow gorse on the high meadows and the thin rain."[59]

Africa came closer to Hemingway's idea of the American frontier. The terrain in which he hunted was more immediately identifiable with that of the American West than Spanish country had been, perhaps because Hemingway's West was the hunter's West more than the rancher's. In "a.d. in Africa" he compared Tanganyika to country in Nebraska, Wyoming and Montana, and to New England orchard country, but still teeming with game—over three million wildebeeste, he estimated.[60] In "Safari" he thought of the Wyoming country west of Cheyenne when he saw the Kenya hills blue with timbered slopes, and saw Nairobi, during the days of the Mau Maus, when many whites carried sidearms, as consciously in imitation of frontier Tombstone, Arizona.[61] As he reported his hunting in *Green Hills of Africa*, the slopes on which he hunted kudu were like the deer slopes of Timber Creek in Wyoming. The discovery of the back country where both kudu and sable were hiding was, he said, like finding the river he had been told about as a child—"a river no one had ever fished out on the huckleberry plains beyond the Sturgeon and the Pigeon."[62]

Beyond the resemblances of terrain, Africa's attraction in Hemingway's eyes was its clearer link with primal time and the springs of vitality. "It was a new country to us," he wrote in *Green Hills of Africa*, "but it had the marks of the oldest countries. . . . The country was so much like Aragon that I could not believe that we were not in Spain." Looking at a kudu bull's track in the grass, he saw it imaginatively as the track of its prehistoric predecessors: "I thought that we had mammoths too, a long time ago, and when they travelled through the hills in southern Illinois they made these same tracks. It was just that

59. *Ibid.*, p. 274.
60. "a.d. in Africa," *Esquire*, I (April 1934), 19.
61. "Safari," *Look*, XVIII (January 26, 1954), 20.
62. *Green Hills of Africa*, pp. 92, 210.

we were an older country in America and the biggest game was gone."[63] A little later on arriving in kudu hunting areas, he found the country like something out of a primeval dream. "It was a country to wake from, happy to have had the dream. . . . This was a virgin country, an un-hunted pocket in the million miles of bloody Africa." And in this country he found a people suitable to it—the tall, friendly, noble Masai.[64]

Africa's further meaning was the meaning Hemingway had seen in America when he interviewed Lloyd George on the "Mauretania." Africa physically was among the oldest of worlds, but culturally, the New World of the twentieth century. His son Patrick, who became a game ranger and safari guide in East Africa, interpreted his father's great frontier concept succinctly: "I know what appealed to my father about Africa. . . . We were given a continent to play with in America, and in some respects it hasn't turned out the way we hoped. The charm of Africa is that we've been given a second chance."[65]

Hemingway himself explained his feeling in *Green Hills of Africa*. Riding back from the kudu and sable country to the base camp, he saw the land in the context of history, and the vision was a Splengerian view of the dry death of nations and a movement toward other fertile frontiers:

A continent ages quickly once we come. The natives live in harmony with it. But the foreigner destroys, cuts down the trees, drains the water, so that the water supply is altered and in a short time the soil, once the sod is turned under, is cropped out, and, next, it starts to blow away as it has blown away in every old country and as I had seen it start to blow in Canada. The earth gets tired of being exploited. A country wears out quickly unless man puts back in it all his residue and that of all his beasts. When he quits using beasts and uses machines, the earth defeats him quickly. The machine can't reproduce, nor does it fertilize the soil, and it eats what he cannot raise. A country was made to be as we found it. We are the intruders and after we are dead we may have ruined it but it will still be there and we don't know what the next changes are. I suppose they all end up like Mongolia.[66]

63. *Ibid.*, p. 250.
64. *Ibid.*, pp. 217-19.
65. *Time*, LXXXVI (July 9, 1965), 41.
66. *Green Hills of Africa*, pp. 284-85.

If the hunter-writer was to be the culture hero of Hemingway's saving frontier, he sought to provide a rationale for that hero, and he tried to cite his own feelings as the basis for that rationale. His *Esquire* article "Remembering Shooting-Flying" went part of the way toward such an explanation. The instinct to hunt, he believed, was a continuing, if repressed, drive in men. In some it had been completely sublimated; in others it was still very much alive, and to him they were the vital ones for the culture. Although he professed no regard for metaphysics, he also argued the teleological point that in the scheme of things, the purpose of existence for game was completed in the hunter's instinct: "I think they were all made to shoot because if they were not why did they give them that whirr of wings that moves you suddenly more than any love of country? . . . Why does the curlew have that voice, and who thought up the plover's call, which takes the place of noise of wings, to give us that catharsis wing shooting has given to men since they stopped flying hawks and took to fowling pieces? I think they were made to shoot and some of us were made to shoot them. . . ."[67] Not only the sound of wings, but the taste of meat, he maintained, evoked the hunter's instinct. In the introduction to François Sommer's *Man and Beast in Africa,* he saw the hunter's instinct as a complement to man's love for the animals worthy of being hunted. It is no hypocrisy to hunt animals and love them, he insisted. To hunt is an instinct on the same order as the instinct to worship and one that can easily become the instinct to worship. "It would be a strange thing if people with hunting in their blood for many hundreds of years would suddenly be without that taste. But it is a taste and a hunger too, that can be satisfied or partially satisfied. . . . In each person the changes come in a different way. There is no sudden thing such as happened to Saint Paul or Saint Ignatius Loyola for anyone who tries to kill cleanly and never to excess." Rather the hunter follows a course of emotion through his hunting life, at seventeen wanting to kill the grizzly bear but feeling happier about killing a boar at forty-five or shooting high-flying pheasants at a more advanced age.[68] He had imagined the basis for such an identification of hunter and hunted, however, during the thirties. When he had

67. "Remembering Shooting-Flying," 152.
68. François Sommer, *Man and Beast in Africa* (London, 1953), p. 6.

been in a Billings, Montana, hospital for weeks, unable to rest or sleep because of the pain from an arm broken in an auto crash, he had come to an imaginative identification with animals hit in the bone, and he vicariously experienced what a bull elk felt when hit by a bullet. Out of the experience came the insight that "what I was going through was a punishment for all hunters" and the feeling that he had earned the right to hunt. Who would give or acknowledge that right was also apparently a religious question, for some mover of events seemed implicit in his observation that "I did nothing that was not done to me."[69]

If Hemingway's mystique of the hunter bordered on some kind of primitive religious feeling, that tendency was hardly denied by his imagined identification with other certifiably primitive hunters. His irregular welts and scars, trophies from wars and hunts, were, he felt, somehow indication of essential kinship with his bearer and tracker Droopy, whose more formal tattoos and tribal scars put him in the tradition of great hunters. And during the later running of the kudu and sable, he felt the unanimity of impulse and instinct that made the hunters do the right things without his calling signals. "I was thinking all the country in the world is the same country and all hunters are the same people."[70] But he knew the metropolitan mind could not understand that mystique. Many Americans, he noted, did not enjoy hunting or fishing and, because they had only "the values they brought with them from the downs they lived in to the towns they live in now," they begrudged the pleasures of those who did find fulfillment in those actions. They were, he observed, the true four-letter people.[71] He noted later that the hunter's experience was incommunicable and incredible, that "nobody ever believes shooting stories ever, and the pleasure has been in the run and trying to hold your heart in when you swing and hold your breath, sweet and clean, and swing ahead and squeeze off lightly with the swing."[72]

So little, indeed, was the hunter's code communicable or capable of being kept pure that Hemingway had to acknowledge that the African and American hunting frontiers were being ruined by too many pseudo-hunters and by transformation of the hunt

69. *Green Hills of Africa*, p. 148.
70. *Ibid.*, pp. 53, 249.
71. "He Who Gets Slap Happy," *Esquire*, IV (August 1935), 19.
72. "The Shot," 27.

into either a massacre or a guided tour. He indicated his disgust at practices by "certain White Hunters in Kenya and
Tanganyika," as detailed by François Sommer, that made safaris
the travesty of a hunt, but noted with satisfaction that the frontier sometimes had its animistic revenge. Several of the worst
offenders had appropriately been killed by the overhunted game.[73]
In Idaho he saw the link between war and a frontierless world.
Where hunting areas became overcrowded, as in Idaho, hunting
conditions resembled warlike conditions, and hunters were more
likely to hit other hunters than to hit game. Indeed, they were
likely to work around to shooting at each other as the frustrations of hunting in overcrowded areas became too great.[74] In
East Africa again in 1953 Hemingway explained why he thought
study of the remaining animals took precedence over study of
the Mau Maus. The animals and hunting were on their way out,
but people and wars were the condition of the future.[75]

Hemingway's next frontier was Cuba. He had led scouting
parties into the area during the thirties while maintaining Key
West as his home base but did not fully settle on Cuba as the
site of his next stand until just before the Second World War.
He explained the meaning of Cuba for himself in "A Situation
Report." It was still an open territory for writing and fishing
and hunting. He explained how it was still unclaimed literary
territory when he chronicled his own literary migrations. "Born
in Cook County, Illinois, I early ceded the territory as writer
to Mr. Carl Sandburg, who had taken it over anyway, and to
Mr. James Farrell and to Mr. Nelson Algren when they came of
age. They have ruled it very well and I have no complaints. . . .
It was possible to stake out a few claims in other places, and I
am glad that not all of these have been jumped. One of these
claims is here."[76]

Explanation of his fishing and hunting claims for Cuba had
been made during the thirties and forties. Though he spoke of
Cuba as an unjumped claim, the real scene was the Gulf Stream.
Asked by a hunter friend why he fished instead of going after
still bigger game such as the elephant, he replied that hunting
elephants was like taking a mouthful of lye water, so strong it

73. Sommer, p. 5.
74. "The Shot," 27.
75. "Safari," 20.
76. "A Situation Report," *Look*, XX (September 4, 1956), 30.

ruined one's taste for subtler pleasures. But more important, "the Gulf Stream and the other ocean currents are the last wild country there is left." And the sea better communicated its primal secrets than did the land: "The sea is the same as it has been since before men ever went on it in boats." While the elephant was awesome, he was known. The sea, though, had its creatures that were yet to be discovered, and its unexplored dimensions included depth as well as breadth: "Because the Gulf Stream is an unexploited country, only the very fringe of it ever being fished, and then only at a dozen places in thousands of miles of current, no one knows what fish live in it, or how great size they reach or what age, or even what kinds of fish and animals live in it at different depths."[77] He confirmed that view in numerous subsequent statements. In 1949 he wrote that having "the great, deep blue river" thirty minutes from his door was the biggest reason for living in Cuba.[78] He told Robert Manning, "It's the last free place there is, the sea. Even Africa's about gone; it's at war, and that's going to go on for a very long time."[79]

That he still tended to see Cuban fishing as an echo of the original American frontier was evident in his repeated analogy between plunging fish and bucking horses. He wrote in *Esquire* in 1936 that a marlin swimming deep had to be convinced and brought to boat "by the same system you break a wild horse"; similarly in *Holiday* in 1949 he wrote that the blue marlin was "as strong as a horse. Treat him like a horse."[80] His use of the fish-horse analogy could not be wholly explained by his reliance on a masculine audience; if *Esquire* aimed at men, *Holiday* was directed at the general reader. In Hemingway's mind the analogy was implicit in the subject.

As with Africa, however, Cuba and the Gulf Stream, in Hemingway's eyes, became overcrowded. The unknown was still in the deeps, but the surface was taken over by sport fishermen who made fishing tournaments trials of equipment engineering rather than of skill, endurance, and luck. The cost of such rigs, he lamented, had made tournament fishing a "social sport" that excluded fishermen of merit. As in African big game hunting,

77. "On the Blue Water," *Esquire*, V (April 1936), 31.
78. "The Great Blue River," *Holiday*, XVI (July 1949), 61. *See also* "A Situation Report," 26.
79. "Hemingway in Cuba," 104-5.
80. "On the Blue Water," 184; "The Great Blue River," 95.

Gulf and Atlantic big game fishing was also being ruined by the bad faith and poor skill of enthusiasts. Too many hooked fish were allowed to get away with severe wounds that would kill them or make them prey of sharks. The result, he saw, was a drop in size and number of fish caught in Cuban and Bahaman waters. While in the thirties he had wondered if laws would deny fishermen their frontier, Hemingway in the forties and fifties advocated international action to close seasons on game fish, much in the way he had admired European forest and game laws in the twenties. Whether such a turn of thinking signified his abandonment of the free frontier idea or whether it was a way of reconciling a diminished frontier with an overcrowded century, Hemingway had personally and intellectually run out of frontiers.[81]

It was significant how the search for frontiers ended. Cuba too became over crowded. Mary Hemingway, in her account of "Lost Resorts: Havana," told how the good restaurants, especially the El Pacifico, in Havana had declined in cuisine as the tourists came.[82] But the overcrowding received its ultimate expression in the war—the Cuban Revolution—that superseded hunting or fishing. Hemingway left Cuba in 1960 after seeing game fishing ceremonially corrupted when Maximum Leader Castro won the spring marlin tournament with the unofficial aid of an insular champion and other manipulations of the fishing gear.[83] His return to Idaho was a retreat to a token frontier. As with his spiritual redskin defenders of the frontier, there was nowhere to go but back to the reservation.

The importance of recognizing the direction of Hemingway's cultural thought is not in finding that such thinking existed but in recognizing that it was Hemingway's thinking. Neither unusual nor extraordinary, it nevertheless provided him with a framework for his actions, decisions, and prejudices. A combination of popularized assumptions from the Pastoralists, Wordsworth, Freud, and Spengler, and of relationships systematically

81. S. Kip Farrington, Jr., *Atlantic Game Fishing* (New York, 1937), pp. xxi-xxii; "Cuban Fishing," *Game Fish of the World*, ed. Brian Vesey-Fitzgerald and Francesca Lamonte (New York, 1949), p. 158; Van Campen Heilner, *Salt Water Fishing* (New York, 1953), pp. vii-viii.

82. *Saturday Review*, LXVIII (January 2, 1965), 74.

83. Leicester Hemingway, *My Brother, Ernest Hemingway* (Cleveland, 1962), p. 280.

described by Frederick Jackson Turner and Walter Prescott Webb, Hemingway's cultural ideology was not a system but a faith. Neither provable nor disprovable, it depended for its authority on its emotional convincingness; and Hemingway, finding it suitable to his background and his temperament, believed it valid. In the long view of his cultural thinking, Hemingway's participation in the Spanish Civil War and his apparent reconciliation to a collectivist society—so much heralded by Marxist critics after 1937—seems to have been an appeal to the metropolis to preserve some pockets of frontier conditions. Except for scale it was the sort of thing that the French game and forest laws represented, or the game and fish laws he advocated in Africa and Cuba. He seemed to believe in the innoculation principle of resistance to the metropolis.

Hemingway's identification of the world's overpopulation problem was ahead of his time, though his reason for concern was more emotional than ecological. While most cultural and social commentators of the thirties were concerned with the conflict of classes and the rise of corporate states, he, except for the 1937-1944 period, saw all states, whether Fascist or Republican, as metropolises, and therefore the enemy of the frontier. His was not a Malthusian dilemma but a fear that too many people would block off the source of vitality, not use it up. As he saw later in Africa, the issue was not British versus Mau Mau or colonialist versus nationalist or white versus black but the problem of keeping the way open to the primal source of emotional energy—the wilderness.

Like the Marxists, though for a different reason, he saw a social value for literature. It was a way of maintaining the freshness of frontier vitality, not of teaching the value of collective man; "Where we go, if we are any good, there you can go as we have been," he wrote as both frontiersman and author in *Green Hills of Africa*. It was his Arminian modification of an otherwise Calvinist view of personality. Only those lucky enough to have some kind of frontier background could know the vitality of the frontier and seek the saving frontier. And only a few were chosen. Others could enter the elect if they read of the frontier and learned "how it was." But most metropolis dwellers, he noted in an early essay, would briefly sense their loss of something vital as the seasons changed, look at the spring sky, and walk on home from the car line. But he wrote for those "beloved of the Red Gods" who wanted more.[84]

If his notion of the sources of vitality was too special for those not of his temperament to find credible, it nevertheless provided a coherent and emotionally consistent response to the world for some. It was important, moreover, because it was translatable into a creative vision of the century, one that depended on fictional presentation, not argument, for its persuasiveness. As long as such thinking explained the actions of his created people or his own actions, Hemingway was content. He presented no schemes for all people. He didn't want them crowding his frontier.

84. "Are You All Set for Trout?" *TSW*, April 10, 1920, p. 11.

VIII. Hemingway's Political Thought

Mourner of Lost Revolutions

"I AM WITHOUT POLITICS," SAID HEMINGWAY'S OLD MAN AT THE
Ebro bridge, and to many readers of Hemingway that fictional
statement has been the epitome of his political awareness, whether
spoken from behind the mask of fiction or said in his own right.
But in spite of such frequent assertions as those by Lionel Trill-
ing and Alvah Bessie that Hemingway lacked politics, his journalism and essays indicate a considerable amount of political
thought and, beyond that, a coherent political view of twentieth-
century events. An understanding of that political vision provides not only insight into the thinking behind a surprising
amount of Hemingway's fiction but also a more dynamic view
of Hemingway's political motives than is generally suspected.

One must recognize that Hemingway's thinking was characteristically pragmatic. It either led to action or explained acts already carried out. In cultural and aesthetic matters it generally sought to explain and justify his own past accomplishments—to tell why he lived in Paris or Spain or Africa and why he hunted and fished or what he had tried to do in his writings. His political thinking was likewise pragmatic, but it more frequently referred to current and future events and sought to prompt others to action. Hemingway's basic political thought was, in short, propagandistic, and as propagandist he sought to carry out the two basic functions of that art—to convince readers by implication or outright denunciation that existing conditions were intolerable and to recommend specific solutions for these conditions.

Hemingway's political reporting and commentary ran from the beginning of his career to the mid 1940's but did not, so far as can be determined, continue significantly beyond that point. To see what he wrote on politics is to see why he stopped at that point. During the intervening twenty-five years, however, he covered a large part of world political action in his reporting: local politics in Chicago and Toronto, European international politics at the Genoa, Mudania, and Lausanne conferences, French politics particularly concerning Poincaré's occupation of the Ruhr, Italian politics and the rise of Benito Mussolini, American New Deal politics, the domestic political backgrounds of the Spanish Civil War, Anglo-Fascist responses to the war in Spain, and in a very general way, early United Nations politics. Throughout his reporting three themes informed his writing, though they were not of equal importance or on the same level of significance. The key theme was Hemingway's belief in the world's readiness for revolution. "The world was much closer to revolution in the years after the war than it is now," he wrote in 1934:

In those days we who believed in it, looked for it at any time, expected it, hoped for it—for it was the logical thing. But everywhere it came it was aborted. For a long time I could not understand it, but finally I figured it out. If you study history you will see that there can never be a Communist revolution without, first, a complete military debacle. You have to see what happens in a military debacle to understand this. It [*sic*] is something so utterly complete in its disillusion about the system that has put them into this, in its destruction and purging away of all the existing standards, faiths, and loyalties, when the war is being fought by a conscript army, that it is the necessary catharsis before revolution.[1]

What aborted the expected revolution, he wrote, was the spurious nationalism generated by wartime politicians and carried over into the postwar period until it culminated in Fascism. His sad summing-up of the course of revolutions in *Green Hills of Africa* was that "They're beautiful. Really. For quite a while. Then they go bad."[2]

The second theme stood in support of the first and helped explain the goal of revolution. Riding the Simplon-Orient express across the Balkans to cover the Greco-Turkish crises in 1922, Hemingway studied the lush Balkan countryside across which he was riding, thought how the peasants must love such a land, and recognized in the light of Balkan history that no peace would come to that part of the world while one people held the land of another.[3] It was a conviction he would repeat often. He saw the Spanish Civil War later as the peasants' attempt to regain and use land kept from them for centuries by land-holding juntas, and he dramatized in *The Spanish Earth* the peasants' fierce satisfaction as they irrigated and tilled lands long denied them. In *Men at War* he digressed from strictly military advice to comment on political goals of the war, noting that no lasting peace would result from the fighting "until *all lands* where the people are ruled, exploited and governed by any government whatsoever against their consent are given their freedom."[4]

The third theme was more attitude than policy, but it permeated Hemingway's political writing widely and deeply. With a few exceptions he distrusted politicians. If there is any basis in critics' claims that Hemingway was politically naïve, its surest ground is at this point. For him, politician was the opposite of soldier, hunter, writer, or honest man, and one must wonder how he expected revolutions to resolve or lands to achieve self-determination without politicians. But in his public and fictional voices Hemingway often retold his distrust. His comment in the *Ken* essay "Call for Greatness" was typical: "One thing you have learned above all others in the last 15 months is that when a

1. "Old Newsman Writes," *Esquire*, II (December 1934), 25.
2. (New York, 1935), p. 192.
3. "Balkans Look Like Ontario: A Picture of Peace, Not War," *TDS*, October 16, 1922, p. 13.
4. *Men at War* (New York, 1942), p. xxiv.

politician cries you are bitched. When they, the big leaders, start to cry and say how unjust and terrible it is but what can we do, our hands are tied, you know just where you stand. They cry for history. But they act to hold their jobs. I think the crying relieves them and they feel that, in a way, they have done a duty. They know how right they were, how good their hearts were, and for a minute they see themselves as statesmen and as historic figures, not as pitiful, conniving, frightened people that they really are."[5] To him, the worst feature of the politicians thus was not their expediency or outright dishonesty, but their ability to delude themselves. Like many of his pitiable fictional persons, they failed to distinguish what they really felt from what they were supposed to feel.

Details of aborted revolutions were the stuff of Hemingway's political reporting and commentary during the twenties and thirties. He witnessed the politics that lost the peace, continued the war—to reverse von Clausewitz—by means of policy, and raised the Fascist dictators who brought finally not revolution but more national wars. In Italy, he noted in his key essay "Old Newsman Writes," the country was ready for revolution after the Caporetto disaster, but the 1918 Piave offensive gave the nationalists—the patriots—enough of a victory that they could shout down the Caporetto defeat and blunt the disgust that would feed the revolution. In Germany and Austria, because the army was never fully discredited, the state kept some vestiges of authority and thwarted the revolution by allowing assassination of such liberals as Karl Leibnecht and Rosa Luxembourg. France too was ready for revolution in 1917 after the failure of the Chemin des Dames offensive, he wrote, but Clemenceau held on to power until American armies came to the trenches. To do so he had to execute most of the liberals in the government and the army, and send the Garde Républicaine against his old veterans. Hemingway saw Clemenceau's betrayal of his old veterans as a classic act of the revolution-aborting politicians:

Because they ended up as winners, revolution was doomed in France and anybody who saw, on Clemenceau's orders, the Garde Républicaine, with their shining breastplates, their horse-hair plumes, and those high-chested, big-hoofed, well-shod horses, charge and ride down the parade of mutilated war veterans who were confident the Old

5. *Ken*, II (July 14, 1938), 23.

Man would never do anything to them, his poilus that he loved, and saw the slashing sabers, the start of the gallop, then the smashed wheel chairs, men scattered on the streets unable to run, the broken crutches, the blood and brains on the cobble-stones, the iron-shod hooves striking sparks from the stones but making a different sound when they rode over legless, armless men, while the crowd ran; nobody who saw that could be expected to think something new was happening when Hoover had the troops disperse the bonus army.[6]

As Hemingway was not in France in 1917 to see the revolution broken, he had to get his details from others. But his conviction was as strong as his report vivid, and in 1934 he had a clear vision of how it had all been.

Hemingway's reports on the 1922 World Economic Conference at Genoa for the *Toronto Daily Star* were, however, made on observed events, and their meaning for him was clear. The war had not stopped. It had only shifted to the conference table. He noted that in the conference hall there were a statue of Columbus and a plaque containing a quotation from Machiavelli. The delegates acted as though Machiavelli's book were a text for the conference and as though Columbus' work had been only to give them more lands to haggle over.[7] The opening day's action was in keeping with the atmosphere. At the close of an apparently routine session, France's Louis Barthou rose to shock the delegates with a denunciation of Russia's disarmament proposal and threatened to walk out of the meeting. Tchitcherin hissed his answer, wrote Hemingway, and retorted that Russia was acting in accordance with Premier Briand's Washington statements. Lloyd George rose to conciliate and Italy's Premier Facta, moderator of the conference, hurriedly adjourned the session. On the second day Tchitcherin rose to challenge the right of Japan, an Eastern power, to participate in a conference on European affairs, but Count Ishii replied that Japan would participate regardless of Russian objections. Only days later a Russo-German treaty was announced, and the other nations' ensuing denunciations of the treaty, Hemingway cabled, all struck the note of "German Machiavellianism" again. French and Belgian delegations protested admission of Russia and Germany to the economics committee. So the Genoa conference went on from crisis

6. "Old Newsman Writers," 25-26.
7. "Two Russian Girls Best Looking at Genoa Parley," *TDS*, April 24, 1922, p. 1.

to crisis until Lloyd George could no longer conciliate, and the conference finally became the shambles it had promised to become. Indeed, the proceedings became so absurd that before he left Genoa, Hemingway was sending back stories on anything but the conference—stories on the betting craze at Genoa night clubs, on the eccentric journalists present, and on the hazards of hotel life in the conference city.[8]

Because Hemingway's reporting of the Lausanne Conference was done without by-line for the International News Service and Universal News Service, we have no contemporary version of his journalistic response to events there, but he wrote years later in his *Esquire* article "The Malady of Power" that the conference to work out terms for the Greco-Turkish peace was almost wrecked by Lord Curzon's pride in power when he referred to the Turkish delegates as Anatolian peasants. It was to Hemingway another evidence of the mentality politicians demonstrated as they tried to thwart revolutions.[9]

His *Star* reports on the French occupation of the Ruhr were, however, Hemingway's fullest initiation into the ways of national politics and one of his clearest insights on the cost to France of a lost revolution. France, he observed in the first of ten articles on the Ruhr occupation and its effects, had refused to make a peace without victory in 1917. Six years later she had victory without peace. Its liberal bloc having been purged by Clemenceau during the war, the French Chamber of Deputies was dominated by the ultra-conservative "bloc national," the wartime coalition of iron, steel, and vintner interests in combination with veterans, royalists, and careerists. Destined to stay in power at least two more years, the bloc was heavily involved in the "devastated areas" scheme whereby numerous uninvestigated repairs and payments were made to claimants and charged off to the German reparations debt. So heavily were the bloc interests committed to full payment of the German debt, in order to cover the "devastated areas" costs and avoid investigations of graft, that they sacrificed Premier Aristide Briand when he offered to reduce reparations payments to get a defense pact. Indeed, wrote Hem-

---

8. "World Economics Conference Opens in Genoa, Tchitcherin Speaks," *TDS*, April 10, 1922, p. 1; "Barthou, Like a Smith Brother, Crosses Hissing Tchitcherin," *TDS*, April 24, 1922, p. 2; "Regarded by Allies as German Cunning," *TDS*, April 18, 1922, p. 1.

9. *Esquire*, IV (November 1935), 198-99.

ingway, the bloc had moved Briand out of power even before he could return to Paris with the proposed pact.[10]

In the second article of the series, "French Royalist Party Most Solidly Organized," Hemingway explained further how Premier Raymond Poincaré, Briand's successor, was maneuvered into the position of having to occupy the Ruhr, a move he had called absurd nine months earlier. But in the meantime Poincaré had come under the influence of the Royalists, suddenly the strongest party of the bloc; and while Poincaré sat in the chief minister's seat, Leon Daudet, head of the Royalists, shook his finger at him and declared, "France will do this, France will do that." Why the sudden ascendancy of Royalist influence? Hemingway asked. His answer suggested two causes. One was the mysterious resurgence of the Fascist-like Camelots du Roi, Royalist bullies who protected and promoted such Royalist enterprises as the party paper *L'Action Française* and who made depredatory sorties into the Socialist-dominated Montmarte district. The second was the probability that in spite of his denials Poincaré was the victim of some Royalist holding an incriminating dossier against him. The result was that Poincaré accepted the Royalist stand on German reparations. The Royalists wanted primarily a weakened Germany and proposed to use the impossibly high reparations costs as a way of occupying part of Germany "until the reparations are paid."[11]

In subsequent articles of the series Hemingway pointed out the full absurdity of such counterrevolutionary politics. The French occupied the Ruhr ostensibly to insure payment of reparations, but their costs of maintaining an occupying army and paying miners double wages for working in an area where they were subject to attack from German mobs had made the venture a money-losing one. The cost of a ton of Ruhr coal had doubled, Hemingway observed, and the only thing that saved the French from greater loss was their failure to get more coal out of the Ruhr. The results in Germany, Hemingway noted after his tour through neighboring provinces, were riots, hate, inflated currency, and starvation for many caught between fixed incomes and inflation. In France the result was only minor inflation but major

10. "A Victory Without Peace Forced the French to Undertake the Occupation of the Ruhr," *TDS*, April 14, 1923, p. 4.
11. *TDS*, April 18, 1923, pp. 1, 4.

deception. The government in fact kept much of the mess out of the papers by buying up the news columns of the major papers and printing only its version of events. A standard item in the French government budget, Hemingway explained—as indeed for many European governments—was the cost of printing the goverment's version of the news; it was so much the major advertiser in French newspapers that no one considered it chic anymore to buy regular advertising space.[12]

To make sure readers took a disapproving view of the conferences and other political deceptions, Hemingway evaluated politics by citing personal characteristics of the politicians, almost all of which were belittling or depreciative. It was his version of the *argumentum ad hominem*. Significant numbers of his articles in the *Toronto Daily Star* during the Genoa and Lausanne conferences were outright personality reviews, and key portions of his Ruhr articles dealt with evaluative personal details of the politicians involved. In a few cases he wrote appreciative portraits. Lloyd George, he noted, was the only statesman who "brought any magic with him" to the Genoa parley, but it was the ingenuous magic of a "boy subaltern just out of Sandhurst." At a news conference he remarked on George's Paderewski-length hair that somehow did not look effeminate and, seeing him sign a portrait of himself drawn by a young Italian artist, Hemingway called George's sprawling signature the most vital part of the portrait. He had good words also for white-haired, aristocratic Chancellor Schober of Austria, who was the only man besides Lloyd George who looked like a real chancellor, and that was because he had forty years' training in dignity as head of the Emperor's police. But the other statesmen received more severe judgments. Russian spokesman Georges Tchitcherin, he noted, was an old-style diplomat with a Talleyrand relationship to the Soviet regime. Generally thought of as a totally intellectual man, a brain supported by a body, the report was, Tchitcherin had lately revealed a new quirk that Hemingway and other newsmen reported with raised eyebrows. He had a weakness for gaudy uniforms; and ranking as a Soviet general because of his Com-

12. "Ruhr Commercial War Question of Bankruptcy," *TDS*, April 25, 1923, pp. 1, 2; "A Brave Belgian Lady Shuts Up German Hater," *TDS*, April 28, 1923, pp. 1, 2; "Hate in Occupied Zone a Real, Concrete Thing," *TDS*, May 12, 1923, p. 19; "Amateur Starvers Keep Out of View in Germany," *TDS*, May 9, 1923, p. 17; "Government Pays for News in French Papers," *TDS*, April 21, 1923, pp. 1, 7.

missar status, he had had his picture made in a specially tailored uniform in Berlin. He had also, as the story went, been kept in dresses until he was twelve years old and from that deprivation had conceived his taste for uniforms. Hemingway was careful to explain the significance of the discovery for his readers: "So that is Tchitcherin's weakness. The boy who was kept in dresses until he was twelve always wanted to be a soldier. And soldiers make empires, and empires make wars."

Bulgarian minister Stambuliski, stocky, mustachioed with a dark red peasant face, stood out like a ripe blackberry among daisies at the conference, wrote Hemingway, and bearded French minister Louis Barthou looked like the left one of the Smith Brothers. He suggested the trustworthiness of Turkish minister Hamid Bey's guarantees of safety for foreigners in Constantinople by noting Bismarck's famous comment that dishonest men in the Balkans wore their shirts tucked in (peasants wore theirs hanging out). Hamid Bey, Hemingway remarked, wore a grey business suit. Russian delegate Rakovsky looked like "an old Florentine nobleman," and Ismet Pasha "like an Armenian lace peddler," who loved to go incognito to Montreux jazz palaces and flirt with the waitresses.

In Hemingway's version of French politics on the Ruhr, former Prime Minister Aristide Briand looked "like a bandit" and was identified as "the natural son of a French dancer and a café keeper of St. Nazaire," and Raymond Poincaré was "the little white-bearded Lorraine lawyer with his patent leather shoes and grey gloves" who had a "methodical accountant's mind" and a "spitfire temper." His Royalist challenger was "fat, white-faced Leon Daudet," the author of a lewd novel called *The Procuress*, "a novel whose plot could not even be outlined in any newspaper printed in English." But it was Benito Mussolini of "the typical Bersaglieri face" who received Hemingway's harshest and most extended depiction. His recitation of damaging details was the result of both general observation and special press interviews, one of which Hemingway had had in private with the Fascist leader. The famous Mussolini scowl, he reported, was a way of hiding a weak mouth, and his dueling boasts were made to hide his fear, for he was "Europe's prize bluffer." There was also, Hemingway observed, something histrionically wrong with a man who wore black shirts with white spats. He reported seeing the future dictator snub a delegation of Italian-Swiss peasant women at Genoa to talk with a flirtatious woman reporter; and when reporters first went into Mussolini's office for their interview, he refused to look up at them, presumably concentrating on a book in hand. But edging beside the desk, Hemingway reported the book was only a French-English dictionary and it was held upside down. He was, Hemingway concluded, more a Bottomley than a Napoleon but still a force to beware in European politics.

Early in his reports on politics in Europe, Hemingway identified Mussolini's Fascism as the real danger for the continent, not the much-talked-about Red revolution that preoccupied most American journalists. His ability to speak Italian and to hear what the Italians in the streets and rail coaches were saying was his key advantage. He observed to Philip Percival later in *Green Hills of Africa* that it was useless to try to find out the truth about revolutions if one did not speak the language of the country. For that reason, he said, he would never try to write about the revolution in Russia.[13] But in Italy he could get around and what he found he reported in such Toronto *Star* articles of 1922 as " 'Pot-Shot Patriots' Unpopular in Italy," "Fascist Party now Half-Million Strong," "Mussolini, Europe's Prize Bluffer," and "Picked Sharpshooters Patrol Genoa Streets." He continued his alarm against rising Fascism in the *New Republic* sketch "Italy, 1927" and in a mounting number of pieces in *Esquire* and *Ken* during the thirties.

Hemingway's version of the Fascist triumph in Italy and later throughout much of Europe was generally the standard interpretation of recent history, but his particular experiences and descriptions gave it special meanings that the standard version lacked. Although he reported background events on the Socialist-Fascist feud that began in 1919, his first writing on the Fascists was done on the occasion of the Genoa World Economic Conference in the spring of 1922. At that time the possibility of northern Italian Red demonstrations, prompted by the appearance of the Soviets at the conference, and answering Fascist demonstrations and raids on Red meeting places, was causing tension in Genoa; and Hemingway reported as a matter of news interest that the Italian government had brought in fifteen hundred mili-

13. *Green Hills of Africa* (New York, 1935), p. 193.

tary policemen to guarantee quiet in the city during the conference. But behind the events Hemingway saw two different sets of
personal and political values at odds, and his interpretation was
keyed on the basic naïveté of the much-feared Reds. He saw the
Reds of northern Italy as politically garrulous but undangerous
workmen. He used his technique of reducing politics to personality traits to show his interpretation: "Now the North Italian
Red is the father of a family and a good workman six days out
of seven, on the seventh day he talks politics. His leaders have
formally rejected Russian communism and he is Red as some
Canadians are Liberals. He does not want to fight for it, or
convert the world to it, he merely wants to talk about it, as he
has from time immemorial." Hemingway's version of the Red
demonstrations was also consistent with his view of the "casual
and childish" Reds:

There is no doubt but that the Reds of Genoa—and they are about
one third of the population—when they see the Russian Reds, will
be moved to tears, cheers, gesticulations, offers of wines, liqueurs, bad
cigars, parades, vivas, proclamations to one another and the wide
world and other kindred Italian symptoms of enthusiasm. There will
also be kissings on both cheeks, gatherings in cafés, toasts to Lenine,
shouts for Trotsky, attempts by three or four highly-illuminated Reds
to form a parade at intervals of two and three minutes, enormous
quantities of chianti drunk and general shouts of "Death to the
Fascisti!"[14]

These men were the Red menace, Hemingway pointed out in
another article, which had conducted a brief reign of lawlessness
in Tuscany in 1919 and 1920. At that time they had hissed and
insulted the "borghese" in the streets, had turned middle-class
passengers out of their first-class train coaches and had themselves
ridden a few miles in first-class cars with third-class tickets. But
after the Fascist counterattacks and raids had gone on for several
months, Hemingway noted, the workers "realized that the millen-
nium, when a man could ride first-class on a third-class ticket,
was still some distance off and settled down to work again."[15]
The opposing Fascists as Hemingway depicted them, however,
were not that innocent. Organized as "a sort of Ku-Klux-Klan"
to combat Red terrorism, initially supported by the outraged

14. "Picked Sharpshooters Patrol Genoa Streets," *TDS*, April 13, 1922, p. 17.
15. "'Pot-Shot Patriots' Now Unpopular in Italy," *TSW*, June 24, 1922, p. 5.

upper and middle classes, and tacitly approved by the government, the Fascists had become "a brood of dragons' teeth." Composed of upper and middle class youths who preferred stalking Reds in the streets to going back to their studies or their fathers' offices, they had gotten a taste of "unpenalized lawlessness, unpunished murder, and the right to riot when and where they pleased" and did not want to give up their militaristic organization or stop having the thrills of war without the dangers. They had ceased to distinguish Communists from any other kind of working men and continued, in the words of their leaders, to prevent the fruits of victory from slipping away in the tide of Communism. As a type, they were fanatic "ex-preservers of their country in time of peril." Wearing their black shirts and black tasseled caps and loaded down with trench knives, clubs, machine guns, and kerosene bombs, they sang the Fascist hymn "Youth" as they marched through streets looking for Reds. "The fascisti are young, tough, ardent, intensely patriotic, generally good looking with the youthful beauty of the southern races, and firmly convinced that they are in the right. They have an abundance of the valor and intolerance of youth," Hemingway warned.[16]

Behind them was Mussolini, editor of the Fascist paper *Popolo d'Italia* when Hemingway first interviewed him. Mussolini boasted of having 250,000 young Fascists in a political party organized on military lines and another quarter of a million ready to be so organized. At the time Mussolini had recently demonstrated the party's strength with a 15,000-man march on Red-dominated Bologna and the burning of several public buildings there. He boasted that the party could take over the government at any time and he was ready to do so if challenged. It was then that Hemingway identified the phases of the Fascist takeover: "Fascism thus enters its third phase. First it was an organization of counterattackers against the communist demonstrations, second it became a political party, and now it is a political and military party. . . . The question is now, what does Mussolini, sitting at his desk in the office of the *Popolo d'Italia* and fondling the ears of his wolfhound pup, intend to do with his 'political party organized as a military force'?"[17] That was in the summer of 1922. Hemingway's next interview came in January of 1923, three

16. "Picked Sharpshooters Patrol," p. 17.
17. "Fascisti Party Now Half-Million Strong," *TDS*, June 24, 1922, p. 16.

months after Mussolini's march on Rome and his assumption of dictatorial powers. That was the time he saw Mussolini scowling, concentrating on his dictionary, and "registering Dictator" for the visiting newsmen. By then Hemingway's view of history was longer, and he wondered if the news correspondents of Julius Caesar's day or Napoleon's saw the same discrepancies in their dictators. More indicative of his changed perspective was the difference in tone of his comments on Mussolini. In June he had observed that Mussolini had agitated so strongly for war in 1914 and 1915 that he had been dismissed from the Milan Socialist daily *Avanti*, had started his own paper, the *Popolo d'Italia*, had enlisted in "the crack Bersaglieri corps as a private," and had been "severely wounded in the fighting on the Carso Plateau and several times decorated for valor. . . ." By January he was writing: "Study his genius for clothing small ideas in big words. Study his propensity for dueling. Really brave men do not have to fight duels constantly to make themselves believe they are brave. And then look at his black shirt and white spats." By 1938, when he advocated open action against Mussolini, he wrote an even more contemptuous view of the Duce's military past:

Fascism in Italy is the bluff of a bully playing at soldier. You have to have known the man Mussolini beforehand; before he was in power and made his legend to know this. You have to know that he was not hot stuff in the war; that he was never even decorated on a front where they decorated plenty of times for attacking when the order was to attack; that he was never wounded in action but took advantage of slight wounds caused by the explosion of an Italian trench mortar to leave the front permanently early in the war; although he was featuring his prowess as an athlete and duelist in 1918 while good men were dying.[18]

Hemingway's subsequent articles on the Fascist counterrevolution measured the changes in Italian temperament as Mussolini made the nation over in his image. In "Italy, 1927," the reportorial sketch Hemingway published in the *New Republic* and later decided to reclassify as a short story, he depicted an Italy of brusque young men imitating the Duce's scowl and acting out his xenophobic doctrines to keep the counterrevolution free of foreign influences.[19] By the 1930's Hemingway defined Fascism

18. "The Time Now, the Place Spain," *Ken*, I (April 7, 1938), 36.
19. *New Republic*, L (May 18, 1927), 350-53.

as "a lie told by bullies" and he wrote several *Esquire* and *Ken* articles to explicate that conclusion. "A successful dictator uses clubs and has constant newspaper triumphs," he noted in "Wings Always Over Africa," an analysis of Mussolini's Ethiopian adventure. In Hemingway's view the Ethiopian campaign was a clear example of the two elements of Fascism. It was a bullying action because Italy sent modern European planes and tanks against a feudal, spear- and old rifle-equipped nation and dared the rest of Europe to stop the expedition. It was a lie for several reasons. One was that it was a war fought in a faraway land and thus one Mussolini could manage for newspaper triumphs on battles and advances and could at the same time hide the bad news of wounded and sick Italian soldiers from their families by sequestering them at "Italian island hospital concentration camps where the sick and wounded are being delivered in order that their return to Italy shall not depress the morale of their relatives who sent them off." Another way the Ethiopian campaign demonstrated Fascism as a lie was that Mussolini dared the rest of Europe to frustrate him on pain of having Italy go Bolshevik if he were defeated or allowed to go bankrupt. Indeed that lie was built on the older one, Hemingway noted, that Mussolini had saved Italy from going Red when the truth was that the Reds could not have won anyway. "Italy was kept from going Red," he explained, "when the workers took over the factories in Turin and not one radical group would co-operate with another radical group," when, also, the workers took over war industries that were scheduled to be closed anyway. And most of all, the workers were doomed to fail because they did not "use their great asset, Italy's defeat at Caporetto, intelligently." A third way Fascism was both a lie and a bully, Hemingway noted, was the dictator's tendency to rewrite history and impose his version on the country. According to Mussolini, Caporetto was not a disaster and the world war not a mistake; but, wrote Hemingway, "There are many people in Italy who remember the last war as it was; not as they have been taught to believe it was." And they were beaten, killed, or put into prison on the Lipari Islands. "It is a dangerous thing in a dictatorship to have a long memory. You should learn to live for the great deeds of the day."[20]

20. *Esquire*, V (January 1936), 31, 174-75.

In "Notes on the Next War" Hemingway explored other implications of Fascist method as seen in the Ethiopian adventure. It indicated for one thing that war is the health of the state, particularly the Fascist state, for it was Mussolini's way of diverting attention from isoluble domestic problems, a way of substituting artificially-maintained patriotism for clear thinking. If that was not an unusual doctrine, Hemingway saw more in it when he surveyed other states' response to Mussolini's move. They were willing to accept his fictions of preserving Italy from bolshevism on the chance that he would get bogged down in East Africa and serve their own purposes thereby: France would be relieved of pressure on North Africa, Germany would have a precedent for African expansion, and Britain could make a deal for Ethiopian water projects to supply the Sudan. But the central meaning was still that in dictatorships—in Italy and Germany—the state was the man, and when the man got in trouble he got out of it by going to war.[21]

While he kept an eye on Mussolini in Italy, Hemingway also saw incipient Fascism spreading to counteract revolution elsewhere in the world, including the United States. He marked the American parallels of Mussolini's methods. "In America as we get premonitions of dictatorships you can see in the newspapers how marvelous everything is every day in the achievements of government and looking back note how lousy is the result of any given year or period of years of governmental activity."[22] And when he wrote in *New Masses* on the veterans left to die on the Florida Keys during the 1935 hurricane, he saw them as successors to the veterans dispersed at Anacostia Flats and, by implication, successors to the wounded veterans destroyed by Clemenceau's Garde Républicaine.[23] Contrary to popular opinion in the country, Hemingway saw the developing Washington bureaucracy as an expression of entrenched Fascist job-holding, not development of a reform-oriented state.

But soon his concern shifted to Spain, for he saw there the next step in the development of Fascism—the attempt to block revolution in foreign countries. Spain demonstrated a combination of counterrevolution and Fascist use of war as the health of

21. *Esquire*, IV (September 1935), 19, 156.
22. "Wings Always Over Africa," 175.
23. "Who Murdered the Vets?" *New Masses*, XVI (September 17, 1935), 9.

the state. As in the European conferences and secret dealings of the early twenties, he saw Spain preparing for counterrevolution by political ineptitude. In his 1934 *Esquire* article "The Friend of Spain," he noted the signs of the times. Someone had called him a friend of Spain, he wrote, but it was a term he could not accept because it had too many possible meanings. To be called a friend of France meant one donated money. Being called a friend of Russia meant one aided and promoted Communism. But "Spain is a big country and it is now inhabited by too many politicians for any man to be a friend to all of it with impunity. The spectacle of its governing is at present more comic than tragic, but the tragedy is very close." The reason for the coming tragedy, he explained, was that politics was the most lucrative profession in Spain. In the shiftings from radical to conservative domination of the Cortes, politicians maneuvered and waited for changes in power to pay their bills. All classes but the bureaucrats were suffering, he noted, but they were getting rich and living at the resorts where kings had formerly played.[24]

At the time Hemingway did not report his witnessing the beginnings of the Spanish Republic. Years later, however, he reported, "I had seen the Republic start. I was there when King Alfonso left and I watched the people write their constitution. That was the last Republic that had started in Europe and I believed in it."[25] What he did report were the fluctuations of the revolution. After Spanish artist Luis Quintanilla was imprisoned for leading a 1934 attack on the royal palace in Madrid, Hemingway wrote a program note, later published as an *Esquire* article, on a exhibition of Quintanilla's work in New York. "Facing a Bitter World" was pessimistic about prospects. "This last revolution," he commented, "it seems was a bad one; not like the good one that brought honor and a chance to work. A good one, you know, is one that succeeds. A bad one is one that fails."[26] After the Falangist invasion from Morocco, however, Hemingway's writing for a year and a half was more military than political. After the war had obviously turned against the Republic because of German and Italian intervention, Hemingway resumed

24. *Esquire*, I (January 1934), 26.
25. A. E. Hotchner, "Hemingway Talks to American Youth," *This Week*, October 18, 1959, p. 11.
26. *Esquire*, III (February 1935), 27.

his interpretation of the Spanish revolution, and it brought him to a new phase of his political writing.

Writing for *Ken* magazine, he began his work as overt political propagandist. He no longer wrote only to provoke a general disgust with the counterrevolutionists. Now he recommended specific actions. If years later he saw failure of the Spanish war as a result of Fascist intervention, at the time he cited political treachery in Spain as an equally important reason. In "Treachery in Aragon" he charged that crucial battles had been lost because Loyalist politicians had sold out to the Gestapo. It was the same technique for breaking open a battle front, he noted, that the Germans had used at Caporetto in 1917. And in light of such techniques of political infiltration and betrayal, he urged Americans to recognize the Fascist weapon that might be used against them.[27] More specifically and pragmatically, his article defended the rightness of executing political turncoats in Spain and regretted that American liberals protested such executions. In "The Cardinal Picks a Winner" he charged the Roman Catholic Church in Spain with supporting the Francoist party and warned American Catholics against being influenced in favor of the Fascists because of their tie with the church in Spain. He cited a photograph showing the Archbishop of Santiago, the Bishop of Lugo, and several other Spanish churchmen giving the Fascist salute and asked rhetorically if they had anything to do with the Fascist bombing of women and children in Barcelona. Cardinal Hayes, he noted, had gone on record saying that he did not believe Franco would bomb children in Barcelona; but, said Hemingway, that "strange outstretched arm salute" of the Spanish churchmen was their sign of agreement with the policy that might makes right, the policy that justified the sending of Fascist bombers over Barcelona.[28]

Besides warning American Catholics and political liberals away from misguided sympathies, Hemingway entered strong pleas with the American public to resist letting the country drift into war. It was not a new plea for him after the Spanish war, however. In 1934 he had noted the European alignments preparatory to war and sounded the warning against American involvement. In "A Paris Letter" he wrote: "What makes you feel bad

27. *Ken*, I (June 30, 1938), 26.
28. *Ken*, I (May 5, 1938), 38.

is the perfectly calm way everyone speaks about the next war. It is accepted and taken for granted. All right, Europe has always had wars. But we can keep out of this next one. And the only way to keep out of it is not to go in it; not for any reason. There will be plenty of good reasons. *But we must keep out of it.* If kids want to go see what war is like, or for the love of any nation, let them go as individuals. Anyone has a right to go who wants to. But we, as a country, have no business in it and we must keep out."[29] Hemingway went to the Spanish war as an individual and saw a brigade of American volunteers who went that way, many of them smuggled across the Franco-Spanish border when the United States State Department refused them permission to go. But his Spanish war experience confirmed his belief that the United States should stay out. In "A Program for U.S. Realism" he acknowledged that a general war in Europe was inevitable and warned Americans against the propaganda appeals that would be made to draw the nation into the conflict: British humanitarian appeals and German brutality would both call for American involvement. In place of participation he advocated strict neutrality as a defensive ploy for Americans. Citing von Clausewitz's doctrine of the negative intention of defense, he argued that America could, as the Prussian strategist suggested, defeat all European combatants by selling to both sides on cash and carry terms and thus accumulate Europe's wealth while Europe exhausted itself in its own wars.[30]

He saw European propaganda as the greatest danger to this policy. But he saw dangers also in the way the U.S. public might be induced to give up control of its destiny to ambitious leaders. In "Notes on the Next War" he warned that "every move that is made now to deprive the people of their decision on all matters through their elected representatives and to delegate those powers to the executive brings us that much nearer war."[31] In "Call for Greatness" he was even more specific. Franklin D. Roosevelt, he acknowledged, had somehow gathered the power to involve the country in war, but he still had the confidence of the country. Hemingway's concern was that Roosevelt's ambition to be

29. *Esquire*, I (February 1934), 156.
30. *Ken*, II (August 11, 1938), 26.
31. "Notes on the Next War," 19.

recorded in history as a great president, even if it meant being a war president, might prompt him to fight a war.[32]

What he thought Roosevelt's policy should be, however, brought Hemingway to advocate a further series of actions. Basic to these recommendations was his contention that the war in Spain was not lost but that the Franco-British policy of neutrality was losing the war for Spain. Because of their unpreparedness for immediate war, France and Britain were reluctant to try to prevent Italy and Germany from pouring men and materials into Spain after the Fascists had agreed not to do so. France and Britain, though, had stopped the supply of war materials to the Spanish Republicans and called on other countries to observe the blockade to help prevent a general war in Europe. Hemingway's contention was that the Republicans could still defeat the Falangists and Fascists if sold the tools of war. His plea thus was for real United States neutrality—selling to both sides if need be, but selling certainly to the Republicans who were crying for arms. American acquiescence to the Anglo-French neutrality policy had prevented such sales and stopped the flow of volunteers to Spain. The essence of Hemingway's propaganda appeal was to allow private American aid to Spain.

A major consideration in favor of lifting the American arms embargo on shipments to the Spanish, Hemingway urged in "The Time Now, the Place Spain," was that with arms the Spanish could defeat the Italians, cause Germany and Japan to take time to repair their alliance with a discredited Italy, and give non-Fascist Europe more time to get armed. "Fascism can still be beaten in Spain the same way Napoleon was beaten in Spain," he declared. Basic to Hemingway's belief that the Italians could be defeated in Spain was his reading of Italian military character. "You have to realize that Italian militarism is not, like German militarism, the expression of a people that history has shown to be suited to be good soldiers. Italian militarism is the romantic thinking of men who were not brave and want to be; of men who were not in the war, and would like to have been; of a race of patriots who like to imagine themselves as soldiers; and are not good at it." They functioned best in battle, Hemingway declared, in conditions approaching assassination. They were generous, brave, hard-working, and panicky in long battles. They

32. *Ken*, II (July 14, 1938), 23.

fought well for two days at Guadalajara, he admitted, but it was an eight-day battle and by the time it ended the Italians had been run off the maps.[33] He thought it could be done again as the Francoists were massing for a crucial drive to the sea. If it could be done, Hemingway argued, it would save Republican Spain from having to surrended *in toto* to the Falangists and at least it would delay the end of the war.

In "Dying Well or Badly" he argued that the battle in Spain was eventually America's battle. Spaniards were fighting for their homeland, but the international brigades fought because they saw clearly that resistance in Spain was "the great holding attack to save what we call civilization." The volunteers fought and died, Hemingway told readers of *Ken*, "knowing that unless they beat the fascists now *you* will have to fight them later." His article was also a defense of the international brigades, which had come under attack by diplomats for violating the neutrality agreements. "Many of them came a long way to die in Spain and none of them, who fought on the ground, got more than 50¢ a day. They, the men of the International Brigades, were not soldiers of fortune or adventurers. They were just very clear thinkers. No one sent them. They came to Spain to fight fascism because they saw, long before the diplomats, how dangerous it was."[34]

To achieve that goal of lifting the embargo he had to clear the air of several matters. One, as he indicated in "Call for Greatness," was to force recognition of Neville Chamberlain as a pawn of the Fascists, if not a Fascist himself. Hemingway's argument for such identification took the Marxist ground that wars were the health of the shareholding class. "Now Mr. Neville Chamberlain is not a fool, and when he makes a deal with Italy it is a deal for the immediate best interests of the shareholding class he represents. It is also a deal for the industries he represents. It is never a deal for the people of England, for any Chamberlain knows that no Chamberlain represents the people of England for long." Thus, Hemingway urged Roosevelt and the American people to recognize that Chamberlain's version of neutrality served the Fascist purposes in Spain, not the interests of real neutrality. The second point he urged was the recogni-

33. *Ken*, I (April 7, 1938), 36.
34. *Ken*, I (April 21, 1938), 68.

tion that the United States State Department was filled with sympathizers of Chamberlain's policy. In "H.M.'s Loyal State Department" he sarcastically recommended that all State Department diplomats be given English old-school ties and decorations as token of their loyalty to British policy. "The most beautiful and inspiring thing is that an American fascist does it all for nothing. He will go against all the natural interests of his country in order to be considered a gentleman. And you will find them doing the dirty work of a very temporary British policy, based on England's not yet being armed. . . ." The State Department Fascists, he charged, "had done their evil, crooked, Roman, British-aping, disgusting, efficient best to end . . . [the war] by denying the Spanish government the right to buy arms to defend itself against the German and Italian aggression."[35] In "False News to the President" he charged that State Department advisers had not only given false information to President Roosevelt and Secretary of State Hull but had also blocked on-the-scene evaluations from American Ambassador to Spain Claude G. Bowers. When the Senate was to decide whether to lift the arms embargo to Spain, State Department men, serving British policy, advised the president, wrote Hemingway, that the war would be over soon and that the arms would fall into Franco's hands. But only a month after the Senate's failure to lift the embargo, both the German General Staff and Franco admitted that the war would last six months or a year.[36]

Besides the larger aim of prompting repeal of the arms embargo, Hemingway wrote pieces calling for specific support of volunteers in Spain. In a telegram signed jointly by him, Vincent Sheean, and Louis Fischer he appealed to the American public for contributions to buy medical supplies and ambulances needed by international volunteers and Spanish Republicans.[37] His foreword to Joseph North's pamphlet *Men in The Ranks*, written in 1939 with the bitter knowledge that the embargo had not been lifted and that the Spanish war was lost, commented on the fates of volunteers. They had either been killed in Spain, captured by Franco's forces, or put in detention camps at Ellis Island for violation of the neutrality policy and for having fought

35. *Ken*, I (June 16, 1938), 36.
36. *Ken*, II (September 8, 1938), 17-18.
37. Preface to *Writers Take Sides*, ed. by League of American Writers (New York, 1938).

for a foreign power. His appeal at this point was for money to defend the Ellis Island volunteers. A year later when he wrote the preface to Gustav Regler's novel *The Great Crusade*, he used the occasion to plead for asylum for refugees from Spain. Gustav Regler, he noted, had been badly wounded fighting for the revolution and should be welcomed in America as the German refugees from the aborted 1848 revolution had been. He had been released with apologies from a French concentration camp, Hemingway observed, but that was only part of the restitution he deserved. "The best citizens we had came in the German migration of 1848, after another revolution failed. America is a big enough country to receive the Reglers who fought in Germany and in Spain; who are against all Nazis and their allies; who would honor America as much by living in it as we would aid them by granting them the right of asylum as we have always accorded to those who have fought in their own land against a tyranny and been defeated."[38] It was a plea consistent with his view that American volunteers' participation in the Spanish Civil War had made that war part of American history.

Hemingway's political vision of the twentieth century reached its climax in the Spanish Civil War. It was all a vast public tragedy, and the Second World War was its denouement. He acted as a propagandist during the world war on two occasions, but the occasions were more military than political. Writing on the prospects for war in the Far East in 1941, he urged as a strategic move that the President and Congress continue aid to Generalissimo Chiang Kai-shek's Nationalist government. For the price of a battleship Chiang could keep the Japanese tied down on the mainland while American, British, and the Netherlands East Indies governments built up defenses and the United States built a two-ocean navy.[39] In *Men at War*, remembering the conditions that almost brought revolution in 1917 after the Chemin des Dames and Caporetto debacles, he called on American politicians and censors to keep faith with the American public by telling the truth, even about military errors. For ultimately it was the public's lack of confidence in the government that produced revolutions.[40]

38. *The Great Crusade* (New York, 1940), p. x.
39. "Aid to China Gives U.S. Two-Ocean Navy Security for Price of One Battleship," *PM*, June 15, 1941, p. 6.
40. *Men at War*, p. xxxi.

But if his statements in *Men at War* had further implications, they were that Hemingway no longer believed in revolution as the way to purify governments, especially the United States government. It is true that Hemingway accepted the discipline of wartime and acquiesced in the deferral of criticism until after the war. But his observations of politics over the preceding twenty-five years had convinced him that revolutions opened the way to Fascist counterrevolution in the confusion of crumbling institutions more than they opened the way to new societies or republics. Italy and Spain were his two harsh examples. In his postwar essay, the introduction to Ben Raeburn's *Treasury for the Free World*, he urged the victors to shun Fascist methods and thus avoid repeating the cycle of Fascism. "It would be easy for us," he wrote, "if we do not learn to understand the world and appreciate the rights, privileges, and duties of all other countries and peoples, to represent in our power the same danger to the world that Fascism did." The positive action he called for was relinquishment of claims over other lands and peoples and thus, presumably, allowing self-determination. In peace "it will be as necessary to relinquish as it was necessary to fight. No nation who holds land or dominion over people where it has no just right to it can continue to do so if there is to be any peace."[41]

His conclusion was Santayanan. Those who do not remember the past are condemned to repeat it, wrote the Cambridge thinker. What Hemingway called for at mid-century was for nations to break the cycle of the past, to conduct peace on different terms from those of war. Whether in his eyes they did so, he did not make a matter of record in his essays. His writing after 1946 focused on the actions of persons rather than nations.

41. *Treasury for the Free World* (New York, 1946), pp. xiii-xiv.

IX. Hemingway's Aesthetic Thought

The Art of Seeing

IN AN OTHERWISE ROUTINE NEWS ARTICLE IN 1923 ON "GENERAL Wolfe's Diaries Saved for Canada" Hemingway lighted upon an insight that expressed the key direction of his later thinking on problems in aesthetics. Wolfe's diaries, he said, showed "how the entire struggle between the British and the French for Canada looked to a man on the job," and with the diaries was a map of the Great Lakes that showed them "as they would appear to a voyageur whose only concern was to traverse them as quickly as possible."[1] Hemingway's aesthetic thought was like that. From 1925 to the end of his career as an essayist he commented frequently on the problems in art, but always those comments had a practical intent. No theorist on art any more than he was on

1. *TSW*, November 24, 1923, p. 19.

history or politics, he wrote on what had been or were at the time his own problems as a writer or, later, wrote practical advice for younger writers. His generalizations came after the fact and gained a hearing only as they helped explain accomplished works. If other writers or critics converted those explanations into prescriptions, they proceeded at their own risk. To Hemingway they were always *ad hoc* pronouncements.

Except for incidental remarks on his practice of journalism, Hemingway's essays in aesthetics concerned the art of fiction. He was, he often insisted, fundamentally concerned with making or inventing, not reporting. Yet, at some periods of his career he emphasized temporarily the value of reporting over creating. During the Spanish Civil War, for example, he called for others, if not himself, to provide a factual account of events. In "The Writer as a Writer" he told of urging James Lardner, son of humorist Ring Lardner, to infiltrate into Madrid and be there to tell the truth about what happened when the city fell to General Franco. Lardner, he noted, had no declared loyalties that would prejudice him in Fascist eyes. "All you have to do," he urged, "is write the truth and be there where you can write it. If no honest man is in Madrid to write about what really happens if it ever falls, it will be one of the tragedies of history."[2] The times were such that he carried his preference a step further in the preface to Gustav Regler's Spanish Civil War novel, *The Great Crusade*. Noting that the characters of the novel had their counterparts in actual persons, that it was confessedly and intentionally a *roman à clef*, he declared that "there are events so great that if a writer has participated in them his obligation is to try to write them truly rather than assume the presumption of altering them with invention. It is events of this importance that have produced Regler's book." Although he did not say so directly, he implied that for limited writers like Regler, fact-based narrative was their best hope for achieving that authority needed to make fiction believable. For better writers the rules were different. "The greatest novels are all made-up. Everything in them is created by the writer. He must create from knowledge, of course, unless his book is to be a tour de force."[3]

Hemingway's aim was imaginative rather than reportorial

2. *Direction*, May-June 1939, p. 3.
3. *The Great Crusade* (New York, 1940), pp. x-xi.

writing and he always returned to four major attributes of the created experience to tell what it was. The first was that created truth transcends facts or any logical inferences to be drawn from facts. What the exact nature of that truth is, he never said and apparently would not analyze it for fear he would dissipate it in the process. "Nobody knows a damned thing about [imagination]," he wrote in 1935, "except that it is what we get for nothing."[4] If part of that truth resided in style, we get an indication of its immunity from analysis in Hemingway's remark to George Plimpton of the *Paris Review* that trying to explain style would make him "so self-conscious that [he] could not write."[5] Consciously or not, he followed Emerson in this refusal to analyze his creative mind. In "Spiritual Laws," for example, Emerson wrote: "Could Shakespeare give a theory of Shakespeare? Could ever a man of prodigious mathematical genius convey to others any insight into his methods? If he could communicate that secret it would instantly lose its exaggerated value, blending with the daylight and the vital energy with the power to stand and to go." A glimpse into the transcendental nature of that truth can be seen, however, in Hemingway's comment in *Men at War*: "A writer's job is to tell the truth. His standard of fidelity to the truth should be so high that his invention, out of his experience, should produce a truer account than anything factual can be. For facts can be observed badly; but when a good writer is creating something, he has time and scope to make it of an absolute truth."[6] He told Plimpton that "a writer, if he is any good, does not describe. He invents or *makes* out of knowledge personal and impersonal and sometimes he seems to have unexplained knowledge which could come from racial or family experience."[7] The writer's knowledge, he suggested, was like the

4. "Monologue to the Maestro," *Esquire*, IV (October 1935), 21.
5. Carlos Baker (ed.), *Hemingway and His Critics* (New York, 1961), p. 30.
6. *Men at War* (New York, 1942), p. xv.
7. Baker, p. 35. C. Hugh Holman suggests in his essay, "Hemingway and Emerson: Notes on the Continuity of an Aesthetic Tradition," *Modern Fiction Studies*, I (August 1955), 12-15, that such knowledge might well come from a cultural tradition shared by both the nineteenth-century transcendentalist and the twentieth-century novelist. See also Earl Rovit, *Ernest Hemingway* (New York, 1963), *passim*. If, as F. I. Carpenter has suggested in "Hemingway Achieves the Fifth Dimension," *PMLA*, LXIX (September 1954), 711-18, and Green D. Wyrick has seconded in "Hemingway and Bergson: The *Élan Vital*," *Modern Fiction Studies*, I (August 1955), 17-19, that Hemingway's intuitive aesthetic was indebted to Henri Bergson, it should also be noted that Bergson acknowledged a similar

homing instinct of the passenger pigeon, the fighting instinct of the bull, or the tracking instinct of the hunting dog. In any case, the writer sensed reality, an innate plausibility in actions, and made his facts to fit that intuition. But the writer's conscience or integrity had to guide him in making sure that intuition was faithful to his grasp of the way the world is, not of the way he wanted it to be. "If you invent successfully it is more true than if you try to remember it. A big lie is more plausible than truth."[8] An instance of the control exercised by the objective world on the created vision can be seen in his admission that his own characters often had real-life origins. Those in *The Sun Also Rises* had identifiable beginnings in actual people, but the characterizations were to the people what the cartoonist's or artist's lines were to their models.[9]

If one accurately rendered an honest vision, he noted in *Green Hills of Africa*, he could get "a fourth and fifth dimension" in his created reality. Timelessness or permanence was one of those dimensions, and it would prevent the vision from dissipating.[10] "From things that have happened and from things as they exist and from all things that you know and all those you cannot know, you make something through your invention that is not a representation but a whole new thing truer than anything true and alive, and you make it alive, and if you make it well enough, you give it immortality."[11] Such fictional renderings constituted a kind of higher reporting. Imagination and honesty were the two indispensable qualities of the writer, and with them he could provide readers with a superior comprehension of factual reality. "If he gets so he can imagine truly enough people will think that the things he relates all really happened and that he is just reporting."[12]

The assimilation and transformation of experience that re-

debt to Emerson. See Joseph Jones, "Emerson and Bergson on the Comic," *Comparative Literature*, I (Winter 1949), 63-72. See also Tony Tanner, *The Reign of Wonder: Naivety and Reality in American Literature* (New York, 1967), pp. 228-57, for further connections between Hemingway's practice and the Transcendentalists' aesthetics.

8. A. E. Hotchner, "Hemingway Talks to American Youth," *This Week*, October 18, 1959, p. 11.

9. Leicester Hemingway, *My Brother, Ernest Hemingway* (Cleveland, 1962), p. 275.

10. *Green Hills of Africa* (New York, 1935), p. 27.

11. Baker, p. 37.

12. "Monologue to the Maestro," 21.

sulted in imaginative knowledge became further the test for vitality in factual knowledge. Stephen Crane, he wrote in *Men at War*, used vicarious experience—old soldiers' stories and the images from Matthew Brady's Civil War photographs—as the raw material for "that great boy's dream of war" in *The Red Badge of Courage*, but it resulted in a created experience of war that was closer to the truth of war than any actual war he later experienced as a correspondent.[13] And in the preface to *A Moveable Feast* Hemingway suggested again that created experience—fiction—could "throw some light on what has been written as fact." In this case he implied that motive and personal vision in actual people could be better understood through the fictional imagination than through facts themselves. His own personal myth of innocence in the Paris memoir was an example.

The second attribute of created experience was its distinctness from an intellectualized view of the actual world. The relationship between a made world and an observed one did not imply to Hemingway direct criticism or intellectual evaluation of the factual world in his fiction. Thinking—abstracting a meaning for the literal world—was for essays, not fiction. The made world of the fiction writer was to be a regiving of the factual world to the reader, an immersion of the reader in enlarged experience, not a drawing away from experience to see it distantly and abstractly. Rather, the whole of experience had to be known microcosmically. "Let those who want to save the world if you can get to see it clear and as a whole. Then any part you make will represent the whole if it is made truly."[14] The thinker and the artist had different roles: one to judge the world by categorical concepts, the other to celebrate its meaning through intensified experience. "As a man," he told one apprentice writer, "things are as they should or shouldn't be. As a man you know who is right and who is wrong. You have to make decisions and enforce them. As a writer you should not judge. You should understand."[15] Similarly, one did not judge the validity of the artist's vision by his acts as a man, he reminded George Plimpton. Verlaine, Rimbaud, Shelley, Byron, Baudelaire, Proust, Gide, and Pound were "not necessarily girl guides nor scoutmasters

13. *Men at War*, p. xvii.
14. *Death in the Afternoon* (New York, 1932), p. 278.
15. "Monologue to the Maestro," 174B.

nor splendid influences on youth." But their ability to create experience made them important to society in other ways.[16]

Hemingway found several applications for this distinction between thinker and artist. Perhaps the most frequently repeated one was his criticism of Tolstoy's mixture of creating and Big Thinking in *War and Peace*. His comment in *Men at War* was typical of his laments about this failing: "I love 'War and Peace' for the wonderful, penetrating and true descriptions of war and of people but I have never believed in the great Count's thinking. I wish there could have been someone in his confidence with authority to remove his heaviest and worse thinking and keep him simply inventing truly."[17] In *Death in the Afternoon* he criticized Aldous Huxley for constructing characters in his novels to present his intellectual persuasions rather than creating people with their own reality and integrity. Putting one's own ideas in fictional form and selling them as novels rather than as less remunerative essays might be smart business, but not good aesthetics. Ideas are not literature, he suggested, much in the way Gertrude Stein had earlier cautioned him that remarks are not literature. And in his interview with Robert Manning, talking not altogether about *The Old Man and the Sea*, Hemingway insisted that intellectually imposed symbols in a writer's work were usually failures, that meanings, including symbolic ones, came out of a created, real experience.[18] If the experience was true, he insisted, the symbols would be there without the writer's trying for them.

The third function of imaginative work was its identification with the experience of both reader and writer. The test of a fictional work—and this was a key to Hemingway's cultural thinking as well as his aesthetics—was that it became part of one's own experience. "A writer's problem . . . is always how to write truly and having found what is true, to project it in such a way that it becomes a part of the experience of the person who reads it."[19] He explained more fully in "Old Newsman Writes" that "all good books are alike in that they are truer than if they had

16. Baker, p. 36.

17. *Men at War*, p. xviii. See also Baker, *Critics*, pp. 36-37, and "Old Newsman Writes," *Esquire*, II (December 1934), 26.

18. "Hemingway in Cuba," *The Atlantic Monthly*, CCXVI (August 1965), 104.

19. "The Writer and War," *The Writer in a Changing World*, ed. Henry Hart (New York, 1937), p. 69.

really happened and after you are finished reading one you will feel that all that happened to you and afterwards it all belongs to you; the good and the bad, the ecstasy, the remorse and sorrow, the people and the places and how the weather was."[20] In a 1922 newspaper review of René Maran's *Batouala*, for example, he praised the novel for its power to take the reader into African village life as it was experienced by the natives: "You smell the smells of the village, you eat its food, you see the white man as the black man sees him, and after you have lived in the village you die there."[21] He certified in *Green Hills of Africa* that this test still worked for him. Tolstoy's action sequences in *Sevastopol* and *The Cossacks*, Stendhal's boudoir and garden scenes in *The Red and the Black*, and Turgenev's country scenes in *A Sportsman's Sketches* were as real for him as if he had been in those created scenes himself.[22]

But equally important, the created experience had to happen imaginatively for the writer. "I write slowly and with a great deal of difficulty," he noted in 1925. "While I write the stuff I have to live it in my head." Years later in *A Moveable Feast* he explained further how the stories of *In Our Time* were lived as they were written—indeed, how their being written followed his discovery and living of the sequences:

Some days it went so well that you could make the country so that you could walk into it through the timber to come out into the clearing and work up onto the high ground and see the hills beyond the arm of the lake. A pencil-lead might break off in the conical nose of the pencil sharpener and you would use the small blade of the pen knife to clear it or else sharpen the pencil carefully with the sharp blade and then slip your arm through the sweat-salted leather of your pack strap to lift the pack again, get the other arm through and feel the weight settle on your back and feel the pine needles under your moccasins as you started down for the lake. . . . When I stopped writing I did not want to leave the river where I could see the trout in the pool, its surface pushing and swelling smooth against the resistance of the log-driven piles of the bridge. . . . But in the morning the river would be there and I would make it and the country and all that would happen.[23]

20. "Old Newsman Writers," 26.
21. "Prize-Winning Book Is Center of Storm," *TSW*, March 25, 1922, p. 3.
22. *Green Hills of Africa*, pp. 108-9.
23. Charles Fenton, *The Apprenticeship of Ernest Hemingway* (New York, 1961), p. 198; *A Moveable Feast* (New York, 1964), pp. 91, 76-77.

Hemingway's further comments on the nature of the created experience indicated his general acceptance of the idea that an artist's vision is influenced heavily by both internal pressures and immediately external stimuli, anything that to him had the feel of truth. El Greco's paintings of saints, he maintained in *Death in the Afternoon*, were influenced by that artist's homosexuality. Not all saints were made the way San Sebastian was, he told a woman art critic, but El Greco painted them that way.[24] Looking with Lillian Ross at Carpaccio's "Meditation on the Passion," he observed that the Italian painter's rendering of Italy as Palestine was another example of the tendency. Picking the parts of Italy they liked best or the parts their mistresses came from, or painting their wives or mistresses as the Madonna was not just a matter of availability of models. They were the places and the people that meant most to the artists. And when the artists got hungry, he noted, they made the picture more meaningful to themselves by putting in rabbits or fowl.[25] Hemingway practiced that art himself, he wrote in *A Moveable Feast*. "I was writing about up in Michigan and since it was a wild, cold, blowing day it was that sort of day in the story. I had already seen the end of fall come through boyhood, youth and young manhood, and in one place you could write about it better than in another. . . . But in the story the boys were drinking and this made me thirsty and I ordered a rum St. James."[26]

His own internal pressures and their role in his writing were factors Hemingway considered when he readied himself for creating an experience. The fear of death was particularly one to be confronted, he wrote in "The Dangerous Summer." Seeing his friends perform in the bull ring had for a time made the fear of death so strong for him that he could not witness or write of such scenes, but finally he had "practically eliminated that fear as a personal problem." The result was that in his writing he became able to communicate to others his new lack of fear. It was a talent, he recognized, that had to be used respectfully and without arrogance, for at any time he could lose both his insight and his ability to render it.[27] In *A Moveable Feast* he noted another relationship between internal pressures and writing abil-

---

24. *Death in the Afternoon*, p. 204.
25. Lillian Ross, *Portrait of Hemingway* (New York, 1961), p. 61.
26. *A Moveable Feast*, p. 5.
27. *Life*, XLIX (September 5, 1960), 85.

ity when he observed that writing served as a way of exorcising harmful knowledge. He had, of course, created fictional people who wrote or talked on such a premise. Nick Adams in "Fathers and Sons" and Robert Jordan and Pilar in *For Whom the Bell Tolls* had attempted to rid themselves of crippling knowledge by bringing it out into the world to wither in the gaze of the community, Nick Adams and Robert Jordan being disturbed by their fathers' suicides, and Pilar by her part in the massacre of Fascists at Pablo's village. But in his own voice as writer Hemingway noted that after hearing Gertrude Stein praise homosexuality he knew he would have to write hard the next day to get rid of the effect of such talk. "Work could cure almost anything, I believed then, and I believe now."[28] He did not say what he wrote the next day.

In general, though, Hemingway's tendency was to make fiction an embracing of experience rather than a shunning of it. He valued experience as the stuff from which stories are made more than he valued a style that existed for itself. Thus he wrote in his 1938 introduction to his collected plays and stories: "In going where you have to go, and doing what you have to do, and seeing what you have to see, you dull and blunt the instrument you write with. But I would rather have it bent and dull and know I had to put it on the grindstone again and hammer it into shape and put a whetstone to it and know that I had something to write about than to have it bright and shining and nothing to say, or smooth and well-oiled in the closet, but unused."[29] That finally this raw experience had to lose its old identity in the inner life of the artist and emerge as something new was clear in Hemingway's Nobel Prize acceptance speech. Ultimately, if not immediately, he declared, a man's writing showed what his inner life was and let the world know the kind of alchemy going on there.[30]

A fourth general characteristic of the created work in Hemingway's eyes was that it had to be uniquely new. The flaw in early American "classic" writers, he said, meaning Emerson, Hawthorne, Whittier and company, was that they wrote to equal, not surpass, their English models. It was one thing to write in

28. *A Moveable Feast*, pp. 20-21.
29. *The Fifth Column and the First Forty-Nine Stories* (New York, 1938), p. vii.
30. Carlos Baker, *Hemingway: The Writer as Artist* (Princeton, 1963), p. 339.

the tradition of certain writers but another to fail to see beyond that tradition. A modern classic, he explained in *Green Hills of Africa*, "could steal from anything it is better than" but could not "derive from or resemble a previous classic."[31] Because his work had to build on but not exactly resemble previous work, the writer had to know the past and run against it as a miler runs against the clock rather than against other runners. The writer, he insisted, should not evaluate his performance by measuring it against the work of his contemporaries, for their value was clear neither to him nor to the critics. Shifting critical fashions prohibited intelligent evaluation of a current scene, but the illustrious dead always were there for measurement.[32] Thus, Hemingway thought that he had equaled Turgenev but was not yet ready to challenge Tolstoy. Even in the light of acknowledged classics, a writer's performance became harder all the time because once a subject was done well, it left a more limited field for the next writer to work with. He had to find a new angle of vision on an established subject or find a new subject.[33] In his Nobel Prize acceptance speech Hemingway, speaking as a certified maker of modern classics, saw the job as not only difficult but approaching the impossible. Writing was trying for something "beyond attainment," for "something that has never been done or that others have tried and failed."[34] The escape clause for such restrictions was that each individual had his own vision, his own style, if he could discover it, and he had to work for that instead of accepting as his own the way others felt and wrote. "Anybody can write like somebody else. But it takes a long time to get to write like yourself and then what they pay off on is having something to say."[35] But having something to say did not mean reading up on a subject and putting it into the created work. Knowledge, even though its eventual source might be external, had to be absorbed and transformed so that it came immediately from within.[36] So the thing to do was to work as an individual and to avoid the failure inherent in alignment with critical schools, regardless of their popularity or persuasiveness.

31. *Green Hills of Africa*, p. 21.
32. "Monologue to the Maestro," 174B.
33. "Old Newsman Writes," 26.
34. *Hemingway: The Writer as Artist*, p. 339.
35. "Notes on Life and Letters," *Esquire*, III (January 1935), 21.
36. "Old Newsman Writes," 26.

Hemingway's version of the artist as individual, in spite of his suspicion of schools and traditions, had much of the Emersonian or Whitmanesque poet about it: "The individual, the great artist when he comes, uses everything that has been discovered or known about his art up to that point, being able to accept or reject in a time so short it seems that the knowledge was born with him, rather than that he takes instantly what it takes the ordinary man a lifetime to know, and then the great artist goes beyond what has been done or known and makes something of his own."[37]

If all that making of a moment or a sequence of moments was the key to achievement of a fictional experience, the key to making the experience was to Hemingway the act of seeing. If Gertrude Stein was a reliable witness on the point, she helped Hemingway learn to see what it was in actual experience that could be transformed into the fictional moment. At any rate, she seemed to have Hemingway's kind of insight into the problem when she wrote: "Gertrude Stein never corrects any detail of anybody's writing, she sticks strictly to general principles, the way of seeing what a writer chooses to see, and the relation between that vision and the way it gets down. When the vision is not complete the words are flat, it is very simple, there can be no mistake about it, so she insists."[38] Hemingway recorded in *Death in the Afternoon* his struggle to learn to see the vision in the experience. It involved for him close study of violence in the bull ring and, as part of that study, learning not to blink emotionally at the moment of impact. One observed and observed and observed, not to record what happened but to take in all the sensations that would in his imagination filter through combined experiences until a lucid sequence emerged. His best illustration of this process of seeing and learning what was memorable and permanent was his seeing the matador Hernandorena tossed and gored. "For myself . . . the problem was one of depiction and waking in the night I tried to remember what it was that was the thing that I had really seen and, finally, remembering all around it, I got it. When he stood up, his face white and dirty and the silk of his breeches opened from waist to knee, it was the dirtiness of the rented breeches, the dirtiness of his

37. *Death in the Afternoon*, pp. 99-100.
38. Gertrude Stein, *The Autobiography of Alice B. Toklas* (New York, 1960), p. 214.

slit underwear and the clean, clean unbearably clean whiteness of the thigh bone that I had seen, and it was that which was important."[39] He told George Plimpton, however, that he had recognized the problem long before his friendship with Gertrude Stein. In Chicago, as early as 1920, he "was searching for the unnoticed things that made emotions such as the way an outfielder tossed his glove without looking back to where it fell, the squeak of resin on canvas under a fighter's flat-soled gym shoes, the gray color of Jack Blackburn's skin when he had just come out of stir and other things I noted as a painter sketches. You saw Blackburn's strange color and the old razor cuts and the way he spun a man before you knew his history. These were the things which moved you before you knew his story." Even as late as his African airplane crashes Hemingway was still, at least satirically, aware of the key role of seeing in inventing. At the time of the crashes, he wrote, he had to observe all the details of the crash, survive, and "according to your own ethics" present a version that "will look good to the insurance company."[40]

In a more didactic manner he wrote in "Monologue to the Maestro" that a writer could train himself to see the potentially useful detail by imaginatively adopting several points of view during an action.[41] One had to remember how things looked and sounded and felt to him and at the same time watch other observers to detect clues on how they saw and felt; one could even ask others' sensations or observations as long as he trusted their responses. But beyond that he had to look inside himself to measure the sensations against his emotional responses and see what made some actions memorable and others unimportant.[42] Then he had to reconstruct events in light of his true emotional response and find a way of recording the newly ordered sequence. In other words, the reporting was for effect, not objective rendering of the unresponded to event. The actual event was still ultimately the source and thus the control of the response, but

39. *Death in the Afternoon*, pp. 2-3, 20.
40. Baker, *Critics*, p. 35; "The Christmas Gift," *Look*, XVIII (May 4, 1954), 83.
41. See John Graham, "Ernest Hemingway: The Meaning of Style," *Modern Fiction Studies*, VI (Winter 1960), 298-313, for a useful study of this technique in the fiction.
42. See Rovit, pp. 30-52, for a useful discussion of this point.

the writer's response to that event was the control of the newly construed event.[43]

The writer's emotional background was the key to what was responded to, and to explain how one's emotional constitution worked in the making of fiction he invoked his iceberg theory of composition. It is significant that Hemingway equated emotional response and knowledge; that is, knowledge is an educated response made up of "the great reserve of things [one] knows or has seen."[44] His passage from *Death in the Afternoon* was his most coherent and complete statement of the idea:

A good writer should know as near everything as possible. Naturally he will not. A great enough writer seems to be born with knowledge. But he really is not; he has only been born with the ability to learn in a quicker ratio to the passage of time than other men and without conscious application, and with an intelligence to accept or reject what is already presented as knowledge. There are some things which cannot be learned quickly and time, which is all we have, must be paid heavily for their acquiring. They are the very simplest things and because it takes a man's life to know them the little new that each man gets from life is very costly and the only heritage he has to leave. Every novel which is truly written contributes to the total knowledge which is there at the disposal of the next writer who comes, but the next writer must pay, always, a certain nominal percentage in experience to be able to understand and assimilate what is available as his birthright and what he must, in turn, take his departure from. If a writer of prose knows enough about what he is writing about he may omit things that he knows and the reader, if the writer is writing truly enough, will have a feeling of those things as strongly as though the writer had stated them. The dignity of the movement of the iceberg is due to only one-eighth of it being above water. A writer who omits things because he does not know them only makes hollow places in his writing.[45]

Or as he said later and more briefly, "If it is any use to know it, I always try to write on the principle of the iceberg. There is seven-eights of it under water for every part that shows. Anything you know you can eliminate and it only strengthens your iceberg."[46]

43. "Monologue to the Maestro," 174B.
44. Baker, *Critics*, p. 34.
45. *Death in the Afternoon*, pp. 191-92.
46. Baker, *Critics*, p. 34.

The writer's educated emotional reserve acted as the seven-eights of the iceberg; his response to particular observations, and therefore the part that became his new fictional vision, acted as the one-eighth. The vaster his reserve of feeling and response, the more knowledgeable was his art, and the greater were the possibilities of observations finding their answering response in the artist. It was this process that he saw working in Gattorno's paintings. The painter, he said, put all his world into each picture and then put it all again, but somehow different, into the next picture. "It is like hauling through the same part of the sea with different dimensions of mesh."[47]

Some special qualities of that iceberg of feeling and knowledge were suggested by Hemingway on several occasions. He noted that dreams, desires, and fears were a large part of one's emotional reserve, and they helped shape one's response to external observations. If they were part of racial experience they provided a common element of the writer's and reader's imaginations for the writer to rely on. He told Plimpton, "I have the nightmares and know about the ones other people have. But you do not have to write them down."[48] They were present and known and therefore omissible. In his essay on "The Circus" he saw that much of the illusion produced by the circus was based on dreams of innocence and fabled animals, of the miraculous performers, and on the clowns. The wild animals obeyed the discipline of man, the exhibition artists defied natural law, and the clowns demonstrated the triumph of innocence and laughter. Even the villains of the acts were part of the dream. "There have to be a few villains in the best of dreams in order that there be Giants for Jack and Goliaths for Young David with the sling and the pebble. There has to be a dragon for St. George to kill."[49] But the important thing was to recognize all the skill and long preparation by the performers that made the illusion possible.

As we can see, Hemingway was talking about two kinds of icebergs. One was that reserve the writer brought to his moments of observation and his reports of that internal observation. The other was the reader's. For the reader's response was also neces-

47. "Gattorno," *Esquire*, V (May 1936), 141.
48. Baker, *Critics*, p. 28.
49. *Ringling Brothers and Barnum & Bailey Circus Magazine* (1953), pp. 7, 62.

sary for the sensing of what the submerged seven-eights might be. The reader had to respond much as the writer did to the stimuli of observation, but the stimuli for him came from the created world rather than the raw, experiential world. His own reservoir of knowledge of course enabled him to respond to the stimuli of a fictional vision, to measure, to accept some and reject others, and to arrive at his own vision. "Read anything I write for the pleasure of reading it," Hemingway told Plimpton. "What ever else you find will be the measure of what you brought to the reading." But because the writer's reserve and the reader's were perhaps similar but not identical, explication by the author was not only undesirable but useless. "You can be sure that there is much more than will be read at any first reading and having made this it is not the writer's province to explain it or to run guided tours through the more difficult country of his work."[50]

That the iceberg theory had too many variables to work exactly as he wanted it to for the reader Hemingway recognized when he saw readers' responses to his story "Out of Season." Written while he still was learning to use the iceberg idea, the story did not state the real end which he thought was implied by events in the narrative. The implied end of the story was "that the old man [Peduzzi] hanged himself," Hemingway wrote, and he had left that out feeling that the omission would strengthen the story. But readers had not understood the story, he admitted years later.[51] Needless to say, however, he did not abandon the principle or the story but worked harder to make the principle function in other stories and waited for other readers to find the ending and meaning of "Out of Season," perhaps through greater comprehension of the principle in other stories.

If the problem of creating involved finding the proper relation between seeing and "getting it down," to use Gertrude Stein's terminology, Hemingway had more to say about how to render the vision; that is, style. Real style, he told Robert Manning, was the plainest, most efficient way of getting the vision on paper. Any gratuitous beauty or anything pleasing about the product was incidental. Efficient rendering was the thing. Finding the right way was important.[52] Amateurs tended to identify

50. Baker, *Critics*, pp. 29, 34.
51. *A Moveable Feast*, p. 75.
52. "Hemingway in Cuba," 105.

as style the marks of inefficiency, "the unavoidable awkward-nesses in first trying to make something that has not heretofore been made."[53] An apprentice writer did wrong to copy the obvious marks of another writer's style. They were the parts the writer most wanted to disown. In writing, as in wine, in architecture, in bullfighting, in fishing and hunting, purity and honesty rated above picturesqueness.

More practically, Hemingway explained the process of getting it down by chronicling his work habits and routines. There was for him a kind of inductive magic in the way he went about writing. Part of the vision and feeling of how to render it came from the way it was approached. Rule one was to work alone. Both seeing and writing were for individuals, not schools or organizations. Incidental reasons for such work were that others distracted the writer from the concentration needed for making his truth and, as he noted while condemning the pseudo-artists of Montmartre and Montparnasse, one had to be careful not to betray himself into substituting public talk and public display for actual writing.[54] And in groups one lost his certainty of how he felt; he was likely to accept the group's feeling for his own. Particularly was this true if the group had its own favorite theories. Watching Reginald Rowe puzzle alone over his paintings in Cuba, Hemingway noted that "as long as an artist is puzzled he has a chance."[55] For a writer with a tragic sense, working alone was the most efficient way to combat the passage of time; time was always short for the artist and the wasting of it became more and more the unforgivable sin.[56] Indeed, the writer, he said in his Nobel Prize speech, had to "face eternity, or the lack of it, each day."[57]

His second rule was to avoid talking about his work while he was doing it. Indeed, he told Harvey Breit, he disliked talking about completed work because such talk destroyed his pleasure in having done it, and requests to explain it made him feel he had not succeeded in conveying the experience.[58] But to talk about work in progress was to endanger the work. One could

53. Baker, *Critics*, p. 30.
54. "American Bohemians in Paris a Weird Lot," *TSW*, March 25, 1922, p. 15; Introduction to *Kiki of Montparnasse* (New York, 1929), pp. 2-3.
55. "Finca Vigía," *Reginald Rowe* (New York, 1952), p. [2].
56. Baker, *Critics*, p. 26.
57. *Hemingway: The Writer as Artist*, p. 339.
58. Harvey Breit, *The Writer Observed* (New York, 1961), pp. 171-72.

talk away his vision, lose the excitement and the mystery of creating before the creation was fully realized, and dissipate the inner tensions that helped get the created experience into writing. The problem was not wholly internal, though. In his writing as in his feeling and thought, Hemingway recognized the power of mysterious external forces on him. That he was superstitious about such powers was evident in remarks like that in *A Moveable Feast*: " 'We're always lucky,' I said [to Hadley] and like a fool I did not knock on wood. There was wood everywhere in that apartment to knock on too."[59] He carried horse chestnuts and rabbit feet for luck and knocked on wood whenever he made proud statements that might offend lurking forces. About his work and his life he practiced a kind of language magic that might be explained away by psychoanalysts but was more than figuratively real to him. Language could either make things real or keep them from being real. Circumstance apparently determined the way the magic worked. In one of his articles on Louis Quintanilla and in another on Gulf fishing he illustrated how talk induced reality. Quintanilla, he said, lost the product of his life's work in painting when his studio was destroyed by bombs in Madrid and found the loss too overwhelming to talk about. Hemingway's coxswain and assistant on the fishing boat *Pilar*, he noted, had an animistic belief about certain hooks, lures, and lines they used, cursed and abused them like sensate beings when they failed, and practiced a kind of incantatory magic on the lines when a large fish was hooked: "Oh, God the bread of my children!" he would chant. "Joseph and Mary look at the bread of my children jump! There it goes the bread of my children! He'll never stop the bread the bread of my children!"[60] That Hemingway thought language could make feeling unreal was evident when he noted in the preface to *The Great Crusade* that he could not write about Hans, commander of the Eleventh Brigade: "We have too much together for me ever to risk losing any of it by trying to write about it."[61] But the important thing was for the writer not to be "spooked," he said, by talking too much and too unwisely.

59. *A Moveable Feast*, p. 38.
60. "Luis Quintanilla: Artist and Soldier," *Quintanilla: An Exhibition of Drawings of the War in Spain* (New York, 1938), p. 7; "a.d. Southern Style," *Esquire*, III (May 1935), 25; "On the Blue Water," *Esquire*, V (April 1936), 185.
61. Regler, p. viii.

Rule three was to wake early, work while his mind was fresh and he could concentrate, to work hard while he worked, then stop. The idea was, he said, to stop when he knew what would come next and not exhaust his imagination. He had exhausted himself while writing his first novel in six weeks and had had to spend extra months rewriting it. Later he found that his imagination functioned like a well, which is "where your 'juice' is. Nobody knows what it is made of, least of all yourself. What you know is if you have it or you have to wait for it to come back." To avoid dry periods he learned "never to empty the well of my writing, but always to stop when there was still something in the deep part of the well, and let it refill at night from the springs that fed it."[62] Another part of the rule was to avoid conscious thinking or worrying about the writing until his next session at the writing board. His mind might, perhaps should, continue to work unconsciously, but he read, fished, and continued observing other things to keep his mind off the next day's writing.[63] That way, he said, all his energy went into the writing.[64]

Rule four was that if one did not worry his work as a dog does a bone, he went fresh to the making of it each day and the coherence of the invention depended on sustained freshness of insight rather than a thought-out plan. He reread each morning what he had written the day before, sometimes read the entire work up to that point if it was not too long, and began again creating within the illusion offered by the work. But, as he said and wrote on several occasions, he seldom knew what was going to happen when he began to write: "I start to make it up and have happen what would have to happen as it goes along."[65] This was as true for novels as for stories. While writing *A Farewell to Arms* and *For Whom the Bell Tolls*, he knew in a very general way what the logic of the story was but "didn't know what was going to happen for sure. . . . I was inventing."[66] He demonstrated the influence of daily experience on day-to-day creation of his fiction when he incorporated family experience in

62. Baker, *Critics*, p. 25; *A Moveable Feast*, p. 26.
63. "Monologue to the Maestro," 174A; *A Moveable Feast*, p. 13.
64. "a.d. Southern Style," 156.
65. "Monologue to the Maestro," 174A.
66. "Hemingway in Cuba," 104; Baker, *Critics*, p. 32; Introduction to *A Farewell to Arms* (New York, 1948), p. viii.

the narrative progress of *A Farewell to Arms*. His wife gave birth to their son by Caesarean section while he was working through the first draft of that novel, and he saw the terrors of a Caesarean birth for Frederic and Catherine's child as imaginatively logical for the novel and made that part of the inventing. In writing *The Old Man and the Sea*, he said, he began knowing "two or three things about the situation, but I didn't know the story. . . . I didn't even know if that big fish was going to bite for the old man when it started smelling around the bait. I had to write on inventing out of knowledge."[67]

Rule five was even more practical. In essence, it was to work slowly. For Hemingway, it was necessary to live the experience as he created and wrote it, and sometimes, as he remembered in *A Moveable Feast*, he wrote only a paragraph in a morning's work. The thing to do was to avoid being facile. He found it useful to write in pencil except for occasional passages of dialogue which he did on the typewriter. Such slow work, he said, gave him more chances to make sure that all the sensations and emotions became available to the reader. Typing up the scenes later gave him another opportunity to revise for vividness, and he did not mind revising for effect even at the proofreading stage. The trick was to keep the writing fluid as long as possible.[68]

Besides noting such concerns with inventing, seeing, and working, Hemingway often thought it useful to review for himself and for his apprentices how he learned to see and to write. Chronicling the process was particularly useful, Hemingway insisted, because he was largely self-taught, or he at least selected his teachers and influences rather than follow a discipline imposed by a college or clique. Although he listened to respected persons like Ezra Pound, Gertrude Stein, William Ryall, and Sylvia Beach, he finally was responsible for choosing his masters and his models. Sylvia Beach's bookshop Shakespeare and Company was his library at his critical learning time, and he recorded having read there most of the books that he later recommended to apprentice writers. They were the books, he remembered, that represented the best of the past for the man who wanted to learn fiction and the books that new writers had to compete against. From time to time and on several occasions he made his lists of

67. "Hemingway in Cuba," 104.
68. "Monologue to the Maestro," 174A.

the books that he "would rather read again for the first time . . . than have an assured income of a million dollars a year" or that he acknowledged as his literary forebears. Those appearing consistently were Tolstoy's *War and Peace* and *Anna Karenina*; Stendhal's *The Red and the Black* and parts of *The Charterhouse of Parma*; Flaubert's *Madam Bovary* and *L'Education Sentimentale*; Mann's *Buddenbrooks*; Joyce's *Dubliners, Ulysses*, and *Portrait of the Artist*; Fielding's *Tom Jones* and usually *Joseph Andrews*; Dostoyevsky's *The Brothers Karamazov* and usually *The Gambler*; Gogol's *Taras Bulba*; several Chekhov stories; Twain's *Huckleberry Finn*; Stephen Crane's *The Red Badge of Courage,* "The Open Boat," and "The Blue Hotel"; Henry James's *The Portrait of a Lady* and frequently *The American, The Turn of the Screw,* and *Madame de Mauves*; Turgenev's *Fathers and Sons* and *A Sportman's Sketches* (though he often simply recommended all of Turgenev); several de Maupassant stories, especially *La Maison Tellier*; and Proust's *Remembrance of Things Past.* Almost as frequently he included books by Captain Marryat; Yeats' *Autobiographies*; stories by Kipling; George Moore's *Hail and Farewell,* D. H. Lawrence's *Sons and Lovers*; parts of Balzac's *La Condition Humaine*; and W. H. Hudson's *Far Away and Long Ago.* He sometimes acknowledged in a general way the influence of Andrew Marvell, John Donne, Thoreau, Hawthorne, Sherwood Anderson, Melville, Shakespeare, Dante, and Vergil.[69] His impetus for writing was not so much a sense of belonging to a certain group of writers and artists in Paris during the twenties as a sense of following the tradition of great masters.

Besides how to see and how to create, what he learned from some of these writers was the value of the honest four-letter word. Joyce's example in *Ulysses,* he told Plimpton, had made it possible to begin the break from genteel restrictions.[70] He argued with Gertrude Stein that use of such words did not make a story either dirty or unpublishable, but they did make the story "come true," he insisted.[71] It was another case of language magic; use of such terms was not so offensive to readers' sense of decorum as it was to their sense of reality, and he insisted that words

69. Baker, *Critics*, p. 27; Ross, p. 18; "Remembering Shooting-Flying," *Esquire,* III (February 1935); "Monologue to the Maestro," 174A-B; *A Moveable Feast,* pp. 36, 133.
70. Baker, *Critics*, p. 26.
71. *A Moveable Feast,* p. 15.

lead to reality, not hide it. In *Men at War* he specifically applied that conviction to war writing, and indicated his debt for the insight to *The Charterhouse of Parma*: "It was at Waterloo that General Cambronne, when called on to surrender, was supposed to have said, 'The Old Guard dies but never surrenders!' What Cambronne actually said was 'Merde!' which the French, when they do not wish to pronounce it, still refer to as 'the word of Cambronne.' It corresponds to our four letter word for manure. All the difference between the noble and the earthy accounts of war is contained in the variance between these two quotations. The whole essence of how men speak in actual war is in Stendahl."[72] Honesty in the use of the four-letter level of experience was what kept writing from going bad, what gave it permanence instead of shackling it to timely slang or temporary sensibilities.[73]

He learned, Hemingway said, not only from great writers. The great painters were his teachers too; they taught how to see and how to pattern one's vision. In actual numbers of expressions of debt and influence, Hemingway had more to say about painters than writers. "I learn as much from painters about how to write as from writers," he told Plimpton. He went to the Luxembourg Museum on foodless lunch hours to study the paintings, particularly those of Cézanne, and found that hunger sharpened his perceptions of the way artists worked. Besides, he had no money for food and the free museum was a powerful teacher for a struggling young man who had stopped his formal education after high school. But an even more fundamental reason for his learning from paintings, he noted on several occasions, was that he wished almost as much to be a painter as a writer. "If I could be something else, I'd like to be a painter," he told Robert Manning on a misty, painter's afternoon.[74] Some emotional states he thought could better be conveyed in paint than in prose. To sense how a picador felt after seeing large bulls in the corrals before a *corrida*, he wrote in *Death in the Afternoon*, one had to see a picture: "If I could draw I would make a picture of a table at the café during a feria with the banderilleros sitting before lunch reading the papers, a boot-black at work, a waiter hurrying somewhere and two returning picadors, one a big brown-faced, dark-browed man usually very cheerful

72. *Men at War*, p. xx.
73. *Ibid.*, p. xvii.
74. Baker, *Critics*, p. 57; Morley Callaghan, *That Summer in Paris* (New York, 1963), p. 102; "Hemingway in Cuba," 108; *A Moveable Feast*, p. 13.

and a great joker, the other a gray-haired, neat, hawk-nosed, trim-waisted little man, both of them looking the absolute embodiment of gloom and depression."[75] The wish was indicative of a key characteristic of Hemingway's invention. He thought and worked in terms of scenes, though they had more movement and fluidity than most painters could suggest.

"Manet could show the bloom people have when they're still innocent and before they've been disillusioned," he commented while looking at the portrait "Mlle. Valtesse de la Bigne." But he learned more about landscapes and patterned actions from such paintings as Cézanne's "Rocks—Forest of Fontainebleau," and this was the debt he commented on most. "I was learning something from the painting of Cézanne that made writing simple true sentences far from enough to make the stories have the dimensions that I was trying to put in them," he remembered in *A Moveable Feast*. What it was he learned we have to guess at, since he was too inarticulate to tell, he said, and besides it was a secret.[76] But while looking at Cézanne's "Rocks—Forest of Fontainebleau," with his wife and son Patrick listening and Lillian Ross recording, he remarked, "This is what we try to do in writing, this and this, and the woods, and the rocks we have to climb over." What "this and this" meant was not recorded, but his remarks shortly before on Francesco Francia's "Portrait of Federigo Gonzago (1500-1540)" indicated the sort of thing he was looking for. Pointing to the trees in the background, he noted that "this is what we try to do when we write. . . . We always have this in when we write."[77] That and his linking Cézanne with "the early painters" provide some basis for interpretation of his cryptic remarks on Cézanne. If insuring that his fictional people lived in an equally well-rendered setting and that the people and the setting functioned mutually on each other was what he learned from Cézanne, it was a lesson well practiced in the protagonists' passage through significant country in such stories as "Big Two-Hearted River," in Jake's trip across the Pyrenees in *The Sun Also Rises*, and in Frederic's encounter with the terrain along the Carso and the Tagliamento River in *A Farewell to Arms*.[78]

75. *Death in the Afternoon*, pp. 56-57.
76. Ross, p. 60; *A Moveable Feast*, p. 13.
77. Ross, pp. 60, 57.
78. See Robert L. Lair, "Hemingway and Cézanne: An Indebtedness," *Modern Fiction Studies*, VI (Summer 1960), 165-68, for other likely parallels.

Still another indication of the way he learned from paintings could be seen in his frequent allusion to paintings as a way of evoking scene-consciousness in his writing, both fictional and non-fictional. In his descriptive accounts, for example, he saw the view from the restaurant and river at Bas Meudon near Paris as a scene from Sisley, and again at the Aranjuez restaurant during his travels on the Ordonez-Dominquin circuit he saw a view of the Tajo River as though Sisley had painted it.[79] In the kudu country of Africa, he noted in 1935, there were parks that looked as though they came out of André Masson's pictures.[80] In Aranjuez at fiesta time the colorful townspeople made the city "Velasquez to the edge and then straight Goya to the bull ring." In Paris the saffron-hued tank wagons working on the Rue Cardinal Lemoine "looked like Braque paintings."[81] And to tell in shorthand what one of his chauffeurs was like in Madrid during the siege, he noted that Tomas looked like a "particularly unattractive, very mature dwarf out of Velasquez, put into a suit of blue dungarees."[82] For scenes of violence he almost always turned to Goya. The broken-legged horses and mules left to drown at Smyrna during the Greco-Turkish war, he noted, called for a Goya to depict them.[83] In his fiction, to cite only a few instances, he used painting and art allusions to evoke scenes and moods. Pablo's proud horse, Robert Jordan notes, "looked as though he had come out of a painting by Velasquez"; and at Velasquez 63, Madrid headquarters of the idealistic International Brigade, Robert Jordan remembers having the religious feeling he knew when looking at Chartres Cathedral windows or seeing paintings by Mantegna, El Greco, and Breughel in the Prado.[84] In *Across the River and into the Trees* Richard Cantwell thinks of death as having a face only Hieronymous Bosch could paint, sees the Venetian market place as if it had been done by Dutch genre painters, and in his elegiac mood sees the Grand Canal "as grey as though Degas had painted it on one of his greyest days."[85] Painting allusions also lent themselves to ironical statement in

79. *A Moveable Feast*, pp. 43-44; "The Dangerous Summer," *Life*, XLIX (September 5, 1960), 80.
80. *Green Hills of Africa*, p. 96.
81. *Death in the Afternoon*, p. 40; *A Moveable Feast*, p. 4.
82. *Fact*, No. 16 (July 15, 1938), 26.
83. *Death in the Afternoon*, p. 135.
84. *For Whom the Bell Tolls* (New York, 1940), pp. 13, 235.
85. *Across the River and into the Trees* (New York, 1950), pp. 254, 191-92, 71.

fiction. The idealistic young Hungarian in "The Revolutionist" carries with him reproductions of saintly paintings by Giotto, Masaccio, and Pierro della Francesca but cannot like the bitter Mantegnas, favorites of his Italian mentor, who has become disillusioned about prospects for revolution in Italy.[86] In *A Farewell to Arms*, when Frederic Henry and Catherine Barkley flee to Switzerland while posing as architecture and art students, they cynically review their clichés on artists in case they are questioned: "Reubens. . . . Large and fat. . . . Titian. . . . Titian-haired. . . . Mantegna. . . . Very bitter . . . lots of nail holes." And with their alibi still in mind after interrogation by the Swiss police, Frederic looks at his raw hands and comments cynically that at least there is no hole in his side.[87]

Hemingway's further insight into the relationship between fiction and painting could be seen in his comments on having his own work illustrated. Charles Scribner, he wrote in the introduction for the 1948 edition of *A Farewell to Arms*, had asked him how he felt about such a prospect. Hemingway's answer indicated his recognition that the two arts met on the level of invention, not observation. Unless the illustrator had a better sense of invention than the writer had, the result would be to limit the imaginative overtones of the novel. What he preferred was to have pictures with their own centers of meaning and let the book and pictures complement each other. "If I could write a book that took place in the Bahamas, I would like it to be illustrated by Winslow Homer, provided he did no illustrating but simply painted the Bahamas and what he saw there. If I were Guy de Maupassant, a good job to have dead or alive, I would like my work to be illustrated by the drawings and paintings of Toulouse-Lautrec, some outdoor scenes of the middle time of Renoir and have them leave my Norman landscapes alone because no painter ever did them better."[88]

If his most instructive analogies for writing came from painting, Hemingway found it useful to think in terms of other arts as well. His family background in music and his own intensive training in music while a boy provided other insights which he later acknowledged. He told George Plimpton that writers should

---

86. *The Short Stories of Ernest Hemingway* (New York, 1955), p. 158.
87. *A Farewell to Arms* (New York, 1963), pp. 280, 284.
88. *A Farewell to Arms* (New York, 1948), pp. viii-ix.

learn what they could from composers on the use of harmony and counterpoint.[89] He provided an example in his interview with Lillian Ross: "In the first paragraph of 'Farewell,'" I used the word 'and' consciously over and over the way Mr. Johann Sebastian Bach used a note in music when he was emitting counterpoint. I can almost write like Mr. Johann sometimes—or, anyway, so he would like it."[90] His counterpointing of two narrative lines in the last third of *For Whom the Bell Tolls*—the partisans' last preparations for the attack on the bridge and Andrés' attempt to ascend the chain of command to reach General Golz—was another instance of his using such strategies from music.

What he learned from the art of bullfighting was both technical and theoretical. His preference for the simple, unadorned line of action with all its meaning implicit, not pointed out either by gesture or by verbalization, was of course a value he shared with the best matadors and *aficionados,* whether or not he learned it at the bull ring. But the fundamental insight behind such a preference was one he could see dramatized at the bull ring and could carry over into his seeing and creating. It was, ironically enough, the decadence of bullfighting rather than its flowering that afforded the insight. The decadent style in bullfighting came with the emphasis on capework rather than on killing the bull. As the popular matadors put on more and more florid shows with their capes, using the butterfly pass and all the other passes with names ending in *illa* and *ina,* they left the true meaning of capework to be carried out by the picadors and banderilleros; that is, to prepare the bull for killing. And with such decadent styles the matadors finally made killing the bull a virtual anticlimax. They emphasized the manner of execution instead of the end result; they ignored the effect of the *suertes* on the bull. To Hemingway it was too often that way with writing also. Style in writing, as he noted more than once, was keyed to efficiency, to attaining the end result of effect on the reader, of giving him the sense of reality that both the good writer and the good bullfighter could provide. But style for itself was meretricious and narcissistic.[91]

Beyond the sense of purpose that style provided, Hemingway also learned more exactly at the bull ring what that ultimate

89. Baker, *Critics,* pp. 27-28.
90. Ross, pp. 60-61.
91. *Death in the Afternoon,* pp. 66ff.

reality for writer and matador was. Both knew that death was the ultimate reality for the living, the reality that with purposeful preparation became the basis for another dimension of living. Men still in rebellion against death as the end to experience sought to remove the effect of death as annihilation and replace it with the effect of immortality. One could get this effect through the temporary art of the bull ring or through the more lasting art of literature. What both matador and writer did was to take the raw material of experience—confrontation of the bull or other terrifying events—and pass it through one's imaginative processes so that it came out a whole new thing. Hemingway frequently wrote of the matador's "creating" the bull, making him do things which his own raw instincts could not conceive but which with man's imagination became true. By his ritual and substitutionary death the bull became the instrument of man's sense of imaginative immortality, not the terrifying threat to but the proof of man's immortality. Man through the substitutionary acts of the matador or the writer became godlike: giving, not receiving, death. And when man's own raw experience, like the bull's, terminated, it had already provided the basis for a new imaginative, created reality. It was art in both cases that produced the transformation of experience into vision, into a new reality.[92]

Hemingway's sense of the comic was also instructed at the bull ring. Indeed, the feelings of tragedy and comedy derived from the same insight—that details of process have their significance as they point to ends. If such an idea had its ethical dangers, they were mitigated, perhaps even lost, in the aesthetic values gained. To say that a moral act is one that makes one feel good afterwards is, in the context of Hemingway's bullfight commentary, a merging of ethical and aesthetic effects. Thus he could say of the disemboweled horses that "there is certainly nothing comic by our standards in seeing an animal emptied of its visceral content, but if this animal instead of doing something tragic, that is, dignified, gallops in a stiff old-maidish fashion around a ring trailing the opposite of clouds of glory it is as comic when what is trailing is real as when the Fratellinis give a burlesque of it in which the viscera are represented by rolls of bandages, sausages and other things. If one is comic the other is;

92. *Ibid.*, pp. 266, 213, 233, 206-7.

the humor comes from the same principle."[93] Even the structure of horses, he pointed out, lent itself to the act of disembowelment by the bull, but at the same time such an action led to the ultimate dignifying of bull and man at the moment of the bull's death and man's imaginative triumph. The timing of the horse's accident, that is, before the bull's death, and the momentary discrepancy between means and end made the horse's death comic. But the true *aficionado*, or artist of the tragic, saw the act of the horses as part of the whole ritual: "The aficionado, or lover of the bull fight, may be said, broadly, then to be the one who has this sense of tragedy and ritual of the fight so that the minor aspects are not important except as they relate to the whole."[94] If formal critics did not see tragedy and comedy in such terms, Hemingway's justification was that such insights worked for him. They might not serve as generalized concepts for all writing situations, but within the context of his observation and writing they had functional significance.

After the writing came the judging of his work by the writer before general readers or critics had their chance. His evaluation was, significantly, for effect, not for abstract excellence. He at one time suggested—no one knows how seriously—the "gooseflesh test," the idea being, he wrote Bernard Kalb, that no one could simulate goose-flesh. At another time he suggested testing by innocents. Again whether he was really serious or not, there was enough plausibility in his statement to give it edge. He knew Reginald Rowe was painting well, he said, when the children of the village learned to see their own village by looking at his paintings. And he implied that it was that way too with writing. But the real test had to come later after the writer had already exposed his failures and small triumphs to the world. Then at some time when the words would not come, he could pick up his book and realize that "this stuff's bloody marvelous."[95]

Self-criticism of specific works, though, indicated better how Hemingway judged his performances. His key critical value was the degree of effective integrity a work maintained. He indicated his later disappointment in *To Have and Have Not* by saying

93. *Ibid.*, p. 7.
94. *Ibid.*, p. 9.
95. "Letter from Hemingway to Bernard Kalb," *Saturday Review*, XXXV (September 6, 1952), 11; "Finca Vigia," p. [2]; "Old Newsman Writes," 26.

what was wrong with it was that it had not been conceived of as a novel but as short stories, and "there is a hell of a lot of difference." After recounting his troubles trying to find a producer for *The Fifth Column*, one of the main ones being producers' demands that he continue to tinker with the play when his tendency was to "go home and take a shower" after writing, he admitted its failure as a play by placing the play with his collected stories and saying that "it makes one story more and brings them a little closer to the present."[96] When he refused *Esquire* permission in 1958 to republish three uncollected Spanish Civil War stories—"The Denunciation," "The Butterfly and the Tank," and "Night Before Battle"—his refusal was again based on recognition of a failure of integrity in the stories. The rhythm was wrong, the use of such euphemisms as "crap" and "s.o.b." or "bastid" was false, and the emotion was timely rather than permanent, he said. "I reserve the right to make my prose as good as it can be. In fact, I have the obligation to do so." Such self-criticism was in line with his earlier remark that the reason Degas' paintings were so good was that all the bad Degas had been destroyed by the artist.[97]

But the writer had to face other critics as well, and he had to learn how to make criticism work for him. He had "learned very much from criticism," he told Harvey Breit, but the valuable criticism was simple and impersonal. His principal experience with critics had been useless because they made criticism the vehicle of personal attacks. They knew little about "the alchemy of the production of literature" and applied irrelevant critical theory—Freudian and Marxist, for example—to a writer's work.[98] What critics should do, he told Robert Manning, is to point living writers toward the best work of dead writers. To insist that a writer work according to current critical fashions would promote a rivalry between critic and writer, each insisting that he had the key insight to contemporary literature.[99]

It was a recommendation Hemingway did not always accept for himself, though he was careful to point out his primary

96. Robert Van Gelder, "Ernest Hemingway Talks of Work and War," *Writers and Writing* (New York, 1946), p. 98; *The Fifth Column and the First Forty-Nine Stories*, p. v.

97. Jerome Beatty, Jr., "Hemingway vs. Esquire," *Saturday Review*, XLI (August 23, 1958), 10-11; Ross, p. 60.

98. Breit, p. 179.

99. "Hemingway in Cuba," 104.

identification as writer rather than as critic of other men's books. He of course did assess the performances of the greats and the classics. His long list of pronouncements on American writers of the nineteenth century in *Green Hills of Africa,* while stated in support of the thesis that American social values prevented full development of American writers, also saw them in light of his own pragmatic standards as a writer. Emerson, Hawthorne, and Whittier, he charged, did not know a classic is new rather than imitative. Melville had vital experience as the raw material for creating a new experience but made the transformational process too intellectualized, too metaphysical, too rhetorical to achieve a fully realized vision. Thoreau he charged with being too concerned with making his observations of nature philosophically and literarily significant to make them real.[100] Stendhal, on the other hand, gave the best account in *The Charterhouse of Parma* of how human beings behaved during "a world shaking event" and Fabrizio at Waterloo became a touchstone beside which battle accounts like Hugo's version of Waterloo and Zola's of Sedan lacked reality.[101] And he recorded that during his apprentice days in Paris he puzzled over how Dostoyevsky could write "so unbelievably badly, and still make you feel so deeply."[102] His comment even then was double-edged. A tribute to the nineteenth-century Russian novelist, it was also a sly dig at Ezra Pound's teaching of the season that writers could learn best from the tradition of Flaubert with its emphasis on the *mot juste.*[103] Also during his apprentice days he had challenged the Swedish Academy as the proper arbiters of world literary recognition. The Nobel Prize committee's selection of W. B. Yeats "made up for a lot of things," he said, but he wondered because of the timing if the selection had more to do with the poet's being named Irish Senator than with his literary work. Some of the failures he thought the Academy had to live down were glorification of such second-rate writers as Maurice Maeterlinck, Rabindranath Tagore, Karl Giellerup, H. Pontoppidan, and Henryk Sienkiewicz while failing to recognize Joseph Conrad, Mark Twain, Henry James, and Thomas Hardy and waiting too late

100. *Green Hills of Africa,* pp. 20-22.
101. *Men at War,* p. xx.
102. *A Moveable Feast,* pp. 137-38.
103. *Ibid.,* p. 134.

for Anatole France's recognition to mean anything.[104] He later charged that Sherwood Anderson and Scott Fitzgerald, among his contemporaries, had been rendered creatively impotent because they listened to and believed the critics. They had believed them when praised and had ruined themselves trying to regain the critics' praise when the critics' standards had shifted.[105]

But the worst kind of critic to beware, and the kind presenting the greatest temptation to writers, was the political critic. For the political critic, he noted in "Old Newsman Writes," could offer the easy satisfaction of doing something worth doing for its time and of being sure one could do it well instead of "working all your life at something that will only be worth doing if you do it better than it has ever been done before." If a writer picked the winning political party, he could receive the plaudits of the party in power and its critics and could have a million copies of his book printed. Even such real artists as Tolstoy and Kipling had submitted to political enlistment, and the result was that parts of their best work had to be passed over as topical. What the writer had to remember, he said, was to make it new and make it true. To approach writing any other way was to cheat oneself and one's readers.[106]

When Gertrude Stein commented that Hemingway looked like a modern but smelled like a museum, she identified an essential characteristic of his work and thought, though it did not have the derogatory meaning she intended. As we can see, for all his supposed primitive simplicity and lack of formal academic training in aesthetics or criticism, Hemingway had a strong sense of the museum and of the past. He pitted his talents against the best of the past and had little reason to feel embarrassed at the result. If modern meant following the shifting literary fashions of the century, he was even more museum-like in his insistence that the true art of the storyteller was an enduring simplicity beyond temporary visions, revisions, and indecisions. But as his aesthetic statements also showed, the key to such apparent simplicity was an incredibly complex and concentrated act of seeing

104. "Learns to Commune with Fairies; Now Wins Nobel Prize," *TSW*, November 24, 1923, p. 35.
105. *Green Hills of Africa*, pp. 23-24.
106. "Old Newsman Writes," 26; "Defense of Dirty Words," *Esquire*, II (September 1934), 158B.

all things at once and yet seeing the act, gesture, or detail that implied all the rest. It may well be that after the siftings of literary analysis and evaluation, Hemingway's techniques of see- ing, together with the ways he used to equate that inner-outer vision, will be thought his most significant contribution to mod- ern literature. If the exact functioning of his reality sense was either too unconscious or too complex to be reduced to expository statement, we have instead a series of metaphors to provide both light and mystery about his creative process. How writing can be like an iceberg, a bullfight, a long-distance race, a hunt, a painting, a fugue, or a ritual of language magic will finally have to find total meaning in the creative imagination of another artist rather than in the categories of critics or other analysts. It may be as Hemingway suggested all along, that no artist or critic can provide guided tours through the more difficult country of his work.

PART FOUR / *Correlations*

The Essay and the Fiction

X. Sources, Analogues, and Echoes

TRUE TO ITS NATURE, HEMINGWAY'S ICEBERG THEORY OF WRITING had more implications than he ever explained. Among other meanings he never brought to the surface for discussion was the fact that his nonfictional work functioned as a kind of substructure for his fiction. If he wrote the kind of fiction that precluded comment or explanation, he also wrote much journalism and other expository material that provided considerable insight into what the fiction was all about. Such nonfictional commentary did not violate his refusal to provide guided tours of his work. Rather it showed the thinking and savoring of experience that went on in the writer's mind before he ever set about creating fictional experience. In many cases the nonfiction existed in its own right as journalism and only later gained recognition in Hemingway's mind as suitable material for imaginative use. In other cases he first recognized the significance of various items of knowledge or personal experience when he remembered them for use in fiction, but, having recognized their significance, he used them again in expository works and sometimes again in later fiction. His vicarious recall of the drowning Greek baggage animals at Smyrna was an example. It emerged first as part of the fictional sketch "On the Quai at Smyrna" and two years later as part of *Death in the Afternoon.* In still other cases his later nonfiction, particularly that of the interview, introduction, and memoir, served to explain not the content of fiction but the influencing circumstances and the sources of his experiences that became part of the fiction. In spite of his frequently repeated statements that using material first in journalism ruined it for later use in fiction, the facts show Hemingway's frequent practice of reusing journalistic materials in his fiction. Such patterns of repetition suggest that, however wide his knowledge and experience were, some elements of that experience called for a kind of understanding that reuse in depth could provide.

Comments and source statements on the fiction are scattered throughout the nonfiction and vary widely in significance. For some stories there is only a single brief mention in the essays. For others the clues to fictional statements are so numerous that a great part of the nonfictional substructure can be identified, both in situations and in persons involved. Sometimes even the phrasing is close enough to prompt identification. Because of the relatively complete and coherent source statements and comments about them, this account is concerned with the nonfictional substructure of *The Sun Also Rises, A Farewell to Arms,* "The Short Happy Life of Francis Macomber," "The Snows of Kilimanjaro," *For Whom the Bell Tolls, Across the River and into the Trees,* and *The Old Man and the Sea.* Statements on other works, which represent a more miscellaneous fund of insights, can be found in Appendix B.

The Sun Also Rises

Hemingway's statements relevant to *The Sun Also Rises* fall into three classes: those concerned with the composition and naming of the novel, those describing general settings and actions incorporated into the novel, and those indicating his own experience as the basis for action and comment in the story. Those concerned with composition of the novel of course came well after it had gained both publication and fame. In his interview with George Plimpton and in *A Moveable Feast* he told how the novel was begun in Valencia on July 21, 1925, was written in six weeks during brief stays in Madrid, Hendaye, and Paris and thoroughly rewritten during the fall and winter of 1925-26 at Schruns in the Vorarlberg.[1] His emphasis in both accounts was on the necessity of places conducive to clear thinking and intense feeling and on the recency of the experiences impelling him to write, particularly his realization that he alone among his contemporaries had not yet written a novel. In *A Moveable Feast* he also explained his thinking when he named the work and gave it the two epigraphs from Gertrude Stein and the Bible: "Later when I wrote my first novel I tried to balance Miss Stein's quotation from the garage keeper with one from Ecclesiastes. . . . I thought of Miss Stein and Sherwood Anderson and mental laziness versus discipline and I thought who is calling who a lost generation?"[2]

In his journalism written before the composition of *The Sun Also Rises* and in *Death in the Afternoon,* published six years after the novel, Hemingway wrote of the world in which Jake Barnes and his friends lived. Principally the worlds of Paris and Pamplona, they were described for other purposes than to serve as settings for the novel, yet they lent themselves to reuse. Indeed much of the authority the novel had came from the detailed and familiar knowledge Hemingway had of those places, their terrain, their colors and smells, their movement, their unspoken secrets. Because of such knowledge he could allude to facts implicit but real in the lives of the people in the novel, and because he knew the facts were there he could pass over them with the barest mention. But in his nonfiction he explained those facts of life for Paris and Pamplona, and the explanations function like a series of commentaries or footnotes on moments in the novel. When Jake attends the Quai d'Orsay briefing for correspondents, listens to the Nouvelle Revue Française diplomat

1. Several identifications of source statements from Hemingway's nonfiction have been made by Carlos Baker, *Hemingway: The Writer as Artist* (Princeton, 1963), pp. 199, 234, 239, 241, 294; by Charles Fenton, *The Apprenticeship of Ernest Hemingway* (New York, 1961), pp. 81, 108, 115, 133, 134, 143, 144, 186, 187; and by A. E. Hotchner, *Papa Hemingway* (New York, 1966), pp. 46, 51-52, 56, 73-74, 94, 103-4, 114-16, 131-36, 161-64, 175-78, 182, 217; all are useful and convincing. But their identifications require supplementation in numerous instances.

2. Baker, *Hemingway and His Critics* (New York, 1961), pp. 30-31; *A Moveable Feast* (New York, 1964), p. 202.

offer routine views on a speech by the President of the Council of State at Lyons, hears sycophantic questions answered and probing questions evaded, the underlying mood of the press briefing is that of perfunctoriness.[3] What is not said in the novel but can be felt during the action is that the briefing is a meaningless ritual. This feeling gains a rationale, however, in light of Hemingway's earlier Toronto *Star* story on the French government's practice of buying news column space in French papers and publishing its version of the news there. "Le Temps is always spoken of as 'semi-official.' That means that the first column on the first page is written in the foreign office at the Quai D'Orsay, the rest of the columns are at the disposal of the various governments of Europe."[4] Both Jake and the reader initiated into the Paris news practices know that only by a lucky accident can anything be learned at the briefing. Within the context of the novel, then, what Hemingway knew from previous acquaintance with the Paris scene becomes a functional scene of futility for Jake. The diplomat's action is as much discounted of meaning or reality as are the later performances by the matador Belmonte, who has selected his bulls for manageability.

In his subsequent conversation with correspondents Woolsey and Krum, Jake finds that they reside in the city of expatriates but live in the manner of suburban Americans, working on a weekly routine and talking of better days to come. But Jake sees also that they long for the freedom and the more intense life that the expatriates are supposed to have. They ask him about the Dingo Bar as the place where the vital people meet, and hope to get some night to the scenes of joy. "I'm coming over some night," says Krum. "The Dingo. That's the great place, isn't it?" (p. 36). Their vision of Left Bank Paris as the happy opposite of their business lives was one Hemingway had noted in Chicago during his brief return to America in 1923. He recorded what he saw in a series of factual vignettes called "So This Is Chicago," and one of them was a rehearsal of Krum's mood: "The boys who went into La Salle Street when you first went on a newspaper now all driving their own cars, lunching at the club, and asking if you think there is any possible way they could

3. *The Sun Also Rises* (New York, 1954, Scribner's Library), p. 36. Subsequent references to the novel will be to this edition and will be parenthesized in the text.
4. *TDS*, April 21, 1923, p. 1.

make a living in Paris."[5] In the novel, however, the ironic turn is that the correspondents are in Paris but have brought their old selves with them and still expect a change of place to make the difference. But Jake has already seen that "You can't get away from yourself by moving from one place to another." (p. 11)

Later in the novel when Frances Clyne tongue-lashes Robert Cohn for sending her away to England to end their affair in favor of Brett Ashley, she recounts in her tirade on betrayals her mother's loss on French war bonds. "Yes, how is my dear mother? She put all her money into French war bonds. Yes, she did. Probably the only person in the world that did." (p. 49) Behind this comment was Hemingway's knowledge of French manipulation of war bond financing. In his 1922 *Star* article "Poincaré Making Good on Election Promises" he explained how the French converted short-term bonds into long-term ones and how finally they paid off, if at all, in devaluated currency. Frances' bitterness over her betrayal by Robert Cohn thus invokes not only her individual feelings but a general sense of betrayal in Paris. Like French and foreign investors, she had believed in a future pay-off and had suffered a loss in money comparable to her loss of hope to marry Robert Cohn.

At another point in the Paris section of the novel Jake takes his prostitute friend Georgette Hobin to the *bal musette*, where, as Mrs. Braddocks says, they have "dancings." The *bal musette* was a Paris phenomenon Hemingway had noted in early 1922, and his description of the dancing club for the Toronto *Star* had much in common, even in phrasing, with the description in the novel. "[A]round the corner somewhere there is a little Bal Musette where the apaches . . . hang out with their girls, sit at long benches in the little smoky room and dance to the music of a man with an accordeon who keeps time with the stamping of his boots. . . . On the gala nights there is a drummer at the Bal Musette, but the accordeon player wears a string of bells around his ankle, and these, with the stamping of his boots as he sits swaying on a dais above the dancing floor, give the accent to the rhythm."[6] Whereas in the newspaper account the *bal musette* is a mark of the real Paris seldom seen by outsiders, in the novel it becomes an affectation of the cafe-hopping crowd, an

5. *TSW*, January 19, 1924, p. 19.
6. *TSW*, March 25, 1922, p. 22.

index to their falseness. They stand in contrast to the working people who use the bal musette the other five nights of the week.

> The dancing-club was a *bal musette* in the Rue de la Montagne Saint Geneviève. Five nights a week the working people of the Pantheon quarter danced there. One night a week it was the dancing-club. . . . There were long benches, and tables ran across the room, and at the far end a dancing floor.
> . . . The proprietor got up on a high stool beside the dancing-floor and began to play the accordion. He had a string of bells around one of his ankles and beat time with his foot as he played. (p. 19).

The original account received further ironic treatment in the novel when Hemingway placed vital characters in the cafes catering to tourists. In the article he described the champagne-selling night clubs of Montparnasse as those where tourists falsely got the impression they were seeing the real Paris while they paid heavily for mock champagne and listened to American-style jazz. But in the novel Count Mippipopolous, a man whose authenticity is certified by his scars, drinks real champagne at the Café Select and knows from wide experience he is getting the best value money can buy. (p. 29) The Count further inverts the meanings of the source article by knowingly savoring the American Negro jazz at Zelli's Bar in Montmartre. (pp. 60-62) If Hemingway provided simple value alignments in his newspaper articles on place, in his creative work he rendered the values more complex and ambiguous. The context of action and feeling, particularly as it is varied through Jake's moody observations, resists easy identification of values. The Braddocks and their crowd render a place of genuine, unselfconscious *joie de vivre* false by their pretensions at joy, and the Count temporarily authenticates an otherwise dubious setting. Then, too, the way the Braddocks' crowd and the Count are to be seen is rendered even more ambiguous by Jake's often unadmitted moods. He is disgusted with himself for picking up Georgette when he arrives at the *bal musette,* and he has just been through a love scene with Brett when he meets the Count at the Select. The observations from the *Star* article are indeed but raw material to be shaped and given meaning by the novelist's imagination.

It is generally recognized that Jake's and Bill's extended conversations, particularly those at the Burguete inn and beside the

Irati River, are loaded with ironic allusions. Much of their humor as well as the thematic elucidation in the scene derives from the technique. Several of the more obscure topical and literary allusions have now been explicated, though several still need such treatment, and later generations of readers will increasingly need explanation of the references to Wayne B. Wheeler, Bishop Manning, and Frankie Fritsch. Hemingway's nonfiction, however, provided some light on the passages. When Bill tells Jake that Irony and Pity are the catch words of the New York scene, "just like the Fratellinis used to be," (p. 114) we find that *Death in the Afternoon* provides not only identification of the Fratellinis as a comedy act but specific indication of their significance in Hemingway's thought. They provided, he said in his discussion of the disemboweling of the picador horses in bullfights, insight into the relationship between tragedy and comic incident. Their burlesque pointed up the essentially comic, not pathetic, role of the horses in a sequence of actions leading to tragic enlightenment. Jake's and Bill's humor, by analogy, serves as a foreshadowing of Jake's drubbing by Robert Cohn and as a comic preparation for later recognitions by Jake, Brett, and Robert Cohn.[7]

The general Pamplona background of *The Sun Also Rises*, both of the *fiesta* and of the bullfights, had already had its initial statement before Hemingway made it the key setting for his novel. In the two *Toronto Star Weekly* articles "Bull Fighting Is Not a Sport—It Is a Tragedy" and "World's Series of Bull Fighting a Mad, Whirling Carnival," and in his "Pamplona Letter" in *the transatlantic review* Hemingway sketched in the manner of the travel writer the key actions of a bullfight and suggested the color and frenzy of a quasi-religious festival. "San Fermin is the local deity in the system of local idolatry which the Spaniards substitute for Catholicism. San Fermin, looking very much like Buddha, is carried through the streets at odd moments during the Feria."[8] So he wrote in 1924. It was an insight on the shifted emphasis in an originally religious *fiesta* that he used in the novel to show Brett as a rival of San Fermin in the eyes of the celebrants. While one group goes inside the cathedral to translate the saint's image to the altar, another group stays in the streets to

---

7. *Death in the Afternoon* (New York, 1932), p. 7.
8. "Pamplona Letter," *the transatlantic review*, II (October 1924), 301; see also *TSW*, October 20, 1923, p. 33; *TSW*, October 27, 1923, p. 23.

dance around Brett. (p. 155) In the *Star* articles he explained the stages of the bullfight—from the ceremonial granting of permission to the marshals to conduct the bullfight to the parade of the *cuadrillas* and the description of the thirds of the actual conflict, those of the picadors, the *banderilleros*, and the matadors. He chronicled them in greater detail later in *Death in the Afternoon*, but they were all there in the prenovel articles. They were implicit in the bullfight scenes in the novel, but the focus there was on Romero and the bullfight details from the journalistic pieces worked as meaningful background for the exploits of the young gypsy matador. The ritual and tradition of the background action, only alluded to in the novel, provide the means for showing Romero both as an individual person in the story and as the epitome of a meaningful system of values.

Hemingway's later commentary in *Death in the Afternoon* showed further factual knowledge on his part that had been implicit in the novel. His fictional hotel keeper Juan Montoya in Pamplona was identified as an actual person—"[Juanito] Quintana the best aficionado and most loyal friend in Spain, and with a fine hotel with all the rooms full."[9] His characterization of Romero as an instinctive matador who "knew everything when he started" (p. 168) found its explanation in the bullfight book. The artist-matador and writer, he observed, "uses everything that has been discovered or known about his art up to that point, being able to accept or reject in a time so short it seems that the knowledge was born with him, rather than that he takes instantly what it takes the ordinary man a lifetime to know. . . ."[10] His description of Vicente Girone's goring and death in the streets of Pamplona by the bull Bocanegra had its previous hearing in the *Star* article on the Pamplona *fiesta* and later its explanation in *Death in the Afternoon*, where Hemingway noted that it was characteristic of a bull to charge an individual rather than a whole crowd.[11] His depiction of scoffers in the novel when Romero dealt with the defective bull (pp. 215-18) had its explanation later when he observed that good bullfights needed a knowledgeable public as well as brave bulls and skillful matadors, "and a good public is not the public of a one bullfight fiesta where

9. *Death in the Afternoon*, pp. 170, 274,
10. *Ibid.*, pp. 99-100, 191-92.
11. *Ibid.*, p. 23.

everyone drinks and has a fine time, and the women come in costume, nor is it the drunken, dancing, bull-running public of Pamplona nor the local, patriotic, bullfighter worshippers of Valencia."[12] His depiction of Juan Belmonte's rejection by the Pamplona public because they believed the legends about the man rather than their eyes had its basis in previous factual knowledge also. In the bullfight book Hemingway told how the critic Guerrita urged people to hurry to see Belmonte because anyone working so close to the bulls was sure to be killed soon. But Belmonte survived, retired, returned from retirement, and was charged with exploiting his name while giving inferior performances. When he retired again, critics discovered his greatness again. The treatment of Belmonte in the novel thus was prejudiced to throw a more heroic light on the fictional Romero, but it had to be understood also that critics and public were fickle in their passions and seldom willing to accord a bullfighter his fame until he was blurred in their memory by retirement or death. (p. 214) In this case the novel, in order to dramatize values, offered an oversimplification in judgment where the nonfiction retained its complexity.

Two other actions in the novel, both concerning Brett Ashley at the bullfights, had their backgrounds in the nonfiction. After Jake's friends see their first bullfight, they compare their sensations and reactions, which range from Robert Cohn's queasiness to Brett's zestful acceptance of all the bloodshed. (p. 166) Brett's enthusiasm for violence, though a matter of congratulation by her friends, was already an established part of Hemingway's view of women. In his Toronto *Star* article on women at prizefights, he saw their applause of bloody fights as an echo of women's applause at the Roman gladiatorial contests. They were, he noted, much more primitive in their tastes than men, and, as their Victorian pretenses dropped away, they showed their really destructive drives.[13] Second, when at the climactic fight Romero sends his cape to Brett, she and Jake prepare to spread it on the *barrera* in front of her, but a swordhandler indicates she should hold it in her lap. (p. 213) No explanation occurs at the point to tell why the usual procedure should not be followed. In *Death in*

12. *Ibid.*, pp. 42, 242.
13. "Toronto Women Who Went to the Prize Fights Applauded the Rough Stuff," *TSW*, May 15, 1920, p. 13.

the Afternoon, however, Hemingway provided a retrospective clue, if not an explanation. Matadors frequently sent their capes to friends, critics, or dignitaries, he said, but it was a potentially embarrassing practice. A matador's performance could sometimes go wrong because of bad luck or bad bulls, and when the hecklers' pillows and bottles started flying down into the ring, it was embarrassing to have the matador's swordhandler come dodging through the missiles to retrieve the cape.[14] The gesture in the novel could have several meanings of intent on Romero's part: his reluctance to acknowledge Brett publicly at the time and his uncertainty of feeling about her and about her image as a matador's favorite. But in narrative terms he is also uncertain of his coming performance at that moment. His drubbing by Cohn still stiffens him and, in light of Hemingway's later comment, it seems he wishes to avoid possible embarrassment for Brett as much as for himself. The nonfictional knowledge thus supplies a general dimension to the action to supplement those meanings implicit in the narrative action.

Few readers have had reason to doubt that the events of *The Sun Also Rises* owed much to Hemingway's personal actions and feelings. Such an account as Harold Loeb's *The Way It Was,* among other memoirs, has made clear how autobiographical the novel was. But Hemingway made much of his personal experience a matter of record in his own nonfiction, both before and after the novel. His statement in "The Dangerous Summer" that Cayetano Ordonez was the model for Romero is believable, but his assertion that only the bull ring incidents of the novel were based on fact while the events outside the ring were all "made up and imagined" needs some interpretation.[15] Too many anticipations and recollections of events occurring both in his recorded experience and in the novel point to a factual base for narrative incident outside the bull ring.

Near the beginning of the novel Jake suggests to Robert Cohn that they fly to Strasbourg and walk to Saint Odile. He knows a girl in Strasbourg who can show them around. The suggestion was an echo of Hemingway's own flight to Strasbourg, which he chronicled in his *Toronto Daily Star* article "A Paris-to-Strasbourg Flight Shows Living Cubist Picture."[16] Flying had train

14. *Death in the Afternoon,* p. 60.
15. *Life,* XLIV (September 5, 1960), 86.
16. *TDS,* September 9, 1922, p. 8.

travel all beat for seeing country, he wrote, and gave a new perspective on the way people reacted to new ideas. That essentially was what Jake suggested for Robert Cohn, but he got instead a kick under the table when he mentioned the girl in Strasbourg. (p. 6).

Other elements of the Paris action of the novel had their origins in experiences Hemingway remembered in *A Moveable Feast*. Mrs. Braddocks' invitation to Jake to bring his friend Georgette Hobin to the *bal musette* was evidently anticipated by Ford Madox Ford's asking Hemingway to "the little evenings we're giving in that amusing Bal Musette near the Place Contrescarpe on the Rue Cardinal Lemoine."[17] Jake takes Georgette to Lavigne's restaurant, which she scorns on sight: "This is no great thing of a restaurant." But after dinner she admits, "It isn't chic, but the food is all right." (p. 16) In his memoir Hemingway identified Lavigne's as the Nègre de Toulouse restaurant, where the Hemingways kept their napkin rings and where even seeing the menu made him hungry. He was thus dealing with solidly known experience when he had Jake take his pickup to an excellent but unshowy place. The associations of Lavigne's were those he knew rang true.[18] Later Jake mentally pauses to watch the barges pass under the bridges crossing the Seine. It is soon after Brett has failed to meet him at the Hotel Crillon, and he is making his way to the Left Bank to join his drinking friends there. Crossing the Seine, he notes the "barges being towed empty down the current, riding high" and the pleasant river. "It was always pleasant crossing bridges in Paris," he observes. (p. 41) E. M. Halliday has suggested that Jake's noting the empty barges is "a metaphorical correlation between certain details of . . . panorama and [Jake's] emotional state at the moment."[19] This perception of the effect the narrative context has on the detail, however, must be modified by Jake's observing the full current as well as the empty barges. Hemingway's notation in *A Moveable Feast* provided an insight into the thematic counterpart to Jake's feeling and a suggestion on the meaning of the river for Jake and his literary creator. "With the fishermen and the life on the river, the beautiful barges with their own life on

17. *A Moveable Feast*, p. 84.
18. *Ibid.*, p. 136.
19. "Hemingway's Narrative Perspective," *Sewanee Review*, LX (Spring 1952), 206.

board, the tugs with their smokestacks that folded back to pass under the bridges, the great elms on the stone banks of the river, the plane trees and in some places the the poplars, I could never be lonely on the river."[20] Jake's notation of the pleasant river as well as the empty barges, in light of Hemingway's later statement, suggests that his personal loneliness is caused by people and is a recognizably passing emotion when measured against his lasting perception of earth's pleasantness. "It was *always* pleasant crossing bridges in Paris," Jake recognizes (italics mine). The paragraph thus provides a glimpse of both basic motifs at work in the book—the lost generation and the abiding earth.

A lighter touch on the Paris scene of the novel is Jake's mention of his overprotective concierge. Only those guests who have been well brought up, are of good family, or are sportsmen manage to pass her station. It costs Brett two hundred francs to convince the concierge of her class. But one of Jake's friends, who meets none of the landlady's tests, "an extremely underfed-looking painter," asks Jake to get a pass for him so the concierge will allow him to visit in the evenings. (p. 53) The touch had its parallel in Hemingway's recorded personal experience. In *A Moveable Feast* he remembered Evan Shipman's telling him that the apartment owner's wife did not like him and refused to let him wait in Hemingway's apartment.[21] Hemingway's alteration of the original experience was significant, though. His change of Shipman from poet to an underfed and unnamed painter was in line with the terms of thematic presentation in the novel. Novelists and poets are in Jake's experience examples of the pseudo-expatriate life in Paris. Both Robert Cohn and Robert Prentiss, novelists without feeling, demonstrate the failure of authenticity by self-consciously artistic writers. Jake and Bill Gorton, writers of journalism and humor, stand in contrast to them. Painters receive less censure. Only Zizi, the Greek portrait painter and friend of Count Mippipopolous, receives low marks, and they are for his sycophantic manner, not his talent. For thematic emphasis, Hemingway thus put writers in contrast to painters in the novel.

Hemingway's personal experience with Pamplona and other bullfight towns provided both background and foreground inci-

20. *A Moveable Feast*, pp. 44-45.
21. *Ibid.*, p. 136.

dent for the novel. Jake's notations of the bouncing *riau-riau* dancers, the throngs in the streets, the wineshops crowded with black-smocked peasants singing hard-voiced songs, the pyrotechnic show by Don Manuel Orquito, the running of bulls in the streets, his standing on the balcony to watch the bulls run, and the rockets announcing the arrival of the bulls at the ring all had their previous appearance in his Toronto *Star* articles. (pp. 153, 155, 160, 178, 196) In "World's Series of Bull Fighting a Mad, Whirling Carnival" he recorded the observations made when he and Hadley Hemingway arrived at Pamplona for the San Fermines in July of 1923:

Bullfight fans from all over Spain jam into the little town. Hotels double their prices and fill every room. The cafés under the wide arcades that run around the Plaza de la Constitucion have every table crowded, the tall, pilgrim father sombreros of Andalusia sitting over the same table with straw hats from Madrid and the flat blue Basque caps of Navarre and the Basque country.

. . . .

All day and all night there is dancing in the streets. Bands of blue-shirted peasants whirl and lift and swing behind a drum, fife and reed instruments in the ancient Basque Riau-Riau dances. And at night there is the throb of the big drums and the military band as the whole town dances in the great open square of the Plaza.

. . . .

We landed at Pamplona at night. The streets were solid with people dancing. Music was pounding and throbbing. Fireworks were being set off from the big public square. A rocket exploded over our heads with a blinding burst and the stick came swirring and whishing down. Dancers, snapping their fingers and whirling in perfect time through the crowd, bumped us before we could get our bags down from the top of the station bus.

. . . .

All night long the wild music kept up in the street below. Several times in the night there was a wild roll of drumming, and I got out of bed and across the tiled floor to the balcony. But it was always the same. Men, blue-shirted, bare-headed, whirling and floating in a wild fantastic dance down the street behind the rolling drums and shrill fifes.

. . . .

Just at daylight there was a crash of music in the street below. Real military music. . . . Down below the street was full of people.

It was five o'clock in the morning. They were all going in one direction.[22]

Hemingway's excitement in the original came from his first seeing the carnival with its strange and often fantastic images. In the novel Jake has seen the *fiesta* in progress before, but that is the basis of the fantastic element for him. He has seen much turmoil in war too, and his recall of bursting rockets goes on back to shrapel bursts. (p. 153) Thus, while Hemingway first approached the *fiesta* as reporter and spectator, in his later view the scene was not different from others of the time but the epitome of the age.

A future use of the article as source of a fictional sequence showed Hemingway's tactic of suppressing some details into an implication and expanding other implications into a dramatized moment. At the Pamplona carnival he asked a newsboy what all the rockets and running of people were about and what was about to happen. Asking what *"encierro"* meant, he got the impatient answer, "Oh, ask me tomorrow." And the boy ran off. Going to a nearby cafe, he and Hadley asked the waiter for explanations while they watched him pour "two streams of coffee and milk into the glass from his big kettles." The waiter's answer was as uninformative as the newsboy's. "All I know is that they let the bulls out into the streets." But they saw a blue-shirted boy run down by the bulls in the streets shortly afterward and soon learned the sequence of events. In the novel Jake's perceptions are sharpened and distorted by his beating from Robert Cohn. He knows the pattern of events, assumes what the newsboy failed to tell Hemingway, is watching through a hole in the street barrier when Vicente Girones is gored in the back, and goes on to a cafe where he hears a waiter express feelings on the absurdity of the running of bulls that the actual waiter had only implied. Watching the waiter pour milk and coffee "in two streams" from the long-handled pots, he learns that one man has been "badly cogido through the back." The waiter is out of sympathy: "A big horn wound. All for fun. Just for fun. What do you think of that?" (pp. 196-98)

Jake's loss of Brett to Romero is another example of what was a possibility in actual reported experience becoming an accom-

22. *TSW*, October 27, 1923, p. 33.

plished narrative incident. Part of the possibility was stated before the novel was written. After Pamplona, Hemingway noted, Maera was his wife's favorite bullfighter:

And if you want to keep any conception of yourself as a brave, hard, perfectly balanced, thoroughly competent man in your wife's mind, never take her to a bullfight. I used to go to the amateur fights in the morning to try and win back a small amount of her esteem but the more I discovered that bullfighting required a great quantity of a certain type of courage of which I had an almost complete lack the more it became apparent that any admiration that she might ever develop for me would have to be simply an antidote to the real admiration for Maera and Villata. You cannot compete with bullfighters on their own ground.[23]

Much of Brett's admiration of Romero in "those green trousers," her not being surprised that she might be falling in love with the matador, and her pressing Jake into introducing her and Romero and then Jake's letting them go off together were implicit in the passage. When Jake later ruefully thinks of the irony of introducing a girl to a man so she can go off with him and signing a telegram to her with "love," he is living out the possibilities of trying to compete with bullfighters on their own ground. Further use of actual events with possibilities realized in fiction occurs in the novel when Romero kills the bull Bocanegra and gives the ear to Brett, who leaves it, wrapped in Jake's handkerchief, in the drawer of her bedside table at the Hotel Montoya. (p. 199) Among the unrecounted experiences in Spain which Hemingway catalogued at the end of *Death in the Afternoon* was this item: "Hadley, with the bull's ear wrapped in a handkerchief, the ear very stiff and dry and the hair all worn off it and the man who cut the ear is bald now too and slicks long strips of hair over the top of his head and he was beau then."[24]

Hemingway's 1927 article "The Real Spaniard" provided insight into his use of another detail in the novel. Jake's friend Juan Montoya tests the American's *afición* by asking indirect questions and by putting his hand on Jake's shoulder. It is a gesture typical of those having *afición*, Jake notes. Montoya's other *aficionado* guests likewise confirm Jake's *afición* by ques-

23. *Ibid.*
24. *Death in the Afternoon*, p. 274.

tion and touch: "When they saw that I had afición, and there was no password, no set questions that could bring it out, rather it was a sort of oral spiritual examination with the questions always on the defensive and never apparent, there was this same embarrassed putting the hand on the shoulder, or 'a Buen hombre.' But nearly always there was the actual touching. It seemed as though they wanted to touch you to make it certain." (pp. 131-32) In *The Boulevardier* article Hemingway wrote of his search for the real Spaniard. "I remember once in Navarre the proprietor of a hotel had a kind way of laying hold of my arm when he talked and not putting the drinks on the bill. The Real Spaniard, I thought."[25] Whatever the original experience was, it had a secrecy about it that led to symbolic depiction in the novel and to satirical indirection in the later essay. In either report it hinted of some intuition too secret, even lewd, said Jake, to say openly.

Jake's role as tutor for his friends at the bullfights is the product of other experience Hemingway recorded in his journalism. Attending his first bullfight in Madrid, he reported having the stages of the *corrida* and the relative merits of the bullfighters present interpreted for him by "a young man in a straw hat, with obviously American shoes" whom he came to know as the Gin Bottle King. Besides what he told Hemingway during the bullfight, the Gin Bottle King continued his instruction during an evening-long dinner of roast pig, mushroom *tortilla*, and red wine. What was reported as true experience also served as an interpretive device in the article. Having the Gin Bottle King explain the actions of Hemingway's first bullfight enabled him as a journalist to understand the events of the ring while first seeing them.[26] In the novel Jake sits beside Brett and explains events "so that she saw what it was all about, so that it became something that was going on with a definite end, and less of a spectacle of unexplained horrors." Where the Gin Bottle King pointed out the veronicas of Chicuelo to Hemingway, Jake shows Brett how Romero smoothly wears down his bull without brusque movements. And where the Gin Bottle tutor put the present bullfighters in the context of other great matadors, Jake tells Brett how Romero has the classic style of Joselito instead of the

25. *The Boulevardier* (Paris), I (October 1927), 6.
26. *TSW*, October 20, 1923, p. 33.

currently popular but less satisfying ornate style of Belmonte. (pp. 167-68) In the novel, however, Brett's initiation into the secrets of *afición* serves to prompt a more personal and dramatically usable passion than that learned by Hemingway. What was for Hemingway a fund of general insight becomes in the novel a critical knowledge serving to complicate and finally resolve the conflicts among characters. Through her new knowledge Brett learns both to value and to renounce Pedro Romero.

The success of *The Sun Also Rises* became a touchstone for Hemingway. He never tried again to render fictionally what he did so well in that novel. Some later short stories dealt with peripheral matters in bullfighting. "The Capitol of the World" concerns the lives of aspiring and defeated matadors, and "The Mother of a Queen" deals with a matador's financial expression of his homosexuality. Some passages in *For Whom the Bell Tolls* embody Pilar's recollections of her matador Finito and his fears. But Hemingway wrote of bullfights in nonfiction as commentaries on that realized fictional experience. In *Death in the Afternoon* he explained that Villar and Miura bulls had the reputation for greatest bravery, power, and size in the Spanish rings during the early twenties, though by 1927 the Villar bulls had been bred down in size to make them more acceptable to matadors. The comment was in effect an explanation of Montoya's anticipatory comment to Jake that "to-night at seven o'clock they bring in the Villar bulls, and tomorrow come the Miuras." (p. 131) He had seen a *corrida* of Villar bulls at Pamplona in 1923, Hemingway noted, and they were well-horned, fast, vicious, and ready to attack.[27] The implication was that the fights in *The Sun Also Rises* occurred during the still heroic age of bullfighting. The presence of Belmonte in the book and Romero's association with him served to enhance that atmosphere of heroism for the time. Cayetano Ordonez—model for Romero—looked like a messiah at the beginning of his career, he wrote, looking back to the novel: "I tried to describe how he looked and a couple of his fights in a book one time. I was present the day of his first presentation as a matador in Madrid and I saw him in Valencia that year in competition with Juan Belmonte, returned from retirement, do two faenas that were so beautiful and wonderful that I can remember them pass by pass to-day. He was

27. *Death in the Afternoon*, p. 161.

sincerity and purity of style itself with the cape, he did not kill badly, although, except when he had luck, he was not a great killer."[28]

As late as "The Dangerous Summer,, he wrote of the novel as though it were established text and only commentaries and reaffirmations by the novelist, not further imaginative creations, could be written. His description of the Pamplona fiesta of 1959 was written as though it were a summation of events in the novel:

Pamplona is no place to bring your wife. The odds are all in favor of her getting ill, hurt or wounded or at least jostled and wine squirted over her, or of losing her; maybe all three. . . . It's a man's fiesta and women always make trouble, never intentionally of course, but they nearly always make or have trouble. I wrote a book on this once. Of course if she can talk Spanish so she knows she is being joked with and not insulted, if she can drink wine all day and all night and dance with any groups of strangers who invite her, if she does not mind things being spilled on her, if she adores continual noise and music and loves fireworks, especially those that fall close to her or burn her clothes, if she thinks it is sound and logical to see how close you can come to being killed for fun and for free, if she doesn't catch cold when she is rained on and appreciates dust, likes disorder and irregular meals and never needs to sleep and still keeps clean and neat without running water; then bring her. You'll probably lose her to a better man than you.

To complete the similarity of actual and fictional experience, he dipicted A. E. Hotchner's running humor as a later counterpart of Bill Gorton's sallies.[29] It is possible that he heard them also as echoes of Donald Ogden Stewart's humor of the 1924 *fiesta*. In any case, the later comments indicated a tendency to see fewer and fewer differences between actual and imagined experience, to let fictional scenes impose themselves on reported personal experience and to serve as his reality, and see actual events as pale ghosts of the fictional account, which he apparently thought he had made "truer than true."

A Farewell to Arms

Hemingway's nonfictional comment relevant to *A Farewell to Arms*, unlike that on the expatriate novel, falls into two cate-

28. *Ibid.*, p. 89.
29. *Life*, XLIX (September 12, 1960), 73; (September 19, 1960), 80-82.

gories—statements made before or after publication of the novel and dealing with general social conditions and scenes made part of the narrative, and statements of personal feeling and personal experiences which became the feeling and thoughts of his created people. He has not stated in public his reasons for naming the novel or offered glimpses of thematic intention through discussion of epigraphs as he did for *The Sun Also Rises*. The closest he came to such a declaration was his statement in the introduction to the 1948 edition that the title was *A Farewell to Arms* and it was written about a century of almost continuous war, much of which he had observed and learned to hate.[30]

His ten-year preparation for writing the novel, however, had a partially documentable history. Much of his observation of postwar Europe prompted him to assumptions and conclusions which became the texture of the novel. Some of those ideas he stated journalistically before the novel was written, others later. Reporting German responses to inflation in 1922, he worked out a metaphor for the times which he later adapted for his novel. German storekeepers, he noted, continued selling goods for an inflating currency which, by the time they were ready to restock, could not even buy an amount of goods equal to what they had sold, much less show a profit. It was like a great national fire sale. "The great national fire sale cannot last forever. While it is going on, however, the German store keeper takes out his wrath on the foreigners who buy from him by acting as nastily as he can without forcing them out of the shop. He believes they are the cause of the fire, but he seems to feel he is in the position of the shopkeeper who is forced to sell goods at a fire sale to the men who set his shop on fire."[31] In the novel he shifted the meaning of the metaphor backward in time, seeing the war as the fire which caused the great fire sale. In his attempts to clarify for himself his desertion from the war, Frederic Henry sees the war as a department store fire for which he, as a floorwalker, cannot be responsible. "You had lost your cars and your men as a floorwalker loses the stock of his department in a fire. . . . If they shot floorwalkers after a fire in the department store because they spoke with an accent they had always had, then cer-

30. *A Farewell to Arms* (New York, 1948), p. x.
31. "Germans Are Doggedly Sullen or Desperate over the Mark," *TDS*, September 1, 1922, p. 23.

tainly the floorwalkers would not be expected to return when the store opened for business."[32] That the foreigner was suspect in both cases became the common element in his extensions of the metaphor; and in the novel, focused on a particular foreigner, it became a dramatically exploitable element.

His identification of the essentials of city and country life in postwar Europe became the basis of thematic contrasts in the novel. His characterizations of the various kinds of night life in Europe, in such articles as "Wild Night Music of Paris Makes Visitor Feel a Man of the World" and "Night Life in Europe a Disease: Constantinople's Most Hectic," pointed out that night life in the city operated on a different scale and with different values from the life of the city by day or that of the countryside.[33] A product of the war, night life ranged from scintillating in Paris to dull in Rome, sordid and vicious in Berlin to sedately conversational in Madrid. In Italy, he said, night life "must be taken to mean not dissipation or dancing places necessarily, but merely that strange, feverish something that keeps people up and about during the hours they would normally sleep." In his prose poem "The Soul of Spain" he described night life much as Frederic Henry remembers it after his night club and brothel tour of Milan, Florence, Rome, Naples, Villa San Giovanne, Messina, and Taormina: "Night Life is when everybody says what the hell and you do not remember who paid the bill. Night life goes round and round and you look at the wall to make it stop. Night life comes out of a bottle and goes into a jar. If you think how much are the drinks it is not night life."[34] Frederic Henry remembers similarly but in more confusing detail because of the added brothel experiences:

I had gone to no such place but to the smoke of cafés and nights when the room whirled and you needed to look at the wall to make it stop, nights in bed, drunk, when you knew that that was all there was, and the strange excitement of waking and not knowing who it was with you, and the world all unreal in the dark and so exciting that you must resume again unknowing and not caring in the night,

32. *A Farewell to Arms* (New York, 1963, Scribner's Library), p. 232. Subsequent references to the novel will be to this edition and will be parenthesized in the text.

33. *TSW*, March 25, 1922, p. 22; December 15, 1922, p. 21.

34. *Querschnitt* (November 1924) quoted in *The Collected Poems of Ernest Hemingway* (Paris, n.d.), p. [7].

sure that this was all and all and all and not caring. Suddenly to care very much and to sleep to wake with it sometimes morning and all that had been there gone and everything sharp and hard and clear and sometimes a dispute about the cost. Sometimes still pleasant and fond and warm and breakfast and lunch. Sometimes all niceness gone and glad to get out on the street but always another day starting and then another night. I tried to tell about the night and the difference between the night and the day and how the night was better unless the day was very clean and cold and I could not tell it; as I cannot tell it now. But if you have had it you know. (p. 13).

What Frederic contrasts with his tour of Italian night life is the life of the country recommended by the priest. Abruzzi is the priest's epitome of life "where the roads were frozen and hard as iron, where it was clear cold and dry and the snow was dry and powdery and hare-tracks in the snow and the peasants took off their hats and called you Lord and there was good hunting." It was the place, he remembers another time, where there were trout fishing and bear hunting on the Gran Sasso D'Italia. (pp. 13, 73) Hemingway's preparation for this part of the contrast could be seen in his 1923 article "More Game to Shoot in Crowded Europe Than in Ontario."[35] There was a Europe of forests, streams, and hunting preserves as well as of crowded cities, he wrote, and all who could get out of the cities hunted. Near Milan they hunted foxes and in the Abruzzi, "the wild, mountainous part of Italy lying up in the country from Naples, there are still bears."

Hemingway's coverage of Swiss winter resorts in 1922 provided him with other scenes for his novel. In his *Toronto Star Weekly* article "Flivver, Canoe, Pram, and Taxi Combined Is the Luge, Joy of Everybody in Switzerland," he described the arrangements made by Swiss railway companies and resort hotels to capitalize on the popularity of luge-ing.[36] The Montreux-Oberland-Bernois Company ran special trains to the top of Col du Sonloup for luge enthusiasts, and the frozen road from Chamby sur Montreux to Montreux was a favorite luge run for British tourists. It was this general background he used as the basis for the Swiss customs official's touting of Montreux winter sports in the novel. When Frederic and Catherine first land in Switzerland, they divert attention from themselves by asking the customs

35. *TSW*, November 3, 1923, p. 20.
36. *TSW*, March 18, 1922, p. 15.

officials about winter sports in Montreux, and the champions of Locarno and Montreux forget their official interrogation to dispute about winter sports in general and luge-ing in particular. Hemingway's comparison of luge-ing and tobogganing in the article becomes a matter of dispute for the officials in the novel. Implicit in their recommendations is the officials' identification of Frederic and Catherine as English in spite of their American and Scottish papers. Their argument assumes that Frederic and Catherine will want to go where other British tourists have gone. Later at Montreux Frederic and Catherine ride the M.O.B. up the mountain, though their luge-ing remains implicit, if done at all. (pp. 282-83, 295-96) But in spite of their professed attempts to live only to themselves and by their own values, they follow a traditional pattern Hemingway had earlier identified as a common one for British tourists.

Hemingway's war scenes in *A Farewell to Arms* owed much to his reports on the Greco-Turkish war of 1922. Although he had been wounded at the Italian front in 1918, his period of service was both too brief and too late for him to witness a retreat like that in the novel. The retreat from Caporetto had occurred the previous autumn, and by June, 1918, with the failure of the Austrians' Piave offensive, it was the Austrians, not the Italians, who were becoming demoralized. Similarly, he missed the fighting in Anatolia in the summer of 1922 but arrived at Constantinople in October in time to cover the Mudania conference and went on to Eastern Thrace to witness the Greek evacuation of the province. His general knowledge of war by the time he wrote his war novel was thus a knowledge of retreats and evacuations. In *Star* articles during October and November of 1922 he tried to convey a sense of defeat and betrayal by describing details of troop movements and peasant refugee columns. His key details in describing the troop columns were of baggage wagons piled high and pulled by buffalo, of telegraph wires cut and left flying from the poles like Maypole ribbons, and of sullenly marching infantry. The general meaning of the retreat, as he interpreted it, was "the end of the great Greek military adventure," an end to dreaming of empires. In the novel the buffalo-drawn baggage carts are replaced by trucks, and the infantry forms a separate column from the machines. But where in the article the Greek soldiers were characterized as a sullen mob herded along by their cavalry and Hemingway used the device of having a British advisor report on the collapse of morale and respect for the Constantine officers, in the novel the Socialist ambulance drivers look at the retreating Bersaglieri and, chorus-like, comment on the deterioration of morale. His description of Adrianople lit up by kerosene flares and presided over by Greek cavalry found its echo in the novel when the *carabinieri* with their torches at the Tagliamento bridge monitor the retreat column. The ambulance drivers fear Austrian cavalry rather than their own.[37]

His depiction of Thracian refugees fleeing across the Maritsa River at Adrianople found its use in his description of Italian peasants joining the retreat column: "In the night many peasants joined the column from the roads of the country and in the column there were carts loaded with household goods; there were mirrors projecting up between mattresses, and chickens and ducks tied to carts. There was a sewing machine on the cart ahead of us in the rain. They had saved the most valuable things. On some carts the women sat huddled from the rain, and others walked beside the carts keeping as close to them as they could. There were dogs now in the column, keeping under the wagons as they moved along." (p. 198) The litter of household goods and the rain were part of the scene from Thrace also, but in the newspaper article he had to make explicit many of the feelings he could let the context suggest in the novel:

> In a never-ending staggering march the Christian population of Eastern Thrace is jamming the roads toward Macedonia. The main column crossing the Maritza River at Adrianople is twenty miles long. Twenty miles of carts drawn by cows, bullocks, and muddy-flanked water buffalo, with exhausted, staggering men, women and children, blankets over their heads, walking blindly along in the rain beside their worldly goods.
>
> This main stream is being swelled from all along the back country. They don't know where they are going. They left their farms, villages, and ripe, brown fields and joined the main stream of refugees when they heard the Turk was coming. Now they can only keep their places in the ghastly procession while mud-splashed Greek cavalry herd them along like cowpunchers driving steers.

37. "Betrayal Preceded Defeat; Then Came Greek Revolt," *TDS*, November 3, 1922, p. 10; "Refugee Procession Is Scene of Horror," *TDS*, November 14, 1922, p. 7. See *A Farewell to Arms*, pp. 194, 198, 207, 221.

It is a silent procession. Nobody even grunts. It is all they can do to keep moving. Their brilliant peasant costumes are soaked and draggled. Chickens dangle by their feet from the carts. Calves nuzzle at the draught cattle wherever a jam halts the stream. An old man marches bent under a young pig, a scythe and a gun, with a chicken tied to his scythe. A husband spreads a blanket over a woman in labor in one of the carts to keep off the driving rain. She is the only person making a sound. Her little daughter looks at her in horror and begins to cry. And the procession keeps moving.[38]

Hemingway had of course reworked this scene into one of the vignettes of *In Our Time*, giving the scene an unspoken meaning and metaphorical unity. In the novel he kept the significant details of household litter and rain-soaked misery but omitted the woman in labor as too special for the Caporetto experience and ruled out the shocked child as suggestive of an experience of initiation, inappropriate in a scene already saturated in weary cynicism. Some echo of the child could be seen in the scared sisters picked up by Aymo. The description appropriately lost its own unity in order to become part of a larger experience observed by Frederic Henry. The refugees are only one more complication in his attempt to get his unit to Pordenone.

But if Hemingway's anonymous soldiers and refugees from Thrace served only as active background in the novel, his mechanics and *carabinieri* had a more dramatically significant role in the narrative, and they had their origins in his reports on the emergence of Fascism in Italy. In his articles on the conflicts between Socialists, Communists, anarchists, and Fascists in northern Italy in 1922 and 1923 he had sketched the state of mind of both his Socialist drivers and their proto-Fascist challengers, the *carabinieri*, at the Tagliamento bridge. In "Picked Sharpshooters Patrol Genoa Streets" and "'Pot-Shot Patriots' Now Unpopular in Italy" he had described the North Italian Socialists and Communists as urban workers disgusted with war governments and war industries. They were politically volatile and talkative but unorganized and given to impromptu demonstrations rather than to plots to take over governments. They had read and believed in the argument that labor was the basis of all economic values and thought that workingmen together could

38. "A Silent, Ghastly Procession Wends Way from Thrace," *TDS*, October 20, 1922, p. 17.

stop the war.[39] This is the belief of Frederic Henry's ambulance drivers as well. "One side must stop fighting," says Passini. "Why don't we stop fighting? . . . We think. We read. We are mechanics. But even the peasants know better than to believe in a war. Everybody hates this war." (pp. 50-51) Later, during the Caporetto retreat, Piani and Bonello tell Frederic that they are Socialists from Imola, that they come from a town where there is a tradition of Socialist belief. (p. 208) That attitude reaches its practical climax in the novel with Bonello's surrendering rather than continuing to fight a war he cannot believe in, and in the shouts of *"a basso gli ufficiali!"* at the Tagliamento bridge when the retreating soldiers throw away their arms to keep the officers from making them fight again. It is probable that Hemingway personally witnessed such actual events, though he did not report them as actual until after he had used the detail fictionally. He used the detail first in the story "In Another Country" two years before it became part of the novel: "The people hated us because we were officers, and from a wine-shop someone called out, 'A basso gli ufficiali!' as we passed."[40] In his article "Wings Always over Africa" he reported as actual events similar episodes: "I can remember in the old days how the mothers and fathers used to lean out of the windows, or from the front of wine shops, blacksmith shops or the door of a cobbler's when soldiers passed and shout *'a basso gli ufficiali!'* 'Down with the officers!' because they saw the officers as those who kept the foot soldiers fighting when they had come to know the war would bring them no good."[41]

The Fascist mentality that Frederic Henry sees exhibited at the Tagliamento bridge serves as antagonist to Socialist sentiment in much the same way Hemingway saw it work in northern Italy in 1922. The young Fascisti had been tacitly encouraged by the middle class in their suppression of worker demonstrations, he reported, and liked their "taste of killing under police protection."[42] In the novel they become the wide-hatted *carabinieri*

39. *TDS*, April 13, 1922, p. 17; *TSW*, June 24, 1922, p. 5.
40. *The Short Stories of Ernest Hemingway* (New York, 1955), p. 268. References to "The Short Happy Life of Francis Macomber" and to "The Snows of Kilimanjaro," which follow later in this chapter, will be to this edition and will be parenthesized in the text.
41. *Esquire*, V (January 1936), 174.
42. "'Pot-Shot Patriots' Now Unpopular in Italy," *TSW*, June 24, 1922, p. 5.

with "all the efficiency, coldness and command of themselves of Italians who are firing and are not being fired on." They have "that beautiful detachment and devotion to stern justice of men dealing in death without being in any danger of it." (pp. 221-223) As Frederic Henry listens to the battle police say their patriotic truisms that "Italy should never retreat" and "It is because of treachery such as yours that we have lost the fruits of victory," he hears echoes of Mussolini's words from 1922. Then the Fascist editor, not yet *Duce*, told Hemingway that he saw the fruits of victory being swept away in a flood of Communism. To prevent that loss, he had organized the Fascisti as shock troops, he said.[43] The xenophobia of the *carabinieri* he saw during his trip through Italy with Guy Hickok in 1927. He first wrote the three sketches of xenophobia presumably as fact in his "Italy, 1927," but presented the sketches as fiction in his short story collection *Men Without Women* that year. In the novel the attitude becomes dramatically functional rather than static as Frederic Henry realizes that his accent, combined with the rumor of German agents in Italian uniforms and the general police suspicion of outsiders, can get him shot. "I saw how their minds worked; if they had minds and if they worked. They were all young men and they were saving their country." (p. 224) It was a statement that could have come from his earlier reports.

The novel contained insights into the life of danger for which Hemingway found later nonfictional expression. Rinaldi's characterization of syphilis as "a simple industrial accident" goes unexplained in the novel. He believes he has it, that Frederic will get it, and that the priest will never get it. In context, syphilis serves as Rinaldi's medical expression of war disgust. But in *Death in the Afternoon* Hemingway saw it further as an expression of personality, and that insight had retroactive significance for Rinaldi's depiction in the novel. "[Syphilis] is a disease of all people who lead lives in which disregard of consequences dominates. It is an industrial accident, to be expected of all those who lead irregular sexual lives and from their habits of mind would rather take chances than use prophylactics."[44] Significantly, the matadors subject to the disease in the bullfight book were central agents in the violence that Hemingway saw as

43. "Fascist Party Now Half Million Strong," *TDS*, June 24, 1922, p. 16.
44. *Death in the Afternoon*, p. 101.

an emotional equivalent of war. Frederic Henry's belief that he cannot be destroyed in the war was Hemingway's dramatic expression of that illusion of immortality he thought all soldiers initially had. "Well, I knew I would not be killed. Not in this war. It did not have anything to do with me. It seemed no more dangerous to me myself than war in the movies. . . ." (p. 37) So thinks Frederic Henry. In his introduction to *Men at War*, however, Hemingway put such a conviction in the context of general military experience. Illusions of immortality, he said, were steps on the way to a greater confrontation with reality; they were what prepared one for his introduction to the knowledge of his place in the long tradition of human pain. And at the end one knew his wounding or death was what happened to all men and that all finally learned to bear it.[45] If the later statement had meaning for the novel, it suggested a growth of awareness on Frederic's part that the war is his life and his reality, even after he has left it. Even in his Swiss retreat he reads the war news and feels like a truant listening for the school bell.

As with his insights on industrial accidents and illusions of immortality, Hemingway found the significance of much personal feeling and experience first in connection with his novel. Later he found other uses for them in his nonfiction, and such later comments served as authentications of the fictional experiences, less often as explanations. Such later recorded experiences, when seen in light of their counterparts in the novel, had the curious function of serving as afterwords and hinting of origins at the same time. Like those passages in "The Dangerous Summer" on *The Sun Also Rises*, these later comments beclouded the line between the created and the actual. How much the later recorded experiences owed to fiction and how much to actual event is unclear. Hemingway's preface to *A Moveable Feast*, with its cryptic statement on the interdependence of fiction and fact, hinted that he wished the line between cause and result to be obscured. "If the reader prefers," he said, "this book may be regarded as fiction. But there is always the chance that such a book of fiction may throw some light on what has been written as fact."

Thus, in *A Moveable Feast* he recorded experience obviously parallel to episodes in the novel and suggestive of source material.

45. *Men at War* (New York, 1942), pp. xiii-xiv.

One day he and Hadley went to the Auteuil race track, learned of a long-shot choice from an acquaintance of his San Siro-Milano days, and won on a 12-to-1 bet. Using another half of their betting capital to bet on an 18-to-1 shot, they won again but found that late betting on their horse had driven the odds down to 8.5-to-1.[46] The episode had close similarities with that in the novel when Frederic and Catherine go to the San Siro track, see the horse Japalac which they rightly suspect is dyed and is running below his class, bet, expecting to win 3000 lire, and find after the race that late betting on Japalac has driven down the odds. They win only 200 lire instead of the expected 3000. Later they receive a tip from the mysterious Mr. Meyers, bet again, and again find the odds driven down. (pp. 128-31) Although the actions in the memoir and novel led to different insights—one on Hemingway's wrestling with distracting pastimes while he was learning to write and the other on the cynicism and betrayal pervading Italy during the war—their similarities suggested an experience that Hemingway saw as an index to several kinds of human behavior and feeling.

Similarly, Hemingway created moments in the novel that had their echoes in later recordings of personal experience. Catherine's doctor advises her to avoid skiing while pregnant (p. 296), but in *A Moveable Feast* Hemingway remembered skiing with Hadley while she was carrying their child: "Hadley and I loved skiing since we had first tried it together in Switzerland and later at Cortina d'Ampezzo in the Dolomites when Bumby was going to be born and the doctor in Milan had given her permission to continue to ski if I would promise that she would not fall down."[47] If the incident in the novel was an ironic twist in a culminating tragedy and that in the memoir part of a personal myth of innocence, they both served as glimpses into strong feeling for the relationship between man and woman, a value in itself whatever use it might be put to. Other insights finding both fictional and expository expression were Frederic's characterization of the sound of artillery shells passing through the air and Hemingway's repetition of the sensation in his Spanish Civil War dispatches. A second before he is wounded by a trench mortar shell, Frederic notes that "[t]hrough the other noise I

46. *A Moveable Feast*, pp. 52-53.
47. *Ibid.*, p. 200.

heard a cough, then came the chuh-chuh-chuh then there was a flash. . . ." (p. 54) Portraying his daredevil chauffer in Madrid, Hemingway later wrote, "He liked the tearing rush of the incomers just as much as the crack and the chu-chu-chu-ing airparting rustle of sound that came from the battery which was firing over our heads on to the rebel positions."[48] And when Frederic is accused by Miss Van Campen, head nurse of the Milan hospital, of inducing jaundice to avoid going back to the front, he answers by describing the sensations of the disease. "I asked you if you had ever known a man who had tried to disable himself by kicking himself in the scrotum. Because that is the nearest sensation to jaundice. . . ." (p. 144) Later in his antiwar, antiMussolini article on the Ethiopian campaign, Hemingway again cited the sensation as one tending to diminish a soldier's enthusiasm for field service. "Malaria and dysentery are even less capable of arousing patriotic fervor and jaundice, as I recall it, which gives a man the sensation of having been kicked in the vicinity of the interstitial glands, produces almost no patriotic fervor at all."[49]

Again, in the novel Frederic tells how he and Catherine on their Swiss mountain wait out the winter and war and the arrival of their child by living close to the inn at Montreux. One of the key details connoting security and peace for them is having Mrs. Guttingen, the innkeeper's wife, come into the room to start the fire in their porcelain stove before they get out of bed. In his memoir later Hemingway remembered going to a chalet below Les Avants, near Montreux, where he and Hadley could have their books and be warm in bed with the windows open and the snow and stars outside.[50] But the recollection in this case was aided by an earlier recorded similar experience. In his nostalgic "Christmas on the Roof of the World," written in Toronto in 1923 and reminiscent of their earlier Christmas in Switzerland, he remembered the beginning of an almost ideal day: "While it was still dark, Ida, the little German maid, came in and lit the fire in the big porcelain stove, and the burning pine wood roared up the chimney. . . . Out the window the lake lay steel gray far down below, with the snow-covered mountains bulking

48. *Fact*, no. 16 (July 15, 1938), 28.
49. "Wings Always over Africa," *Esquire*, V (January 1936), 31.
50. *A Moveable Feast*, p. 7.

jagged beyond it, and far away the massive tooth of Dent du Midi beginning to lighten with the first touch of the morning."[51] The moment was evidently a magical one for Hemingway and full of imaginative possibilities.

Not all Hemingway's personal feelings that found their uses in the novel had their first recording there, however. His 1922 *Toronto Daily Star* article "A Veteran Visits Old Front, Wishes He Had Stayed Away" was a rehearsal of several states of feeling that later informed the novel. An account of his return to Schio, the town where his ambulance group was stationed in 1918, the article told not only of his disappointment with the place but also his memories of how things had been there during his stay. His 1922 memories of the summer of 1918 took the same viewpoint and much of the same tone used in the opening pages of the novel seven years later. The vantage point was the window and garden of the house he had lived in, from which he could watch troop movements as Frederic Henry does in the novel.

I remember lying in the squeaky bed in the hotel and trying to read by an electric light that hung high up from the centre of the ceiling and then switching off the light and looking out the window down at the road where the arc light was making a dim light through the rain. It was the same road that the battalions marched along through the white dust in 1916. They were the Brigata Ancona, the Brigata Como, the Brigata Tuscana and ten others brought down from the Carco [*sic*] to check the Austrian offensive that was breaking through the mountain wall of the Trentino and beginning to spill down the valleys that led to the Venetian and Lombardy plains. They were good troops in those days and they marched through the dust of the early summer, broke the offensive along the Galio-Asagio-Canoev line, and died in the mountain gullies, in the pine woods on the Trentino slopes, hunting cover on the desolate rocks and pitched out in the soft-melting early summer snow of the Pacubio.

It was the same old road that some of the same old brigades marched along through the dust in June 1918, being rushed to the Piave to stop another offensive. Their best men were dead on the rocky Carso in the fighting around Goritzia [*sic*], on Mount San Gabrielle, on Grappa, and in all the places where men died that nobody ever heard about. In 1918 they didn't march with the same ardor that they did in 1916, some of the troops strung out so badly that after the battalion was just a cloud way up the road you would

51. *TSW*, December 22, 1923, p. 19.

see poor old boys hoofing it alongside of the road to ease their bad feet, sweating along under the packs and rifles and the deadly Italian sun in a long, horrible, never-ending stagger after the battalion.[52]

What Frederic sees is similar:

In the late summer of that year we lived in a house in a village that looked across the river and the plain to the mountains. . . . Troops went by the house and down the road and the dust they raised powdered the leaves of the trees. . . .

Sometimes in the dark we heard the troops marching under the window and guns going past pulled by motor-tractors. . . . [The King] lived in Udine and came out this way nearly every day to see how things were going, and things went very badly.

. . . .

I sat in the high seat of the Fiat and thought about nothing. A regiment went by in the road and I watched them pass. The men were hot and sweating. Some wore their steel helmets but most of them carried them slung from their packs. Most of the helmets were too big and came down almost over the ears of the men who wore them. The officers all wore helmets; better fitting helmets. It was half of the brigade Basilicata. I identified them by their red and white striped collar mark. There were stragglers going by long after the regiment had passed—men who could not keep up with their platoons. They were sweaty, dusty and tired. Some looked pretty bad. (pp. 3-4, 33)

Hemingway also remembered that "there was a garden in Schio with the wall matted with wistaria where we used to drink beer on hot nights with a bombing moon making all sorts of shadows from the big plane tree that spread above the table."[53] Frederic remembers that they "lived in a house in Gorizia that had a fountain and many thick shady trees in a walled garden and a wistaria vine purple on the side of the house." (p. 5)

Also a part of Hemingway's visit to the old front was his return to the Piave banks where the fighting had occurred: "In Mestre we hired a motor car to drive out to the Piave and leaned back in the rear seat, studied the map and the country along the road that is built through the poisonous green Adriatic marshes that flank the coast near Venice."[54] At Stresa Frederic Henry reads the papers about the fighting as the army withdraws from

52. *TDS*, July 22, 1922, p. 7.
53. *Ibid.*
54. *Ibid.*

the Tagliamento to the Piave: "I remembered the Piave. The railroad crossed it near San Dona going up to the front. It was deep and slow there and quite narrow. Down below there were mosquito marshes and canals." (p. 253)

What was perhaps most remarkable about these earlier observations and their later fictional restatement was Hemingway's early tendency to see more than the scene actually showed. Although his actual presence at Schio during the war occurred only during the early summer of 1918, he could imaginatively place himself there in 1916 as well. His report on the troop columns of the later year was imposed on a vision of how it had been, by contrast, in 1916. He made this imagined continued presence at the billet house window a part of Frederic Henry's war experience and afforded him the advantage of reporting the emotional course of the war through his own observation. And of course Frederic's observations were for 1915, 1916, and 1917, if his observations were climaxed by the Caporetto retreat. Noticeable also was the way Hemingway dramatized the feelings he had merely stated in the newspaper article. Frederic notes the contrast between the better troops of the earlier years and the culls of the later summer by noting their slackness in wearing helmets and in their being too young or too small to fit their helmets. Only the officers fit their helmets or the war. He identifies the brigade by their collar markings rather than knowing abstractly that they are the Brigata Basilicata.

The relationship between Hemingway's nonfiction and *A Farewell to Arms*, in sum, was twofold. The nonfiction pointed to a fund of experience that Hemingway grasped in terms of key details, motifs, and metaphors; and when he reused that experience as the basis of created vision for the novel, he carried over those details, motifs, and metaphores as the foci of moods and scenes. Secondly, the nonfiction pointed largely to a postwar world. He altered the context of the nonfiction record to show how it was the continuation of what had gone on in war. He wrote the novel as a probe into the roots of the nonfictional world he had reported.

"The Short Happy Life of Francis Macomber"

The two chief groups of nonfictional analogues for "The Short Happy Life of Francis Macomber" were Hemingway's hunting accounts in *Green Hills of Africa* and in *Esquire* and his discussions of war, written before and echoing after, the hunting story. That these two recorded funds of knowledge and insight should both point to the story is not surprising when we recognize the linkage of the two kinds of experience in the story. Robert Wilson's machine-gunner eyes and his recollection of young men's sudden attainment of maturity in battle are two reminders of the connection between hunting and warring in Hemingway's thought.

Hemingway's *Esquire* articles on hunting, written soon after his return from the first safari to East Africa, contained much of his personal response to Africa, of his delight in the land, and of his satisfaction at hunting well. But for that part reappearing later in fiction, these articles were important for their understanding and presentation of the hunter's code—that ethic so briefly and expensively learned by Francis Macomber. In "Shootism versus Sport" Hemingway sketches the exigencies of lion hunting much as Macomber learns them on his first lion hunt, but the *Esquire* account was generalized and didactic, the fictional account a specific and dramatic event. The *Esquire* account made explicit the code assumed by Robert Wilson and gradually recognized by Macomber:

[The hunt] will be exactly as dangerous as you choose to make it. The only way the danger can be removed or mitigated is by your ability to shoot, and that is as it should be. You are out to kill a lion, on foot and cleanly, not to be mauled. . . . Once you are on the ground and the car is gone, lion hunting is the same as it always was. If you wound the lion in any way but a vital spot he will make for the donga and then you will have to go after him. . . . If you wound the lion and he gets into cover it is even money you will be mauled when you go in after him. A lion can still cover one hundred yards so fast toward you that there is barely time for two aimed shots before he is on you. After he has the first bullet, there is no nervous shock to further wounds and you have to kill him stone dead or he will keep coming.[55]

In the story Francis Macomber fails initially to recognize the code. He fails to control the danger when he tries to shoot with the safety still on his gun and when his hands shake during the moment of aiming. He wounds the lion, lets him get into the

55. *Esquire*, II (July 1934), 150.

thicket, flinches at the idea of going in after him, and fails to understand how the lion could feel the bullet tearing through him and still charge. As a result he misses that primitive exultation in killing, in finding lion hunting "the same as it always was"—a test of intelligent skill against furious strength. In the *Esquire* article "On Being Shot Again" Hemingway recited the technical lesson that Robert Wilson has to tell Macomber before they go into the bush for the wounded buffalo. Again the instruction had its general statement before Hemingway found its dramatic application: "If you want to kill any large animal instantly you shoot it in the brain if you know where the shot is and can call it. If you want to kill it, but it does not make any difference whether it moves after the shot, you can shoot for the heart. But if you want to stop any large animal you should always shoot for the bone. The best bone to break is the neck or any part of the spinal column, then the shoulders. A heavy four-legged animal can move with a broken leg but a broken shoulder will break him down and anchor him."[56] Thus Wilson tells Macomber to shoot for the brain through the buffalo's nose or to try for the neck or shoulders—a technical lesson, but still part of the code.

In the articles on Africa and in *Green Hills of Africa* Hemingway also defined and demonstrated a key moral term later used in the story. When Margot Macomber audibly wonders about the legality of chasing buffalo in the car, Wilson silently calls Francis a four-letter man and Margot a five-letter woman. Besides the obvious and obscene four- and five-letter names suggested by the situation, Hemingway evidently intended the special meaning for the term as he explained it in "He Who Gets Slap Happy." A sportsman, he noted, is the opposite of a four-letter man. "A four-letter man is one who because he does not enjoy doing a thing believes it impossible for anyone else to enjoy it and so sneers at them."[57] In *Green Hills of Africa* he remembered feeling like a four-letter man himself and hating himself for feeling that way when his hunting rival Karl consistently shot larger game; and again he knew the feeling when he failed to appreciate his wife's pain from the badly-cut hunting boots.[58]

56. *Esquire*, III (June 1935), 25.
57. *Esquire*, III (August 1935), 19.
58. *Green Hills of Africa* (New York, 1935), pp. 84, 95.

The term thus referred to another element of the code. A four-letter man perverted the hunting code by making the trophy the only end to the hunt and short-circuiting the emotional course of the hunt.

Green Hills of Africa, however, was even more relevant to the story in its rehearsal of several personal observations and responses. Francis Macomber's initial fright at the lion when he hears him roar from the river thickets before dawn had its parallel and possibly its origin in Hemingway's personal recollection of hearing "a lion roaring just before daylight when we were getting up," but he did not record his own response.[59] His naming of Mrs. Macomber quite possibly was suggested by his personal acquaintance with a beautiful woman named Margot, though no other of her characteristics were cited.[60] Margot Macomber's fatal shooting of Francis in the back of the head had possible origins in Hemingway's being surprised and shaken by his wife's coming up unexpectedly behind him while he and his white hunter stalked a buffalo in tall grass and by his other discovery, while stalking a rhino, that his gun bearer M'Cola was holding a cocked Springfield behind Hemingway's back.[61] His having Wilson advise Macomber to use the Springfield for greater accuracy against the charging buffalo had its possible origin in Hemingway's own self-castigation for wounding a buffalo with his stiff-triggered .470 piece when he might have made a fatal shot with his Springfield. And his own elation—"the best elation of all, of certain action to come, action in which you had something to do . . . and no responsibility except to perform something you feel you can perform"—he projected onto Francis Macomber when that young man finally discovers the elemental simplicity of killing well.[62]

"Notes on Dangerous Game" furnished the actual experience of shooting a galloping buffalo and having the white hunter also fire to help bring down the escaping animal. "You shot twice, Mr. P.," he remembered. "Correct me if I'm wrong. Once at the leopard's mate when she broke back and you spun her over like a rabbit, and the other time when we caught the bull in the open and had two down and the third bull with four solids in

59. *Ibid.,* p. 139.
60. *Ibid.,* p. 65.
61. *Ibid.,* pp. 115, 78.
62. *Ibid.,* pp. 101, 116.

him going at the same gallop, all one solid piece, the neck a part of the shoulders, dusty black and the horns blacker, the head not tossing in the gallop. You figured he would make the bush so you shot and the gallop changed into a long slide forward on his nose."[63] In the story the sequence was changed so that it became the basis for the safari's downing of the first two bulls: ". . . then [Macomber] was shooting at the bull as he moved away, hearing the bullets whunk into him, emptying his rifle at him as he moved steadily away, finally remembering to get his shots forward into the shoulder, and as he fumbled to re-load, he saw the bull was down. Down on his knees, his big head tossing, and seeing the other two still galloping he shot at the leader and hit him. He shot again and missed and he heard the *carawanging* roar as Wilson shot and saw the leading bull slide forward onto his nose." (p. 28) It was the third bull that had "the steady, plunging, heavy-necked, straight moving gallop" that Hemingway remembered. But though he shifted the narrative circumstances of the kills, the image of the galloping and sliding bull was the center of Hemingway's vision in the moment of usable reality. That was the image that grasped one's imagination.

In his essays on war Hemingway rehearsed or reused other images that found their place in the story. In his antiwar essay "Notes on the Next War" in 1935 he found a key image for the story. Francis Macomber's education is climaxed by "a sudden white-hot, blinding flash" exploding in his head. What personal or vicarious experience enabled Hemingway to imagine the sensation is not clear, but it was evidently a convincing image for him. Trying to make his readers realize the horrors of a war which he thought Americans should not get into that year, he listed, among other unpleasant moments of war, one's being hit in the head with a "white blinding flash that never stops. . . ."[64] Other insights from war in the story had their real origins explained later in his 1942 introduction to *Men at War*. Robert Wilson's moral tutoring of Macomber, the introduction revealed, was really war-engendered. His quotation from Shakespeare on every man's owing God a death was an echo of a moral talisman Hemingway had received from a fellow patient: "I remember the

63. *Esquire*, II (July 1934), 94.
64. *Esquire*, IV (September 1935), 156.

sudden happiness and the feeling of having a permanent protecting talisman when a young British officer I met when in the hospital first wrote out for me, so that I could remember them, these lines: 'By my troth, I care not: a man can die but once; we owe God a death . . . and let it go which way it will, he that dies this year is quit for the next.' " The implication of that precept, as Macomber sees in the story and as Hemingway spelled out in 1942, was that one could not worry about the time of his death when he was properly occupied with living up each moment. "Cowardice, as distinguished from panic, is almost always a lack of ability to suspend the functioning of the imagination. Learning to suspend your imagination and live completely in the very second of the present minute with no before and no after is the greatest gift a soldier can have."[65] But then it was also the kind of thing a bullfighter had to know, he wrote in *Death in the Afternoon*. To know how to ignore and despise consequences was the way to achieve that elation that only the brave could know.[66]

The didactic tone of the nonfiction correlated with the story indicates how fundamental is the relationship of tutor and learner in "The Short Happy Life of Francis Macomber." The *Esquire* articles on the hunter's code; the bullfight book, which Hemingway called a didactic work; and *Men at War*, which was compiled and edited to instruct young men on how to face danger in war—all presume the value of instruction through art and adage. They point up the story as an adventure in the failure and success in teaching the morality of courage. Robert Wilson's failure to tell Macomber the old Somali proverb about men's responses to lions and his later advancement of the Shakespearean quotation to celebrate the moment of Macomber's insight underscore the theme of morality through knowledge in the story.

"The Snows of Kilimanjaro"

"The Snows of Kilimanjaro" had perhaps a greater number of nonfictional analogues, sources, and echoes than any piece of comparable length in Hemingway's work. The reason for that abundance can be seen in the story itself. Among other things, it is a story about unwritten stories. As such, it catalogues situa-

65. *Men at War*, pp. xiv, xxvii.
66. *Death in the Afternoon*, p. 58.

tions and feelings that stories grow out of. It is, in a way, an index to Hemingway's raw material for fiction as well as Harry's last inventory. But the difference between Hemingway's fictional voice and his public one is important here too. Harry laments that he never has written down those things he thinks of during his last evening and now never will write them. The refrain running through his elegiac lament is that *"he had never written a line of that.* . . . Now he would never write the things that he had saved to write. . . . *He had been in it and he had watched it and it was his duty to write of it; but now he never would."* Hemingway did write those things, though. Some occurred in his fiction, but most in his journalism and memoirs. Harry's recollection of skiing after the war with the Austrians he had fought during the war had its echo in Richard Cantwell's similar memory of skiing with his German adversaries between wars.[67] And in his nonfiction, both before the writing of "The Snows of Kilimanjaro" and afterwards, Hemingway made most of Harry's memorable moments a part of the public record.

Harry begins his recall with a scene of betrayal in Thrace comparable to his betrayal of himself by drinking his whiskey and soda. His memory of the railway station at Karagatch and Nansen's callous arrangement to send Thracian refugees trekking into the snows of western Thrace and Macedonia had its previous hearing in Hemingway's articles in the *Toronto Daily Star*—"Betrayal Preceded Defeat, Then Came Greek Revolt" and "Refugee Procession Is Scene of Horror."[68] Hemingway's journalistic depiction of the straggling columns of troops and peasant refugees passing through Adrianople was the reality behind Nansen's exchange of populations, and he had made the term "betrayal" meaningful in his *Star* reports and later in his vignettes of *In Our Time*. Later Harry thinks again of the Greco-Turkish wars, remembering his whoring in Constantinople, his picking up the "hot Armenian slut," and his fighting the British gunner subaltern for her. In his *Star* articles " 'Old Constan' in True Light: Is Tough Town" and "Night Life in Europe Is a Disease" Hemingway had sketched the background for Harry's frenzied dissipation. Constantinople, he had reported, was doing its dance of death before Mustafa Kemal's troops entered the city. "Constanti-

67. *Across the River and into the Trees* (New York, 1950), p. 122.
68. *TDS*, November 3, 1922, p. 10; November 14, 1922, p. 7.

nople before the Mudania armistice was probably the most hectic town in the world. . . . Nobody slept much during the day and nobody slept at all during the night. . . . No good restaurants opened up before ten at night and the theatres opened at midnight. . . . As the evening advanced fights would break out among the sailors of the different nationalities in the various Galata beer emporiums. . . . All of Constantinople was in a feverish sort of wildness."[69] In another report he wrote that "Galata, half way up the hill from the port, has a district that is more unspeakably horrible than the foulest heyday of the Barbary Coast. It festers there, trapping the soldiers and sailors of all the allies and of all the nations."[70] Later Harry sees in Anatolia the betrayal of the Greek army by the newly-arrived and incompetent officers of the Constantine party. They had directed fire into their own troops and "the British observer had cried like a child." In his article on betrayal and revolt in the Greek army in 1922, Hemingway explained the backgrounds of such a sight. He had not himself reached Anatolia in time to see the fighting, but he had heard the account told by Captain Wittal of the Indian cavalry and learned how the regular Greek army officers had been replaced by political supporters of newly installed King Constantine, "from the commander-in-chief down to platoon commanders." Wittal's account was a close parallel, and probably the source of Harry's recollection: " 'In the one show in Anatolia,' Captain Wittal said, 'the Greek infantry were doing an absolutely magnificent attack and their artillery was doing them in. Major Johnson (the other British observer who later acted as liaison officer with the press at Constantinople) is a gunner, you know. He's a fine gunner too. Well, Major Johnson cried at what the gunners were doing to their infantry. He was wild to take over the artillery. But he couldn't do a thing. We had orders to preserve strict neutrality—and he couldn't do a thing.' "[71] After Anatolia Harry had "seen the things that he could never think of and later still had seen much worse." Hemingway's report's on "The Quai at Smyrna," again told through the mouth of a British observer, suggested what those worse things were—wailing refugees, brutal officers, and crippled baggage animals.

69. *TSW*, December 15, 1923, p. 21.
70. *TDS*, October 28, 1922, p. 10.
71. *TDS*, November 3, 1922, p. 10.

Another locus of Harry's significant but unwritten memories is the Vorarlberg skiing area of Austria. The snows of Mount Kilimanjaro make him think of the snows of the Gauertal and the Vorarlberg districts. Then he remembers Christmases at Schruns, and staying in the Madlener-Haus and other ski stations to make the glacier runs, rushing down the mountain to stop finally and kick off skis and go into the barroom of the inn. Hemingway's nonfictional memories, though, were much the same, as he showed in *A Moveable Feast.* From Thanksgiving to Easter, he and his wife and young son would go to Schruns and Bludenz, stay at the Hotel Taube, use the Madlener-Haus, the Lindauer-Hütte, the Wiesbadener-Hütte as ski camps, and make glacier runs with Herr Lent's ski school group.[72] Hemingway also reported in his *Star* article "Christmas on the Roof of the World" how it felt to ski down the mountain, feeling the air and snow slip by, and then stop beside the inn to kick off skis and go inside for drinks, supper, and long evenings of talk.[73] Harry's secret memory and Hemingway's public memory were also close on the fact of Herr Lent's gambling. During a week-long blizzard, they played cards at the Madlener-Haus, Harry remembers, *"and the stakes were higher all the time as Herr Lent lost more. Finally he lost it all. Everything, the ski schule money and all the season's profit and then his capital. He could see him with his long nose, picking up the cards and then opening, 'Sans Voir.'"* In his memoir Hemingway also remembered, "Once or twice a week there was a poker game in the dining room of the hotel with all the windows shuttered and the door locked. Gambling was forbidden in Austria then and I played with Herr Nels, the hotel keeper, Herr Lent of the Alpine ski school, a banker of the town, the public prosecuter and the captain of the Gendarmerie. It was a stiff game and they were all good poker players except that Herr Lent played too wildly because the ski school was not making any money."[74]

Harry's memories of fishing in the Black Forest trout streams were echoes of the fishing trips Hemingway reported in his travel articles for the Toronto *Star.* Where Harry remembers renting a trout stream and getting to it by following the valley roads from

72. *A Moveable Feast*, p. 201.
73. *TSW*, December 22, 1923, p. 19.
74. *A Moveable Feast*, p. 201.

Triberg or by crossing the hills and going through pine forests
and passing small farms to reach the birch-covered pools, Hemingway earlier told of trying to rent a trout stream in Baden and
being frustrated by German feeling against *ausländers* and by
municipal red tape. Finally he had fished where he saw good
streams and paid off wardens or landowners on the spot when
challenged. "Following this method of fishing without permits,"
he wrote in 1923, "we fished all through the Black Forest. With
rucksacks and fly rods, we hiked across country, sticking to the
high ridges and the rolling crests of the hills, sometimes through
deep pine timber, sometimes coming out into a clearing and
farmyards, again going for miles without seeing a soul except
wild-looking berry pickers. We never knew where we were. But
we were never lost because at any time we could cut down from
the high country into a valley and know we would hit a stream.
Sooner or later every stream flowed into a river and a river meant
a town."[75] There was, in fact, similarity of mood as well as
image in the two accounts. Hemingway's article for the *Star* was
written out of nostalgia for Europe while he was back in Toronto
for the birth of his and Hadley's son. His uncertainty that he
would ever get back to such places as the trout streams of Baden
carried over with a minimum of dramatic shaping into Harry's
lyric tribute to an irrecoverable past.

In his evocation of Paris Harry remembers much that Hemingway had already recorded about his quarter and that he would
record again, in more nostalgic detail, later in his Paris memoir.
He had reported in a *Star* article that on making his first flight
from Paris to Strasbourg he and Hadley had gotten up at four,
taken a cup of coffee with the man who acted as operator of the
bal musette and taxi driver, and had been invited to try the
white wine with him before leaving home for the airline company office.[76] Harry likewise remembers that: "*The husband of
the woman who ran the Bal Musette drove a taxi and when he,
Harry, had to take an early plane the husband knocked upon the
door to wake him and they each drank a glass of white wine at
the zinc of the bar before they started.*" Later in *A Moveable
Feast* Hemingway remembered that it had been a glass of white

75. "Fishing All Across Europe—Spain Has the Best, Then Germany," *TSW*,
November 17, 1923, p. 11.
76. "Paris-to-Strasbourg Flight Shows Living Cubist Picture," *TDS*, September
9, 1922, p. 8.

wine he had taken, as he assured Ford Madox Ford that he knew about the *bal musette*: "I lived above it for two years. . . . The man who owned it had a taxi and when I had to get a plane he'd take me out to the field, and we'd stop at the zinc bar of the Bal and drink a glass of white wine in the dark before we'd start for the airfield."[77]

In *Green Hills of Africa* he also remembered the quarter, where he rode a bicycle on the asphalt and cobble streets in the rain, and recalled the pavilion in the Notre Dame des Champs, the whine and smell of the sawmill, and the apartment where he wrote and received his rejection slips through the mail slot.[78] In his vision Harry remembers that version of Paris too:

> . . . *the Place Contrescarpe where the flower sellers dyed their flowers in the street and the dye ran over the paving where the autobus started and the old men and the women, always drunk on wine and bad marc; and the children with their noses running in the cold; the smell of dirty sweat and poverty and drunkenness at the Café des Amateurs. . . . There was never another part of Paris that he loved like that, the sprawling trees, the old white plastered houses painted brown below, the long green of the autobus in that round square, the purple flower dye upon the paving, the sudden drop down the hill of the rue Cardinal Lemoine to the River, and the other way the narrow crowded world of the rue Mouffetard. The street that ran up toward the Pantheon and the other that he always took with the bicycle, the only asphalted street in all that quarter, smooth under the tires, with the high narrow houses and the cheap tall hotel where Paul Verlaine had died. There were only two rooms in the apartments where they lived and he had a room on the top floor of that hotel that cost him sixty francs a month where he did his writing, and from it he could see the roofs and chimney pots and all the hills of Paris.*[79]

In *A Moveable Feast* those images of Paris again appeared. "The leaves lay sodden in the rain and the wind drove the rain against the big green autobus at the terminal and the Café des Amateurs was crowded. . . . It was a sad, evilly run café where the drunkards of the quarter crowded together and I kept away from it because of the smell of the dirty bodies and the sour smell of drunkenness. . . . The Café des Amateurs was the cesspool of the

77. *A Moveable Feast*, p. 84.
78. *Green Hills of Africa*, p. 70.
79. *Short Stories*, pp. 69-70.

rue Mouffetard, that wonderful narrow crowded market street which led into the Place Contrescarpe . . . [and there was] the hotel where Verlaine had died where I had a room on the top floor where I worked."[80]

If Hemingway's iceberg theory had extensions into time as well as space, these nonfictional records worked as icebergs before and after the fiction of "The Snows of Kilimanjaro," for they showed that fiction came out of experiences that had continuing meaning in terms of mood and image for Hemingway the writer. The key to his fictional use of such scenes, implicit in the story itself, was clearer in the expository accounts. In both *Green Hills of Africa* and *A Moveable Feast*, key personal experiences were linked with key vicarious experiences available in works by other artists. In the African book they were mingled with remembered scenes from great novels by Tolstoy and Stendhal; he remembered Tolstoy's *Sevastopol* in connection with the Boulevard Sevastopol in Paris. In the Paris memoir they were observed as though by a painter. The scene at the Place Contrescarpe was worthy of a Braque painting, Hemingway remembered, and while he was daily walking through scenes, he was learning to see by studying the pictures at the Luxembourg Museum. That such observed places and people would find their way into a story was already half-decided even as Hemingway noted them, for they were seen through the eyes of a man learning to see the world in terms of pictures. The curious staticity of the memory pictures in the Kilimanjaro story, the containment of all action within the frame of an individually remembered scene, suggested the matrix in which they had been originally conceived.

Harry's career among the rich, his self-betrayal through sloth and talent-bought comfort, his exchange of vitality for security too had their counterparts in Hemingway's memoir. "He had sold vitality, in one form or another, all his life," Harry recalls. In his success he let himself be taken over by the rich, gave them the vitality and the vision he had put into his work, and at last had left only a talent for hunting with cameras, not guns. His gangrenous leg was the result of such pseudo-hunting. He had scratched his knee while trying to photograph a herd of waterbuck and had even missed that shot when they bolted. (pp. 61-62) In *A Moveable Feast* Hemingway recorded his own encounter

80. *A Moveable Feast*, pp. 3-4.

with the rich. In his innocence and first success he too had attracted the rich by his happiness and performance, but when the party was over, "when they [had] passed and taken the nourishment they needed, [they left] everything deader than the roots of any grass Attila's horses hooves have ever scoured."[81] The dramatic proof of such loss for both Harry and Hemingway was estrangement from first loves. Separated from his, Harry remembers writing and waiting for the answer. *"So then the letter in answer to the one he'd written came in on a platter one morning and when he saw the handwriting he went cold all over and tried to slip the letter underneath another. But his wife said, 'Who is that letter from, dear?' and that was the end of the beginning of that."* (p. 66) In his own fable of lost innocence Hemingway remembered how the "unmarried young woman" from among the rich admirers moved in with his family, ingratiated herself into their lives, and later met him in Paris on his return from a trip to New York to see his publishers. If there was no telltale letter when he arrived in Schruns to join his family, the guilt was there, and the beginning of the end of innocence had come. If Paris had been equated with innocence before, it was the city of self-knowledge afterward. "Paris was never to be the same again although it was always Paris and you changed as it changed."[82]

For that portion of the story outside the remembrance of past things Hemingway had other experiences to call on, some already recorded, others to be recalled later. Two of the key situations in "Snows" grew out of events recorded in *Esquire* articles based on his own safari in late 1933 and early 1934. Harry's point of view on and in relation to narrative incidents—that of an invalid lying under a large mimosa tree and watching the vultures, like fates, hover and move in—had its parallel in Hemingway's own temporary invalidism because of amoebic dysentery while on safari and in his own recorded observations on the tactics of carrion birds. In "a.d. in Africa" his descriptions of the mental confusions produced by emetine and his attempts to write while in that confused state had their reappearance as Harry's confused remembering and "writing."[83] Harry's notation of "three of the

81. *Ibid.*, p. 208.
82. *Ibid.*, pp. 209-11.
83. *Esquire*, I (April 1934), 19, 146.

birds squat[ting] obscenely, while in the sky a dozen more sailed" and his observation later that "the birds no longer waited on the ground. They were all perched heavily in a tree. There were many more of them . . ." were dramatic adaptations of general notes on carrion birds Hemingway had recorded in "Wings Always over Africa." "If you want to see how long it takes them to come to a live man lie down under a tree, perfectly still, and watch them, first circling so high they look as small as specks, then coming, dropping in concentric circles, then plummeting down in a whish of rushing wings to deal with you. You sit up and the ring jumps back raising their wings. But what about if you do not sit up?"[84] The second situation in the story to come from journalistically recorded experience was Harry's proposed flight from the safari camp on the Serengetti Plain to Nairobi by way of Arusha. In the *Esquire* article "a.d. in Africa," written from the hospital in Nairobi, Hemingway reported having flown there from the camp on the Serenea River.

In "The Christmas Gift," written twenty years later after a second safari to East Africa, Hemingway noted the night sounds outside the camp, sounds that both confirmed and echoed those evening and early night sounds picked up by Harry. But more than confirming them by echo, the later recorded sounds occurred in a more explicitly meaningful context than those in the story and by analogy suggested more clearly functional meanings for those sounds at Harry's camp. The beasts outside Hemingway's later camp, he indicated, often had human sounds that suggested human traits: "night, which is the loveliest time in Africa," seemed to give the animals a dreamlike, fabulous overtone. He could hear the talking and laughing of the hyenas, the wildebeeste's "terrifying noise" to make him sound like a dangerous beast, and the coughing grunts of Mr. Chui, the leopard. It was a mood quite similar to Harry's as he notes the "filthy" hyena slinking across the camp area and watches the small plains animals feeding closer to the camp as the sun goes down. Later Helen hears the "strange, human, almost crying sound" of the hyena's whimpering in her half-sleep before she discovers Harry has died. (pp. 63, 74, 76-77) Hemingway's personal acceptance of different levels of feeling, thought, and perhaps even of allegorical significance in the later article were commensurate with

84. *Esquire*, V (January 1936), 31.

the shifts in memory and perception levels in the story and went far in making plausible and psychologically appropriate the shift in Harry's scale of perception in the next-to-last section of the story. Compton's Charon-like office in that section and the bestiary-like overtones of the questing leopard and of the hyena, devourer of the dead and robber of crypts, become likelihoods rather than possibilities. To be flown from a primitive camp on the plain to the top of Kilimanjaro or to the different world of Nairobi was a movement of translation with which Hemingway was familiar, and to be lifted from the plain by airship or by thought was the stuff from which death visions were made.[85]

The chief importance of the nonfictional background to "The Snows of Kilimanjaro" is its clarification of the relationship between the foreground of narrative incident in the story and the memory sequences. Where the predicament of Harry, dying on his cot in an African camp and being translated to some kind of glory symbolized by Mount Kilimanjaro, was a possible denouement to Hemingway's own illness and flight, the memory sequences, which were for the most actualities in Hemingway's own recorded experience, became the basis for Harry's might-have-beens. They were assuredly memories for Harry but only potential writings. Thus Hemingway wrote one of his best stories by using the technique of inverting actuality and possibility. In doing so, he showed the imaginative reality in both.

For Whom the Bell Tolls

In his introduction to the narrative text for the film *The Spanish Earth*, Jasper Wood wrote, "It would be a most interesting story if Hemingway would write a book based upon his experiences while in Spain working on the film. He has not and says he will not. . . ."[86] Whether Jasper Wood was thinking of such a book as *For Whom the Bell Tolls* was not clear. His call, though, indicated the need for a full and expert fictional response to the Spanish Civil War. Since Hemingway was well into the novel less than a year after Wood's report, Hemingway's denial of intent to write such a book was quite probably either made in disgust after his troubles with producers of *The Fifth Column* or simply made as part of his refusal to discuss his work. For

85. *Look*, XVIII (May 4, 1954), 87.
86. *The Spanish Earth* (Cleveland, 1938), p. 9.

Hemingway had already begun the novel in that he had written in his nonfiction much of the background incorporated into the later fiction. His journalistic reports on the Spanish war, his observations of Spanish scene and character in *Death in the After-noon,* and his occasional comparisons of the Spanish Civil War to the American Civil War were the chief sources he adapted to the novel.

Hemingway's use of his Spanish Civil War experiences in *For Whom the Bell Tolls* was, except for a very few instances, concerned with the presentation of emotions and attitudes rather than with images of war. He reported on battlefield actions rather than guerilla activities in his journalism, and, except for El Sordo's stand on the hilltop and the guerrillas' attack on the bridge, action in the novel included no battle scenes. Although it was an always present assumption in the journalistic reports that the war had its emotional course to run, the reports were concerned primarily with such actual public events as the defense of Madrid, the attack on Teruel, or the Ebro River defense. This sort of action is in the background of the novel. General Golz's planned attack on Segovia and the German bombers flying over are reminders of the larger war. But the part of the war reports most relevant to the novel were Hemingway's interpretations of political manipulations and faulty military planning. One of the key attitudes toward war in the novel was that spoken by Robert Jordan when he told Karkov, "I like it better at the front. . . . The closer to the front the better the people."[87] In his introduction to the 1948 edition of *A Farewell to Arms* Hemingway made plain that this was his attitude as well: ". . . it is the considered belief of the writer of this book that wars are fought by the finest people that there are, or just say people, although the closer you are to where they are fighting, the finer people you meet. . . ."[88]

So although the attack on the bridge is a climactic event in the novel, most of Robert Jordan's energies are spent in his attempt to understand the meaning of the war. Hemingway's articles in *Ken* magazine which analyzed the political meanings of military actions were the real background for the novel. His

87. *For Whom the Bell Tolls* (New York, 1940, Scribner's Library), p. 248. Subsequent references to the novel will be to this edition and will be parenthesized in the text.

88. *A Farewell to Arms,* p. x.

concern there was with the betrayal of the Spanish Republican movement by Spanish politicians and churchmen. In "Treachery in Aragon" he noted, for example, that Fascist military successes usually followed an act of betrayal by some politician, and even the politicians most believed in by liberal Americans were among the traitors. He cited the example of one American novelist who tried to secure the release of a Spanish friend caught in a betrayal. The novelist refused to believe in the treachery of his friend, but Hemingway wrote from his own knowledge of the man's guilt and of many politicians' similar guilt. "But we who have seen this war for a long time have learned that there are all sorts of treachery just as there are all sorts of heroism in war. And very shortly the true story of the role played by treachery in the Aragon break-through will be able to be written."[89] Robert Jordan is forced again to recognize this fact of war when Pablo steals the detonator, and he generalizes his recognition of such a betrayal:

Muck the whole treachery-ridden country. Muck their egotism and their selfishness . . . and their conceit and their treachery. . . . God muck Pablo. Pablo is all of them. God pity the Spanish people. Any leader they have will muck them. One good man, Pablo Iglesias, in two thousand years and everybody else mucking them. . . . They always muck you instead from Cortez, and Menendez de Avila down to Miaja. Look what Miaja did to Kleber. . . . Muck all the insane, egotistical, treacherous swine that have always governed Spain and ruled her armies. Muck everybody but the people and then be damned careful what they turn into when they have power. (pp. 369-370)

In "The Cardinal Picks a Winner," another *Ken* essay, Hemingway noted the alignment of the church and Falangism in Spain, particularly noting a photograph of prominent churchmen with their hands raised in the Fascist salute.[90] That identification of Church and Fascist viewpoints had its reappearance in the novel in the partisans' talk of the republic as a replacement for religion and in the priest's siding with the local Fascists during the massacre at Pablo's village. (p. 127)

Robert Jordan's recognition of the Spanish people's betrayal by their military leaders had its probable origins in Hemingway's earlier articles in *Ken* and in the war reports. In "Good Generals

89. *Ken*, I (June 30, 1938), 26.
90. *Ken*, I (May 5, 1938), 38.

Hug the Line" he noted how both Republican and Insurgent generals followed the old Spanish practice of staying miles behind the lines. Because they were so far from the place of action and out of touch with tactical changes, they constantly betrayed their own fighters. General Mola of the Falangist army had been one of the worst offenders, he wrote, and in the same article he applauded Republican General Mangada for being one of the few Loyalist commanders who stayed at the line. Mangada he described as an old eccentric who perched in a tree between the lines, studied the enemy position with his field glasses, and talked to spirits while he planned the battle. But he had beaten Mola in the Sierra. More typical of the Republican leaders' betrayal of their troops' interests though was their refusal to let Republican bombers hit Pamplona when government intelligence learned that Fascist leaders would gather there for the funeral of Generals Mola and Sanjurjo, both killed in air crashes.[91] Another flaw in Spanish military thinking, Hemingway noted in his war dispatches, was the Republicans' inability to think beyond their own districts. After the Ebro delta had fallen into Fascist hands, he returned briefly to Madrid and found the commanders there only casually interested in any front but their own, although they were virtually isolated by the Ebro defeat. "There you have it," he wrote. "That is the one unaccountable factor foreigners never figure when analysing the Spanish campaign. This factor is the regionalism of the Spanish. . . . Today I have talked with a dozen Spanish officers that I knew well and not one asked anything but perfunctory questions about how things are going on the coast or Ebro fronts. All they wanted to do was to tell how well things were going in their sector."[92] In the novel these realities of Spanish military practice become crucial when Robert Jordan sends Andrés to General Golz and Andrés is delayed by Anarchist troops and Spanish officers higher up the command line until his message arrives too late to matter. But as Golz acknowledges, he himself could not call off the attack. It would have to be canceled by political generals even further from the fighting, and the party at Karkov's apartment shows how little the planners understand. They interpret the report on the bombing of

91. *Ken*, II (August 25, 1938), 28.
92. *Fact*, 71.

Sordo's hilltop as evidence the Fascists have been fighting among themselves. (pp. 375, 396-401, 357)

In his nonfictional commentaries on the Spanish war, Hemingway saw discipline as the answer to the political and military unreliability, and he carried over that solution into Robert Jordan's thinking in the novel. In his report on the army at Teruel he noted that Anarchist regiments had stayed in the hills outside the Teruel-Mansueto fortress eight months without attacking the Fascists, had kept their lines three kilometers from the rebel position, and had often deserted their lines to make trips to Valencia for drunken weekends. But when battalions of the reorganized and well-disciplined Army of the Levante, commanded by Col. Hernandez Sarabia, had replaced the Anarchists, they closed the lines, put the fortress under siege, and captured 2000 tons of wheat standing on formerly neutral ground.[93] In *The Spanish Earth* he applauded the early holding actions of the hastily organized government militia but noted that real military results had to wait until regular army groups were trained and commanded by officers schooled in Soviet army methods.[94] Enrique Lister was one of that new tough, disciplined breed. In the novel Robert Jordan similarly, if perhaps more cynically, notes the value of the new disciplinarians. By following the instructions of their Soviet military advisors they have overcome their provincial outlook. "Lister's and Modesto's and Campesino's Spanish troops had all fought well in that battle of Guadalajara, Hans had told him, and that was to be credited to their leaders and to the discipline they enforced. But Lister and Campesino and Modesto had been told many of the moves they should make by their Russian military advisors. They were like students flying a machine with dual controls which the pilot could take over whenever they made a mistake." And at Gaylord's, Madrid headquarters for the Soviet advisors, he had met those peasant leaders who, so the papers said, had risen from the people but who spoke Russian and used methods learned from Soviet military schools. (pp. 229-36)

Robert Jordan's acceptance of Communist discipline for the duration of the war and his declaration to Karkov that his mind is "in suspension till we win the war" were not, however, Hem-

93. *Ibid.*, 36-37.
94. *The Spanish Earth*, pp. 23-24, 27.

ingway's public position on thinking in wartime. In his preface
to Luis Quintanilla's book of drawings on the Spanish war, he
noted that a writer had to renounce the luxury of blind obedience to orders and make his own mistakes in getting at the truth.
"To write about [war] truly you have to know a great deal about
cowardice and heroism. For there is very much of both, and of
simple human endurance, and it is a long time since anyone has
balanced them truly."[95] Even more to the point for Robert Jordan's dilemma of limited action and ranging thought, Hemingway noted in his 1937 essay "The Writer and War" that when a
man went to seek truth in war, he could find death instead.[96]
Robert Jordan, as both soldier and writer in the novel, has to
face the contradictions of the two kinds of demands made on
him. In his talks with the intelligent Russian journalist Karkov
and during his seventy-hour wait with the partisan group to destroy the bridge, he tries to resolve the dilemma only to note at
the end that the action and its rationale still fail to coincide.
The only harmony he can find is between action and feeling,
and the feeling is not one Hemingway ever advanced in his public voice. Jordan attacks the bridge knowing irrationally that the
attack is foredoomed by all the physical and supernatural forces
he is aware of, whether they operate through human perversity,
weather, or gypsy superstition. His intuitive, though only half-
admitted, vision of the warring world is of one governed by
capriciously cruel and dark forces. In that context he can match
action and understanding. It is not a vision that Hemingway
ever projected in his nonfictional public writing, however, and
Robert Jordan's intuitive resolution is not, therefore, necessarily
the author's. In both *Men at War* and in his postwar introduction to Ben Raeburn's *Treasury of the Free World*, Hemingway
still saw an essential contradiction between the act of the soldier
and the thought of the writer but advanced no argument for
reliance on an intuitive and irrational view. The writer, he said
in the war anthology, should continue to think critically though
he might refrain from publication of his views until after the
war; refrain, that is, unless his criticism could help win the war.[97]
In his postwar essay he seemed to assume that criticism had main-

95. *All the Brave* (New York, 1939), p. 11.
96. *The Writer in a Changing World* (New York, 1937), p. 72.
97. *Men at War*, p. xv.

tained a discreet silence during wartime: "We have come out of the time when obedience, the acceptance of discipline, intelligent courage and resolution were most important into that more difficult time when it is a man's duty to understand his world rather than simply fight for it."[98]

But if the novel differed from its journalistic matrix in Hemingway's handling of the reconciliation between action, thought, and feeling, it followed the journalism in assuming an emotional course of the war. In the war reports Hemingway traced the rise and fall of Republican morale—the army's belief in the possibility of ultimate victory after the victories at Brihuega and Guadalajara, the successful resistance to the siege of Madrid, and the falling off of morale after the Fascist victories at Irun and on the Ebro. In the novel Robert Jordan has also participated in some of the early battles in the Sierras and at Madrid and has been elated at news of other victories. He remembers the early idealism of the Fifth Regiment, the crusade-like feeling, before the cynical Russian advisors set up in Gaylord's. At Valasquez 63, Madrid headquarters of the International Brigade, he felt an atmosphere of consecration and duty that was "like the feeling you expected to have and did not have at your first communion." And only two weeks before he has heard Hans, one of the new army commanders, tell of the victory at Brihuega, when for a time the Republicans faced defeat but knowing they faced Italian troops, tried a bold but risky maneuver and won. (pp. 233-36) He also notes for individual soldiers and units that after six months of fighting they have lost that purity of feeling and have begun to concentrate on surviving. That was when hard thinking and discipline became important.

Hemingway's thought on the large-scale significance of the war in Spain also entered the novel. Although the time of Robert Jordan's partisan adventure in the novel is the late spring of 1937, a time when there was still good hope that the Falangist-German-Italian combine might be defeated, Hemingway put into Robert Jordan's mind the urgency that he himself did not begin to put into his journalism and propaganda until 1938. In such *Ken* articles as "The Time Now, the Place Spain" and "Dying, Well or Badly," he called for major aid for the Republicans so they could concentrate on beating the Italian units in Spain. The

98. *Treasury for the Free World* (New York, 1946), p. xiii.

Italians, he asserted, were the weakest part of the Fascist ring tightening on the Republican government and army; and if they could be soundly defeated in another Brihuega or Guadalajara, their German and Japanese allies would have to take time to repair their alliance. Such delay would give the rest of the world time to arm, he argued. Temporary Republican success would constitute "the great holding attack to save what we call civilization."[99] In the novel Robert Jordan similarly sees the action at the bridge as a holding attack and part of the tradition of Thermopylae, Horatius at the bridge, and the Dutch boy with his finger in the dike. "But remember this," he tells himself, "that as long as we can hold them here we keep the fascists tied up. They can't attack any other country until they finish with us. If the French help at all, if only they leave the frontier open and if we get planes from America they can never finish with us." (pp. 164, 432) He was evidently thinking of the Franco-British non-intervention pact of November, 1936, when he surveyed his contingencies.

It was those circles of significance surrounding the bridge, as Carlos Baker has called them,[100] that Hemingway had in mind when Robert Van Gelder interviewed him in New York. Hemingway was reading proof on the novel at the time and consulting with Gustavo Duran, one of those Loyalist generals who had escaped after the collapse of the Republic. Robert Jordan's agony of decision was analogous to Duran's, so Hemingway acknowledged. "It was suggested by Duran that perhaps because the military decision is so difficult to make, that is why when it is made rightly it pays off so well. There is nothing in finance, for example, to compare with it, or in internal politics, and perhaps for twenty years the importance of the military decision has been underestimated and aims that are practically inferior have been mistakenly rated above the real pay-off, which is still in strength at arms. Hemingway exclaimed: 'That's what the new novel is about!' "[101]

Although the chief use of Hemingway's war reports for the novel was to supply the contexts of thought and feeling in the narrative, he also recorded a number of situations later adapted

99. *Ken*, I (April 7, 1938), 36-37; (April 21, 1938), 68.
100. Baker, *Hemingway: The Writer as Artist*, pp. 245ff.
101. *Writers and Writing* (New York, 1946), p. 97.

to the fictional account. It is probable that his depiction of Robert Jordan as a university professor on leave to fight in Spain was suggested by his encounter with "Robert Merriman, a former California university professor and now chief of staff of the fifteenth brigade," who had led the assault at Belchite much as Robert Jordan had fought at Carabanchel and Usera.[102] Hemingway did not report any tie to Spain for Merriman as he did in his account of Jordan's ten years' travel in the country, but he did have Jordan recognize the prospect of being black-listed by the State Department and by his university for activity in Spain contrary to the State Department's policy of refusing permits to American volunteers for Spain. (pp. 165, 237) In his preface to Joseph North's *Men in the Ranks*, Hemingway pointed out that many volunteers had been refused repatriation and had been detained on Ellis Island.[103] Jordan was thus a dramatic application of the general condition Hemingway sketched in his nonfiction.

Hemingway's depiction of La Pasionaria was satirically executed in the novel, where in *The Spanish Earth* he presented her with the seriousness appropriate to propaganda. La Pasionaria, he said in the movie narration, was "the most famous woman in Spain today. . . . She is not a romantic beauty, nor any Carmen. She is the wife of a poor miner in Asturias. But all the character of the new Spanish woman is in her voice."[104] She is the Republican Virgin to whom young Joaquin briefly appeals as the bombs fall on El Sordo's hilltop, but her failure as the replacement for the Virgin of Catholicism becomes evident as the boy soon reverts to his *Ave Marias* and the bombs fall closer. Under her real name of Dolores Ibarruri she is known to the people of Karkov's party in Madrid, and the irony of Joaquin's calling on her becomes clear when she is the one who reports the erroneous version of the fight on the hilltop. There Karkov mocks the journalist from *Izvestia* who rhapsodizes over "that great face." (pp. 309, 321, 357) Hemingway provided no external reasons for altering his portrait of La Pasionaria, but within the novel it is clear that she is linked to the betrayal of

---

102. *Fact*, 35. Cecil D. Eby has supplied additional evidence of the identification between Robert Jordan and Robert Hale Merriman in his article "The Real Robert Jordan," *American Literature*, XXXVIII (November 1966), 380-86.

103. *Men in the Ranks* (New York, 1939), pp. 3-4.

104. *The Spanish Earth*, pp. 31-32.

the peasants. Her presence in the cynical, callous group from Gaylord's makes her genuineness as suspect as that of the peasant battalion commanders. It is probable also that between 1938 and 1940 Hemingway learned some disillusioning facts about the Russian presence in Spain. Certainly the Stalin-Hitler pact of 1939 did nothing to reassure one's illusions.

Robert Jordan's investigation of the dead Navarrese cavalry scout's papers was a touch Hemingway brought to the novel from his war reports. The partisan's discovery of the letters from the young scout's sister and his fiancée and his insight into how the war looked from the village of Tafalla were reminiscent of both *The Spanish Earth* and the *Ken* essay "Dying, Well or Badly." In the film narration he mentioned the tearful and anxious letters from home found on the Italian dead at Brihuega, and in the essay he wrote of another dead Italian: "You remember this man quite well because you turned him over to look at his papers and among them was a letter from his wife that you kept until you lost it. She wrote how badly things were going in the village, how pleased she was to get his pay allotment; but that she cried every night because he was not there. She also told how many times she prayed each day to keep him safe and that she had never ceased to thank St. Joseph for sending her such a good husband."[105] Jordan's reading of the sister's invocation of the talismanic protection of the sacred Heart of Jesus, which the young cavalryman wears over his heart, not only tends to balance Fascist suffering against Republican suffering in the novel but also provides further thematic emphasis on the workings of the dark powers in the novel, an emphasis Hemingway did not consider in the nonfiction.

Rafael's remarkable if unprintable obscenities in the novel had their rehearsal and probably their source, including Hemingway's technique of suggesting the complete rawness of the obscenity by use of the word *unprintable*, in his characterization of one of his chauffeurs in Madrid. In one report on the city under siege he wrote, "David was an Anarchist boy from a little town near Toledo. He used language that was so utterly and unconceivably [*sic*] foul that half the time you could not believe what your ears were hearing. Being with David has changed my whole conception of profanity. . . . He liked the war and he

105. *Ibid.*, pp. 46-47; *Ken*, I (April 21, 1938), 68.

thought shelling was beautiful. 'Look at that! Olé! That's the stuff to give the unmentionable unspeakable absolutely unutterables,' he would say in delight."[106] It is likely also that Hemingway picked up the chauffeur's Anarchist background as the basis of Rafael's unreliable and anarchistic behavior in the narrative.

El Sordo's stand on the hilltop and his destruction of Fascist bombers quite probably had their origins in two incidents Hemingway witnessed and recorded during the Republican withdrawal to the Ebro. He reported in April, 1938, that after the Fascist breakthrough at Gandesa the Lincoln-Washington Battalion and a British volunteer battalion were last seen holding out on a hilltop near Gandesa. He later heard that 150 of the 450 trapped there had escaped.[107] Near Tortosa he reported seeing another company cornered on a hilltop and bombed:

Ahead of us fifteen Henkel light bombers, protected by Messerschmidt pursuit planes, swung round and round in a slow circle like vultures waiting for an animal to die. Each time they passed over a certain point there was the thud of bombs. As they swung over the bare hillside, keeping their steady formation, every third ship would dive, guns spitting. They kept that up for 45 minutes unmolested, and what they were bombing and diving on was a company of infantry making a last stand on the hillside and the bare ridge at noon on this hot spring day to defend the Barcelona-Valencia road. . . . Ahead of us all this time the Henkels were circling and diving with the mechanical monotony of movement of a quiet afternoon at the six-day bicycle race. And under them one company of men lay behind rocks in hastily dug foxholes and in simple folds of the ground, trying to hold up the advance of an army.[108]

If Hemingway's war reports seemed most direct in their influence on *For Whom the Bell Tolls*, his observations on Spanish life and character in *Death in the Afternoon* had most relevance for his depiction of Pablo's band. That he relied so heavily on what he had put in the bullfight book to connect the peasants with their prewar lives gave perhaps further support to Arturo Barea's charge in "Not Spain but Hemingway" that the only Spain Hemingway knew well was the Spain of bullfights.[109] Yet

106. *Fact*, 28.
107. *Ibid.*, 55-56.
108. *Ibid.*, 62.
109. Reprinted in Baker, *Hemingway and His Critics* (New York, 1963), pp. 202-12. See especially pp. 211-12.

if Hemingway wrote mostly about the world of bullfighters in that book, he at times looked beyond the bullfight circles to note how the *corrida* was an expression of cultural forces in the country. When he wrote that in Castile the people "know death is the inescapable reality, the one thing any man may be sure of; the only security" and that they "think a great deal about death and when they have a religion they have one which believes that life is much shorter than death" and that "when they can see it being given, avoided, refused and accepted in the afternoon for the nominal price of admission they pay their money and go to the bull ring,"[110] Hemingway was rehearsing Robert Jordan's insight, gained through ten years' travel and study in the country, that death "is their extra sacrament. Their old one that they had before the new religion came from the far end of the Mediterranean, the one they never abandoned but only suppressed and hid to bring it out again in wars and inquisitions. They are the people of the Auto de Fé [*sic*]; the act of faith. Killing is something one must do. . . ." (pp. 286-87) And Hemingway's own lyric farewell to a Spain that was more than the bullfighter's Spain had its echo in El Sordo's lyric farewell to life. Hemingway's personal comprehension that if one could "make clouds come fast in shadows moving over wheat and the small, careful stepping horses; the smell of olive oil; the feel of leather, rope soled shoes; the loops of twisted garlics; earthen pots; saddle bags carried across the shoulder; wine skins; the pitchforks made of natural wood (the tines were branches); the early morning smells; the cold mountain nights and long hot days of summer, with always trees and shade under the trees, then you would have a little of Navarra" had its answer in Sordo's thoughts.[111] "Dying was nothing and he had no picture of it nor fear of it in his mind. But living was a field of grain blowing in the wind on the side of a hill. Living was a hawk in the sky. Living was an earthen jar of water in the dust of the threshing with the grain flailed out and the chaff blowing. Living was a horse between your legs and a carbine under one leg and a hill and valley and a stream with trees along it and the far side of the valley and the hills beyond." (pp. 312-13)

More specifically, Hemingway drew on his topographical

110. *Death in the Afternoon*, p. 266.
111. *Ibid.*, p. 275

knowledge of Ronda when he described Pablo's village as the site for the massacre of local Fascists. "It is built on a plateau in a circle of mountains and the plateau is cut by a gorge that divides the two towns and ends in a cliff that drops sheer to the river and the plain below where you see the dust rising from the mule trains along the road," he wrote in *Death in the Afternoon*. And after bullfights they dragged dead horses to the edge of the cliff and toppled them over.[112] In the novel Pilar similarly describes the unnamed village: "The town is built on a high bank above the river and there is a square there with a fountain and there are benches. . . . On three sides of the plaza is the arcade and on the fourth side is the walk shaded by the trees beside the edge of the cliff with, far below, the river." (p. 103) At this plaza Pablo organizes the massacre like a *capea*, an amateur bullfight, and the townsmen throw the dead Fascists over the cliff. Significantly, the Fascists, for the most part, die like comic and shameful horses rather than brave bulls during the massacre.

Hemingway's description of the *capea* in the bullfight volume had applicability to his conception of Andrés in the novel. The amateur bullfights, he noted, were occasions for young men of the villages to get free experience with bulls if they aspired to professional standing as matadors and occasions for others to prove to themselves or their townsmen that they had the courage to face charging bulls. Sometimes the bull was killed when the amateurs, frenzied enough, swarmed over him to beat and stab him to death.[113] Carrying the message to General Golz, Andrés remembers not only the *capeas* of his home village but also that sense of relief he sometimes knew when they canceled the *capea* and he did not have to face the bulls. Escaping the action at the bridge is, in his mind, like escaping his yearly self-trial at the *capea*. For he is one of those amateurs who fight because the other townsmen expect him to. His identity in the village as the Bull Dog, because of his trick of biting the bull's ear in the final onslaught, must be yearly renewed. (pp. 364-66) But beyond the similarity of the general and specific accounts of *capeas*, the significance of Hemingway's using bullfight backgrounds for Andrés' feeling was that he showed again the the-

112. *Ibid.*, p. 43.
113. *Ibid.*, pp. 23-24.

matic link between the war and the messy and ultimately disgusting amateur *capeas*. Andrés' identification of the coming action at the bridge with the *capea* is not only restatement of the association made between the two kinds of violence in Pablo's massacre of Fascists. It is also an omen of the uncontrolled violence to develop at the bridge.

Pilar's matador Finito, whom she had before Pablo, had his apparent origins in sketches of Varelito, Zurito, Maera, and "Alfonso Gomez, called Finito de Valladolid"—all found in *Death in the Afternoon*. Varelito, Hemingway remembered, in a *corrida* at Seville in 1922 put a sword in the bull, turned his back, and received a horn wound in the rectum, which perforated his intestine and caused his death a few weeks later.[114] Pilar similarly remembers her Finito's rectal wound and his complaint that "having killed him as I should and him absolutely dead, swaying on his legs and ready to fall of his weight, I walked away from him with a certain amount of arrogance and much style and from the back he throws me this horn between the cheeks of my buttocks and it comes out my liver." (p. 55) Zurito, as Hemingway described him in the bullfight book, was a brave and honest matador who insisted on putting the sword into the proper place at the top of the bull's shoulders, even though he often received blows in the chest from the flat of the horns and would often faint from them and have to be carried from the ring.[115] "Finito," Pilar recalls, "did not eat much because he had received a *palotazo*, a blow from the flat of the horn when he had gone in to kill in his last corrida of the year at Zaragosa, and it had rendered him unconscious for some time and even now he could not hold food on his stomach and he would put his handkerchief to his mouth and deposit a quantity of blood in it at intervals throughout the banquet." (p. 185) Maera, Hemingway described as one of the most nearly complete matadors, with a perfect knowledge of bulls and an absolute valor, but who died of tuberculosis and pneumonia. "I thought that [last] year he hoped for death in the ring but he would not cheat by looking for it."[116] Pilar remembers how Finito died after five years of wounds in the bull ring and the aggravation of his tuberculosis

114. *Ibid.*, p. 253.
115. *Ibid.*, p. 257.
116. *Ibid.*, p. 82.

by the heat and the cold of the bull ring, blows on the chest, and the exhaustion of the bullfight tours. For all his fear of bulls he never displayed fear in the ring, Pilar recalls, and he died after a hard winter of pain when he could let no one touch his chest or legs. (pp. 184-90) He was a second-rate matador, Pilar concedes, but he kept his dignity in the ring, and outside it "took everything with great seriousness." (pp. 185-86) In 1931 Hemingway saw "Alfonso Gomez, called Finito de Valladolid, well over thirty-five, once handsome, a failure in his profession, yet very dignified, intelligent and brave, who has been fighting in Madrid ten years without ever interesting the public enough to justify a move from *novillero* to full matador."[117]

Pilar also sees Finito's tubercular apprenticeship while he followed the *capeas* about the country as typical of the limited opportunities allowed the poor in Spain:

Who wouldn't be tubercular from the punishment he received? In this country where no poor man can ever hope to make money unless he is a criminal like Juan March, or a bullfighter, or a tenor in the opera? Why wouldn't he be tubercular? In a country where the bourgeoisie over-eat so that their stomachs are all ruined and they cannot live without bicarbonate of soda and the poor are hungry from their birth till the day they die, why shouldn't he be tubercular? If you travelled under the seats in third-class carriages to ride free when you were following the fairs learning to fight as a boy, down there in the dust and dirt with the fresh spit and dry spit, wouldn't you be tubercular if your chest was beaten out by horns? (p. 184)

In his 1930 *Fortune* article, "Bullfighting, Sport and Industry," Hemingway similarly pointed out that there were two ways to get into bullfighting; one, for those who could afford it, was to go through schools for bullfighters. The other was to survive the *capea* circuits, much as Finito is said to have done in the novel. "Poor boys, without any financial protection, follow the bullfights as boot blacks, eager to get into the ring in any kind of amateur fight no matter how dangerous, practicing the various passes on each other, a passing waiter, a cab horse; riding under the seats of trains with their fighting capes rolled up as pillows; going for days without food when they have been put off a train somewhere by a conductor who catches them without a ticket;

117. *Ibid.*, p. 227.

going through all the hell of the *capeas* or village fights. . . ."[118] Finito's portrait was thus constructed from both individual instances and general conditions. His life and fate, while remembered singularly, provided insight into his whole class as well.

There was nothing in Hemingway's nonfiction to suggest sources or echoes of Pilar's brilliant narration of the massacre at Pablo's village or of her attempt to describe the smell of mortality, but that other set piece of narration given her in the novel—the description of *fiesta* time in Valencia—had its apparent source in Hemingway's celebration of Valencian beach life in *Death in the Afternoon*. But where the delights of Valencia, as told in the bullfight book, were catalogued with both nostalgia and anticipation—a repeatable cluster of sensations—in the novel Pilar's memory of Valencia has the poignancy of an irrecoverable past. Her recall of the pleasures of seeing oxen dragging fishing boats onto the beach from the surf, of eating *paellas* covered with prawns and sprinkled with lime juice, of tasting small eels cooked in oil, of eating the Valencian melons, and of drinking the cold white wine had its parallel in Hemingway's own recorded memories. But in her mind Valencia was also part of that world of Finito and prewar Spain, a tribute to a Spain that was vanishing with the Republic.[119] In a significant way in the novel, Hemingway generally contrasted those glimpses of old Spain, drawn mostly from *Death in the Afternoon*, with the newer, more vicious and cynical Spain whose formation he recorded in the war reports.

His third point of reference for bringing insights from his nonfiction into the novel was the American experience of many international brigade volunteers of whom he wrote. The American Civil War and the American frontier were the cultural reference points he found relevant to the Spanish Civil War. In his portrait of Milton Wolff he saw the young volunteer as a latter-day member of that tradition that sent young men off to learn to fight and brought them back home as accomplished field officers in their early twenties, much as his own grandfather had been. Milton Wolff, he wrote, "is a retired major now at twenty-three and still alive and pretty soon he will be coming home as other men his age and rank came home after the peace at Appo-

118. *Fortune*, I (March 1930), 146.
119. *Death in the Afternoon*, p. 44; *For Whom the Bell Tolls*, pp. 85-86.

mattox Courthouse long ago.[120] Robert Jordan calls on his family memory of his own grandfather, veteran of the Civil War, as guide for his own feeling and courage. Indeed he tries to establish his own identity within the remembered tradition of his grandfather. (p. 338) Jordan's comparison of Fascist and Republican commanders to American Civil War generals is another point of reference between the two civil wars. If there are no Grants, Shermans, Jacksons, or Jeb Stuarts so far, he thinks, there are any number of McClellands, on both sides. It was not until his discussion of generals' merits in *Men at War*, however, that Hemingway made his nonfictional evaluations relevant to Jordan's comparisons. What he mostly applauded in that context was the ability of several American generals to use common sense and adapt to new methods of fighting.[121] In the novel Robert Jordan similarly thinks of the Republican army's adaptation to new methods of warfare, of using guerrilla tactics, and of imposing new political and military disciplines. (pp. 233, 336)

Robert Jordan's call on his frontier heritage for guidance and example in his Spanish Civil War experience had its rehearsal in Hemingway's occasional comparisons of Spanish irregular warfare and Indian wars of the American frontier. Jordan calls on the example of his grandfather to guide him—the grandfather who was pacifier of Indians at Fort Kearny after the American Civil War as well as cavalryman during the war. His grandfather's cavalry pistol and sword and the war bonnet trophies and the arrowheads are reminders to Jordan in his moments of despair that he comes from a frontier that was much like the pre-Fascist Spain he has known. In his war reports Hemingway similarly wrote of American volunteers calling on their frontier heritages for guidance in the conflict. Robert Merriman, probably the prototype for Jordan, evidently knew his frontier history as he led American volunteers in their attack on Belchite. They had surprised the Rebel defenders, Hemingway wrote, by marching twenty miles across country from Quinca, working their way through the woods Indian-style, and bursting onto the defenders. Such Indian tactics, Hemingway noted, were "still the most life-saving [tactics] that any infantry can know."[122]

120. "Milton Wolff," *An Exhibition of Sculptures by Jo Davidson* (New York, 1938), p. 22.
121. *Men at War*, p. xiii.
122. *Fact*, 34-35.

But also part of Jordan's frontier heritage is his own memory of the American West. The images of the West, mingled with those he has gathered from his life in Spain, act as touchstones of the good for him and reminders of the kind of life he wants to save by saving the Republic. His recollections of the smell of clover, crushed sage, woodsmoke from the burning autumn leaves at Missoula, of Indian grass and smoked leather are in many respects repetitions of those smells, sights, and sounds Hemingway had evoked the year before in his *Vogue* sketch "Clark's Fork Valley, Wyoming," celebration of a place representative of essential America for him. Like Pilar's reminiscences on Valencia, Jordan's recall of the West takes on the sadness of a lost era and of a world recharacterized by cities and wars.

The three major nonfictional source areas for Hemingway's novel, seen together, suggest that in his mind *For Whom the Bell Tolls* was not simply a war novel or a novel about his experiences in Spain, as Jasper Wood called for, but a fictional merging of the three worlds of war, Spain, and the American past. What Hemingway seemed to be doing through the use of these sources was showing how Americans with their Civil War and frontier pasts were confronting the twentieth-century European world through the catalyst of war and finding the ties that united them to other men who had their pasts and were now having their civil war. He was in close, if uneasy, agreement with Gertrude Stein that Americans were the oldest people of the twentieth century because they had entered it at the time of the Civil War.

Across the River and into the Trees

In his interview with Harvey Breit, after *Across the River and Into the Trees* had become a best seller, Hemingway explained what he thought the book was about by telling for whom it had been written. "This last book was written for people . . . who had lived and would die and be capable of knowing the difference between these two states. It was also written for all people who had ever fought or would be capable of fighting or interested in it. It was written, as well, for people who had ever been in love or were capable of that happiness."[123] Though he did not say so, it was written also for those who had read his

123. "Success, It's Wonderful," *New York Times Book Review*, December 3, 1950, p. 58.

earlier works. For the novel was a fictional reprise of themes, characters, situations, and sometimes phrases found in the novels, stories, and nonfiction of the quarter-century before—so much so that critics would charge him with imitating himself. Readers could recognize the jokes on La Pasionaria's slogans from *For Whom the Bell Tolls*, could recognize Cantwell's hunting and skiing between wars with his German counterparts as similar to Harry's in "The Snows of Kilimanjaro," or Cantwell's return to the site of his wounding as similar to Nick Adams' imagined return in "A Way You'll Never Be."[124] Readers of his journalism and other nonfictional pieces, if there were any, could recognize also that Hemingway drew upon ideas, passages, and situations from that body of work, which ranged from some of his earliest articles to those as late as the war reports on the invasion of Germany. Later readers might also recognize that in the novel Hemingway tried out some ideas and phrases that he would reuse in his later nonfiction.

Indeed, in a novel in which the protagonist does most of the talking there were remarkable similarities with the technique Hemingway used in *Green Hills of Africa*. Richard Cantwell's being prodded into talking about things he would rather leave unsaid was a retrial of the technique used in the African book when Hemingway was urged by Kandisky to talk about literature, writers, and the craft of writing. His surly answers there in quasi-justification of his writing and hunting had their parallels in Cantwell's grudging explanation to Renata of his sad profession of soldiering. Though both spoke reluctantly, they spoke at length. A further technique borrowed from the African book was the way of getting into the narrative. Both books begin with a spoiled wait in a hunting blind, and both proceed in a mood of frustration and urgency—one because of the coming rains that will spoil the hunt, the other because of coming death.

For some of the incidents and moods in the novel Hemingway reached back to the Toronto *Star* article which in its time told the essential story of Richard Cantwell's return to Venice. In "A Veteran Visits Old Front, Wishes He Had Stayed Away," written in 1922, Hemingway told of his return to the town where

124. *For Whom the Bell Tolls*, p. 321; *Short Stories*, pp. 57, 409; *Across the River and into the Trees* (New York, 1950), pp. 40, 122, 18. Subsequent references to the novel will be to this edition and will be parenthesized in the text.

his unit had been billeted, to the river banks where the old trenches had been, and to the marsh country between Schio and Venice where the battles of his youth had been fought. His conclusion then had been that it was better not to revisit old places one had illusions about. The real place without its setting in imagination was a diminished thing and was better left in the country of memory.[125] To return to such sites was to find that the magic places were smaller and duller than remembered. But in Richard Cantwell's situation this recognition is not the end but the beginning of things. He has learned, Cantwell says, that "each day is a new and fine illusion. But you can cut out everything phony about illusions as though you would cut it with a straight edge razor." (p. 232) His return to Venice, the magic city of his youth, is his last attempt to determine what has been substance and what has been illusion in his life and to celebrate the substantial part.

At Fossalta di Piave, Hemingway said, he "climbed the grassy slope above the sunken road where the dugouts had been to look at the Piave and looked down an even slope to the blue river. The Piave is as blue as the Danube is brown. Across the river were two new houses where the two rubble heaps had been just inside the Austrian lines." It was a sight evidently that haunted him, for the house beside the canal was an image he used repeatedly to denote a place of past or coming danger. In "A Way You'll Never Be" the yellow house in the willows beside the canal is Nick Adams' place "that meant more than anything." That it meant something to Hemingway in his public writing was evident too when, of all things to see, he saw another ominous house beside a river as the battle of the Ebro delta was taking shape. In his Spanish war report of April 18, 1938, he told of the hasty Republican defenses set up on the eastern bank of the Ebro and desultory shelling from Fascist guns as the lines of infantry dug in. "You crossed a stretch of road that in another day would be worth your life to sprint across and headed for a white house that stood above a canal that paralleled the Ebro and dominated all the yellow town across the river where the Fascists were preparing their attack."[126] The deadliness of the fight at nearby Tortosa was creeping toward the house and canal, he noted. In

125. *TDS*, July 7, 1922, p. 7.
126. *Fact*, 66.

Across the River and into the Trees Richard Cantwell too re-
turns to the "low red farmhouse" and the canal of the dead and
sees the willows on the other side and at the spot where he was
first badly wounded carries out his rite of exorcism to rid the
place of its terror for him. (pp. 13, 18, 20, 23) Near Porto Grande
was the place, Hemingway remembered, where "Austrians and
Italians attacked and counter-attacked waist deep in the swamp
water. . . ." Richard Cantwell similarly remembers shooting "the
men who came wading across the marshes, holding their rifles
above the water and coming as slow as men wade, waist deep." (p.
32) It was another of those memorable images that one had to
use and reuse until its reality was confirmed or vanished.

Other incidents from the 1922 visit that found fictional use
were Hemingway's encounter with the war profiteers at Mestre
and his discovery of Venice seen across the marshes. Richard
Cantwell too sees the postwar rich from Milan in the garage bar
at Venice and admires a profiteer's expensive mistress, "a beautiful, hard piece of work," he guesses. More important for the
later novel, though, was the way Hemingway saw Venice: "Then
a wind blew the mist away from the Adriatic and we saw Venice
way off across the swamp and the sea standing grey and yellow
like a fairy city." Richard Cantwell anticipates such a view when
he sees across the marshes the campanile of Burano and the slate-
blue sea with "the sails of twelve sailing barges running with the
wind for Venice." Then after a turn of the road he sees the city
beyond the fishing boats, ". . . and it was like going to New York
the first time you were ever there in the old days when it was
shining, white and beautiful. . . . They made the left turn and
came along the canal where the fishing boats tied up, and the
Colonel looked at them and his heart was happy because of the
brown nets and the wicker fish traps and the clean, beautiful
lines of the boats." (pp. 26, 34) But the causeway approach to
the city has no counterpart in his or Hemingway's recorded
earlier experience, and Cantwell thinks it is "a miserable view of
Venice" from that point on.

From another early *Star* article Hemingway drew his attitude
toward Gabrielle D'Annunzio, whom Cantwell, in his memories
of the first war, recalls as a purveyor of the old, dead patriotism
in Italy. In his article on Mussolini as Europe's prize bluffer
Hemingway had noted in 1923 that, should Mussolini falter in

his attempt to establish his superpatriotic Fascist movement, his place might be taken by "that old, bald-headed, perhaps a little insane but thoroughly sincere, divinely brave swashbuckler—Gabrielle D'Annunzio."[127] Cantwell similarly remembers D'Annunzio as the orator who during the first war exhorted the troops to sacrifice for the fatherland and as the adventurer who had worn the patch over his eye, had told the infantry how to die, and had been "writer, poet, national hero, phraser of the dialectic of Fascism, macabre egotist, aviator, commander, or rider in the first of the fast torpedo attack boats, Lieutenant Colonel of Infantry without knowing how to command a company, nor a platoon properly, the great, lovely writer of *Nottorno* whom we respect, and jerk." (pp. 49-52) The intensity of Cantwell's feeling over Hemingway's of 1923 was to be measured by the extent of Hemingway's later knowledge of Fascism.

From Hemingway's *Esquire* articles of the 1930's came the recollections of bird shooting during his boyhood, recollections that Cantwell cites as one of the reasons for going hunting on his last weekend. During his army physical examination before the weekend begins, he tells the army doctor that he wants to go on a duck shoot at the mouth of the Tagliamento and return imaginatively to the hunting he had known "at home when we were kids." It is a memory and a passion that the city-bred doctor cannot know or share. (pp. 10-11) In his 1935 article "Remembering Shooting-Flying" Hemingway similarly celebrated his early hunting of snipe, pheasant, ducks, partridge, and quail near the Des Plaines River during his boyhood and called it the proper beginning for one who would later see and hunt across most of the world. It was the beginning of a passion that a fifty-year-old colonel, facing mortality and trying to identify the real passions of his full life, might later return to.[128]

From *Death in the Afternoon*, especially the view of death found in "A Natural History of the Dead," Hemingway took both attitude and image for Cantwell's responses. His catalogue there of how men died like animals was instructive: some from wounds hardly severe enough to kill a rabbit—"of little wounds . . . from three or four small grains of shot that hardly seem to break the skin"; others with wounds in the head that made them

127. "Mussolini, Europe's Prize Bluffer," *TDS*, January 27, 1923, p. 11.
128. *Esquire*, III (February 1935), 21, 152.

die slowly like cats; others from such maladies as Spanish influenza, so that they died in a final flow of the bowels.[129] The context for the catalogue there was Hemingway's scorn for the Humanists' claims of human dignity. In "Notes on the Next War" he wrote another catalogue of sickening ways to die, this time in scorn of the professional patriots who told how sweet and fitting it was to die for one's country:

> But in modern war there is nothing sweet or fitting in your dying. . . . Hit in the head you will die quickly and cleanly and even sweetly and fittingly except for the white blinding flash that never stops, unless perhaps it is only the frontal bone or your optic nerve that is smashed, or your jaw carried away. . . . But if you are not hit in the head you will be hit in the chest, and choke in it, or in the lower belly, and feel it all slip and slide loosely as you open, to spill out when you try to get up, it's not supposed to be so painful but they always scream with it, it's the idea I suppose, or have the flash, the slamming clang of high explosive on a hard road and find your legs are gone above the knee. . . .[130]

In the novel Cantwell imagines a further list of ways to die, but the catalogue keeps different company this time. Richard Cantwell has run the gauntlet of all the ways to die listed in the catalogues and now recognizes the irony that death is closest to the ecstasy of love, not the horrors of war:

> He only thought of her and how close life comes to death when there is ecstasy. . . . It comes to you in small fragments that hardly show where it has entered. . . . It can come from unboiled water; an unpulled-up mosquito boot, or it can come with the great, white-hot, clanging roar we have lived with. It comes in small cracking whispers that precede the noise of the automatic weapon. It can come with the smoke-emitting arc of the grenade or the sharp, cracking drop of the mortar. . . . I have seen it come, loosen itself from the bomb rack, and falling with that strange curve. It comes in the metallic rending crash of a vehicle, or the simple lack of traction of a slippery road. . . . It comes in bed to most people, I know, like love's opposite number. (pp. 219-20)

Besides the general tactics already mentioned that he adapted from *Green Hills of Africa*, Hemingway found a key metaphor from that book useful for Cantwell's review. For the hunter, he

129. *Death in the Afternoon*, pp. 138-39.
130. *Esquire*, IV (September 1935), 156.

learned, terrain was reality, regardless of its covering of trees or grass. Like Twain discovering the deadly reality of the river bottom beneath the innocent and romantic surface in *Life on the Mississippi*, Hemingway found that an innocent-looking meadow could be cut with ravines and ambush points for lurking animals.[131] The nightmare terrain that Twain the river pilot and Hemingway the hunter learned about becomes the stuff of dreams for Cantwell also. He has dreams of combat and "strange dreams about places mostly," he tells Renata. "We live by accidents of terrain, you know. And terrain is what remains in the dreaming part of your mind." (p. 123)

Hemingway's 1942 anthology *Men at War* was perhaps one of the most fertile sources for the novel. There he brought together much of what he had learned and decided about war up to that time, and those conclusions were the basis of Cantwell's talk to his two principal listeners during the weekend in Venice. To the Gran Maestro of the Gritti Palace Hotel he talks of their early initiation to war's obscene secrets, one of which was that men will find ways to mutilate themselves rather than go to battle. They remember those who shot each other in the leg and others who induced gonorrheal infections from match boxes filled with pus and others who produced jaundice symptoms by putting ten centime pieces under their armpits or others who had paraffin injected under their kneecaps. (p. 59) In *Men at War* Hemingway catalogued a similar, almost identical, list of dodges. "There was much trouble with self-inflicted wounds in Italy during the last war. The men became very skillful at it and often a pair would team up to shoot each other, usually wrapping sandbags around the arm or leg, to avoid any evidence of a close discharge of the rifle. Others would hold copper coins in their armpits to get a yellow cast of complexion and simulate jaundice. Others deliberately contracted venereal disease in order to leave the lines. There were doctors in Milan who did a thriving trade in injecting paraffin under the kneecaps of their clients to induce lameness."[132] If the context of the war book suggested that even the then-victorious Italians could be afraid of war, the novel suggested that such actions were a temptation for all men who recognized the obscenity of war.

131. *Green Hills of Africa*, p. 259.
132. *Men at War*, p. xxviii.

To Renata, Richard Cantwell talks of the false generalship in the Second World War, while in *Men at War*, written for soldiers likely to go into battle, Hemingway criticized only the generals of the first war and publicly hoped that generals of the second had learned from earlier mistakes. "The worst generals it would be possible to develop by a process of reverse selection of brains carried on over a period of a thousand years could never make a worse mess than Passchendaele and Gallipoli," he said in the war anthology. In the novel, Cantwell's sad recognition though is that the butcher generals triumphed again during the second war. (pp. 237-42) His critique of political generals, bullying generals, and generals playing to the grandstands of public opinion, however, must be dramatically weighed in light of his own loss of a regiment, committed piecemeal under orders from above and sent against a cleverly entrenched enemy in the Hürtgen Forest with prepared lanes of fire. It was, he says, "Passchendaele with tree bursts." (p. 254) To Renata he also confides his infantryman's view of armored units, a view also elaborated on in *Men at War*.[133] There Hemingway noted that armor gave men false courage. At first tank men would take their armor where they as men would not go, but when they learned that tanks too could be destroyed, they left the hard fighting and holding to the infantry, and he concluded that "finally no mechanized vehicle is any better than the heart of the man who handles the controls." Richard Cantwell's anger at armored soldiers is directed both at the type of generals developed by that kind of fighting and at the morality of men who would substitute invulnerability for courage. "Georgie Patton," he says, was the new type of general who was protected by his money and his armor and "possibly never told the truth in his life." The trouble with armor, he tells Ranata, is "the people inside of it. It makes men into bullies which is the first step toward cowardice; true cowardice, I mean. Perhaps it is a little complicated by claustrophobia." (pp. 115, 145)

To himself Richard Cantwell reviews other insights Hemingway had previously stated in *Men at War*. Cantwell is, in fiction, the dramatization of Hemingway's earlier statement that the history of the century is all one piece, that American involvement in foreign wars begun in 1917 was irrevocable and did not end

133. *Ibid.*, pp. xi, xix-xx.

in 1918. "Once a nation has entered a policy of foreign wars, there is no withdrawing. If you do not go to them then they will come to you. It was April, 1917 that ended our isolation—it was not Pearl Harbor." Cantwell's involvement with the century is signaled by his recognition that he has lost three countries to Fascism and regained two. (p. 172) Spain is still to be retaken. Cantwell likewise has experienced that loss of the illusion of immortality that in *Men at War* Hemingway described as the common experience of most soldiers initiated into their profession by serious wounding.[134] Cantwell had received the small wounds that made one think himself immune to death and then the serious wound. "Finally he did get hit properly and for good. No one of his other wounds had ever done to him what the first big one did. I suppose it is just the loss of the immortality, he thought." (p. 33) In the war anthology Hemingway had similarly written that "when you go to war as a boy you have a great illusion of immortality. Other people get killed; but not you. It can happen to other people; but not to you. Then when you are badly wounded the first time you lose that illusion and you know it can happen to you."[135]

Cantwell's running account of his army's experience during the Normandy invasion, the capture of Paris, and the breaking of the Siegfried Line drew heavily on Hemingway's *Collier's* reports of the same events of 1944. But the colonel's purposes and the war correspondent's were different. Whereas Hemingway's war reports sought to chronicle and interpret events that were already weeks-old news to newspaper readers, Cantwell's account was presented as essentially a self-justification of his brief career as regimental commander and brigadier general. Perhaps the closest Hemingway the war reporter came to Cantwell's point of view in the *Collier's* stories was in "The G.I. and the General" when he contrasted a general's sympathy for his division with a private's complaints about the general as a "slave driver."[136]

Cantwell's story that his group landed in Normandy without serious opposition, presumably at Utah Beach, stood in contrast to Hemingway's account in "Voyage to Victory" of the confused and hard-fought landing at Omaha Beach; and Cantwell's sum-

134. *Ibid.*, p. xxiii.
135. *Ibid.*, p. xiii.
136. *Collier's*, CXIV (November 4, 1944), 44, 47.

mary of a relatively easy sweep through Normandy after the Saint-Lô breakthrough had no parallel in Hemingway's articles, as he was back in England covering the buzz bomb attacks at the time of the hedgerow fighting.[137] But Cantwell's version of the capture of Paris, with the chief fighting at Rambouillet, had specific parallels with the accounts in "The Battle for Paris" and "How We Came to Paris." Hemingway's own reported experience was with French guerrilla units near Rambouillet, though he recorded joint actions by guerrilla and army reconnaissance units. Cantwell mentions no guerrillas but tells of fighting twelve times between Rambouillet and the outskirts of Paris. (pp. 221, 133) His statement that only two of the engagements, those at Toussus le Noble and Le Buc, were real fights had origins in Hemingway's previous accounts of duels between French armor and German artillery at those points.[138] Cantwell's story of the return to Paris and Americans' difficulties with the French General LeClerc had closer parallels with the journalistic reports. "The taking of Paris was nothing," he says. "It was only an emotional experience. We killed a number of typists and the screen the Germans had left, as they always do, to cover their withdrawal. I suppose they figured they were not going to need a hell of a lot of office workers any more and they left them as soldiers." (p. 134) In "How We Came to Paris" Hemingway told of German soldiers captured by the guerrillas as Chateaufort identifying themselves as office workers who had been brought to the front at one o'clock in the morning. Arrival in Paris was an emotional experience for himself too, Hemingway reported: "I couldn't say anything more then, because I had a funny choke in my throat and I had to clean my glasses because there now, below us, gray and always beautiful, was spread the city I love best in all the world."[139]

Cantwell's scorn of the entry into Paris by General LeClerc's armored divisions after the fighting had been done by French guerrillas and American armor apparently grew out of Hemingway's encounter with LeClerc's column while he was operating with the guerrillas. Outside Toussus le Noble, he reported, Le-Clerc's staff and military police had caught up with the guerrillas

137. "Voyage to Victory," *Collier's*, CXIV (July 22, 1944), 11-13, 56-57; "London Fights the Robots" (August 19, 1944), 17, 80-81.
138. *Collier's*, CXIV (September 30, 1944), 1, 83-86; (October 7, 1944), 65, 67.
139. *Collier's*, CXIV (October 7, 1944), 67.

and ordered them to stay behind until the column had moved ahead, and LeClerc had personally tongue-lashed the commander of the guerrilla force. "In war, my experience has been that a rude general is a nervous general," Hemingway afterwards concluded.[140] Cantwell's stronger feelings, whether dramatically called for in light of his own disastrous and brief career as a general or prompted by Hemingway's later and more acid response to insult, called for depiction of LeClerc as an incompetent political general. "We were also requested not to enter [Paris] too rapidly as the General Leclerc was to take the city. I complied with this request and entered as slowly as I could. . . ." Later: "The people of Leclerc, another jerk of the third or fourth water . . . shot a great number of rounds to make it seem important and because we had given them what they had to shoot with. But it was not important." (pp. 140, 134)

Perhaps most important of the war reports for the novel was "War in the Siegfried Line," for in the Hürtgen Forest Richard Cantwell's military career reached its tragic climax. Hemingway's opening claim in the article was already slanted in the argumentative, infantry-boosting mode that Cantwell was later to adopt:

A lot of people will tell you how it was to be first into Germany and how it was to break the Siegfried Line and a lot of people will be wrong. . . . The infantry broke the Siegfried Line. They cracked it on a cold rainy morning when even the crows weren't flying, much less the Air Force. Two days before, on the last day before the weather broke for the bad, we had come to the end of the rat race. It had been a fine rat race from Paris up as far as Le Cateau, with bitter fighting at Landrecies that few saw and fewer still are left to remember. Then there had been the forcing of the passes of the Ardennes Forest in country like the illustrations for Grimm's Fairy Tales only a lot grimmer.[141]

Cantwell's review of the similar time in his career also had the sound of Hemingway's earlier identification of the conditions for fighting if not the same place: "It was cold and raining and blowing half a gale, and ahead of us was the dark forest wall of the Schnee Eifel range where the dragon lived, and behind us on the first hill behind was the German reviewing stand that had been built for high officers to occupy when they watched

140. *Ibid.*, 14, 65.
141. *Collier's*, CXIV (November 18, 1944), 18.

the maneuvers that proved the Westwall could never be broken. We were hitting it on the point that the Germans had chosen to prove, in sham battles, that it was impregnable."[142] Cantwell tells Renata: "It was not really the Hurtgen Forest. That was only a small sector. It was the Stadtswald and it was where the German High Command had figured, exactly, to fight after Aachen had been taken and the road into Germany breached." (pp. 235-36)

Other details from the *Collier's* account that found their way into the novel included Hemingway's contrast between the way battles are planned and the way they develop. The detail had its dramatic amplification in Cantwell's account of the briefing session at Paris. There General Walter Bedell Smith, he remembers, "explained to all of us how easy the operation that later took the name of Hurtgen Forest would be." (p. 235) It was the operation that cost Cantwell his regiment. The article mentioned further the well-hidden German 88's that opened fire on the infantry and their tank support as they crested the hill. Cantwell similarly remembers the 88's, the mortars, and "the fire-lanes taped for machine gun and automatic weapon fire. . . ." (p. 256) And where Hemingway reported the faltering of the five tanks and tank destroyers under the pounding by the German guns, with the infantry drawing back, Cantwell remembers losing four infantry companies in the Hürtgen draws and the quick destruction of five tanks, with the tankmen running crazily from the burning tanks. (p. 233) But the detail from the journalistic account that was most vivid for Cantwell was the bursting of shells in the trees. "The woods were close-planted fir trees, and the shell bursts tore and smashed them, and the splinters from the tree bursts were like javelins in the half-light of the forest, and the men were shouting and calling now to take the curse off the darkness. . . ."[143] Cantwell's recall was bitter for it was his only regiment that had been lost in the exploding trees: "He looked up at the light on the ceiling and he was completely desperate at the remembrance of his loss of his battalions, and of individual people. He could never hope to have such a regiment, ever. . . . Now every second man in it was dead and the others nearly all were wounded. In the belly, the head, the feet or the hands,

142. *Ibid.*, 70.
143. *Ibid.*, 70, 73.

the neck, the back, the lucky buttocks, the unfortunate chest and the other places. Tree burst wounds hit men where they would never be wounded in open country. And all the wounded were wounded for life." (p. 242).

But if Richard Cantwell is a synthesizer of much previously recorded nonfiction by Hemingway, he is also an anticipator of effects still to come in Hemingway's journalism and memoirs. The *True* article "The Shot," like the *Holiday* fable "The Good Lion," both published a year after the novel, retained mannerisms and attitudes of Colonel Cantwell, hints of the close imaginative identity of Hemingway and his character. If "The Good Lion" got off a few leftover Cantwellian jokes on Venice, "The Shot" re-celebrated the frontier traits Cantwell had displayed. In the opening paragraphs of the article Hemingway showed he still found literary use of Cantwell's necessity to guard his rear approaches. Where Cantwell sits in the Gritti Palace Hotel dining room with his flanks covered, Hemingway recorded the need to sit watchfully even in his own backyard to guard against unseen approaches by his fellow Cubans. "I didn't see these two Negroes until they were by the table where it was set under the arbor to be in the shade," he noted, ". . . and when I looked up and saw these two by the table I knew that I was slipping."[144] Such Old West instincts easily allowed him to slip into his other story of hunting in Wyoming and Idaho. There he re-argued the points Cantwell and his Wyoming-bred driver discuss on the way to Venice. That Hemingway saw significance in characterizing Goldburg, Idaho, as a "rough town" in comparison to Sun Valley or Ketchum was indication of the significance he attached to Cantwell's and Jackson's talk on Cheyenne and Casper, Wyoming, and Cooke City, Montana, as "tough towns." "The Shot" verified the importance of Cantwell's Old West background in the novel. For the Colonel's tribute to Venice as a "tough town" had, in the mind of the novelist, the authority of wide and rough experience, that of the later frontier as well as of an army career. (pp. 115, 35-36)

When Cantwell tells the Gritti Palace Hotel waiter, "I'll damn well find happiness, too. . . . Happiness as you know is a movable feast," (p. 68) he finds the phrase for Hemingway's later equation of the young author's Paris and happiness: "If you are lucky

144. *True,* XXVIII (April 1951), 25.

enough to have lived in Paris as a young man, then wherever you go for the rest of your life, it stays with you, for Paris is a moveable feast." So said Hemingway the same year that the novel was published, and perhaps he meant it then for the epigraph to his memoir. It was a fitting linkage, for both Hemingway and his fictional counterpart expected to find that happiness by looking backward and inward.

The Old Man and the Sea

The Old Man and the Sea was Hemingway's clearest example of fiction finding its germ in the essays. "On the Blue Water," published in *Esquire* for April, 1936, contained in a paragraph the narrative essentials of the short novel. Within the context of his argument that fishing was more exciting than hunting because one never knew what he would pull up from the depths of the sea, he wrote:

Another time an old man fishing in a skiff out of Cabañas hooked a great marlin that, on the heavy sashcord handline, pulled the skiff far out to sea. Two days later the old man was picked up by fishermen sixty miles to the eastward, the head and forward part of the marlin lashed alongside. What was left of the fish, less than half, weighed eight hundred pounds. The old man had stayed with him a day, a night, a day, and another night while the fish swam deep and pulled the boat. When he had come up the old man had pulled the boat up on him and harpooned him. Lashed alongside the sharks had hit him and the old man had fought them out alone in the Gulf Stream in a skiff, clubbing them, stabbing at them, lunging at them with an oar until he was exhausted and the sharks had eaten all that they could hold. He was crying in the boat when the fishermen picked him up, half crazy from his loss, and the sharks were still circling the boat.[145]

The novel was also one of the best certified examples of the iceberg relationship between Hemingway's fiction and nonfiction. When Hemingway elaborated on his iceberg theory for George Plimpton of the *Paris Review*, he cited *The Old Man and the Sea* as a work particularly created according to that theory. He could have made the book a thousand pages long, he said, and filled it with the lives of all the people of Santiago's village and all the fishing legends the villagers knew about, but he made it

145. *Esquire*, V (April 1936), 184.

a spare story with all but the essential experiences of the old man and the boy left in the suspension of implied knowledge.[146] He also told another group of listeners about his twenty-year preparation to write the novel: "I knew about a man in that situation with a fish. I knew what happened in a boat, in a sea, fighting a fish. So I took a man I knew for 20 years and imagined him under those circumstances."[147]

Much of that twenty-year-old iceberg of knowledge could be found in Hemingway's fishing and hunting articles of the 1930's and afterward in his introductions to books on hunting and fishing. One major part of that information concerned the natural history of game fish, sharks, birds, and other denizens of the sea. In "Marlin off Cuba," for example, he told how hooked blue or striped marlin made a run to the northwest though they ordinarily traveled deep from east to west against the Gulf Stream. And the big ones, he noted, did not appear until September.[148] Santiago similarly fishes deep, finds his big marlin in September, and observes that the giant fish strikes in a northwesterly direction until, tiring, he turns northeast to follow the current.[149] In the same article Hemingway wrote that the largest marlin yet caught by commercial fishermen off Cuba dressed out to 1175 pounds of salable meat, which meant that a fourth to a third of its total weight had been lost in dressing. Santiago estimates his big fish to weigh close to 1500 pounds. In "Marlin off the Morro" Hemingway reported the presence of mako sharks off Havana, even though they were allegedly found only in the waters off New Zealand and Tahiti.[150] One of the first types of sharks to hit Santiago's marlin is the mako. (p. 100) And in "There She Breaches" Hemingway chronicled an ornithological phenomenon he later used when the small warbler lights on the old man's skiff: "So we drifted like that all morning, and, in the fall, the small birds that are going south are deadly tired sometimes as they near the coast of Cuba where the hawks come out to meet

146. Baker, *Critics*, p. 34.
147. A. E. Hotchner, "Ernest Hemingway Talks to American Youth," *This Week*, October 18, 1959, p. 11.
148. Eugene V. Connett, ed., *American Big Game Fishing* (New York, 1935), pp. 57, 62, 59, 67.
149. *The Old Man and the Sea* (New York, 1952, Special Student's Edition), pp. 60, 39, 51, 65. Subsequent references to the novel will be to this edition and will be parenthesized in the text.
150. *Esquire*, I (Autumn 1933), 8.

them, and the birds light on the boat to rest and sometimes we would have as many as twenty on board at a time in the cabin, on the deck, perched on the fishing chairs or resting on the floor of the cockpit."[151] Not only is Santiago with a friend, as he confides to the bird (pp. 52-53), but if the fishing note was relevant, he is also a part of such natural cycles as the migrations of birds.

Another part of that iceberg of substructural knowledge was Hemingway's acquaintance with numerous instances of sharks attacking hooked but unboated game fish. At Bimini, he said, sharks would swarm over a hooked tuna so that "you are lucky to land more than the head and skeleton." But they were more wary of marlin than of tuna because of the marlin's sword. And he reported Henry Strater's loss of half a marlin to the sharks, which took two bucketfuls of meat away, he said, while the boat party was bringing the marlin over the side of the boat. Taking marlins at Bimini, he generalized, was "complicated by the fact that they feed, when on the surface, on schools of bonito and small tuna along with the fish sharks and the big brown, wide-finned sharks we call Galanos and as soon as a hooked marlin is killed the sharks will attack him. They will hit him sooner, of course, if he is hooked deeply and bleeding."[152]

Santiago's careful preparation and tying of the bait to the hooks had their backgrounds in Hemingway's sports fishing accounts of the thirties, as did his harpooning and clubbing of the sharks. Santiago's hiding of the hook inside the bait fish, his tying and sewing of the fish over the curve of the hook, and his sweetening of the bait fish with fresh sardines all had their rehearsals in Hemingway's prescriptions for bait preparation in "Marlin off the Morro" and "Marlin off Cuba." The expertness with which Santiago harpoons the marlin and later the sharks was also presented by example and prescription in "Marlin off the Morro" and "On Being Shot Again." His fishing companion Carlos Gutierrez of Havana, Hemingway bragged, could gaff dolphin and marlin backhanded and with accuracy as a result of forty years' fishing in the Gulf Stream. And his advice on how and exactly where to shoot or club a shark was made in much

151. *Esquire*, V (May 1936), 35.
152. "a.d. Southern Style," *Esquire*, III (May 1935), 156; "The President Vanquishes," *Esquire*, III (July 1935), 23.

the same terms Santiago thinks in when he fights the makos. "If you ever have to shoot a shark shoot him anywhere along a straight line down the center of his head, flat, running from the tip of his nose to a foot behind his eyes. If you can, with your eye, intersect this line with a line running between his eyes and can hit that place it will kill him dead. . . . What paralyzes him is clubbing his head."[153] With his harpoon Santiago similarly rams "at a spot where the line between his eyes intersected with the line that ran straight back from his nose." He clubs sharks later in the melee. (pp. 101, 113)

But important as such physical and technical knowledge was to the novel, the nonfictional statements on the morality of fishing and hunting had even greater relevance to a novel that invited allegorical readings. One of the most relevant types of statement was that which implied consideration of the game fish in human terms. In the *Esquire* article "The President Vanquishes" Hemingway told of Henry Strater, president of the Maine Tuna Club, who had hooked a large marlin, "had fought himself out and killed the fish at the same time the fish had finished him." Santiago's determination to "stay with you [the marlin] till I am dead" emphasized such an identification. (p. 51) And in the *Esquire* article "On the Blue Water" he provided both technical and moral insight for the old man's later fight. Fishing from a small boat was effective in finally beating the fish, he said, because making the fish tow a skiff would kill him in time. "But the most satisfaction is to dominate and convince the fish and bring him intact in everything but spirit to the boat as rapidly as possible." In "Marlin off Cuba" Hemingway had similarly seen that the merit of the fisherman was in his ability to work as close as possible to the breaking point of his tackle without breaking it—much as in *Death in the Afternoon* he had noted the matador's merit in working as close to the limit of his skill with the cape without going past the point of total self-exposure. "It is better to convince [the fish] than to try to kill him," he saw. And in "The Great Blue River," written only the year before the novel, he saw more clearly the analogy between working a fish and working a bull. A fishing partner, he said, was "playing [the fish] as a bull-fighter might play a bull. . . ."[154]

153. *Esquire*, III (June 1935), 25.
154. "Marlin off Cuba," p. 68; *Holiday*, VI (July 1949), 63.

In the novel Hemingway picked up such bullfight terms as *dominate* and *convince* and enhanced the man-fish struggle with overtones of the *corrida*, which he had already established as a moral struggle aesthetically presented. After maneuvering the marlin as a matador might a bull, Santiago tells himself, "Now I must convince him and then I must kill him." (p. 86)

In his 1937 introduction to *Atlantic Game Fishing* and in his 1949 essay "Cuban Fishing," Hemingway further argued the morality of identifying men and game fish. If men were to claim merit for landing a large game fish, he said, they ought to compensate for the fish's having a hook in his mouth by using their own strength to beat the fish rather than depend on heavy equipment. "But until fishermen agree to be hooked in the mouth or stomach (depending on the system they follow) I think they exaggerate somewhat when they employ the term 'fight.' "[155] In the novel he had Santiago embody the moral point by holding the slashing cord with his bare hands. He and the fish are equally caught on opposite ends of the handline. (pp. 54, 84)

After winning his struggle with the marlin, Santiago recognizes that "I am only better than him through trickery. . . ." (p. 99) The term "trickery" in the context, however, had special meanings, both technological and moral, as Hemingway indicated in "There She Breaches," his *Esquire* account of an attempt to catch or kill a sperm whale near Cabañas. Although Hemingway's *Pilar* had chased the whale most of a day, the whale had finally eluded the fishing party. One of the group then observed that they failed to take the whale because they were ignorant of the trick needed to catch him. During the ensuing conversation, the term gathered other meanings as one thought that "everything's a trick. . . . Life is a very difficult trick to learn," and another concluded, "No, . . . Life is a combat. But you have to know lots of tricks to make a living."[156] Evidently Hemingway drew on the conversation later, for the technical meaning of the term applies when Santiago thinks that his tying the oar to the stern of the skiff as a drag is a "good trick" against the fish. Later the moral meanings emerge when Santiago recognizes

155. S. Kip Farrington, Jr., *Atlantic Game Fishing* (New York, 1937), p. xix; Brian Vesey-Fitzgerald and Francesca Lamonte, eds., *Game Fish of the World* (New York, 1949), p. 157.

156. *Esquire*, V (May 1936), 35, 205.

that human intelligence and spirit are the real tricks he has used to overcome the marlin.

One of the special tricks used by Santiago is that of talking to himself and the fish and sometimes of saying prayers. The talk and the prayers become a kind of incantatory language magic, a magic by which he induces the desired to happen by saying it. His refrain-like wishes for the strength of DiMaggio and the presence of Manolin, his talking to his hand to make it strong, and his saying of "Our Fathers" and "Hail Marys" are all part of the incantatory process. It was a phenomenon that Hemingway had witnessed among his own Cuban boatmen. Carlos' chant after a large marlin was hooked and was being played into the boat was an anticipatory model for Santiago's chants: "Oh God the bread of my children! Joseph and Mary look at the bread of my children jump! There it goes the bread of my children! He'll never stop the bread the bread the bread of my children!"[157] If Santiago's talk magic is more coherent and serene than Carlos', it is a matter of degree, not kind, that distinguishes them.

Two climactic insights in the novel had their prior statement and elucidation in *Green Hills of Africa*, significantly another, if nonfictional, account of quest and frustration. Both were in effect statements of the illumination common to Hemingway protagonists who win morally while losing physically. At the end of Santiago's adventure all that is physically left of his great victory is "the long backbone of the great fish that was now just garbage waiting to go out with the tide." In the African book Hemingway supplied the philosophical context for the image when he observed that all physical triumphs are finally nullified in the sweep of time and natural decay. It was, however, his metaphor for that dissolution that most pertained to the image in the novel. The monuments of today become the debris of tomorrow and disappear into the Gulf current, he said, ". . . and the palm fronds of our victories, the worn light bulbs of our discoveries and the empty condoms of our great loves float with no significance against one single, lasting thing—the stream." But if such happens to the physical gains, the spiritual ones endure because they are made of the same stuff the current is—individual flux and generic identity. One knows, he said in the same long paragraph, that "things you find out about [the stream] . . . are

157. "On the Blue Water," 185.

permanent and of value because that stream will flow. . . ." Or as the white hunter tells Hemingway when Karl consistently comes back with more impressive trophy heads than those taken by Hemingway, "You can always remember how you shot them. That's what you really got out of it. . . ."[158] That is the old man's consolation too when he tells Manolin of the great fish. (pp. 125-27)

That Hemingway continued to think on the themes running through *The Old Man and the Sea* could be seen in his subsequent essays. Santiago's expressions of love for the marlin he is killing found some explication in Hemingway's 1953 introduction to François Sommer's *Man and Beast in Africa*. There he wrote that a hunter's profession of love for the animals he hunts is no hypocrisy but an acceptance of "his deep and ancient faults" along with "his good parts," and a recognition that hunting was itself an action shared by hunter and animal—or fish, he might have added.[159] Santiago's recognition that he had to go "far out" beyond ordinary limits to get his marlin furnished a metaphor for Hemingway's Nobel Prize acceptance speech two years later. Applying the metaphor to writing, he said, "How simple the writing of literature would be if it were only necessary to write in another way what has been well written. It is because we have had such great writers in the past that a writer is driven far out past where he can go, out to where no one can help him."[160]

The *Old Man and the Sea* with its supporting nonfiction exemplified the general relationship between Hemingway's fiction and nonfiction. The origin of the novel could be identified in earlier journalistic statements. It demonstrated a blend of personal insights and impersonal descriptions previously made. It reused, within an altered context, images and metaphors used earlier or anticipated statements used later in nonfictional statements. It carried over moods and ideas. It gathered authority for a convincing fictional statement from fully reported public and private experience. It demonstrated, as Hemingway said fiction and nonfiction did, the interdependence of a writer's knowledge of the actual world and his created vision, so that each

158. *Green Hills of Africa*, pp. 149-50, 293.
159. (London, 1953), p. 6.
160. Reprinted in Baker, *Hemingway: The Writer as Artist*, p. 339.

became a check on the writer's realistic relationship to the other. It showed how a creative work could draw primarily from one part of a writer's recorded experience and yet draw generally from his whole work. It showed how a created work could have internal consistency and at the same time be faithful to the writer's inner life and to the public world.

Beyond that, the relationship between the fiction and nonfiction exemplified Hemingway's statements on the way actual experience became the raw material for the imagination to transmute into a created vision. When that raw material of personal and public experience had received an initial processing for the purposes of journalism or didactic writing, it began to show its lasting elements and relationships. As these were valid for a coherent nonfictional view of the actual world, they revealed their potentialities for significant use in an imaginative view of experience. In his nonfiction Hemingway found a useful intermediate step in the processing of experience into art. To paraphrase Thoreau on poetry, Hemingway made his fiction imply the whole truth, his nonfiction express a part of it.

PART FIVE / *Uses of the Essay*

XI. Hemingway's Art of the Essay

HENRY THOREAU SPOKE OF SENTENCES "UTTERED WITH YOUR BACK
to the wall." Hemingway should have read more of Thoreau
than he apparently did, for he would have liked the conceit. It
described the way he wrote at times in his essays and other nonfiction. Not always though. For like Juan Belmonte, whom he
described in *The Sun Also Rises*, he could bring himself to do
only sometimes what he would have liked to do always. Perhaps
because he shrugged off much of his nonfiction as a second-best
effort he did not concentrate and revise and polish as thoroughly
as he did for his fiction. That he did not do so was quite probably a loss to discursive prose style in English during the twentieth
century. That he wrote as much nonfiction as he did, though,
increased the percentages of his writing some hard, clear, and
unforgettable passages, and these are part of what we have for
our time. Both for themselves and for their relevance to his
more widely recognized fiction, his better nonfictional achieve-

ments have a value that should be determined and recognized.

True to the best tradition of the informal essay, Hemingway practiced the art of self-exploration and self-revelation. If we say that his developing art of the essay was closely linked to his growing recognition of how much he could put himself into his public utterances, we at the same time recognize how much he was a part of the whole movement to develop the essay during the nineteenth and twentieth centuries. If his own experience was a control on one end of the communications link, his readers' experience was a control on the other. And since in his nonfiction he aimed at a ready and immediate public, not one that would come to understand his efforts as in the fiction, he wrote with a sound and sometimes cynical knowledge of the predilections of newspaper and magazine readers who were his major public. He spoke more than once of writing journalism that could evoke predictable responses from readers. When he wrote a nonfiction book—*Death in the Afternoon, Green Hills of Africa,* or *A Moveable Feast*—he wrote in the wake of a fictional success and could expect his readers to accept the books as the other voice of a major fiction writer. As it turned out, the nonfiction books, aside from their ostensible subjects, were discussions on the art of writing, hints of attitude and method that had helped the fiction writer to gain his triumphs. If readers of the bullfight and African books got discussion when they had anticipated fiction, they nevertheless knew they were hearing from the young novelist who had proved he could write a second major novel that was as good as the first. And readers of his Paris memoir undoubtedly read it with the knowledge that they read a Nobel Prize novelist who had proved his talent for endings.

Hemingway's nonfiction can be seen for what it was against the background of journalism within the memory of his readers. One of the traditions he followed was that of the native American humorists, particularly of Mark Twain. His exaggerations in the Toronto *Star* articles and his Westerner-in-Europe pose in the early journalism were reminiscent of *Innocents Abroad* and of the later Twain imitators that flourished up to the First World War. Beefsteak in Constantinople, he reported, was rare and likely to be "the last appearance of one of the black, muddy, sad-eyed buffalo with the turned back horns . . . or the last charge of Kemal's cavalry. My jaw muscles are beginning to bulge like a bull-dog's from chewing, or chawing, Turkish meat." The marc drunk by hunters on the Cote D'Or, he reported in an article on hunting in Europe, was so powerful that "three drops of it on the tongue of a canary will send him out in a grim, deadly, silent search for eagles." And to repel rug vendors in Paris it was necessary to say "with a dirty look, that you hate all rugs and have just come out of jail after having served twenty years for killing rug sellers on the slopes of Montmartre. . . ." After one had nevertheless been conned into buying a "tiger skin" rug he knew was goat, one put the skin across the back of a chair and watched the rug "commence . . . his life-long job of getting hair on your clothing."[1] Although his articles on the low price of war medals in Toronto pawn shops and on the ease with which small time war profiteers could reingratiate themselves into post-war society mercifully lacked the comic spelling of Mister Dooley, they had much of the sardonic bite of that school of journalism. He showed he knew how to find the satiric edge to popular clichés when he wrote: "During the late friction with Germany a certain number of Torontonians of military age showed their desire to assist in the conduct of the war by emigrating to the States to give their all to laboring in munitions plants. . . . Through a desire to aid these morally courageous souls who sup-plied the sinews of war we have prepared a few hints. . . ." That was the beginning of "How to Be Popular in Peace Though a Slacker in War."[2] Such early essays as "Taking a Sporting Chance for a Free Shave" and "Keeping up with the Joneses" had Lard-nerian overtones in both their humor and their social criticism.

A more immediate tradition for reference was that of Richard Harding Davis and Stephen Crane, war correspondents and chroniclers of their own exploits. If Davis and Crane covered their Greco-Turkish war at Valestino and saw their refugee col-umns, Hemingway reported the human results of the Mudania Conference and saw a new Balkan struggle. Whereas Crane and Davis had described the Rough Riders' charge up San Juan Hill, Hemingway described for a larger audience what he thought was a more crucial assault, the taking of Teruel and the Mansueto

1. "'Old Constan' in True Light; Is Tough Town," *TDS*, October 28, 1922, p. 17; "More Game to Shoot in Crowded Europe Than in Ontario," *TSW*, Novem-ber 3, 1923, p. 20; "Rug Vendor Is Fixture in Parisian Life," *TDS*, August 12, 1922, p. 5.
2. *TSW*, March 13, 1920, p. 11.

fortress during the Spanish Civil War. And like Davis' brilliant life in London society between wars, Hemingway had his Stork Club period. Like Crane, he reported wars for the papers but considered writing fiction his true work. Like Davis, he was gratified by the world's applause of his journalism and the increasingly personal role it allowed him in his public writing.

If he wrote no book examining in detail the rise of Fascism in Italy as William Bolitho did in *Italy Under Mussolini*, his articles on Mussolini and the young Fascisti in the *Toronto Star Weekly* and the *Daily Star* had more than casual parallels with Bolitho's articles in the *New York World*. Hemingway's *Esquire* and *Ken* articles later, especially "The Malady of Power," acknowledged their indebtedness of insight to the South African's work and tutelage. Bolitho's flair for making his personal manner a part of the writing was congenial to Hemingway's predilections, though the younger writer had already found some of the possibilities of the method before he met Bolitho.

His bullfight book had to be seen against the background of travel books on the soul of Spain, particularly Waldo Frank's *Virgin Spain*. But it was also a corrective for the Baedeker view of that country. Not a land of picturesque cathedrals or museums devoted to costumery and Velasquez, it was Goya's Spain of men trying to make themselves brave in plain settings of sand and wall. Not a country possessed by a Freudian death wish, it was a land of olive groves, wine skins, and black-smocked peasants who admired dignity in the presence of danger. His African book was written in the manner of Baroness von Blixen's *Out of Africa*, Sir Samuel Baker's book on the Nile tributaries, and Hans Meyers' book on climbing Mount Kilimanjaro, not the Martin and Osa Johnson sagas.

The memoir of Paris was in the manner of and an answer to Gertrude Stein's version of Paris in the twenties. It also joined the swarm of other less recriminatory accounts such as Janet Flanner's *An American in Paris*, Samuel Putnam's *Paris Was Our Mistress*, and Malcolm Cowley's *Exile's Return*. If those memoirs suggested a group spirit that encouraged young writers from provincial America, a heyday of the youthfully courageous who were not afraid to put art above business, his was the more introspective and retrospective account of the older, well-honored man who could still marvel at his youthful innocence and talent. If it too had the bite of unflattering portraits, it was not so much a matter of evening accounts with old enemies as of an older man's insistence on the rightness of his earlier judgments. He knew his place in the history of the times and saw no reason to sacrifice perception to tact. He wanted on record his version of the world that helped make him a writer, and the distracters as well as the encouragers had to be accounted for.

In a less immediate way he wrote in the tradition of those New England essayists and journal keepers who thought their personal responses to the world worth recording. If in *Green Hills of Africa* he stated his high opinion of the writer who refused to join movements and faced his own lonely individuality, he might well have recognized his spiritual kinship with Henry Thoreau. He had not been able to read Thoreau, he said, "because I cannot read other naturalists unless they are being extremely accurate and not literary." He must have been put off by Thoreau's idealism more than by his observation, for they both were admirers of technique and of simplification of society's demands on the person. Hemingway said in *Death in the Afternoon* that he went to the bull arenas to begin with the simple things to learn how to feel and how to write. His remark could have been a later version of Thoreau's reasons for going to Walden. But closer perhaps to the hearts of both was their belief in a prose that could rival or surpass poetry, meaning verse, in its intensity and vision. Where Thoreau could remark that he had a notebook for facts and another for poetry but found the distinction increasingly difficult to preserve, Hemingway could write of trying to achieve extra dimensions in his prose and of attempting prose "more difficult than poetry . . . a prose that has never been written." Thoreau said, "I see that if my facts were sufficiently vital and significant—perhaps transmuted into the substance of the human mind—I should need but one book of poetry to contain them all."[3] That was almost a preliminary summary of Hemingway's program of writing. *Walden* and Thoreau's *Journals* and Hemingway's *Death in the Afternoon* and *Green Hills of Africa* shared a tradition more profoundly than surface details might initially suggest.

3. Bradford Torrey and Francis H. Allen, eds., *The Journal of Henry D. Thoreau* (Boston, 1949), III, 311.

Hemingway began his career of writing nonfiction for pay with his few months spent in the newsroom and on the beats of the *Kansas City Star.* There, he said later, they taught him to write a simple declarative sentence. There also, notes Charles Fenton, he began to learn the technique of reporting through narration.[4] But because he was under strict supervision appropriate for a cub reporter, he was writing according to the formula for a news report. Not until he worked for the more permissive Toronto *Star* did he begin to write articles showing the structures he found natural to his presentation of public and private matters. That his work was feature-writing rather than straight reporting gave him the needed flexibility to develop a characteristic approach. From his early articles on the Toronto scene to his late accounts of hunts in Africa and bullfights in Spain, his journalistic work and his expository writing in general showed a growing conception of what a nonfictional work could be. And basic to it all was his increasing awareness of the value of the personal response, the exploitation of his own view of the world as one to which the public would respond.

His first articles for the *Toronto Star Weekly* had a personal but not individual touch. As reporter he was very much in some of the accounts, but the reporter could have been any aggressively humorous young man. "Taking a Chance for a Free Shave" was typical of the early articles. It began with a provocative lead that reeked of post-adolescent brashness. "The land of the free and the home of the brave is the modest phrase used by certain citizens of the republic to the south of us to designate the country they live in. They may be brave—but there is nothing free. Free lunch passed some time ago and on attempting to join the Free Masons you are informed that it will cost you seventy-five dollars. . . . The true home of the free and the brave is the barber college." This was followed by a dramatized account of his passing through the low-cost salons of the soon-to-graduate barbers and on to the free chairs of the beginners. In the chair he endured the taunts of the beginner's fellows and the uncertainty of an irresponsible razor at his throat. Following the dramatized portion of the article was a miscellaneous survey of other free or low-cost services available in Toronto—at the dental college, the public clinic at Grace Hospital, the Fred Victor Mission. It

4. *The Apprenticeship of Ernest Hemingway* (New York, 1954), p. 44.

ended on an even more adolescent note, with the observation that free room and board were available at the jail for those who took the trouble to hit a policeman.[5] The provocative lead—a startling statement or a challenging question—was a tactic he practiced often at the beginning. "What is the market price of valor?" he asked at the beginning of his 1923 article on the unsalability of war medals, and concluded that "the market price of valor remained undetermined" after his dramatized survey of pawn shops and second-hand stores. Sometimes he began with a dramatic situation and followed it with explanations. "Gun Men's Wild Political War on in Chicago" opened with a description of Anthony d'Andrea's murder as he approached his apartment door from the street. Also, within the ensuing paragraphs were sentences predictive of Hemingway's future tough-guy writing: "For months D'Andrea [*sic*] had been entering his home, gun in hand, in the expectation of such a death. He knew he was doomed—but he wanted to protest the verdict."[6]

By the time he wrote his series on French politics and the occupation of the Ruhr in early 1923 he was beginning his articles with a surer sense of his right to be heard and with less brashness dependent on formulaic and falsely personal openings. The tone was flatter and quieter, but the details had sharpness and functioned to suggest personality. "Raymond Poincaré is a changed man," he wrote at the beginning of "French Royalist Party Most Solidly Organized." "Until a few months ago the little white-bearded Lorraine lawyer in his patent leather shoes and his gray gloves dominated the French chamber of deputies with his methodical accountant's mind and his spitfire temper. Now he sits quietly and forlornly while fat, white-faced Léon Daudet shakes his finger at him and says, 'France will do this. France will do that.' " An orderly exposition of personalities and issues involved followed and ended with a one-sentence paragraph that summed the French dilemma. "Meanwhile the French government has spent 160 million francs (official) on the occupation and Ruhr coal is costing France $200 a ton."[7] His account of the effect of the occupation on a German town began as quietly and succinctly as a practiced travel writer could make it.

5. *TSW*, March 6, 1920, p. 13. The pattern has been noted by Fenton, p. 106.
6. *TSW*, May 28, 1921, p. 21.
7. *TDS*, April 18, 1923, pp. 1-2.

"Offenburg is the southern limit of the French occupation of Germany. It is a clean, neat little town with the hills of the Black Forest rising on one side and the Rhine plain stretching off on the other." What followed though was an account of quiet resistance to the French by townspeople caught between quarreling governments. The tactic here was again mostly exposition with one dramatized informal interview of a German motor truck driver included. The article ended with the truck driver's laugh at himself and his townsmen for believing that even revolutions could help them.[8]

What Hemingway found out about the essay style while he wrote for the Toronto *Star* was that he could make the writing more personal by what he saw and recorded than by forcing his funny-man persona on the material and twisting it for chuckles. He had taken other masters than Ring Lardner. There were, to be sure, vestiges of unpurged cuteness. When his wife figured in the articles, she was usually referred to as "Herself." But when he felt engaged by the subject, he could write such thoroughly personal yet instructive essays as "Bull Fighting Is Not a Sport— It is a Tragedy" and include sentences filled with contained pleasure such as this: "It was very exciting sitting out in front of a café your first day in Spain with a ticket in your pocket that meant that rain or shine you were going to see a bullfight in an hour and a half."[9]

In his articles for the little magazines in Paris and for the New York magazines during the late twenties, Hemingway made no significant advances in style. Such pieces as "The Real Spaniard" in the *Boulevardier* (Paris) and "My Own Life" in the *New Yorker* were apparently written as jokes for literary insiders. The first was a close and not very witty parody of Louis Bromfield's serious piece in search of "The Real French," and the second had a giveaway subtitle, "After Reading the Second Volume of Frank Harris' 'My Life.' " It ended with more parody, a closing promise to tell "How I Broke with Dos Passos, Coolidge, Disraeli, Lincoln, and Shakespeare." His *Fortune* article "Bullfighting, Sport and Industry" contained some of the unsavory details about bullfight management he would later put into *Death in the After-*

8. "Ruhr Commercial War Question of Bankruptcy," *TDS*, April 25, 1923, pp. 1-2.
9. *TSW*, October 20, 1923, p. 33.

noon, but the treatment of the subject was almost completely according to the formula for articles done by staff writers. The slant was toward an entrepreneur's view of bullfighting. The article described problems of bullfight managers and was well supplied with dollars-and-cents figures and names of marketable bullfighters. It was a businessman's view of the industry, and though he called bullfighting a sport and tragedy as well as a business, those aspects received no real consideration. His celebration of matadors as artists and men of courage had to wait for *Death in the Afternoon.*

By the time he began writing his articles for *Esquire,* however, he had decided that the informal essays Arnold Gingrich wanted could best be written as a correspondent's letters to his home journal. They were not polished essays with evident thinking out and ordering of effects decided on before the writing began. Rather they showed the man in the process of reporting his sensations and experiences much as they happened. "Remembering Shooting-Flying: A Key West Letter," for example, began with a look out the window: "There is a heavy norther blowing: the Gulf is too rough to fish and there is no shooting now. . . . But when you cannot shoot you can remember shooting and I would rather stay home, now, this afternoon and write about it than go out and sail clay saucers in the wind, trying to break them and wishing they were what they're not." Or "The President Vanquishes: A Bimini Letter" begins with an "as-I-take-this-pen-in-hand" mood: "You write this at three o'clock in the morning lying at anchor outside of Bimini harbor. There is nearly a full moon and you dropped out of the harbor to avoid the sand-flies."[10]

Such an approach influenced the structure of the letter-articles as well. Some achieved coherent development of a central theme, but others could only be described as a succession of moods with little unifying force except that furnished by the author's personality. "Shootism versus Sport" presented a coherent view of the hunter's code, and "On the Blue Water" was a unified argument for deep sea fishing as opposed to more sensational forms of hunting. But essays like "A Paris Letter," "Defense of Dirty Words," "The Sights of Whitehead Street," "a.d. Southern Style," and "On Being Shot Again," to mention a few, resembled per-

10. *Esquire,* III (February 1935), 21; III (July 1935), 23.

sonal letters, each with its grab bag of themes and topics. "Defense of Dirty Words" began with a citation of Westbrook Pegler's recent column on the lamentable use of profane and obscene words in postwar writing and cited Pegler's applause of Ring Lardner, who, said the columnist, dealt with earthy people but used clean language. Hemingway's rebuttal of Pegler's thesis followed as he argued that Lardner had accepted limitations harmful to his work. Besides, Lardner, feeling superior to his people, had never really gotten inside them and had not seen the need to use their real language. Hemingway then shifted to a contrast between Maupassant's achievements in earthy language and story and the achievements of critically acceptable Lardner and O. Henry. Following the contrast was a report on summer fishing, and following that a qualified tribute to Lardner in spite of his language.

Articles like "Notes on Dangerous Game" and "He Who Gets Slap-Happy" were illustrative of another kind of division in his personal essays. Each presented a sustained development of a topic but was interspersed with asides to readers and critics who had written to the magazine or to Hemingway complaining of his slack writing. The answers to the implied criticism indicated a fundamental difference between Hemingway and many of his readers on what his nonfiction should be. If one can judge from Hemingway's answers, his critics, both professional and amateur, expected him to write highly polished, felicitously phrased, conventionally organized essays typical of the formula articles in the big-pay magazines. Some apparently wanted the tense prose with an implicitly suffering narrator he had given them in his fiction. Some who thought of him still as the Paris expatriate wanted accounts of the avant-garde literary world. Others with Marxist persuasions wanted social relevance and attention to the problems of unemployment and class conflict. Others, following the lead of *Esquire*'s celebration of the male cult, wanted more swashbuckling and discussion or demonstration of the sexual freedom he had seemed to favor in his fiction. Hemingway's conception of his task, however, was something more personal and less formulaic. He proposed to write intimate essays that developed, and showed their development, as they were written. The language was to be that of an authoritative man talking casually, not writing and revising. If there was something of the male cultist in his attitude, it was that of Hemingway the man, not the elements of a supposed general complex of maleness. And his social relevance and commentary were what he experienced and thought, not what the literary fashion makers were calling for. His comments to readers in "Notes on Dangerous Game" indicated his recognition of the difference and his insistence on writing his way: " (*There are too many supers in these last two sentences. Re-write them yourselves and see how easy it is to do better than Papa. Thank you. Exhilarating feeling, isn't it?*). . . . *(All right now, better that one. Getting harder, what?* . . .) . . . . *(You see, this is where Papa scores. Just as you learn to better one of these awful sentences . . . you find it is the thing he is writing about that is interesting, not the way it's written. Any of you lads can go out there and write twice as good a piece, what?*)" At another point he answered those who "wrote letters to the magazine about how lousy letters such as this one are." His answer essentially was that he was of a different breed. He had made, he said, "an extensive study of the four letter man at home and abroad; what he will wear and what he will say on different occasions including social, domestic, sporting, and dramatic and there is no pleasure like seeing a perfect specimen in print. Let the boys write."[11]

What Hemingway was doing in his letter-articles for *Esquire*, and what his publishing-center-oriented critics failed to recognize, was that he, like the journal and diary keepers of America's earlier generations in the hinterlands, was both living and recording his life and taking his poetry where he found it, or making it when the vision allowed. Though they imagined themselves at the center of things and him in the hinterlands, he found his moments of poetry and truth and wrote them, even if they were not recognized and certified as belles-lettres by critics. The writing, like the living, went on during the wretched moments as well as the brilliant. And he was self-confident enough to believe that even his prosaic moments had something in them to mirror, if not instruct, some of his readers. No one can pretend that his twenty-seven letters and articles in *Esquire* are unalloyed felicity, but if he had his moments of ill-humor with readers and critics and his other moments of banality and others of unsuccessful wit, he still had moments that were worth reading for. In the

11. *Esquire*, III (August 1935), 19.

midst of the surliest essays could come paragraphs of passionately alive description. Arguing for the subtler thrills of fishing over more sensational ones of big game hunting, he wrote of the breath-holding joy of seeing a marlin play the line: "Then the heavy rod arc-ing out toward the fish, and the reel in a band-saw zinging scream, the marlin leaps clear and long, silver in the sun long, round as a hogshead and banded with lavender stripes and, when he goes into the water, it throws a column of spray like a shell lighting." Or in an essay on the horrors of an Ethiopian war he could break into a celebration of ordinary men who get caught in those horrors: "Certainly no knowledge of the last war will help boys from the little steep-hilled towns of the Abruzzi where the snow comes early on the tops of the mountains, nor those who worked in garages, or machine shops in Milano or Bologna or Firenze or rode their bicycles in road races on the white dust-powdered roads of Lombardy, nor those who played football on their factory teams in Spezia or Torino, nor mowed the high mountain meadows of the Dolomites and guided skiers in the winter, or would have been burning charcoal in the woods above Piombino, or maybe sweeping out a trattoria in Vicenza, or would have gone to North or South America in the old days."[12] If they contained no symbolic insights, the passages, more in the mood of the present century, found significance for actions in their natural and social settings—their existential settings—rather than in contexts of ideas.

If by the phrase "[sentences] uttered with your back to the wall" Thoreau meant writing as if one's life depended on the truth of his statement, Hemingway occasionally achieved such seriousness in his *Esquire* pieces. Some of his hunting and shooting admonitions evidently had the authority of personal proof in them. His instructions on where to aim for the shot that could stop the charging buffalo had both his own emotional backing and some corroborating photographic evidence to vouch for their reality. If his readers expected to shoot no buffalo, they could learn from hunting, something about shooting men, he suggested in his commentaries on the coming war in Europe. His statement on the realities behind the word "revolution" had something of

12. "On the Blue Water," *Esquire*, V (April 1936), 185; "Wings Always over Africa," *Esquire*, V (January 1936), 175.

that "back-to-the-wall" urgency. It also happened to be a vivid piece of writing:

Now this may possibly be a good time to suggest that a small tax be levied on the use of the word revolution, the proceeds to be given to the defence of, say, such people as Luis Quintanilla, or any of your friends who are in jail, by all those who write the words and never have shot nor been shot at; who never have stored arms nor filled a bomb, nor have discovered arms nor had a bomb burst among them; who never have gone hungry in a general strike; nor have manned streetcars when the tracks are dynamited; who have never sought cover in a street trying to get their heads behind a gutter; who never have seen a woman shot in the head, in the breast or in the buttocks; who never have seen an old man with the top of his head off; who never have walked with their hands up; who never have shot a horse or seen hooves smash a head; who never have sat a horse and been shot at or stoned; who never have been cracked on the head with a club nor have thrown a brick; who never have seen a scab's forearms broken with a crow-bar; or an agitator filled up with compressed air with an air hose; who, now it gets more serious— that is, the penalty is more severe—have never moved a load of arms at night in a big city; nor standing, seeing it moved, know what it was and afraid to denounce it because they did not want to die later; nor . . . stood on a roof trying to urinate on their hands to wash off the black in the fork between finger and thumb from the back-spit of a Thompson gun, the gun thrown in a cistern and the troops coming up the stairs; the hands are what they judge you by—the hands are all the evidence they need although they won't acquit you on them being clean if they are sure of the roof; nor even came up with the troops.[13]

In quite another vein, but no less seriously, he told of his longing to see Africa again and reported the interest among Negro soldiers at Cabaña fortress, Havana, in his African experiences, and after they had asked their questions, he realized the truth of archetypal memory: "Many people are homesick for Africa without knowing it."[14]

In his *Ken* articles Hemingway shifted his idea of what his journalistic essays should be. He wrote them soon after his return from Europe where the Republican situation in Spain was deteriorating rapidly and the probability of new Fascist moves

13. "Facing a Bitter World," *Esquire*, III (February 1935), 26-27.
14. "Sailfish off Mombasa," *Esquire*, III (March 1935), 156.

was great. In *Ken* he was not so much reporter or miscellaneous columnist as editorial writer. His structure and diction became formal in keeping with that role. In almost every article an action or response was called for, and the essay was organized to lead to that call. Whether it was the call to send arms to Republicans while there was still time or to purge the State Department of Fascist sympathizers, the mood was imperative. In only one or two articles was there dramatization of a point. Rhetorical questions, statistics, sensational statements of fact, and vivid imagery were the techniques used. The punch line of "Call for Greatness" was typical of the mood and public voice of Hemingway's editorials and of the *Ken* program in general: "There is no reason, either, why our president, unless he is afraid of offending voters whose vote is controlled by foreign agencies, should not oppose fascism and support publicly those things that he admits to believe in privately. He can refuse to allow our neutrality legislation to become a tool for Chamberlain's, and Mussolini's, and Hitler's foreign policy. And the first step in this is never to believe the fascist lie which always goes, 'Don't do anything. It is useless. It's too late.' "[15]

When he reported the Spanish Civil War for the North American Newspaper Alliance and the Allied invasion of Europe for *Collier's*, he returned to his dramatic style. War was primarily a matter of sensation, not policy, for him, and his articles took the form and language suitable for reporting scene and incident. His own narrative of events or that furnished by one of his soldier subjects commonly furnished the structure for the articles. In the Spanish war dispatches the form of the essay was frequently that dictated by the events of a particular day. Standard elements included an account of getting to the scene of action, description of the day's action, and an interpretation of the day's action in light of larger movements of armies in campaign. Because the subject was movement and action, it yielded well to Hemingway's spare but vivid descriptions. Often the actions were described in the context of some historical or metaphorical parallel. "The battle was spread out at our feet," wrote Hemingway in a typical passage. "The government artillery with a noise which sounded like many freight trains was registering shell after shell of direct hits on an insurgent strong point, a church with castle-

15. *Ken*, I (July 14, 1938), 23.

like towers of yellow stone. The dust was roaring up in steadily
rising clouds." Or another: "Below was the great yellow battle-
ship-shaped natural fortification of Mansueto, the city's main protection which the government forces had slipped past to the north,
leaving it helpless as a stranded dreadnought."[16] In his *Collier's*
stories Hemingway similarly followed the events of the Normandy
landing and the approach to Paris in narrative summary and dramatized passages. In his account of the breaching of the Siegfried
Line he described the approaches to the Westwall area and told
in the words of his informant, Captain Blazzard, the details of
the advance through the enfiladed forests and of the envelopment
of German bunkers. Blazzard's laconic account, as rendered by
Hemingway, contrasted with the furious battle described and was,
on Hemingway's part, a tactic as effective as those that broke open
the bunkers.

The *Collier's* series was uneven, however, and Hemingway's
intrusive personality accounted, in part at least, for the highs and
lows. In "London Fights the Robots" he was hobbled by security
measures in his attempts to tell either about German rocket performances or those of the British interceptors. In place of facts
he attempted to substitute manner and the result was an unhappy failure to convey the interceptor pilots' lyric feeling for
their planes and a false jocularity when Hemingway rode American bombers over the rocket-launching sites: "These sites," he
reported, "can be readily identified by the merest tyro by the
quantity of old Mitchell bombers which are strewn around them
and by the fact that, when you get close to them large, black
circular rings of smoke appear alongside the vehicle you are riding in. These circular black rings of smoke are called flak, and
this flak is the author of that old piece of understatement about
two of our aircraft failed to return." But if he revealed his failure to understand the feeling of air war, he was in a familiar
situation when he reported on the land war of infantry and tanks
in France. His evocation of the infantryman's war as one of dis-
connected episodes, accidents of terrain, and forgotten maneuvers
was as true in feeling and detail as such a statement could be:

No one remembered separate days any more, and history, being
made each day, was never noticed but only merged into a great blur
of tiredness and dust, of the smell of dead cattle, the smell of earth

16. *Fact*, no. 16 (July 15, 1938), 23.

new-broken by TNT, the grinding sound of tanks and bulldozers, the sound of automatic rifle and machine-gun fire, the interceptive dry tattle of German machine-pistol fire, dry as a rattler rattling: the quick, spurting tap of the German light machine guns—and always waiting for others to come up.

It was merged in the memory of the fight up out of the deadly hedgerow country out to the heights and through the forest and on down into the plain, by and through the towns, some smashed, and some intact, and on up into the rolling farm and forest country where we were now.

History now was old K-ration boxes, empty fox-holes, the drying leaves on the branches that were cut for camouflage. It was burned German vehicles, burned German tanks, many burned German Panthers and some burned Tigers, German dead along the roads, in the hedges and in the orchards, German equipment scattered everywhere, German horses roaming the fields, and our own wounded and our dead passing back strapped two abreast on top of the evacuation jeeps. But mostly history was getting where we were to get on time and waiting there for others to come up.[17]

Such passages were the payoff when Hemingway's author-permeated style worked at its best. Although he injected no directly personal statement in the paragraphs, the details, the mood, the sentences were patently Hemingway of the middle-period style.

After the war his journalistic essays were more obviously focused on the writer than on the events described. "The Great Blue River" concerned Hemingway's reasons for living in Cuba and fishing the Gulf Stream, not the great ocean river itself. "Safari" and "The Christmas Gift" were important because they told about Hemingway's return to East Africa and his two air crashes, not because they were about a part of the world where some of the bloodiest anti-colonialist fighting was going on. And in "The Dangerous Summer" the Ordonez-Dominguin rivalry was the ostensible subject. The real subject was the return of the century's most celebrated Hispanophile to Spain and to the kind of life he had made famous a quarter century before. The suspense was not whether Ordonez or Dominguin would survive the rivalry but whether Hemingway could bring off his celebration of Spain and bullfighting as well as before and how he would judge the new generation of matadors and *fiesta*-goers.

17. "London Fights the Robots," *Collier's*, CXIV (August 19, 1944), 80; "The G.I. and the General," *Collier's*, CXIV (November 4, 1944), 11.

The structural consequences were an exaggerated return to the shifting mood pieces reminiscent of the *Esquire* letters of the thirties, but these pieces were occasionally-contracted magazine articles, not letters from a retained correspondent. In "The Shot" he began with a Damon Runyan-style account of a Cuban Negro on the run from political assassins, then shifted to an account of hunting antelope in Idaho with a transition like this: "So with a background of this sort of shooty-shooty, I'm going to write 2,000 words about an antelope hunt where you kill one antelope that can't shoot back."[18] In "The Christmas Gift" he told a straightforward story of events up to the point of his auto ride from Masindi to Entebbe after the second air crash. But the account broke apart at that point while he spent pages describing his inner sensations and incoherent musings on Senator McCarthy, Leonard Lyons, Toots Shor, Joe Russell, George Brown, Sherman Billingsley, Bill Corum, Ben Finney, Earl Wilson, Walter Winchell, and Damon Runyon. More mock-Freudian musings occurred later in the account as he satirized the press speculations on his supposed life-long quest for death. "The Dangerous Summer" built up to the climatic fight at Bilbao in an ominously suspenseful progression of events and choric interpretations. But the dramatic effect was diffused by frequent pauses for Hemingway to mark parallels between his present visit to Spain and his earlier visits. Such procedure was of course suitable for an account of return to familiar ground, but if the subject was coverage of an important *mano a mano*, the secondary purpose tended to challenge the primary subject in emphasis.

Hemingway used the choric commentary to achieve a sense of coming and inevitable catastrophe in the matadors' rivalry, an effect suitable for a nonfiction account because of his role as reporter and narrator. It is doubtful that he could have made the technique work in his non-discursive fiction. It presumed an intrusive and omniscient author alien to his fictional practice. But in the journalistic account the choric passage had the right proportions of impersonal prescience and personal involvement to be one of the more effective innovations in his later writing. As the two matadors approached the feria at Bilbao, for example, Hemingway wrote:

18. "The Shot," *True*, XXVIII (April 1951), 26.

He [Ordonez] was at the top of a form that had been great all year and he was living in complete confidence in his ability and his immortality. He wanted to go to Bilbao now, the most difficult public in Spain, where the bulls are the biggest and the public the most severe and exigent so that no one could ever say that there was ever anything doubtful or shady or dubious about this campaign of 1959. If Luis Miguel wanted to go too that was fine. But it would be a dangerous trip. If Luis Miguel had been managed by his father, who was wise and cynical and knew the odds, instead of by his two nice brothers, who got ten per cent from him and from Antonio each time they fought, he would never have gone to Bilbao to be destroyed.[19]

In his magazine essays of the fifties Hemingway showed himself wrestling with most of the problems of a writer working in a medium he considered second best but writing, at the same time, for a large audience before whom he had to justify his reputation as a leading author. If, as he wrote in "A Situation Report," he considered himself a fool to take time away from the novels in progress, he at the same time had to save some of his best concentration for the magazine articles that kept him alive in the mind of his public. The result was a run of facilely impressive journalism with occasional moments of clarity and naked strength of line. His account of the crash at Murchison Falls was an example of action smothered in words: "As we broke away from the falls, we encountered a flight of large birds which I identified as black and white ibis. We had seen this same flock on our way up the river. A bird of this type can easily go through the Plexiglass and could eliminate the pilot of an aircraft of this type or the co-pilot. Since the co-pilot's seat was occupied by Miss Mary, Roy Marsh dove sharply under these birds which we observed passing overhead and I had the chance to admire their black and white markings and their down-swept black bills."[20] And in his characterization of Luis Miguel Dominguin he abandoned vividness to give a lusterless account of a colorful person and family. He substituted telling for showing. "He [Dominguin] had a mocking humor and was very cynical and I learned much from him about many things when we had the good luck to have him stay with us at the finca in Cuba for a while. He is

19. *Life*, XLIX (September 19, 1960), 84.
20. "The Christmas Gift," *Look*, XVIII (April 20, 1954), 31-32.

very intelligent, completely articulate, talented in many ways that have nothing to do with bullfighting and he comes from a family of the most intelligent people I have ever been fortunate enough to know."[21]

But he could still find moments of clarity. In a sentence he could still make a scene, as when Antonio Ordoñez prepared at Bilbao to kill a bull in the dangerously difficult *recibiendo* style: "He squared the bull up and the plaza was so quiet I could hear the click behind me as a woman's fan closed." And when in the same series he described the actions of his dangerously incompetent chauffer on the hill roads of central Spain, he achieved a blending of image and emotion as he noted landscape details in relation to the movement of the careening car: "He was wrong on every turn . . . and he chilled me and spooked me hollow both climbing and descending. I tried to watch the valleys and small stone towns and farms spread out below us as we climbed and looked back at the broken ranges running to the sea. I looked at the naked dark trunks of the cork trees where the bark had been cut and stripped a month before and I looked down into the deep crevasses on a town and at the fields of gorse with limestone jutting out that rolled away to the high stone peaks and took the stupid driving as it came. . . ."[22] At such moments he accomplished his real purposes in writing for the mass-circulation magazines. By showing millions how to feel the immediate moment and make it theirs, he did in nonfiction what they remembered he did in his stories. But without a fictional mask he took them more directly into partnership in the moment.

The books *Death in the Afternoon, Green Hills of Africa,* and *A Moveable Feast* expanded the tendencies Hemingway practiced in his last two periods of nonfiction writing. They were more careful in general structure than were the articles but contained digressions similar to the shifting mood principle of organization in the shorter pieces. The bullfight book was arranged analytically, with chapters on the *corrida* as an entire act, others on the different skills associated with the thirds of the bullfight, and later others evaluating the performers. But the dialogues with the Old Lady and the intrusive essay on "A Natural History of the Dead" were examples of the associative rather

21. *Life*, XLIX (September 5, 1960), 88.
22. *Life*, XLIX (September 19, 1960), 95; (September 5, 1960), 92.

than logical scheme of organization. The African book used many of the techniques of fiction, even though the action was certified as factual. The middle part, with its account of the previous month's hunt, was written according to the same narrative pattern of recall Hemingway used in "The Short Happy Life of Francis Macomber" and "The Snows of Kilimanjaro." But it was also similar to the organization in several of the *Esquire* letters. In "Remembering Shooting Flying," for example, the comment began with the present scene, shifted to his memories of boyhood hunting and reading, then returned to his present justification of hunting. That the article, the stories, and the book all came from approximately the same time and experience suggested a particular way of thinking for Hemingway during 1934 and 1935. The comments linking reading and hunting in both book and articles suggested further relationships between method and feeling in Hemingway's nonfiction. He was exploring both the values and techniques of reflection.

A Moveable Feast, though revised and published late, avoided most of the fuzziness of the later period. The scenes and moods were those of the earlier period, when indeed much of the phrasing as well as observation had been made. The succession of sketches, though ostensibly on randomly remembered people and events, was unified by a personal myth of innocence and despoliation that becomes clear only with the last sketch. Because the subject was well in the past, rather than a current experience, Hemingway enjoyed both the perspective of thirty years and the freedom from the press of a deadline. His careful polishing, an advantage he could not afford in the journalistic pieces, and his certitude produced a style of simple, sensuous statement that was consistently what the journalism achieved only sometimes. The preface suggested, in its ambiguity about whether the memoir should be read as fact or fiction, an answer to the question posed in the foreword of *Green Hills of Africa*: whether a factual account "can, if truly presented, compete with a work of the imagination." The answer seemed to be affirmative, if one let thirty-five years' memories compete with the imagination.

It is perhaps impossible to imagine what value would be placed on Hemingway's nonfiction if it stood independent of his novels and stories. Critics, editors, and anthologists have in recent years, however, turned to some of the journalistic essays and chapters from the expository books as examples of the best prose of the century, and this new interest seems to indicate a belated recognition of their high value, even when seen in the shadow of Hemingway's fiction. To be true to Hemingway's own intentions, we should perhaps always place the nonfiction in a secondary rank in our estimates. But as William White and others make his prolific nonfictional work more generally accessible, the significance of that work should emerge and its values should find corresponding recognition. It may then be that, though we value the fiction more, we shall accord the nonfiction a considerably higher place in American writing than it has heretofore been assigned. Moreover, in a time when nonfiction is received with increasingly greater enthusiasm, Hemingway's accounts of himself and his world—his public voice—will help establish a new dimension of American literary awareness. Generations' taste do differ and the way a generation of readers finds access to literary values is not to be prescribed. Hemingway's nonfiction should reveal that, in spite of his frequent self-depiction as a lonely man at work outside the mainstream of literary and political fashions, he was very much a public writer for his times.

Appendices / Index

A Chronological List of Hemingway's Nonfiction

(According to Date of Publication)

I AM INDEBTED TO THE CHECK LIST IN CARLOS BAKER, *Hemingway: the Writer as Artist* (Princeton, 1963), for identification of unsigned articles by Hemingway in the *Toronto Star Weekly* and the *Toronto Daily Star* (listed below as *TSW* and *TDS*). I acknowledge further indebtedness to Louis Henry Cohn, *A Bibliography of the Works of Ernest Hemingway* (New York, 1930); to Lee Samuels, *A Hemingway Check List* (New York, 1951); and to Audre Hanneman, *Ernest Hemingway: A Comprehensive Bibliography* (Princeton, 1967). Juvenilia—contributions to the Oak Park High School *Trapeze, Tabula*, and *Senior Tabula*, to the *Kansas City Star*, and to *Ciao*—are not included, as they are outside the scope of this study. Hemingway's private letters are also excluded, but those that are part of his public statement are deemed relevant. Signed contributions to the *Toronto Star Weekly* and the *Toronto Daily Star*, except for those written under the pseudonyms "John Hadley" or "Peter Jackson," were published with the by-line "Ernest M. Hemingway."

"Sporting Mayor at Boxing Bouts," *TSW*, March 13, 1920, p. 10.

"How to be Popular in Peace Though a Slacker in War," *TSW*, March 13, 1920, p. 11.

"Store Thieves Use Three Tricks," *TSW*, April 3, 1920, pp. 9, 12.

"Are You All Set for the Trout?" *TSW*, April 10, 1920, p. 11, unsigned.

"Toothpulling Not a Cure-for-All," *TSW*, April 10, 1920, p. 12.

"Lieutenants' Mustaches the Only Permanent Thing We Got Out of War," *TSW*, April 10, 1920, p. 17.

"Stores in the Wilds Graveyards of Style," *TSW*, April 24, 1920, p. 11.

"Fishing for Trout in a Sporting Way," *TSW*, April 24, 1920, p. 13.

"Keeping Up with the Joneses, the Tragedy of the Other Half," *TSW*, May 1, 1920, p. 12.

"Toronto Women Who Went to the Prize Fights Applauded the Rough Stuff," *TSW*, May 15, 1920, p. 13.

"Galloping Dominoes, alias African," *TSW*, May 22, 1920, p. 21.

"Prices of 'Likenesses' Run From 25 cents to $500 in Toronto," *TSW*, May 29, 1920, p. 13.

"Canadian Fox-ranching Pays Since the Wild-cats Let the Foxes Alone," *TSW*, May 29, 1920, p. 32.

"Canuck Whiskey Pouring into U.S.," *TSW*, June 5, 1920, p. 1.

"It's Time to Bury the Hamilton Gag, Comedians Have Worked It to Death," *TSW*, June 12, 1920, p. 1.

"When You Camp Out Do It Right," *TSW*, June 26, 1920, p. 17.

"When You Go Camping Take Lots of Skeeter Dope and Don't Ever Lose It," *TSW*, August 5, 1920, p. 11.

"The Best Rainbow Trout Fishing in the World Is at the Canadian Soo," *TSW*, August 28, 1920, p. 24.

"The Average Yank Divides Canadians into Two Classes—Wild and Tame," *TSW*, October 9, 1920, p. 13.

"Carpentier Sure to Give Dempsey Fight Worth While," *TSW*, October 30, 1920, p. 3.

"The Wild West Is Now in Chicago," *TSW*, November 6, 1920, pp. 1, 13, general and fiction section.

"No Danger of Commercial Tie-Up Because Men Carry Too Much Money," *TSW*, November 6, 1920, p. 11.

"A Fight with a 20-Pound Trout," *TSW*, November 20, 1920, pp. 25, 26.

"Plain and Fancy Killings, $400 Up," *TSW*, December 11, 1920, pp. 25, 26.

"Will You Let These Kiddies Miss Santa Claus?" *Co-operative Commonwealth*, II (December 1920), 27-28.

"Why Not Trade Other Public Entertainers Among the Nations as the Big Leagues Do Baseball Players?" *TSW*, February 19, 1921, p. 13.

"Our Confidential Vacation Guide," *TSW*, May 21, 1921, p. 21.

"Gun-Men's Wild Political War On in Chicago," *TSW*, May 28, 1921, pp. 21, 22.

"Chicago Never Wetter Than It Is To-day," *TSW*, July 2, 1921, p. 21.

"Condensing the Classics," *TSW*, August 20, 1921, p. 22.

"Cheap Nitrates Will Mean Cheaper Bread," *TSW*, November 12, 1921, p. 11.

"On Weddynge Gyftes," *TSW*, December 17, 1921, p. 15.

"Tourists Are Scarce at Swiss Resorts," *TSW*, February 4, 1922, p. 3.

"A Canadian with One Thousand a Year Can Live Very Comfortably and Enjoyably in Paris," *TSW*, February 4, 1922, p. 16.

"At Vigo, in Spain, Is Where You Catch the Silver and Blue Tuna, the King of All Fish," *TSW*, February 18, 1922, p. 15.

"Builder, Not Fighter, Is What France Wants," *TDS*, February 18, 1922, p. 7.

"Exchange Pirates Hit by German Export Tax," *TSW*, February 25, 1922, p. 10.

"Influx of Russians to All Parts of Paris," *TDS*, February 25, 1922, p. 29.

"Behind the Scenes at Papal Election," *TSW*, March 4, 1922, p. 3.

"Queer Mixture of Aristocrats, Profiteers, Sheep and Wolves at the Hotels in Switzerland," *TSW*, March 4, 1922, p. 25.

"Try Bob-Sledding If You Want Thrills," *TDS*, March 4, 1922, p. 9.

"Wives Buy Clothes for French Husbands," *TSW*, March 11, 1922, p. 12.

"How'd You Like to Tip Postman Every Time?" *TSW*, March 11, 1922, p. 13.

"Poincaré Making Good on Election Promises," *TDS*, March 11, 1922, p. 13.

"Sparrow Hat Appears on Paris Boulevards," *TSW*, March 18, 1922, p. 12.

"Flivver, Canoe, Pram and Taxi Combined Is the Luge, the Joy of Everybody in Switzerland," *TSW*, March 18, 1922, p. 15.

"Prize-Winning Book Is Center of Storm," *TSW*, March 25, 1922, p. 3.

"American Bohemians in Paris a Weird Lot," *TSW*, March 25, 1922, p. 15.

"Wild Night Music of Paris Makes Visitor Feel a Man of the World," *TSW*, March 25, 1922, p. 22.

"The Mecca of Fakers Is French Capital," *TDS*, March 25, 1922, p. 4.

"Much-Feared Man Is Monsieur Diebler," *TDS*, April 1, 1922, p. 7.

"95,000 Now Wearing the Legion of Honour," *TDS*, April 8, 1922, p. 13.

"Anti-Alcohol League Is Active in France," *TDS*, April 8, 1922, p. 13.

"World Economic Conference Opens in Genoa; Tchitcherin Speaks," *TDS*, April 10, 1922, p. 1.

"Jap Presence at Genoa Protested by Russia," *TDS*, April 11, 1922, p. 1.

"Picked Sharpshooters Patrol Genoa Streets," *TDS*, April 13, 1922, p. 17.

"French Politeness," *TSW*, April 15, 1922, p. 29.

"Regarded by Allies as German Cunning," *TDS*, April 18, 1922, p. 1.

"Barthou Refuses to Confer with Russians and Germans," *TDS*, April 18, 1922, p. 1, unsigned.

"Two Russian Girls the Best Looking at Genoa Parley," *TDS*, April 24, 1922, pp. 1, 2.

"Barthou, Like a Smith Brother, Crosses Hissing Tchitcherin," *TDS*, April 24, 1922, p. 2.

"Strongest Premier in Parley Is Stambouliski of Bulgaria," *TDS*, April 25, 1922, p. 5.

"Schober of Austria, at Genoa, Looks Every Inch a Chancellor," *TDS*, April 26, 1922, p. 9.

"Russian Delegates at Genoa Appear Not to Be of This World," *TDS*, April 27, 1922, p. 9.

"German Delegation at Genoa Keep Stinnes in Background," *TDS*, April 28, 1922, p. 9.

"Getting a Hot Bath an Adventure in Genoa," *TDS*, May 2, 1922, p. 5.

"Russian Delegation Well Guarded at Genoa," *TDS*, May 4, 1922, p. 10.

"German Journalists a Strange Collection," *TDS*, May 8, 1922, p. 3.

"All Genoa Goes Crazy over New Betting Game," *TDS*, May 9, 1922, p. 2.

"Lloyd George Gives Magic to Parley," *TDS*, May 13, 1922, p. 7.

"There Are Great Fish in the Rhone Canal," *TDS*, June 10, 1922, p. 5.

" 'Pot-Shot Patriots' Unpopular in Italy," *TSW*, June 24, 1922, p. 5.

"Fascisti Party Now Half-Million Strong," *TDS*, June 24, 1922, p. 16.

"A Veteran Visits Old Front, Wishes He Had Stayed Away," *TDS*, July 22, 1922, p. 7.

"Expecting Too Much in Old London Town," *TSW*, August 5, 1922, p. 17.

"Latest Drink Scandal Now Agitates Paris," *TSW*, August 12, 1922, p. 11.

"Did Poincaré Laugh in Verdun Cemetery?" *TDS*, August 12, 1922, p. 4.

"Rug Vendor Is Fixture in Parisian Life," *TDS*, August 12, 1922, p. 5.

"Old Order Changeth in Alsace-Lorraine," *TDS*, August 26, 1922, p. 4.

"Takes to the Water, Solves Flat Problem," *TDS*, August 26, 1922, p. 8.

"Germans Are Doggedly Sullen or Desperate over the Mark," *TDS*, September 1, 1922, p. 23.

"Once Over Permit Obstacle, Fishing in Baden Perfect," *TDS*, September 2, 1922, p. 28.

"German Inn-Keepers Rough Dealing with 'Auslanders,' " *TDS*, September 5, 1922, p. 5.

"A Paris-to-Strasbourg Flight Shows Living Cubist Picture," *TDS*, September 9, 1922, p. 8.

"Crossing to Germany Is Way to Make Money," *TDS*, September 19, 1922, p. 4.

"Riots Are Frequent Throughout Germany," *TSW*, September 30, 1922, p. 16.

"British Strong Enough to Save Constantinople," *TDS*, September 30, 1922, p. 1.

"Hubby Dines First, Wife Gets Crumbs," *TDS*, September 30, 1922, p. 9.

"Turk Red Crescent Propaganda Agency," *TDS*, October 4, 1922, p. 1.

"Hamid Bey Wears Shirt Tucked In When Seen by Star," *TDS*, October 9, 1922, p. 1.

"Balkans Look Like Ontario, a Picture of Peace, Not War," *TDS*, October 16, 1922, p. 13.

"Constantinople, Dirty White, Not Glistening and Sinister," *TDS*, October 18, 1922, p. 17.

"Constantinople Cut-Throats Await Chance for an Orgy," *TDS*, October 19, 1922, p. 4.

"A Silent, Ghastly Procession Wends Way from Thrace," *TDS*, October 20, 1922, p. 17.

"Russia to Spoil the French Game with Kemalists," *TDS*, October 23, 1922, p. 13.

"Turks Beginning to Show Distrust of Kemal Pasha," *TDS*, October 24, 1922, p. 17.

"Censor Too 'Thorough' in the Near East Crisis," *TDS*, October 25, 1922, p. 7.

" 'Old Constan' in True Light; Is Tough Town," *TDS*, October 28, 1922, p. 17.

"Kemal Has Afghans Ready to Make Trouble for Britain," *TDS*, October 31, 1922, p. 5.

"Betrayal Preceded Defeat, Then Came Greek Revolt," *TDS*, November 3, 1922, p. 10.

"Destroyers Were on Lookout for Kemal's One Submarine," *TDS*, November 10, 1922, p. 12.

"Refugee Procession Is Scene of Horror," *TDS*, November 14, 1922, p. 7.

"Mussolini, Europe's Prize Bluffer, More Like Bottomley Than Napoleon," *TDS*, January 27, 1923, p. 11.

"Gaudy Uniform Is Tchitcherin's Weakness, a 'Chocolate Soldier' of the Soviet Army," *TDS*, February 10, 1923, p. 2.

"A Victory Without Peace Forced the French to Undertake the Occupation of the Ruhr," *TDS*, April 14, 1923, p. 4.

"French Royalist Party Most Solidly Organized," *TDS*, April 18, 1923, pp. 1, 4.

"Government Pays for News in French Newspapers," *TDS*, April 21, 1923, pp. 1, 7.

"Ruhr Commercial War Question of Bankruptcy," *TDS*, April 25, 1923, pp. 1, 2.

"A Brave Belgian Lady Shuts Up German Hater," *TDS*, April 28, 1923, pp. 1, 2.

"Getting into Germany Quite a Job, Nowadays," *TDS*, May 2, 1923, pp. 1, 28.

"Quite Easy to Spend a Million, if in Marks," *TDS*, May 5, 1923, pp. 1, 34.

"Amateur Starvers Keep Out of View in Germany," *TDS*, May 9, 1923, p. 17.

"Hate in Occupied Zone a Real, Concrete Thing," *TDS*, May 12, 1923, p. 19.

"French Register Speed When Movies Are on Job," *TDS*, May 16, 1923, p. 19.

"King Business in Europe Isn't What It Used to Be," *TSW*, September 15, 1923, p. 15.

"Search for Sudbury Coal a Gamble; Driller Tells of What He Has Found," *TDS*, September 25, 1923, p. 4.

"Anthraxolite, and Not Coal, Declares Geologist Again, *TDS*, September 25, 1923, p. 4, unsigned.

"Tossed About on Land Like Ships in a Storm," *TDS*, September 25, 1923, p. 16, unsigned. Identified by William White, reprinted in *By-Line: Ernest Hemingway* (New York, 1967), pp. 83-89.

"He's a Personality, No Doubt, But a Much Maligned One," *TDS*, October 4, 1923, p. 12, unsigned.

"Lloyd George Willing to Address 10,000 Here," *TDS*, October 5, 1923, p. 1.

"Lloyd George Up Early as Big Liner Arrives," *TDS*, October 5, 1923, p. 14.

"Cope Denies Hearst Paying Lloyd George," *TSW*, October 6, 1923, p. 1.

"Lloyd George Attends Theatre in New York," *TSW*, October 6, 1923, p. 2.

"Little Welshman Lands; Anxious to Play Golf," *TDS*, October 6, 1923, p. 3.

"Wonderful Voice Is Chief Charm of Lloyd George," *TDS*, October 6, 1923, p. 17.

"Miss Megan George Makes Hit; 'A Wonder' Reporters Call Her," *TDS*, October 6, 1923, p. 17.

" 'A Man of the People, Will Fight for People,' " *TDS*, October 8, 1923, p. 14.

"Hungarian Statesman Delighted with Loan," *TDS*, October 15, 1923, p. 21, unsigned.

"Bull Fighting Is Not a Sport—It Is a Tragedy," *TSW*, October 20, 1923, p. 33.

"World's Series of Bull Fighting a Mad, Whirling Carnival," *TSW*, October 27, 1923, p. 33.

"More Game to Shoot in Crowded Europe Than in Ontario," *TSW*, November 3, 1923, p. 20.

"Trout Fishing All Across Europe; Spain Has the Best, Then Germany," *TSW*, November 17, 1923, p. 13.

"Cheer Up! The Lakes Aren't Going Dry; High Up and Low Down Is Just their Habit," *TSW*, November 17, 1923, p. 18, signed John Hadley.

"General Wolfe's Diaries Saved for Canada," *TSW*, November 24, 1923, p. 19.

"The Sport of Kings," *TSW*, November 24, 1923, p. 17, signed Hem.

"The Big Dance on the Hill," *TSW*, November 24, 1923, p. 18.

"Wild Gastronomic Adventures of a Gourmet," *TSW*, November 24, 1923, p. 18, signed Peter Jackson.

"Tancredo is Dead," *TSW*, November 24, 1923, p. 20.

"Learns to Commune with the Fairies, Now Wins the $40,000 Nobel Prize," *TSW*, November 24, 1923, p. 25.

"Fifty-Ton Doors Laugh at Robbers' Tools; Bank Vaults Defy Scientific Cracksmen," *TSW*, December 1, 1923, p. 33.

"German Marks Make Last Stand as Real Money in Toronto's 'Ward,' " *TSW*, December 8, 1923, p. 18, signed John Hadley.

"Lots of War Medals for Sale but Nobody Will Buy Them," *TSW*, December 8, 1923, p. 21.

"Night Life in Europe a Disease; Constantinople's Most Hectic," *TSW*, December 15, 1923, p. 21.

"Dose Whole City's Water Supply to Cure Goiter by Mass Medication," *TSW*, December 15, 1923, pp. 33, 34, signed John Hadley.

"Christmas on the Roof of the World," *TSW*, December 22, 1923, p. 19.

"A North of Italy Christmas," *TSW*, December 22, 1923, p. 19.

"Christmas in Paris," *TSW*, December 22, 1923, p. 19.

"Toronto 'Red' Children Don't Know Santa Claus," *TSW*, December 22, 1923, p. 33, unsigned.

"W. B. Yeats a Night Hawk; Kept Toronto Host Up," *TSW*, December 22, 1923, p. 35, unsigned.

"The Blind Man's Christmas Eve," *TSW*, December 22, 1923, p. 16, signed John Hadley.

"Toronto Is Biggest Betting Place in North America; 10,000 People Bet $100,000 on Horses Every Day," *TSW*, December 29, 1923, p. 17.

"Wild New Year's Eve Gone Forever; Only Ghost of 1914 Party Remains," *TSW*, December 29, 1923, p. 20, signed John Hadley.

"Weird, Wild Adventures of Some of Our Modern Imposters," *TSW*, December 29, 1923, pp. 20, 21.

"Ski-er's Only Escape from Alpine Avalanche Is to Swim! Snow Slides off Mountain as Fast as off Roof of House," *TSW*, January 12, 1924, p. 20.

"So This Is Chicago," *TSW*, January 19, 1924, p. 19.

"Must Wear Hats Like Other Folks if You Live in Toronto," *TSW*, January 19, 1924, p. 33, signed John Hadley.

"And to the United States," *the transatlantic review*, I (May-June 1924), 355-57.

"And Out of America," *the transatlantic review*, II (August 1924), 102-3.

"Tackling a Spanish Bull Is 'Just like Rugby': Hemingway Tells How He Surprised the Natives," *TSW*, September 13, 1924, p. 18, based on a Hemingway letter.

"Pamplona Letter," *the transatlantic review*, II (October 1924), 300-302.

"Conrad, Optimist and Moralist," *the transatlantic review*, II (October 1924), 341-42.

"Homage to Ezra," *This Quarter*, I (May 1925), 221-25.

"My Own Life," *New Yorker*, II (February 12, 1927), 23-24.

"Italy, 1927," *New Republic*, C (May 18, 1927), 350-53.

"The Real Spaniard," *The Boulevardier* (Paris), No. 8 (October 1927), 6.

"Valentine," *The Little Review*, XII (May 1929), 41-42, poem with covering letter.

"Who Knows How?" *Creating the Short Story*, ed. Henry Goodman. New York: Harcourt, Brace & Co., 1929, p. 121; introductory note to "The Killers."

"Introduction," *Kiki of Montparnasse*. New York: Edward W. Titus at the Sign of the Black Manikin, 1929, no pagination. Book reissued as *Kiki's Memoirs*, trans. Samuel Putnam. Paris, 1930.

"Bullfighting, Sport and Industry," *Fortune*, I (March 1930), 83-88, 139, 140, 150.

Letter excerpt in *Bibliographical Notes on Ernest Hemingway*. Chicago: The Walden Book Shop, 1930. Letter dated "Spring, 1927." Four unnumbered pages.

Published letters in Louis Henry Cohn's *A Bibliography of the Works of Ernest Hemingway*. New York: Random House, 1931.

Death in the Afternoon. New York: Scribner's, 1932.

Untitled tribute to Ezra Pound. *The Cantos of Ezra Pound*. Testimonies by Hemingway and others. New York: Farrar & Rinehart, 1933, p. 13.

"Marlin off the Morro," *Esquire*, I (Autumn 1933), 8-9, 39, 97.

"The Friend of Spain," *Esquire*, I (January 1934), 26, 136.

"A Paris Letter," *Esquire*, I (February 1934), 22, 156.

"a.d. in Africa," *Esquire*, I (April 1934), 19, 146.

"Shootism versus Sport," *Esquire*, I (June 1934), 19, 150.

"Notes on Dangerous Game," *Esquire*, II (July 1934), 19, 94.

"Out in the Stream," *Esquire*, II (August 1934), 19, 156, 158.

"Defense of Dirty Words," *Esquire*, II (September 1934), 19, 158B.

"Genio after Josie," *Esquire*, II (October 1934), 21, 22.

"Old Newsman Writes," *Esquire*, II (December 1934), 25, 26.

[Joan Miro's] "The Farm," *Cahiers d'Art*, IX (1934), 28, 29.

"Introduction," *This Must Be the Place* by James Charters (Jimmie the Barman), illus. Ivan Opffer and Hilaire Hiler. London: Herbert Joseph, Ltd., 1934, pp. 11-13.

"Death in the Afternoon Cocktail," *So Red the Nose, or Breath in the Afternoon*, ed. Sterling North and Carl Kroch, illus. Roy C. Nelson. New York: Farrar and Rinehart, 1935, pp. 8-9.

"Notes on Life and Letters," *Esquire*, III (January 1935), 21, 159.

"Remembering Shooting-Flying," *Esquire*, III (February 1935), 21, 152.

[With John Dos Passos] "Facing a Bitter World: A Portfolio of Etchings by Luis Quintanilla," *Esquire*, III (February 1925), 25-27.

"Sailfish off Mombasa," *Esquire*, III (March 1925), 21, 156.

"The Sights of Whitehead Street," *Esquire*, III (April 1935), 25, 156.
"a.d. Southern Style," *Esquire*, III (May 1925), 25, 156.
"On Being Shot Again," *Esquire*, III (June 1935), 25, 156.
"The President Vanquishes," *Esquire*, IV (July 1935), 23, 167.
"He Who Gets Slap Happy," *Esquire*, IV (August 1935), 19, 182.
"Who Murdered the Vets? A First-Hand Report on the Florida Hurricane," *New Masses*, XVI (September 17, 1935), 9-10.
"Notes on the Next War," *Esquire*, IV (September 1935), 19, 156.
"Monologue to the Maestro," *Esquire*, IV (October 1935), 21, 174A, 174B.
Green Hills of Africa. New York: Scribner's, 1935.
"The Malady of Power," *Esquire*, IV (November 1935), 31, 198, 199.
"Million Dollar Fright," *Esquire*, IV (December 1935), 35, 190B.
"Marlin off Cuba," *American Big Game Fishing*, ed. Eugene V. Connett. New York: Derrydale Press, 1935, pp. 55-81.
"Hemingway," *Portraits and Self-Portraits*, collected and illus. Georges Schreiber. Boston: Houghton Mifflin, 1936, pp. 55-57.
"Wings Always over Africa," *Esquire*, V (January 1936), 31, 174-75.
"On the Blue Water," *Esquire*, V (April 1936), 31, 184-85.
"There She Breaches! or Moby Dick off the Morro," *Esquire*, V (May 1936), 35, 203-5.
[With John Dos Passos] "Gattorno: Program Note," *Esquire*, V (May 1936), 111, 141.
"Hemingway on Mutilated Fish," *Outdoor Life*, LXXVII (June 1936), 70-72.
"Rabelais in a Smock," *Esquire*, VI (July 1936) 101, 118, 121-22. Contains quotations by Hemingway.
"Greetings on Our Twenty-Fifth Anniversary," *New Masses*, XXI (December 1, 1936), 21.
"Preface," *All Good Americans* by Jerome Bahr. New York: Scribner's, 1937, pp. vii-viii.
"Introduction," *Atlantic Game Fishing* by S. Kip Farrington, Jr., illus. Lynn Bogue Hunt. New York: Kennedy Brothers, 1937, pp. xvii-xxii.
"The Writer and War," *The Writer in a Changing World*, ed. Henry Hart. New York: Equinox Cooperative Press, 1937, pp. 69-73.
"Hemingway Reports Spain," *New Republic*, XC (May 5, 1937), 376-79.
"Death in Spain: The Civil War Has Taken 500,000 Lives in One Year," *Life*, III (July 12, 1937), 19-25.
"Hemingway Reports Spain," *New Republic*, XCIII (January 12, 1938), 273-76.
"Luis Quintanilla: Artist and Soldier," *Quintanilla: An Exhibition*

of Drawings of the War in Spain by Luis Quintanilla. New York: The Museum of Modern Art, March 1938, p. 7.

"The Time Now, the Place Spain," *Ken*, I (April 7, 1938), 36-37.

"Dying, Well or Badly," *Ken*, I (April 21, 1938), 68-70.

"Hemingway Reports Spain," *New Republic*, XCIV (April 27, 1938), 350-51.

A section of "Inquiry into the Spirit and Language of Night," ed. Eugene Jolas, *Transition*, No. 27 (April-May 1938), 233-38.

Letter about the war in Spain, *Writers Take Sides*, collected by the League of American Writers. New York: The League of American Writers, May 1938, p. 30.

"The Cardinal Picks a Winner," *Ken*, I (May 5, 1938), 38-39.

"United We Fall upon Ken," *Ken*, I (June 2, 1938), 38.

"Hemingway Reports Spain," *New Republic*, XCV (June 8, 1938), 124-26.

"H. M.'s Loyal State Department," *Ken*, I (June 16, 1938), 36.

"Treachery in Aragon," *Ken*, I (June 30, 1938), 26

The Spanish Earth, with an introduction by Jasper Wood and illustrations by Frederick K. Russell. Cleveland: The J. B. Savage Company, June 1938.

"Call for Greatness," *Ken*, II (July 14, 1938), 23.

"The Spanish War," *Fact*, No. 16 (July 15, 1938), 7-72. A compilation of Hemingway's North American Newspaper Alliance dispatches, syndicated and published in various newspapers and partially in the *New Republic*.

"My Pal the Gorilla Gargantua," *Ken*, II (July 28, 1938), 26.

"A Program for U.S. Realism," *Ken*, II (August 11, 1938), 26.

"Good Generals Hug the Line," *Ken*, II (August 25, 1938), 28.

"False News to the President," *Ken*, II (September 8, 1938), 17-18.

"Fresh Air on an Inside Story," *Ken*, II (September 22, 1938), 28.

"Milton Wolff," *An Exhibition of Sculpture by Jo Davidson.* New York: Arden Gallery, November 18-December 3, 1938.

"Preface," *The Fifth Column and the First Forty-Nine Stories.* New York: Scribner's, 1938, pp. v-vii.

"Three Prefaces," *All the Brave* by Luis Quintanilla, text by Elliot Paul and Jay Allen. New York: Modern Age Books, 1939, pp. 7-11.

"The Next Outbreak of Peace," *Ken*, III (January 12, 1939), 12-13.

"The Clark's Fork Valley, Wyoming," *Vogue*, XCIII (February 1, 1939), 68, 157.

"On the American Dead in Spain," *New Masses*, XXX (February 14, 1939), 3.

"The Writer as a Writer," *Directions* (May-June 1939), p. 3.

"Foreword," *Men in the Ranks: The Story of 12 Americans in Spain* by Joseph North. New York: Friends of the Abraham Lincoln Brigade, 1939, pp. 3-4.

"War Writers on Democracy," *Life*, VIII (June 24, 1940), 8.

"Man, What a Sport!" *Rotarian*, LVI (May 1940), 19, 21.

"Ernest Hemingway Talks of Work and War," interview by Robert Van Gelder in *New York Times Book Review*, August 11, 1940, section VI, p. 2. Reprinted in *Writers and Writing* by Robert Van Gelder. New York: Scribner's, 1946, pp. 95-98.

"Preface," *The Great Crusade* by Gustav Regler, trans. Whittaker Chambers and Barrows Mussey. New York: Longmans, Green, 1940, pp. vii-xi.

[Catalogue note] *Henrietta Hoopes*. New York: Knoedler Galleries, December 18, 1940-January 4, 1941, p. [2].

"Story of Ernest Hemingway's Far East Trip to See for Himself if War with Japan Is Inevitable," interview by Ralph Ingersoll, *PM*, June 9, 1941, pp. 6-10.

"Ernest Hemingway Says Russo-Jap Pact Hasn't Kept Soviet from Sending Aid to China," *PM*, June 10, 1941, pp. 4-5.

"Ernest Hemingway Says We Can't Let Japan Grab Our Rubber Supplies in Dutch East Indies," *PM*, June 11, 1941, pp. 6-7.

"Ernest Hemingway Says Japan Must Conquer China or Satisfy USSR Before Moving South," *PM*, June 13, 1941, pp. 6-7.

"Ernest Hemingway Says Aid to China Gives U.S. Two-Ocean Navy Security for Price of One Battleship," *PM*, June 15, 1941, pp. 6-7.

"After Four Years of War in China Japs Have Conquered Only Flat Lands," *PM*, June 16, 1941, pp. 6-9.

"Ernest Hemingway Says China Needs Pilots as Well as Planes to Beat Japanese in the Air," *PM*, June 17, 1941, p. 5.

"Ernest Hemingway Tells How 100,000 Chinese Labored Night and Day to Build Huge Landing Field for Bombers," *PM*, June 18, 1941, pp. 16-17.

"Introduction," *Men at War*, ed. Ernest Hemingway, based on a plan by William Kozlenko. New York: Crown Publishers, 1942, pp. xi-xxxi.

Note on Martha Gellhorn, *Collier's*, CXIII (March 4, 1944), 43.

"Voyage to Victory," *Collier's*, CXIV (July 22, 1944), 11-13, 56-57.

"London Fights the Robots," *Collier's*, CXIV (August 19, 1944), 17, 80-81.

"Battle for Paris," *Collier's*, CXIV (September 30, 1944), 11, 83-84, 86.

"How We Came to Paris," *Collier's*, CXIV (October 7, 1944), 14, 65, 67.

"The G.I. and the General," *Collier's*, CXIV (November 4, 1944), 11, 46-47.

"War in the Siegfried Line," *Collier's*, CXIV (November 18, 1944), 18, 70-71, 73.

"Golden Jubilee Greetings," *Cincinnati Symphony Orchestra Program*, March 23-24, 1945, p. 618.

"Introduction," *Studio: Europe* by John Groth. New York: The Vanguard Press, 1945, pp. 7-9.

"Introduction," *Treasury for the Free World*, ed. Ben Raeburn. New York: Arco Publishing Company, 1946, pp. viii-xv.

"Hemingway in the Afternoon," *Time*, L (August 4, 1947), 80.

"Introduction," *A Farewell to Arms*, illus. Daniel Rassmusson. New York: Scribner's, 1948, pp. vii-xi.

"Cuban Fishing," *Game Fish of the World*, ed. Brian Vesey-Fitzgerald and Francesca Lamonte, illus. A. Fraser-Brunner. New York: Harper, 1949, pp. 156-60.

"The Great Blue River," *Holiday*, VI (July 1949), 60-63, 95.

"The Position of Ernest Hemingway," *New York Times Book Review*, July 31, 1949, p. 1.

"Introduction," *In Sicily* by Elio Vittorini, trans. Wilfrid David. New York: New Directions, 1949. No pagination.

Letter on Nelson Algren's *The Man With the Golden Arm*, *Book Find News*, January 1950, p. 5.

"How Do You Like It Now, Gentlemen?" interview by Lillian Ross, *New Yorker*, XXVI (May 13, 1950), 36, 38-40, 42-56. Reissued with Ross's introduction as *Portrait of Hemingway*. New York: Simon and Schuster, 1961.

" 'Hemingway Is Bitter About Nobody'—But His Colonel Is," *Time*, LVI (September 11, 1950), 110.

"Important Authors of the Fall Speak for Themselves: Ernest Hemingway," *New York Herald Tribune Book Review*, October 8, 1950, p. 4.

"Success, It's Wonderful," interview by Harvey Breit, *New York Times Book Review*, December 3, 1950, pp. 4, 58.

"Books I Have Liked," *New York Herald Tribune Book Review*, December 3, 1950, p. 6.

"Hemingway Rates Charles for *Gazette*," *National Police Gazette*, CLVI (January 1951), 16.

"The Shot," *True*, XXVIII (April 1951), 25-28.

Letter advertisement for Ballantine Ale, *Life*, XXXI (November 5, 1951), 90-91. Run again with different introductory material on September 8, 1952.

"Preface," *A Hemingway Check List* by Lee Samuels. New York: Scribner's, 1951, pp. 5-6.

"Finca Vigia, San Francisco de Paula, Cuba," *Reginald Rowe*. New York: Wellons Gallery, February 18-March 1, 1952.

"A Tribute to Mamma From Papa Hemingway," *Life*, XXXIII (August 18, 1952), 92-93.

"From Ernest Hemingway to the Editors of Life," *Life*, XXXIII (August 25, 1952), 124.

"A Letter from Ernest Hemingway," *New York Post*, August 31, 1952, p. 8.

"A Letter from Hemingway," letter interview with Bernard Kalb, *Saturday Review*, XXXV (September 6, 1952), 11.

"Hemingway Comments on His Life and Work," interview with Harvey Breit in *New York Times Book Review*, September 7, 1952, section VII, p. 20. Reprinted in Harvey Breit, *The Writer Observed*. New York: Collier Books, 1961, pp. 171-72.

Note on books of 1952, *New York Herald Tribune Book Review*, December 7, 1952, p. 9.

"Preface," *Salt Water Fishing* by Van Campen Heilner, illus. W. Goadby Lawrence. Second Revised Edition. New York: Alfred A. Knopf, 1953, pp. vii-viii.

"The Circus," *Ringling Brothers and Barnum & Bailey Circus Magazine and Program* (1953), pp. 7, 62.

"Foreword," *Man and Beast in Africa* by François Sommer, trans. Edward Fitzgerald. London: Herbert Jenkins, Ltd., 1953, pp. 5-7.

"Hemingway Pays His Respects to Oak Park Library," *Library Journal*, LXXIX (February 15, 1954), 292.

Cable on death of Robert Capa, *Life*, XXXVI (June 7, 1954), 25.

"Ernest Hemingway," interview with Harvey Breit, *New York Times Book Review*, November 7, 1954, section VII, p. 1. Reprinted in *The Writer Observed*, pp. 179-82.

"Safari," *Look*, XVIII (January 26, 1954), 19-34.

"The Christmas Gift," Part I, *Look*, XVIII (April 20, 1954), 29-37; Part II (May 4, 1954), 79-89.

Ezra Pound at Seventy by Hemingway, E. E. Cummings, and others. Norfolk, Connecticut: New Directions, 1955, 16 unnumbered pages.

Testimonial for Pan American Airline, *Holiday*, XIX (February 1956), 60.

"A Situation Report," *Look*, XX (September 4, 1956), 23-31.

"My Life and the Woman I Love," London *Daily Express*, September 10, 1956, pp. 4-5.

"Hemingway on the Town," London *Daily Express*, September 11, 1956, p. 4.

"The Art of Fiction," interview with George Plimpton, *The Paris*

Review, XVIII (Spring 1958), 61-82. Reprinted as "An Interview with Hemingway" in *Hemingway and His Critics,* ed. Carlos Baker. New York: Hill and Wang, 1961, pp. 19-37.

"Foreword," *A Fly Fisher's Life* by Charles Ritz. Introduction by Bernard Venables, trans. Humphrey Hare. London: Max Reinhardt, 1959, p. 7.

"A Matter of Wind," *Sports illustrated,* XI (August 17, 1959), 43.

"Hemingway Talks to American Youth," interview recorded by A. E. Hotchner, *This Week Magazine* (October 18, 1959), pp. 10-11, 24.

"Two Prideful Rivals and a Prideful 'Life,' " *Life,* XLIX (September 5, 1960), 2.

"The Dangerous Summer," *Life,* XLIX, Part I: "The Dangerous Summer" (September 5, 1960), 78-109; Part II: "The Pride of the Devil" (September 12, 1960), 60-82; Part III: "An Appointment with Disaster" (September 19, 1960), 74-96.

"Last Words Hemingway Wrote," *Life,* LI (August 25, 1961), 7.

"Letter to a Young Writer," *Mark Twain Journal,* XI (Summer 1962), 10.

"A Man's Credo," *Playboy,* X (January 1963), 120, 124, 175.

"Advice to a Young Man," *Playboy,* XI (January 1964), 153, 225-27.

A Moveable Feast. New York: Scribner's, 1964.

"Hemingway in Cuba," interview by Robert Manning, *The Atlantic,* CCXVI (August 1965), 101-8.

Ernest Hemingway Reading. Caedmon Record TC 1185. New York: Caedmon Records, Inc., 1965.

More Sources, Analogues, and Echoes

ITEMS BELOW ARE ARRANGED CHRONOLOGICALLY ACCORDING TO THE original publication date of the fictional work for which there is a correlated nonfictional passage. Within the short story collections—*In Our Time, Men Without Women,* and *Winner Take Nothing*—the arrangement is according to their order of appearance in *The Short Stories of Ernest Hemingway,* Scribner's Modern Standard Authors edition.

In Our Time

Chapter II, p. 97 Refugee column described.	"A Silent Ghastly Procession Wends Way from Thrace," *TDS,* October 20, 1922, p. 17; "Refugee Procession Is Scene of Horror," *TDS,* November 14, 1922, p. 7.
"The Three Day Blow," pp. 115-25.	"I was writing about up in Michigan and since it was a wild, cold, blowing day it was that sort in the story. I had already seen the end of the fall

come through boyhood, youth and young manhood, and in one place you could write about it
better than in another. . . . But in the story the
boys were drinking and this made me thirsty and
I ordered a rum St. James. This tasted wonderful
on the cold day and I kept on writing. . . ." (*A
Moveable Feast*, p. 5.)

Chapter V, p. 127.
Shooting of six cabinet
members.

Among Lloyd George's Genoa contemporaries who
have disappeared since the conference: "Gournaris,
the Greek premier, was carried from his bed sick
with typhoid to stand before the firing squad in
the rain in the courtyard of the military hospital."
("Lloyd George Up Early as Big Liner Arrives,"
TDS, October 5, 1923, p. 14.)

"The Battler"
Nick's observation of
the Ad Francis-Bugs re-
lationship, pp. 133-38.

Hemingway's mental note after being told by
Gertrude Stein that he is uneducated about sex
and prejudiced against homosexuality: "I knew it
was why you carried a knife and would use it
when you were in the company of tramps when
you were a boy in the days when wolves was not
a slang term for men obsessed by the pursuit of
women." (*A Moveable Feast*, p. 18.)

Chapter VI, p. 139
Nick's wound, his sight-
ing of Rinaldi sprawled
face downward in street
near a church wall, his
declaration of a separate
peace.

"So we walked along through the street where I
saw my very good friend killed, past the ugly new
houses toward the motor car whose owner would
never have had a motor car if it had not been
for the war, and it all seemed a very sad business."
("A Veteran Visits Old Front, Wishes He Had
Stayed Away," *TDS*, July 22, 1922, p. 7.)

"Soldier's Home"
Harold Krebs reads in a
war history about en-
gagements in which he
fought, wishes for more
maps, more details, p.
148.

On how to appear to be a war veteran: "Buy or
borrow a good history of the war. Study it carefully and you will be able to talk intelligently on
any part of the front. In fact, you will more than
once be able to prove the average returned veteran
a pinnacle of inaccuracy if not unveracity. The
average soldier has a very abominable memory for
names and dates. Take advantage of this. With a
little conscientious study you should be able to
prove to the man who was at first and second
Ypres that he was not there at all. You of course
are aided in this by the similarity of one day to
another in the army." ("How to Be Popular in
Peace Through a Slacker in War," *TSW*, March
13, 1920, p. 11.)

Krebs' loss of belief in his own war experiences after talking about them, pp. 145-46.

"Don't go back to visit your old front. If you have pictures in your head of something that happened in the night in the mud at Paschendaele, or of the first wave working up the slope of Vimy, do not try and go back and verify them. . . . Go to someone else's front if you want to. There your imagination will help you out and you may be able to picture the things that happened. But don't go back to your own front, because the change in everything and the supreme, deadly, lonely dullness, the smooth green of the fields that were once torn up with shell holes and slashed with trenches and wire, will combine against you and make you believe that the places and happenings that had been the really great events to you were only fever dreams or lies you had told to yourself." ("A Veteran Visits Old Front, Wishes He Had Stayed Away," *TDS*, July 22, 1922, p. 7.)

"The Revolutionist"
Young Hungarian's faith in successful revolution in Italy, p. 157.

Account of Socialist revolution defeated in Italy by Mussolini's young Fascisti. ("Picked Sharpshooters Patrol Genoa Streets," *TDS*, April 13, 1922, p. 17; " 'Pot-Shot Patriots' Unpopular in Italy," *TSW*, June 24, 1922, p. 5; "Fascisti Party Half-Million Strong," *TDS*, June 24, 1922, p. 16.)

Chapter IX, p. 159
Young matador has to kill five bulls, vomits when finished killing them.

Algabeno rescues wounded member of Olmos' cuadrilla by holding on to bull's tail, then kills five bulls after other matadors wounded. "There are no substitute matadors allowed. Maera was finished. His wrist could not lift a sword for weeks. Olmos had been gored badly through the body. It was Algabeno's bull. This one and the next five [*sic*]. He handled them all. Did it all. Cape play easy, graceful, confident. Beautiful work with the muleta. And serious, deadly killing. Five bulls he killed, one after the other, and each one was a separate problem to be worked out with death. At the end there was nothing debonair about him. It was only a question if he would last through or if the bulls would get him." ("World Series of Bull Fighting a Mad, Whirling Carnival," *TSW*, October 27, 1923, p. 33.)

Chapter X, p. 165.
Picador horse entrails hang out as horse canters jerkily into position for another charge by bull.

Stiff, old-madish movements of disemboweled horse are the comic element of a tragic bullfight. (*Death in the Afternoon*, p. 7.)

"Out of Season"
Peduzzi, the young gentleman, and the young wife walk through the village to do illegal fishing while watched by people at the Fascist café and in other shops, p. 174.

Hemingway and William Bird fish illegally in the Black Forest after finding German bureaucrats unfriendly and impossible to deal with in their attempts to obtain a fishing permit. ("Once over Permit Obstacle, Fishing in Baden Perfect," *TDS*, September 2, 1922, p. 280.)

Peduzzi makes tentative appointment to take young couple fishing next day, p. 179.

"Then I started to think in Lipp's about when I had first been able to write a story after losing everything. It was up in Cortina D'Ampezzo when I had come back to join Hadley there after the spring skiing which I had to interrupt to go on assignment to the Rhineland and the Ruhr. It was a very simple story called 'Out of Season' and I had omitted the real end of it which was that the old man hanged himself." (*A Moveable Feast*, p. 75.)

"Cross-Country Snow"
Sensations of ski run down slopes after ride up mountain by funicular, p. 183.

Description of ride up mountain on funicular, of Christmas noon on slopes, then sensations of a ski run down the mountainside for Christmas dinner at the inn. ("Christmas on the Roof of the World," *TSW*, December 22, 1923, p. 19.)

Nick observes Swiss all have goiter, p. 188.

"In Switzerland the disease is almost universal among the men and women of the mountains. In the Canton of Zurich one district was found to be 100 per cent goiterous." ("Dose Whole City's Water Supply to Cure Goiter by Mass Medication," *TSW*, December 15, 1923, p. 33.)

"Big Two-Hearted River"
Nick rides through burned-out country, gets off the train at Seney, looks at the river near the bridge, begins his hike into the green countryside and on toward the river camp, pp. 209-12.

"I sat in the corner with the afternoon light coming in over my shoulder and wrote in the notebook. The waiter brought me a *café creme* and I drank half of it when it cooled and left it on the table while I wrote. When I stopped writing I did not want to leave the river where I could see the trout in the pool, its surface pushing and swelling smooth against the log-driven piles of the bridge. The story was about coming back from the war but there was no mention of the war in it.

"But in the morning the river would be there and I would make it and the country and all that would happen." (*A Moveable Feast*, pp. 76-77.)

Nick sees remains of the burned-out Mansion House Hotel at Seney, p. 209.	A porcupine skin, a stuffed owl, a chuck-wills-widow, old magazines, boys' letters—"Yesterday's tribute is gone/Along with youth/. . . when the hotel burned down/At Seney, Michigan." ("Along with Youth" in *Three Stories and Ten Poems*, Paris, 1923, reprinted in *The Collected Poems of Ernest Hemingway*, Number one of the Library of Living Poetry, Paris, no date [p. 18].)
Nick shoulders his pack, strides off into the rising hill country beyond the burned-out areas, pp. 212-13.	"Some days it went so well that you could make the country so that you could walk into it through the timber to come out into the clearing and work up onto the high ground and see the hills beyond the arm of the lake . . . then slip your arm through the pack again, get the other arm through and feel the weight settle on your back and feel the pine needles under your moccasins as you started down for the lake." (*A Moveable Feast*, p. 91.)
Nick methodically makes camp, clears the ground of roots for his bed roll, pitches his tent tautly, puts up cheesecloth against mosquitoes, eats beans and spaghetti brought in cans, eats canned apricots, boils coffee, drinks it slowly; cooks buckwheat cakes for breakfast, pp. 214-17, 221.	Description of correct way to make mosquito-proof tent, to lay a bed on bare ground to avoid bumps or chill, to fry trout and bacon, cook pancakes, bake a fruit pie, and to boil coffee so a camping trip will not be ruined by indigestion. ("When You Camp Out Do It Right," *TSW*, June 26, 1920, p. 17.); Hemingway recommends the use of cheesecloth instead of commercial mosquito netting. ("When You Go Camping Take Lots of Skeeter Dope and Don't Ever Lose It," *TSW*, August 5, 1920, p. 11.)
Nick gathers grasshoppers for bait by taking them early in the morning while they are still stiff with cold, finds them at grass stems and under a log, p. 221.	"The big difficulty about fishing with grasshoppers has always been the difficulty in catching them. The classic way is to get up early in the morning before the sun has dried the dew, and catch the hoppers while they are still stiff and cold and unable to hop more than a feeble foot or two. They are found under the side of logs in a clearing and along the grass stems." ("Fishing for Trout in a Sporting Way," *TSW*, April 24, 1920, p. 13.)
Nick ties gut leaders to fly line, uses small, springy hook, p. 223.	Hemingway recommends use of leaders on a line as big trout will strike at bait on an invisible leader but avoid bait on a visible line. ("Are You All Set for Trout?" *TSW*, April 10, 1920, p. 11.)

Nick hooks a grasshopper under the chin, runs the hook through the thorax and abdomen, p. 224.

"Put the hook in under the chin of the grasshopper and carry it back through the thorax." ("Fishing for Trout in a Sporting Way," *TSW*, April 24, 1920, p. 13.)

Nick loses leader to biggest trout he has ever seen, p. 226.

Account of losing a leader to a large though unseen fish in trout stream; Jock Pentecost's account of hour-and-a-half struggle with giant trout before losing him in deep pool. ("A Fight with a 20-Pound Trout," *TSW*, November 20, 1920, pp. 25-26.)

Chapter XV, p. 219.
Sam Cardinella's paralysis, loss of control of sphincter muscle occur before he is hanged.

"But in the case of an execution by a firing squad, or a hanging, this is not true, and if these very simple things were to be made permanent, as, say, Goya tried to make them in *Los Desastros de la Guerra*, it could not be done with any shutting of the eye. I had seen certain things, certain simple things of this sort that I remembered but through taking part in them, or, in other cases having to write of them immediately after and consequently noticing the things I needed for instant recording, I had never been able to study them as a man might, for instance, study the death of his father or the hanging of someone, say, that he did not know and would not have to write of immediately after for the first edition of an afternoon newspaper." (*Death in the Afternoon*, p. 3.)

"*L'Envoi*"
Interviewer-visitor finds the Greek king and queen eager to please, submissive to revolutionary government, wistful about America; "Like all Greeks he wanted to go to America," p. 232.

News cameraman Shorty Wornall reports on interview with King George of Greece: "I ran off a lot of film of him and the queen all around the palace and out in the field. He wanted me to take him with an old binder they had in one of the big fields inside the walls. 'This will look fine in America, won't it?' he said. . . . When I left the king said: 'Well, maybe we'll meet in the States sometime.' Like all the Greeks he wants to get over to the States." ("King Business in Europe Isn't What It Used to Be," *TSW*, September 15, 1923, p. 15.)

Men Without Women
"The Undefeated"
Fuentes, the gypsy *banderillero*, causes the bull to run into the *barrera* after a dazzling placement of the barbs, p. 256.

"Maera planted his first pair of banderillos sitting down on the edge of the little step up that runs around the barrera. He snarled at the bull and as the animal charged leaned back tight against the fence and as the horns struck on either side of him, swung forward over the brute's head and planted the two darts in his hump. He planted the next pair the same way, so near to us we would have leaned over and touched him. Then he went out to kill the bull and after he had made absolutely unbelievable passes with the little red cloth of the muleta, drew up his sword and as the bull charged Maera thrust. The sword shot out of his hand and the bull caught him. He went up in the air on the horns of the bull and then came down. Young Algabeno flopped his cape in the bull's face. The bull charged him and Maera staggered to his feet. But his wrist was sprained.

Maera hits bone, loses his sword, is repeatedly tossed, and is gored before killing the bull Campagnero, pp. 261-64.

"With his wrist sprained, so that every time he raised it to sight for a thrust it brought beads of sweat out on his face, Maera tried again and again to make his death thrust. He lost his sword again and again, picked it up with his left hand from the mud floor of the arena and transferred it to the right for the thrust. Finally he made it and the bull went over. The bull nearly got him twenty times. As he came in to stand under us at the barrera side his wrist was swollen to twice normal size. I thought of prize fighters I had seen quit because they had hurt their hand." ("World's Series of Bull Fighting a Mad, Whirling Carnival," *TSW*, October 27, 1923, p. 33.)

"Maera had trouble with his wrists, once had to go in over the horns six times before he killed his bull. His wrist was swollen to double its size." (*Death in the Afternoon*, pp. 80-81.)

Manuel Garcia earns 300 pesetas for a nocturnal bull fight, p. 238.

"There were six matadors in Spain last year who had only one fight. None of them received over 4,000 pesetas for their single appearance and it is safe to say that they had to give at least 1,000 of that to their aides and the manager who put them on the program, and the 3,000 pesetas that remain is the money they made the year of Our Lord 1929. There were thirty-one bullfighters, that is, officially consecrated *matadors de toros*, who made less than $4,000 last year. So it is not the bullfighters in general who made the money but rather the twenty or so who are in the first flight of their profession." ("Bullfighting, Sport and Industry," *Fortune* I [March 1930], 144.)

Manuel Garcia has gone into decline as a matador because of his frequent wounds; now has to fight in the nocturnals, pp. 237-43.

"After the matador has been wounded, and until he has his nerves back, he does only one thing—avoids the bull's horn, and each day he loses popularity and drawing power. There are new fighters coming up each season and after two or three bad years a bullfighter finds himself without contracts, out of training because he has no chance to keep his judgment of distance and confidence by fighting. Then he has to accept what fights he can get as a substitute, kill the bulls no one else will kill and, being out of practice, if he tries anything brilliant the serious horn wound is nearly inevitable." ("Bullfighting, Sport and Industry," *Fortune* I [March 1930], 144.)

Manuel Garcia wants Zurito as his picador. Zurito says he gets more than 300 pesetas per fight for pic-ing, p. 243.

Old Zurito, father of the matador Zurito and of a picador son, was "the last and one of the greatest of the old-time picadors." (*Death in the Afternoon*, pp. 254, 258.)

"In Another Country"
During the cold fall in Milan, the narrator sees game hanging stiff and heavy outside the shops, p. 267.
Officer patients from hospital go to Café Cova, next to La Scala, p. 268.

"Milan, the sprawling, new-old, yellow-brown city of the north, tight frozen in the December cold.
"Foxes, deer, pheasants, rabbits hanging before the butcher shops. Cold troops wandering down the streets, from the Christmas leave trains. All the world drinking hot rum punches inside the cafés.
"Officers of every nationality, rank and degree of sobriety crowded into the Cova Café across from the Scala theatre. . . ."
("A North of Italy Christmas," *TSW*, December 22, 1923, p. 19.)

Officer patients walk together through the Communist quarter of Milan, hear people shout from wine shops, "A Basso gli Ufficiali!" p. 268.

"I can remember in the old days how the mothers and fathers used to lean out of windows, or from the front of wine shops, blacksmith shops or the door of a cobbler's when soldiers passed and shout *'Abassa gli ufficiali!'* 'Down with the officers!' because they saw the officers as those who kept the foot soldiers fighting when they had come to know the war would bring them no good." ("Wings Always over Africa," *Esquire*, V [January 1936], 174.)

"Hills like White Elephants"
Girl and young man talk about abortion without ever mentioning the word, pp. 273-78.

"I met a girl in Prunier where I'd gone to eat oysters before lunch. I knew she'd had an abortion. I went over and we talked, not about that, but on the way home I thought of the story, skipped lunch, and spent that afternoon writing it." (Baker, *Hemingway and His Critics*, p. 34.)

"The Killers"
Al and Max come to Summit to kill Ole Andreson "for a friend." They have no quarrel with their victim, p. 283.

Hemingway's interview in Chicago with an ex-gunman about American gunmen going to Ireland to perform assassinations for the Irish Republican Army: "In the course of the afternoon I learned a number of things about the trade. Yes, there were American 'bump-off' artists in Ireland. Yes, he knew some that were there personally. Well, he didn't know who was in the right in Ireland. No, it didn't matter to him. He understood it was all managed out of New York. Then you worked out of Liverpool. No, he wouldn't particularly care about killing Englishmen. But, then, they gotta die sometime.

"He's heard that most of the guns were Wops—Dagoes, that is. Most gunmen were Wops, anyway. A wop made a good gun. They usually worked in pairs. In the U.S.A. they nearly always worked out of a motor car, because that made the getaway much easier. . . . That's the type of mercenary that is doing the Irishmen's killings for them." ("Plain and Fancy Killings, $400 Up," *TSW*, December 11, 1920, p. 26.)

"Fifty Grand"
Jack Brennan bets on his opponent Walcott, intentionally loses by fouling Walcott, pp. 313, 325.

After seeing the disappointing performance of Max Baer in his fight with Joe Louis, Hemingway reports the rumor that Baer had bet on Louis, reports from his own observation that Baer tried to end the fight early by fouling Louis, hitting him after the gong had sounded. ("Million Dollar Fright," *Esquire*, IV [December 1935], 35, 190B.)

"An Alpine Idyll"
Narrator and John, carrying skis and rucksacks, hike into Gultar, greet priest with "Grüss Gott," go into the dining room of their inn to drink beer, watch the peasants drink wine and schnapps, pp. 343, 345.

"I remember the snow on the road to the village squeaking at night when we walked home in the cold with our skis and ski poles on our shoulders, watching the lights, and then finally seeing the buildings, and how everyone on the road said, 'Grüss Gott.' There were always country men in the Weinstube with nailed boots and mountain clothes and the air was smoky and the wooden floors were scarred by the nails." (*A Moveable Feast*, p. 202.)

"Now I Lay Me"
Narrator at night reviews all the kinds of fishing bait for different streams and remembers where to find different baits—worms, beetles, grubs, wood ticks, angle worms, salamander, crickets, grasshoppers, p. 364.

Hemingway rejects expensive tackle and flies advertised in sporting magazines, reviews suitable, cheaper baits for different streams, different conditions: "Worms, grubs, beetles, crickets, and grasshoppers are some of the best trout baits. But worms and hoppers are those most widely used." Night crawlers can be caught in grass at night with the aid of a flashlight, are better for bass than trout. Angle worms can be dug up after a rain, kept in moist coffee grounds. ("Fishing for Trout in a Sporting Way," *TSW*, April 24, 1920, p. 13.)

Winner Take Nothing

"A Way You'll Never Be"
Nick Adams passes through the litter of personal papers and equipment and swollen bodies left after an attack has swept across an open field, pp. 402-3.

Description of the swollen, smelling dead and their pulled-out pockets with the litter of personal papers left around them after the Austrian offensive of June, 1918, and the Italian counterattacks: "The surprising thing, next to their progressive corpulence, is the amount of paper that is scattered about the dead. Their ultimate position, before there is any question of burial, depends on the location of the pockets in the uniform. In the Austrian army these pockets were in the back of the breeches and the dead, after a short time, all consequently lay on their faces, the two hip pockets pulled out and, scattered around them in the grass, all those papers their pockets had contained." (*Death in the Afternoon*, pp. 137-38.)

Nick Adams looks over the shattered town as he passes through it to trenches at the Piave, travels the road along the river, sees the bank where the Austrian position had been, thinks the river has not changed much since becoming historical. He finds the country surprisingly lush and green, remembers it before as arid and shell-pocked, pp. 403-4.

Returning to Fossalta di Piave after the war, Hemingway sees the road beside the river, sees the rebuilt town, remembers it as "a shelled to pieces town that even the rats couldn't live in," climbs the slope above the sunken road where the dugouts had been, looks across the river to the place where old Austrian positions had been located, sees all lushly overgrown. ("A Veteran Visits Old Front, Wishes He Had Stayed Away," *TDS*, July 22, 1922, p. 7.)

In his semi-hysterical talk to Italian infantrymen in the dugout, Nick Adams speaks of fishing, catching grasshoppers as bait, says all young officers should be instructed on how to catch grasshoppers by holding mosquito netting in the wind like a seine, letting the hoppers fly into the netting, pp. 411-12.

"Any fisherman who has chased a lively grasshopper in the heat of the day will appreciate the method of catching them invented by Jacques Pentecost, an old north shore trout fisher. In a clearing or around an old lumber camp where hoppers usually abound, they can be obtained in plentiful quantities by the Pentecost method. Let two men each hold the end of a ten yard strip of mosquito netting and run into the wind with it. The netting bellies out like a seine, and the grasshoppers flying down wind are soon swarming in the net seine, which is held only a few inches above the ground. Then you flop the netting together and pick the hoppers out and put them in your hopper bottles. This method takes all the labor out of hopper catching." ("Fishing for Trout in a Sporting Way," *TSW*, April 24, 1920, p. 13.)

"Homage to Switzerland"
Three Americans wait an extra hour at Swiss railway station cafes for their trains, reveal their private obsessions during the isolation of the extra hour among the Swiss, pp. 422, 425, 431.

"I have never seen the town of Aigle, it struggles up the hillside, but there is a café across the station that has a galloping gold horse on top, a great wistaria vine as thick through as a young tree, that branches out and shades the porch with hanging bunches of purple flowers, that bees go in and out of all day long and that glisten after a rain, green tables with green chairs and seventeen per cent dark beer. The beer comes foaming out in great glass mugs that hold a quart and cost forty centimes, and the bar maid smiles and asks about your luck. Trains are always at least two hours apart in Aigle, and those waiting in the station buffet, this café with the golden horse and the wistaria hung porch is a station buffet, mind you, wish they never would come." ("There Are Great Fish in the Rhone Canal," *TDS*, June 10, 1922, p. 5.)

"The Gambler, the Nun, and the Radio"
Mr. Frazer listens to the Mexican serenaders play outside his room, asks them to play "the Cucaracha, which has the sinister lightness and deftness of so many of the tunes men have gone to die to," p. 485.

Report on a Ukranian Communist meeting in Toronto:
"Finally the united mandolin, violin groups and choruses sang and played the march of the Red army and the Internationale. The first is a good stirring march. The second is the most uninspiring tune I know.

"They used to say in Italy that if the Reds had possessed any tune as good as the Fascisti hymn 'Giovanezza,' Italy would have gone Bolshevist for good when the workers seized the factories. But nobody can fight or feel like dying to the strain of the 'Internationale.' " ("Toronto 'Red' Children Don't Know Santa Claus," *TSW*, December 22, 1923, p. 33.)

"The Capital of the World"

Paco, aspiring to be a matador, practices passes in the dining room of the pension Luarca with the dishwasher Enrique acting as the bull with two butcher knives tied to the legs of a chair, pp. 48-49.

"Poor boys, without any financial protection, follow the bullfights as bootblacks, eager to get into the ring in any kind of amateur fight no matter how dangerous; practicing the various passes on each other, a passing waiter, a cab horse; riding under the seats of trains with their fighting capes rolled up as pillows. . . ." ("Bullfighting, Sport and Industry," *Fortune*, I [March 1930], 146.)

To Have and Have Not

Harry Morgan dodges behind the bar in the Pearl of San Francisco Café in Havana, watches a gun battle between three pro-revolution smugglers and a carfull of gunners from the opposition party, swigs from bottles to dull the impact of the sight, pp. 6-8.

Pauline Hemingway's version of the Cuban revolution told to white hunter Philip Percival: "I was crouched down behind a marble-topped table while they were shooting in Havana. They came by in cars shooting at everybody they saw. I took my drink with me and I was very proud not to have spilled it or forgotten it." (*Green Hills of Africa*, p. 192.)

Between deep-sea fishing trips Harry Morgan smuggles liquor from Cuba to Key West, p. 5.

Hemingway fishes for marlin from the launch *Anita* run by Joe Russell of Key West, "who brought the first load of liquor that ever came into that place from Cuba." ("Marlin off the Morro," *Esquire*, I [Autumn 1933], 3.)

Harry Morgan goes broke when a high government official, "Mr. Johnson," carelessly loses expensive tackle, flies away without paying for the ruined equipment or his fishing trips, p. 27.

In a satirical article on having his children write his material for him, Hemingway notes, "Johnson [of the N.R.A.] cracked down on us about the kids. . . . Tried to call it child labour [*sic*], and the oldest boy over ten. I had to go to Washington on it. 'Listen Hugh,' I said to him. 'It's no skin off the ants of conscience in my pants what you do to Richberg. But the little boy works, see?' " ("The Sights of Whitehead Street," *Esquire*, III [April 1935], 25, 156.)

On one liquor run from Cuba Harry and his helper Wesley are shot up by Cuban customs officials, are identified as smugglers by the Washington bureaucrat, Dr. Frederick Harrison, and Harry's boat is impounded by the Coast Guard, pp. 86, 80,

During preparations at Key West for a hurricane, Hemingway secures his boat in the submarine basin. "There is a booze boat seized by the Coast Guard tied next to you and you notice her stern lines are only tied to ring-bolts in the stern and you start belly-aching about that." ("Who Murdered the Vets?" *New Masses*, XVI [September 1935], 9.)

Harry Morgan, when he goes broke because of Mr. Johnson's default, begins the more dangerous business of smuggling liquor and aliens into the country. He accepts the greater dangers, he tells himself, because of his responsibility to his family, pp. 28, 81, 147, 174.

On the sea one does not consider danger to himself but danger to his dependents and loved ones if he is lost. "When you have a family and children . . . you don't have to look for danger. There is always plenty of danger when you have a family.

"After a while the danger of others is the only danger and there is no end to it nor any pleasure in it nor does it help to think about it." ("On the Blue Water," *Esquire*, V [April 1936], 185.)

Veterans from the Matecumbe and Tortugas work camps come into Freddy Wallace's bar to drink and fight each other. One masochist enjoys having his friends beat his head on the pavement or hit him over the head with a bottle. His brag is that he can "take it," p. 201-2.

"The finest lot of Slap Happies your correspondent has ever been privileged to hoist a beer with hang around Mr. Josie Grunts's bar in Key West when the veterans from the C.C.C. camp at Matecumbe come in on pay day." One sadist delights in calling unsuspecting newcomers to the bar, then hits them with a crutch. ("He Who Gets Slap Happy," *Esquire*, IV [August 1935], 19.)

As Richard Gordon stands at the bar in Freddy Wallace's saloon, he sees one veteran suddenly turn on another at the bar and break his jaw. The assailant explains that the other puts his pay in postal

"I'd known a lot of them [dead veterans after the September, 1935, hurricane] at Josie Grunts's place and around the town when they would come in for pay-day, and some of them were punch drunk and some of them were smart; some had been on the bum since the Argonne almost and some had lost their jobs the year before last Christmas; some had wives and some couldn't remember; some were good guys and others put their pay checks in the

savings, then hangs around the bars picking up free drinks, pp. 204-5.
One veteran brags to Richard Gordon that he has a loving and loyal wife somewhere but can't remember where, pp. 211-12.

Postal Savings and then came over to cadge in on the drinks when better men were drunk; some liked to fight and others liked to walk around the town; and they were all what you get after a war." ("Who Murdered the Vets?" *New Masses*, XVI [September 1935], 10.)

One drunken veteran quarrels with Freddy over the cost of drinks, starts to swing on Freddy, is hit by Freddy with a saltcellar covered in a bar towel. Another veteran at the bar expresses a preference for seeing Freddy hit people with his sawed-off billiard cue. Another veteran, seeing the beaten veterans recovering their senses while lying against the barroom wall, remembers once seeing the barroom handyman mopping up blood from the floor by the bucketful, pp. 207-9.

Joe Russell, called Josie Grunts, runs his Key West bar according to the code that he can handle his customers without calling in the law. He lets them pay for broken things when they sober up. He keeps a cut-off billiard cue behind the bar in case some one makes the mistake of swinging at him. He tells Hemingway, "Ernest, you ought to have seen it. Skinner had to mop the blood off the floor with a mop and bucket. Fights! I never saw better fights in the ring. And all night long." ("Genio after Josie," *Esquire*, II [October 1934], 21.)

The tall, scarred Communist veteran at Freddy's bar rasps that the veterans are political burdens on Washington after the Anacosti Flats march and have been sent to the work camps in the Keys to die of disease, but have refused to die in the Keys. He thinks Washington will have to find some way to get rid of them because the brutalized vet-

After the September, 1935, hurricane destroys the Matecumbe veterans' camp with great loss of life because Washington bureaucrats waited too late to send an evacuation train, Hemingway sees them treated like troublesome troops during the war and left in exposed positions. "But veterans, especially the bonus-marching variety of veterans, are not property. They are only human beings, and all they have to lose is their lives. They are doing coolie labor for a top wage of $45 a month and they have been put down on the Florida Keys where they can't make trouble." ("Who Murdered the Vets?" *New Masses*, XVI [September 1935], 9.)

erans are desperate enough to cause trouble, pp. 205-6.

Harry Morgan rejects the revolutionary movement in Cuba as only another sequence of betrayals of working people by those who understand killing better than governing, p. 168.

Hemingway's summation of the Cuban revolution (Gerardo Machado's dictatorship versus Fuigencio Batista's revolt): "Beautiful, then lousy. You couldn't believe how lousy." (*Green Hills of Africa*, p. 192.)

The Fifth Column

When two international Brigade guards careless-ly allow a fifth columnist to escape, Philip Rawl-ings reprimands them for lack of professionalism, tells them idealism is no substitute for discipline. The one thing about orders, he says, is to obey them, p. 21.

"It was all very simple in the old days [before the war]. The old days were so simple that now they seem almost pitiful. If you want to have it simple now, you can do one thing: take orders and obey them blindly. That is the only simplicity that is left now." (Preface, *All the Brave* by Luis Quintanilla, p. 11.)

Security Colonel Antonio expresses supreme con-tempt for the cowardice of politicians. He has seen them crumble dur-ing questioning but has never seen one die well. Most soldiers die well, he contends, but politi-cians never, p. 42.

Hemingway regrets the political naïveté of his liberal American friends who believe their Spanish political friends would not betray their cause. He cites several cases where political commissars fail to maintain the loyalties their military counter-parts maintain. ("Treachery in Aragon," *Ken*, I [June 30, 1938], 6.)

Philip Rawlings helps Dorothy Bridges concoct a vision of escape from the frugalities and ten-sions of Madrid to the luxuries and pleasures of Paris, Havana, Saint Moritz, and other places, but then tells her he doesn't believe in those

In a tent waiting for the battle for the Ebro delta to begin, Hemingway thinks of the Stork Club and the food there instead of the water soup, single fried egg, and single orange that are the usual ration in Spain. "You keep The Stork, though, as a symbol of how you would like to eat. Be-cause this war in Spain is not being fought so that everyone will be reduced to the level of block-ade rations but so that everyone can eat as well as the best." (Preface, *All the Brave*, pp. 10-11.)

places. He just likes to say their names as a kind of hope and illusion, pp. 97-98, 67.

After savoring the memory of all the luxurious hotels, spas, and clubs he has known and made Dorothy Bridges think he wants to return to them, Philip Rawlings tells her he has "left them all behind," he goes to other places for other reasons, pp. 97-98.

"Paris is very beautiful this fall. It was a fine place to be quite young in and it is a necessary part of a man's education. . . . But me, I now love something else. And if I fight, I fight for something else." ("A Paris Letter," *Esquire*, I [February 1934], 156.)

"The Faithful Bull"

The young bull so well demonstrates his bravery in pasture fights that the rancher decides to keep him for breeding to upgrade the line. But the young bull becomes faithful to only one female. He is later sent to the bull ring and provides such a brave fight he earns tribute from the matador who kills him. Told of the bull's faithfulness, the matador suggests, "Perhaps we should all be faithful . . . ," p. 51.

"I will tell you of an odd occurrence. The bull is polygamous as an animal, but occasionally an individual is found that is monogamous. Sometimes a bull on the range will come to so care for one of the fifty cows he is with that he will make no case of all the others and will have only to do with her and she will refuse to leave his side on the range. When this occurs they take the cow from the herd and if the bull does not then return to polygamy he is sent with the other bulls that are for the ring.

"I find that a sad story, sir.

"Madame, all stories, if continued far enough, end in death, and he is no true-story teller who would keep that from you. Especially do all stories of monogamy end in death, and your man who is monogamous, while he often lives most happily, dies in the most lonely fashion. There is no lonelier man in death, except the suicide, than that man who had lived many years with a good wife and then outlived her. If two people love each other there can be no happy end to it." (*Death in the Afternoon*, pp. 121-22.)

Index